Marriages and Related Items
Abstracted from

THE CLAYTON ENTERPRISE

Newspaper of
Clayton, Adams County
Illinois

1879–1900

Mrs. Joseph J. Beals
&
Sandra Kirchner

HERITAGE BOOKS
2015

HERITAGE BOOKS
AN IMPRINT OF HERITAGE BOOKS, INC.

Books, CDs, and more—Worldwide

For our listing of thousands of titles see our website
at
www.HeritageBooks.com

Published 2015 by
HERITAGE BOOKS, INC.
Publishing Division
5810 Ruatan Street
Berwyn Heights, Md. 20740

International Standard Book Numbers
Paperbound: 978-0-7884-0766-6
Clothbound: 978-0-7884-6261-0

Table of Contents

The marriage related items in this book were abstracted from The Clayton Enterprise newspapers of Clayton, Illinois. These papers were dated from 1879 through 1900. In the early 1960's while doing research on my own genealogy in the Clayton Enterprise, I found so much valuable information that I decided to start writing them on index cards. Items that mentioned a family name would be written on a 3 x 5 index card. Cards for any advertising, jury lists, criminal courts and letter remaining at the post office were also made. Remaining items will be worked up for publishing as time permits.

The town of Clayton was established, Feb 9, 1836, by order of its proprietors, Charles K. McCoy, John McCoy and Reuben K. McCoy. It is situated on the T.W. Railroad, at the junction of a road running to Quincy and the road diverging to Keokuk, Iowa. The country surrounding Clayton is one of the finest and wealthiest in the state. It has a large scale manufacturing and a woolen mill, has 2 hotels, several stores, churches etc. and does a large and profitable trade.

ACHLY, Roe Elm Grove Nov 13, 1884
Roe Achly was married recently.

ADAIR, Mr Ad Golden Jun 17, 1886
Wedding bells Thursday night for Mr Ad Adair and Miss Laura MrCray, of this place by Rev Powell of Bowen.

ADAIR, Arthur P. Personal Jun 17, 1886
A marriage license was issued last week to Arthur P. Adair and Laura McCray.

ADAMS, Mr Eugene E. Jan 10, 1884
SEE BARKER, Miss Elizabeth F.

ADAMS, Mr Kit Local Jun 9, 1881
Last Sunday eve Kit Adams of the Quincy Argo was married to Miss Mary Idella Day.

ADEN, Ehnne Apr 14, 1887
SEE GOOST, George

ADEN, Heye Golden Mar 1, 1883
Heye Aden of this and Miss Bert, of Carthage were married in that town on Thursday.

ADEN, Miss Katie Apr 14, 1887
SEE GOOST, George

ADKINSON, Flora Sep 27, 1883
SEE MCCLAIN, Joseph L.

ALESHIRE, Wm Neighborhood News Jan 12, 1888
The Burnside Correspondent to a Carthage paper says: The event of 1887 was the golden wedding at the hotel in honor of Wm Aleshire, better known as Uncle Billy.

ALEXANDER, Alice Elm Grove Jan 22, 1885
Married on the 8th inst at the home of brides father, John Alexander, Elbert Vermillion to Alice by Rev E.M. Rice. Took the night train for Tiskilwa, Bureau County Illinois.

ALEXANDER, Miss Della M. Oct 25, 1888
SEE THOMPSON, Mr Elsworth

ALEXANDER, Mrs Emily Jan 17, 1884
SEE EYMAN, Daniel

ALEXANDER, John Elm Grove Oct 13, 1887
Married on the 21st ult, Mr John Alexander to Miss Lou Paxon.

ALEXANDER, Miss Olive Married Jan 10, 1889
Married at the home of the brides parents, on Jan. 1st, 1889 Miss Olive Alexander, daughter of Mr and Mrs J.E. Alexander to Mr W.N. Robbins, son of Hon. Nathan Robbins at 7 PM by Rev J.B. King of Lomax, Ill.

ALEXANDER, Philip Elm Grove Apr 9, 1885
Married, Philip Alexander to Miss Maggie Shank.

ALLEN, Miss Fannie Sep 21, 1882
SEE BAIRD, S.A.

ALLEN, G.H. Feb 3, 1887
SEE DAVIS, Miss Ella

ALLEN, Miss Hattie Local Jul 21, 1887
Miss Hattie Allen, only daughter of the late Dr J.N. Allen, and George H. Lee, Supt. of Schools of this county were married at the home of brides mother, this city, 8 AM last Wednesday by Rev Smith of the Presbyterian Church.

ALLEN, Mrs Sarah E. Feb 23, 1888
SEE MILLER, Oliver C.

AMEN, Miss Frona Feb 26, 1885
SEE WEAR, Zeke

AMEN, Miss May Oct 12, 1882
SEE ELSON, John

AMENT, Miss Blanche Jul 5, 1888
SEE BAIRD, David O.

AMON, Mary Jan 29, 1880
SEE WEST, Milton'

ANDERSON, Miss Belle May 31, 1888
SEE BROWN, Andrew A.

ANDERSON, Miss Clara Local Nov 7, 1889
Miss Clara Anderson of Kellerville and Mr Jos. Richardson of Beverly Prairie will be married at the home of Mrs Amen, the brides mother, at Kellerville today.

ANDERSON, Mr Elmore Feb 24, 1887
SEE HUMPHREY, Miss Angie

ANDERSON, Florence F. and Wm E. Local Mar 29, 1888
The divorce case of Florence F. Anderson vs Wm E. Anderson will be tried in the Adams County Court today, Wednesday.

ANDERSON, George A. Local Jun 17, 1886
The marriage of George A. Anderson of Quincy to Miss Cora Sweet, occurred Tuesday eve June 12th.

ANDERSON, J.E. Jan 26, 1888
SEE COLLIER, Miss Viola

ANDERSON, Mr Josiah B. Local Oct 26, 1882
Married at the Presbyterian parsonage Tuesday eve at 4 October 24th Mr Josiah B. Anderson and Miss Lillie Anderson, of Concord township by Edwin J. Rice. Couple went to the home of Mr Anderson's father afterwards.

ANDERSON, Miss Lillie Oct 26, 1882
SEE ANDERSON, Mr Josiah B.

ANDERSON, Maggie Hazel Dell Apr 28, 1881
She who was Maggie Anderson returned from Meredosia bringing a husband with her.

ANDERSON, Maude Married Jan 13, 1887
Married at John S. Anderson's, their daughter Maude and Mr M.W. Kirkpatrick of the U.S. Mail Service by Rev S.H. Whitlock of Quincy.. (Mt Sterling Democrat-Message)

ANDERSON, Ruth H. Oct 17, 1889
SEE REED, Henry F.

ANDERSON, W.E. Jun 9, 1887
SEE STOUT, Miss Flora

ANDERSON, Will Local Jan 13, 1881
Married Miss Carrie Kendall and Mr Will Anderson of Quincy over the holidays.

ANGLE, Mrs H.C. Oct 9, 1884
SEE EVERETT, Rev W.P.

ARNTZEN, Leopold Locals Mar 3, 1887
Marriage license issued to Leopold Arntzen and Mary Dissler all of this vicinity.

ARNTZEN, Mr Leopold Local Mar 10, 1887
Married, Mr Leopold Arntzen and Miss Mary Disler, both of this place at the Methodist parsonage Wednesday eve March 2nd, 1887.

ARTZ, Miss Helen Neighborhood News Sep 9, 1886
Married at Augusta on Thursday, Miss Helen Artz, daughter of Mrs Edwin Artz to Dr D.D. Waldeck of Wellington, Ohio.

ATCHINSON, Sarah Jun 23, 1881
SEE PERKINS, Jackson

ATKINS, Miss Alice M. Sep 15, 1887
SEE LEMON, S.P.

ATWATER, Sarah Neighborhood News Sep 12, 1889
SEE DELANEY, John L.
AUSTIN, Miss Nanny Chestline Jan 13, 1887
Miss Nanny Austin and Mr Lykes, both of Chestline were lately married.
AUSTIN, Nanny Chestline Jan 6, 1887
SEE LIKES, James
BABB, Mrs Mary E. Married Sep 5, 1889
Married at Grand Marias, Cook Co. Minnesota, Jun 20, 1889, Mrs Mary E. Babb, of Quincy to Mr C.S. Durfee of Grand Marias. They have a pleasant home on the N. shore of Lake Superior, a thousand miles from Clayton 30 miles from Canadian line.
BACON, Miss Lily Jan 3, 1884
SEE THOMAS, Luther
BADGLEY, Ed 5 Years Ago Sep 20, 1888
SEE GILBIRDS, Miss Lulu
BADGLEY, Edward L. Local Sep 20, 1883
Quincy "News" The marriage of Edward L. Badgley and Miss Lulu F. Gilbirds took place at Clayton a few evenings ago, by Rev Hays.
BAGBY, Miss Addie Oct 18, 1883
SEE BURNS, James and Ed
BAGLEY, Miss Eva Mar 2, 1882
SEE DEWEY, Al A.
BAIRD, David O. Golden Jul 5, 1888
Mr David O. Baird of Villisca, Iowa and Miss Blanche Ament, of Warsaw, formerly of this vicinity were married in Warsaw on Thursday, June 21st.
BAIRD, John Neighborhood News Oct 4, 1883
Brown County "Gazette" The marriage of Mr John Baird and Miss Ollie Newhouse, both of Clayton occurred at the courthouse in this city Wednesday afternoon by Elder S.R. Patton.
BAIRD, S.A. Local Sep 21, 1882
S.A. Baird of Camp Point and Miss Fannie R. Allen of Pearidge were married at the Tinnen House in Mt Sterling Saturday eve Sept. 9th.
BAKER, Miss Anna 5 Years Ago Aug 25, 1887
Miss Anna Baker was married to Melvin Lawler by Rev Lee at the home of Jas. Gillenwater.
BAKER, Mr Oliver Jul 24, 1884
SEE COX, Miss Mary L.
BAKERBOWER, Miss Caroline Local Sep 9, 1886
Miss Caroline Bakerbower was married to Mr Joseph Miller at Mt Sterling Sunday by Rev Harper. Mr Miller is a mechanic, living in Jacksonville. Miss Carrie made a good choice.
BALDWIN, Mr T.S. Local Dec 15, 1887
Thursday eve at the home of the bride in Quincy, the marriage of Mr T.S. Baldwin the aeronaut, to Miss Carrie Pool by Rev Corbyn of the church of the Good Shepherd.
BALFOUR, Mr J.O. May 5, 1887
SEE WORKING, Miss Ida M.
BALLAGH, O.W. Mar 17, 1887
SEE WELBORN, Miss Margaret
BALLOW, Hon C. Married Jun 16, 1881
Married at the Hampton House Tuesday afternoon at 4 June 14th by Rev E.J. Rice, Hon C. Ballow of Clayton and Mrs C.L. Kinnear of Trinadad, Col. Mrs Kinnear has been visiting at Hon H.C. Craig's house past few months.

BALLOW, Charles B. Married Jun 28, 1883
At the home of Dr Spencers, Murphysboro, Illinois June 17th 1883 by Rev. M. House, Mr Charles B. Ballow to Miss Lou Pullis, both of Murphysboro, Illinois.

BARKER, Miss Elizabeth F. Quincy Jan 10, 1884
Miss Elizabeth F. Barker, daughter of Judge Barker and Mr Eugene E. Adams of New York were married Thursday afternoon at the home of bride's parents by Rev S.H. Dana of the Union Congregational Church. Will live Orange, New York.

BARKER, Miss Nora Apr 21, 1887
SEE HUGHES, George

BARROWS, Mr Bushrod W. Neighborhood News Jul 18, 1889
Quincy Whig Mr Bushrod W. Barrows of Mt Sterling and Mrs Buttorph of this city were married at the home of brides sister, Mrs Henry Root on Wednesday 2 PM by Rev Dr Dana of the First Congregational Church. Will live Mt Sterling.

BARRY, David S. Apr 10, 1884
SEE BRADSHAW, Mrs

BARRY, John Oct 4, 1888
SEE WASH, Miss Prina

BARRY, Miss Katie L. Sep 13, 1883
SEE MUNFORD, Mr Wm.

BARTHOLEMEW, A.H. Golden Dec 22, 1881
A.H. Bartholemew of this place, and Miss Lizzie Carlin of Clayton were married in Camp Point last Thursday.

BARTHOLOMEW, Mr James Local Sep 8, 1887
Married at the Methodist parsonage September 1st Mr James Bartholomew and Mrs Evaline L. McKinney, both of Kellerville.

BARTLETT, Miss Laura Nov 2, 1882
SEE KUNTZ, Frederick

BASS, Miss Jan 13, 1887
SEE GRABEL, Mr

BASSET, Chas. R. Sep 30, 1880
Chas. R. Basset, editor of the Plymouth Phonograph was married last Thursday to Laura A. Whitson of Rushville.

BATES, Miss Mamie Local May 23, 1889
Camp Point Journal Last Wednesday eve at the home of Mr and Mrs Frank Bates, the marriage of their only daughter, Miss Mamie to Mr Chas. E. Shank of Clayton.

BATTERSHELL, Chas. E. Dec 13, 1883
SEE JOHNSON, Miss Hilda

BAUGHMAN, Miss Cora Happy Reunion Aug 1, 1889
Last nights Wabash train brought here, Mr John Nevins and bride from Camp Point where they were married early last evening at the home of the brides parents, Mr and Mrs Samuel Baughman. The bride, Miss Cora Baughman is well known in this city and will receive a hearty welcome into Quincy's society. Mr Geo. Baughman of 623 Jersey St is her uncle. Groom is the Superintendant of the Board of Public Works in this city. "Herald"

BEALL, William Pea Ridge Oct 11, 1883
Married Mr William Beall and Miss Lina Bradley, on Thursday by Rev E.J. Rice.

BEAN, Mr Feb 16, 1888
SEE BOWMAN, Miss Rosa

BECKETT, Miss Carrie Golden Jan 26, 1888
On Tuesday eve at the home of her father, Mr Resia Beckett, two miles - south of town, Miss Carrie Beckett was married to Mr A.E. Beers of Iowa, formerly of Camp Point.

BECKETT, Miss Hittie Dec 5, 1889
SEE MOORE, Mr

BECKETT, Miss Lizzie 5 Years Ago Jan 27, 1887
Miss Lizzie Beckett was married to Mr Daily C. Lewis.

BECKETT, Robert Jr. Golden Feb 17, 1881
Robert Beckett, Jr is married. He sold his buggy last fall and is in the market now for a three seat spring wagon.

BECKETT, Mr and Mrs Robert A.Sr. Camp Point Mar 6, 1884
Last Wednesday Mr and Mrs Robert A. Beckett Sr celebrated their 50th wedding anniversary.

BECKMAN, Celestie Dec 23, 1880
SEE STEVENS, James

BECKMON, Miss Celeste Dec 2, 1880
SEE STEVENS, James A.

BEERS, Mr A.E. Jan 26, 1888
SEE BECKETT, Miss Carrie

BELFORD, John Golden Feb 16, 1882
John Belford was married to a blooming widow on Wednesday eve. Both of Houston.

BELL, Miss Ann E. Local Dec 16, 1880
Miss Ann E. Bell of Pearidge and Mr Benj. Dodd of Clayton were married last Sunday by Rev Coats.

BELL, Miss Jennie Mar 6, 1884
SEE BRATTON, Walter

BELL, Mr Louis D. Sep 13, 1883
SEE MUNFORD, Mr Wm.

BELL, Miss Martha E. Mar 31, 1887
SEE BROWN, Wesley S.

BELLIMEYER, Maggie T. Jul 21, 1887
SEE DAUGHERTY, Charles S.

BELLMEYER, David Locals Apr 28, 1887
Mr David Bellmeyer, of Chestline was married to Miss Curtis of the same vicinity, last week.

BELLOMY, Mac Concord Feb 8, 1883
Mac Bellomy was down to Quincy last week and got that thing which will bind him and Miss Lizzie Franks in the bonds of matrimony for life.

BELLOMY, Mac Concord Feb 22, 1883
Mac Bellomy and Lizzie Franks were married Feb 18th by Rev Crawford of Mt Sterling.

BELLOW, Miss Anna Mar 9, 1882
SEE MOTTER, L.H.

BENNET, Miss Adda 5 Years Ago Oct 4, 1888
Miss Adda Bennet was married to Mr Rankin Smith.

BENNETT, Miss Nov 25, 1886
SEE GUNN, Johnny

BENNETT, Miss Adda Oct 4, 1883
SEE SMITH, Mr Rankin

BENNETT, Judge T. Eddy Local Mar 31, 1887
Judge T. Eddy Bennett and Miss Victoria L. Brown were married at York, Nebraska on the 17th inst. Judge Bennett was a Quincy lawyer who went west a few years ago. Was raised in North-East township near Chatten and is son of the venerable Elisha Bennett still living here.

BENNETT, Mr Edgar 5 Years Ago Aug 2, 1888
SEE WYLIE, Miss Ida M.

BENNETT, Miss Fredonia L. Nov 25, 1886
The marriage of Miss Fredonia L., daughter of Mr and Mrs Z.F. Bennett, living just north of this city, to Mr Geo. Farmer, took place in Quincy Monday by Elder F.N. Calvin.

BENNETT, Mr Josiah Married Nov 23, 1882
In this city at the home of the brides father, Jacob Miller, Nov 18th by Rev F.M. Hayes, Mr Josiah Bennett and Miss Emma A. Miller.

BENNETT, Miss Maggie 5 Years Ago Sep 22, 1887
Miss Maggie Bennett and Geo. Hill were married at Mounds.

BENNETT, Robert Golden Dec 21, 1882
Married in this town Sunday eve the 10th inst at the home of Jacob Bennett, by Rev Sir William Hanna J.P., N.P., P.M., Mr Robert Bennett to Miss Tracy Smith all of Houston.

BENT, Fred Mound Station Aug 23, 1888
Capt. Mumford, J.P. married his first couple Friday, they were Fred Bent and Miss Wear of Clayton.

BERKETT, Alden S. Married Jul 5, 1883
At the home of Jas. Long, Clayton, June 27th by Eli Loyd, Esq., Alden S. Berkett, of Camp Point to <u>Mrs</u> Ellen Noakes of Clayton.

BERKITT, A.S. 5 Years Ago Jul 5, 1888
SEE NOKES, <u>Mrs</u> Ellen

BERNSEN, Mr Chas. F. Sep 1, 1887
SEE REEDER, Miss Connie

BERRIER, David Local Feb 9, 1888
A marriage license has been issued to David Berrier, of Clayton and Alice Hoke of Clayton.

BERRY, Mr Leon W. Married Jun 1, 1882
At the home of Mrs Mary Kirkpatrick at 5 <u>AM</u> May 31, 1882 by Rev J.C.H. Hobbs and Rev R.G. Hobbs, Mr Leon W. Berry and Miss Ida E. Smith of Clayton. Left on the 6 o'clock train for a trip to the eastern cities.

BERRY, Leon W. Oct 3, 1889
SEE CRAWFORD, Miss Fanny L.

BERT, Miss Mar 1, 1883
SEE ADEN, Heye

BICKERS, Mr N. Kellerville Jan 18, 1883
Married Mr N. Bickers and Miss Sarah Herman Sunday.

BINNEY, James Jr. Neighborhood News Jul 18, 1889
At Springfield on Saturday night James Binney Jr and Miss Bertha Wood were married in the show window of a furniture dealer.

BISSELL, Mr F.I. Married Nov 6, 1884
Married at Mount Pleasant on the 30th of October by Rev Vanway, Mr F.I. Bissell of Brown County to Miss Lona Davis of Camp Point.

BISSELL, Myron Kellerville Dec 2, 1880
Married during the week in the neighborhood Myron Bissell to Miss Sarah Durbin.

BLACK, Bill and Clara Bill Black Jul 8, 1886
Lexington, Missouri on June 2nd he by attorney J.G. Young of Kansas City filed for divorce against his wife, Clara of this place. They were married Nov 25, 1880 in McDonough County Illinois. They lived together until Jan 29, 1885. Charged herewith cruel treatment. Lived Missouri one year.

BLACK, Dr C.E. Personal Jun 13, 1889
Dr J.N. Black and wife and Mrs Black went to Jacksonville today to attend the wedding of Dr C.E. Black, who is to wed Miss Bessie McLaughlin at 9 AM today. Dr recently returned from Europe.

BLACK, Mrs Clara and W.L. Local Sep 9, 1886
Mrs CLara Black has begun proceedings for divorce from W.L. Black. She alleges cruelty and desertion in the catalogue of offences of which Mr Black is supposed to be guilty.

BLACK, Prof J.H. and wife Concord Apr 27, 1882
Prof J.H. Black and wife celeberated their China wedding last Thursday.

BLACK, John Hazel Dell Nov 3, 1881
Mr John Black and Miss Berintha Orton were married last Saturday.

BLACK, John D. Local Nov 3, 1881
Married by Rev J.V. Pringle at his home October 29th Mr John D. Black and Miss Berinthia Orton, daughter of Mr Clark Orton.

BLACK, Dr Joseph N. Black-McBratney Sep 13, 1883
Married 4 PM Wednesday the 5th inst, Dr Joseph N. Black and Miss Maude L. McBratney both well known from infancy by our readers by Rev F.M. Hayes at the home of the brides mother, Mrs M.L. McBratney. Dr J.N. graduated from Rush Medical College some months ago.

BLACK, Mary C. 5 Years Ago May 9, 1889
Mary C. Black was married to Mr Wm Kee. Mrs Kee has since died.

BLACK, Miss Mary F. 5 Years Ago Nov 17, 1887
Miss Mary F. Black was married to Samuel R. Wallace.

BLACK, Miss Mattie 5 Years Ago Dec 2, 1886
Miss Mattie Black was married to Mr Lee Wells on Thanksgiving day.

BLACK, W.L. Personal May 27, 1886
W.T. Henly of Good Hope, was in town Monday on his way to K.C. to appear before the grand jury in the W.L. Black case. It appears that there is no record in the county clerks office of the marriage of Black to Mr Henley's daughter and he is going to tell the jury he was present and witnessed the ceremony.

BLACK, Will Local Jan 5, 1882
Miss Clara Henley and Will Black were married at the home of the brides father in Good Hope Wednesday the 28th ult. by Rev Taylor. Will live Clayton.

BLAIR, Richard G. Local Apr 24, 1887
Married, in La Grange, Missouri April 21st by Rev W.W. Whipple, Richard G. Blair, of Colfax, Washington territory, to Miss Julia Hogwood, daughter of J.N. Hogwood of La Grange.

BLAKE, Leander May 19, 1881
Leander Blake of Barry, age 60 years tired of his lonely condition married Miss Ida Larimore age 22. "Democrat"

BLANK, Miss Nettie Local Dec 6, 1888
Invitations are out for marriage of Mr Prigmore of Kansas City to Miss Nettie Blank. Wedding will be in Quincy on 27th of this month.

BLOCK, Mr Alfred Elm Grove Dec 21, 1882
Married on the 14th inst, Mr Alfred Block and Miss Mary Lanes.

BLOOD, Miss Katie Oct 4, 1888
SEE HINCHMAN, James L.

BLUE, Miss Annie 5 Years Ago Mar 10, 1887
Miss Annie Blue was married to L.H. Motter, by Rev Frank C. Bruner.

BOBBITT, Miss Minnie E. Aug 24, 1881
SEE SHANK, Mr Jacob

BOEHM, Mr Frank Feb 3, 1881
SEE GROSS, Miss Amelia

BOLT, Miss Emma Oct 15, 1881
SEE KENDRICK, Mr H.B.

BOLTON, Miss Anna B. Oct 13, 1887
SEE SMITH, Charles E.

BONNEL, Miss Lizzie Dec 1, 1881
SEE BURLEIGH, DeMoin

BOOTHE, Miss Ella Local Dec 16, 1880
Miss Ella Boothe, sister of Mrs R.S. Curry was married at Independence, Kansas December 2nd to Mr Jonas Pickler.

BOREN, Dug Local Feb 21, 1884
It is a false alarm, Dug Boren is not married, but would like to be.

BOREN, James A. Married Sep 21, 1882
Early last Tuesday AM at the home of the brides father, B.A. Curry, Mr James A. Boren and Mrs Linnie Simmons by Elder Stewart of Mt Sterling.

BOREN, Lennie and Jas A. Local Apr 4, 1889
Divorce cases heard in Adams county at this term, Lennie Boren vs Jas A. Boren.

BOREN, Rhoda E. Feb 3, 1881
SEE WILLIAMS, Wm C.

BOREN, Mrs Rhoda Feb 24, 1881
SEE WILLIAMS, Billy

BOSS, Miss Jan 6, 1887
SEE GABREL, Mr

BOSTICK, Miss Cad Jan 17, 1889
SEE BOSTICK, Miss Nellie

BOSTICK, Miss Nellie Local Jan 17, 1889
Miss Nellie Bostick was married to Mr Chas. A. Price in Kansas City December 20th, 1888. Miss Cad Bostick was married to Mr Edward Kelly on November 29th. Mr Kelly is foreman of a newspaper office and Mr Price is employed by a tea and grocery house. They will live in Kansas City.

BOTTORFF, Miss Sallie May 19, 1881
SEE KERN, Samuel

BOTTORFF, Mr and Mrs William Local May 12, 1887
Mr and Mrs William Bottorff, who married May 11, 1820, 67 years ago. Mr Bottorff was born in 1779 and yet is a vigorous old man with good prospects for several years more. "Journal"

BOUKER, Miss Minnie Jan 24, 1884
SEE CLARK, Henry

BOWERS, Miss Emma Oct 27, 1887
SEE HUDDLESTON, Clemens H.

BOWLING, Miss May Nov 7, 1889
SEE CANNON, Ollie G.

BOWMAN, Miss Rosa Siloam Springs Feb 16, 1888
The marriage of Mr Bean and Miss Rosa Bowman at the home of brides parents last Sunday.

BOWMAN, Susan Sep 27, 1883
SEE MCCLAIN, Joseph L.

BRADLEY, Mr E. Mound Station Feb 21, 1889
Married, Mr E. Bradley and Miss Emma Crawford, both of this place, Sunday February 17th at the brides home at 2 PM by Rev E. Knock of Rushville.

BRADLEY, Miss Hallie May 26, 1887
SEE SWOPE, Mr Homer

BRADLEY, Miss Hattie May 19, 1887
SEE SWOPE, Homer M.

BRADLEY, Miss Lina Pea Ridge Oct 11, 1883
SEE BEALL, William

BRADLEY, Miss Mary Nov 10, 1881
SEE BREWER, Mr Percival

BRADLEY, Mr Wm A. Wedding Feb 23, 1882
Married, Mr Wm A. Bradley and Miss Effie Cox at the home of J.A. Cox Esq of Bowen, Illinois on Sunday eve Feb 19th at 7 PM. Grooms father Benj. A. Bradley two miles northeast of Clayton gave them a reception on Monday eve.

BRADNEY, Miss Mary Jan 3, 1889
SEE HODGSON, Harry

BRADSHAW, Mr and Mrs Quincy Feb 28, 1884
A divorce was granted to Mrs Bradshaw and the right to resume her maiden name, Miss Maggie Young.

BRADSHAW, Mrs Local Apr 10, 1884
Mrs Bradshaw, of Quincy recently divorced from her insane husband was married Tuesday of last week to Mr David S. Barry of Bismark, Dakota.

BRATTON, Walter Pea Ridge Mar 6, 1884
Married yesterday afternoon, Walter Bratton and Miss Jennie Bell by Rev Palmer at the home of the brides father.

BRAWNER, Mrs Mary E. May 8, 1884
SEE WEENS, Mr Jesse E.

BRAY, Miss Florence R. Jul 5, 1888
SEE CREEKMUR, Mr J.W.

BREWER, Mr Percival Local Nov 10, 1881
Rev Kent and wife have been called to Roseville to attend the wedding of Mr Percival Brewer, the Roseville druggist and Miss Mary Bradley, only daughter of Theodore Bradley, M.D.

BREWER, Percival Local Nov 17, 1881
Married at the home of Dr Theodore Bradley in Roseville, Ill. Nov 9th by Rev G.D. Kent, Mr Percival Brewer and Mary A. only daughter of T.E.J. Bradley of Roseville.

BREWSTER, Miss Maggie Sep 21, 1882
SEE HILL, Mr Henry

BRIDGES, Miss Alice Dec 8, 1881
SEE WATSON, Robert

BRIDGES, Miss Alice 5 Years Ago Dec 9, 1886
Miss Alice Bridges was married to Robert Watson at Hamilton.

BRIDGES, Miss Ella Local Mar 30, 1882
Miss Ella Bridges, daughter of W.C. Bridges was married Sunday March 19th at Hamilton to Mr Elmer Dennis.

BRIDGES, W.C. Oct 14, 1880
W.C. Bridges and wife celebrated their china wedding anniversary Thursday.

BRIDGES, Mr and Mrs W.C. Local Nov 4, 1880
China wedding of Mr and Mrs W.C. Bridges at Hamilton on the 14th ult.

BRIERTON, Mr Henry Apr 7, 1887
SEE HILL, Miss Mollie

BRIGGS, Miss Luisa Oct 14, 1880
SEE CAMPBELL, Mr Allen

BROCKMAN, Mrs Bertha Feb 2, 1888
SEE WHEELER, Hiram N.

BROOKS, Miss Maggie Mar 13, 1884
SEE SPILLARS, John

BROWN, Mr Alonzo Local Feb 1, 1883
Married at Mt Sterling, Jan 25th by Rev J.G. Lowry, Mr Alonzo Brown of Concord township and Miss Mary J. Smith of Lee township, Brown County.

BROWN, Andrew A. Local May 31, 1888
Mr Andrew A. Brown and Miss Belle Anderson of Concord, were married Monday of last week at Mt Sterling.

BROWN, Flora J. Jul 15, 1880
SEE MULKEY, Horace B.

BROWN, Mr and Mrs Lon Local Jan 28, 1888
Mr and Mrs Lon Brown celebrated their 5th wedding anniversary Friday in their newly made home in Concord.
BROWN, Miss Victoria L. Mar 31, 1887
SEE BENNETT, Judge T. Eddy
BROWN, Virgil A. Local Apr 14, 1881
Married at the home of brides parents, by Rev E.J. Rice on Thursday eve April 7th Mr Virgil A. Brown and Miss Sarah E. Franks.
BROWN, Wesley S. Local Mar 31. 1887
From the Kingman (Kansas) News we clip the following Married at South Kingman March 2nd 1887 by Rev J.H. Marshall, Wesley S. Brown and Miss Martha E. Bell. Miss Bell known in Clayton and is daughter of Joseph Bell who lived here years ago and grandaughter to Mrs Robinson of this city.
BRUPHY, Wm Golden Oct 13, 1881
Married in Houston at the home of the brides parents, Mr Wm Bruphy of Iowa to Mary, daughter of John Rice.
BRYANT, Mr and Mrs B.W. Local Feb 12, 1880
Mr and Mrs B.W. Bryant celebrated their 10th wedding anniversary last Saturday eve.
BRYANT, Everett P. Local Apr 29, 1880
Married, at the home of H.P. Coe, Thursday eve April 22nd, 1880, Mr Everett P. Bryant of Camp Point and Miss Joeann LaSage of Clayton by Rev P.L. Turner.
BRYANT, Mr O.E. Married Jun 10, 1886
Mr O.E. Bryant and Miss Nora Smith Monday at 7 PM at the home of Mr and Mrs Tom C. Smith by Elder F.M. Calvin. Grooms parents are Mr and Mrs B.W. Bryant who had a reception Tuesday eve. Good wishes to Mr and Mrs Orion Ellsworth Bryant.
BRYANT, Will Married Nov 1, 1888
The Peoria Daily transcript of the 26th ult contained the wedding of Miss Mollie Warner, daughter of Mayor and Mr Will Bryant of Clayton by Rev George B. Stocking at 8 PM last evening at 203 Park Place. Will live Clayton.
BUCHANAN, Miss Lulu Feb 12, 1880
SEE GROVER, Mr M.D.
BULLEIN. Ludwig Neighborhood News Sep 19, 1889
At Carthage, Illinois, Wednesday, Ludwig Bullein, age 18 years and Lucinda Vaughan, age 14 years were married. The parents of both present at the ceremony.
BURGESS, Miss Sallie Apr 3, 1884
SEE CARTER, Samuel C.
BURGESSER, Mr J.Q. 5 Years Ago Mar 29, 1888
SEE STAKER, Miss Addie
BURGESSER, John Q. Wedding Bells Mar 29, 1883
Married at the home of the brides parents, Mr and Mrs Wm Staker, by Rev M.M. Davidson of Carrolton, Ill., Mr John Q. Burgesser and Miss Adda Staker at 7:30 on eve of the 22nd. Grooms parents are Mr and Mrs Q. Burgesser. Gifts from brides brother, Dick Staker, grooms sister, May Burgesser, Clara Burgesser, grooms brother, Freddie Burgesser, grooms brother, Frank Burgesser and wife.
BURGESSER, Miss Mae Local Sep 16, 1886
The marriage of Miss Mae Burgesser, daughter of Mr and Mrs Q. Burgesser to Mr George L. Young takes place at the family home this eve. (Wed.)
BURGESSER, Mr and Mrs Q. 25 Years Jan 26, 1882
Mr and Mrs Q. Burgesser celebrated their 25th wedding anniversary Jan. 24th. Children Misses May and Clara and son Frank and his wife and Master Fred.

BURGISS, Miss Blanche — Aug 15, 1889
SEE STROTHER, Frank
BURKE, Miss — Elm Grove — Mar 5, 1885
SEE HACKNEY, Joe Bryant
BURKE, Miss Addie B. — Oct 6, 1881
SEE COATS, Rev H.C.
BURKE, Emma — Mar 6, 1884
SEE SMITH, W.
BURKE, George — Apr 10, 1884
SEE WALKER, Miss Mary
BURKE, Henry — Golden — Feb 22, 1883
Henry Burke of Bently and Lena Ellumira daughter of Frederick Ellumira of Houston were married in Quincy on Thursday.
BURKE, Miss Letha — Jun 7, 1888
SEE OSBORN, Robert
BURKE, Lilburn — Elm Grove — Jan 1, 1885
A wedding dinner was given Lilburn Burke and wife by their parents, Mr and Mrs Burke.
BURKE, Mr T.T. — Apr 4, 1889
SEE ROY, Miss Mary
BURKE, Mr Thadeus — Elm Grove — Sep 28, 1882
Married on the 21st inst, Mr Thadeus Burke of Virginia and Miss Ollie Walker of Elm Grove, in Quincy.
BURKINSHA, Geo. W. — Camp Point — Jan 22, 1880
Married at the home of the brides parents by W.A. Crawford, D.D., Geo. W. Burkinsha to Miss Anna Jacobs.
BURLEIGH, De Moin — Local — Dec 1, 1881
De Moin Burleigh and Miss Lizzie Bonnel daughter of Dr W.W. Bonnel of Astoria, Illinois were married at the brides home last Thursday.
BURNS, James and Ed — Elm Grove — Oct 18, 1883
Miss Addie Bagby and James Burns were married last week. Also Miss Pet Dorsett and Ed Burns.
BURNS, Nick — Local — Aug 12, 1880
Married Wednesday eve of last week by Squire Ballow, Nick Burns and Miss Crissie Kroll.
BURT, Miss Mary — Local — Dec 25, 1884
Pittsfield Old Flag Cards are out announcing the marriage of Miss Mary Burt to Rev Wm R. Shank on Tuesday December 23rd.
BURT, Miss Mary — Neighborhood News — Jan 1, 1885
Pittsfield Old Flag One of the most notable society events in 1884 was the marriage of Miss Mary Burt to Rev Wm H. Shank at the home of brides parents, Mr and Mrs Thos. Burt at 3 PM Tuesday Dec 23rd by Rev W.W. Rose of this city and Rev G.D. Kent of Clayton. Nearly 100 persons attended wedding.
BURT, Miss Mary A. — Married — Dec 25, 1884
Married December 23rd at 3 PM at the home of Mr Thomas Burt, Pittsfield father of the bride by Rev W.W. Rose and Rev G.D. Kent, Rev Wm H. Shank to Miss Mary A. Burt, all of Pittsfield, Pike County Illinois.
BUSBY, James — Married — Mar 16, 1885
Married at the home of Mr John Elder, in Carthage, Ill. Tuesday March 17th Mr James Busby of Eldorado Springs, Missouri to Miss Anna E. Cranston of Clayton. Will live Missouri.
BUSH, Mr E.J. — Local — May 17, 1888
Wedding of Mr E.J. Bush, secretary of the board of health in Quincy and city license collector, to Mrs Jennie Farrer took place Monday at 8 PM at the home of the bride, 505 Locust St. by Elder Calvin of the Christian Church.

BUSS, Gerd G. Gölden Apr 19, 1888
Gerd G. Buss was married on Friday April 6th to Miss Ihnen, daughter of Harm Ihnen of Houston.
BUSS, John G. Golden Mar 1, 1883
John G. Buss pf Clayton township and Miss Wubke Ihnen daughter of Gerd Ihnen of Houston were married yesterday.
BUSS, John J. Dec 18, 1884
Marriage license issued Saturday to John J. Buss and Catherine F. Port of Clayton.
BUSS, John J. 5 Years Ago Dec 19, 1889
SEE POST, Catherine F.
BUSS, Miss Kate Elm Grove Feb 23, 1888
To be married on Wednesday of this week, Miss Kate Buss and Mr Herman Kollmann at the home of brides parents.
BUSS, W.J. Golden Jan 27, 1887
W.J. Buss went to Quincy last Thursday and married Miss Bertha Tausman of Quincy and brought her back that night to take charge of his household matters.
BUTTLER, Miss Clara L. Jan 6, 1887
SEE DOOCY, Judge Edward
BUTTORPH, Mrs Jul 18, 1889
SEE BARROWS, Mr Bushrod Jr.
CAIN, James Harvey Local Oct 11, 1888
Mr James Harvey Cain, son of John Cain and Miss Mary O. Robbins, daughter of highly respected parents in Northeast township were married last week.
CAIN, Miss Margaret Mar 29, 1888
SEE CRAWFORD, Henry C.
CAIN, Mr and Mrs Philip Elm Grove Mar 9, 1882
Mr and Mrs Philip Cain celebrated their 55th wedding anniversary.
CALDWELL, Addie 5 Years Ago Mar 21, 1889
SEE MCDOWELL, S.K.
CALDWELL, Miss M. Mar 20, 1884
SEE MCDOWELL, Sam
CAMERON, Miss Hattie M. Sep 15, 1887
SEE MCCULLUM, H.E.
CAMP, Dr J.E. Local Apr 14, 1881
Married at the home of brides parents in Brooklyn, Schuyler County Ill. April 6th by Rev Stead of Augusta Dr J.E. Camp and Miss Nettie Taylor.
CAMP, Mr and Mrs L.W. Silver Wedding Mar 18, 1880
Mr and Mrs L.W. Camp celebrated their silver wedding on the 9th.
CAMP, Miss Maymie L. Locals Dec 16, 1886
Invitations are out for the marriage of Miss Maymie L. Camp, to Mr Harvey B. Henderson a prominent young business man of Columbus, Kansas at the home of the brides parents, Mr and Mrs L.W. Camp in the west end on Wednesday. Will live Kansas.
CAMP, Miss Maymie L. Wedding Dec 23, 1886
Married, at the home of brides parents, Mr and Mrs L.W. Camp in the west side Wednesday eve December 15th, Miss Maymie L. Camp, Clayton to Mr Harvey B. Henderson of Columbus, Kansas by Rev C.F. McKown.
CAMP, Samuel Local Jan 26, 1888
Miss Mary E. Macomber was married to Mr Samuel Camp in Quincy Monday. Sam and bride came out Monday eve to visit his mother and relatives.
CAMP, W. Edward Feb 7, 1889
SEE RIPPETOE, Miss Nellie
CAMPBELL, Mr Allen Local Oct 14, 1880
The Mt Sterling Democrat says: Mr Allen Campbell of Clayton and Miss Luisa Briggs of Bukhorn were married at the home of Elder Stewart October 2nd.

CAMPBELL, Allen D. Married Nov 2, 1882
At the Baptist parsonage in Clayton, Illinois October 26th by Rev G.D. Kent, Allen D. Campbell and Miss Ollie M. Wright all of Adams County.

CAMPBELL, Mr Chas. Pea Ridge Oct 4, 1883
Married Mr Chas. Campbell and Sophronia Clark, all of Brown County by J.J. Pevehouse.

CAMPBELL, Thomas A. Married Nov 27, 1879
Married at the ME parsonage, on the eve of the 22nd inst by Rev P.L. Turner, Mr Thomas A. Campbell of Clayton to Miss Geneva Noakes, of Mound Station, Brown County.

CAMPBELL, Mr Thos. A. 10 Years Ago Nov 28, 1889
Mr Thos. A. Campbell and Miss Geneva Nokes were married.

CANNON, Ollie G. Neighborhood News Nov 7, 1889
At the result of the elopement of Ollie G. Cannon of Carthage, and Miss May Bowling of Kansas City, Missouri, uoung Cannon and Will C. Newton, deputy County Clerk of Hancock have been arrested. The former for subordination of perjury and the latter for perjury. The lady is not of legal age. It is said the father intends pushing the ciminal case with vigor.

CAPEL, Mr Neighborhood News Dec 11, 1884
Griggsville Press Cards are out for double wedding at Perry next Wednesday, parties are Mr Capel of St Louis and Miss FAnnie Hinman and Mr S.K. Strother of Abilene, Kansas and Miss Mamie Hinman.

CARLIN, George Golden Jan 3, 1889
Married, George Carlin of Clayton township and Miss Mattie Duse of Golden at Quincy on Thursday.

CARLIN, Miss Lizzie Dec 22, 1881
SEE BARTHOLEMEW, A.H.

CARN, Mrs Richard 5 Years Ago Mar 24, 1887
Mrs Richard Carn's at Girggsville eloped with the hired man.

CARTER, Joel Neighborhood News Mar 8, 1888
Joel Carter, a manufacturer of Peoria, has eloped from his home with the hired girl. He has been gone several weeks. Before leaving he drew out $30,000 from the bank, leaving his wife $5000 in cash and $15,000 in property.

CARTER, Lawson G. Neighborhood News May 8, 1884
Carthage "Gazette" A young couple from McDonough County suspected to being runaways were married in County Clerks office by Hon. Judge Risse last Tuesday. The groom age 67 years was Lawson G. Carter and blushing bride age 62 years was Mrs Josephine Paughburn.

CARTER, Miss Rhoda Sep 7, 1882
SEE WING, Theodore

CARTER, Samuel C. Local Apr 3, 1884
Samuel C. Carter of Augusta, Illinois was married on the 19th ult to Miss Sallie Burgess of Joplin, Missouri.

CASTLE, Miss Mattie J. Nov 9, 1882
SEE MILEHAM, Dr Samuel

CATE, Mr Horatio W. Neighborhood News Mar 20, 1884
Quincy Whig Married in Gilmer township, March 11th at the home of brides father, Mr Horatio W. Cate of San Jose, California and Miss Susie A. Powell, by Rev Dr Goodwin. Will live California.

CATLIN, Mr and Mrs Isaac Quincy Apr 24, 1884
Last Monday, Mr and Mrs Isaac Catlin celebrated their 60th wedding anniversary at the home of J.R. Dayton, a son in law. Both are natives of Connecticut and came west in 1839 settling first in Augusta and to Quincy in 1850 till now.

CHAMBERS, Rice Elm Grove Jan 3, 1884
Married in the township during the past week Rice Chambers and Miss Libbie Ewing.

CHAMBERS, Will C. Feb 24, 1887
SEE THOMAS, Miss Laura

CHAMBERS, William Mar 3, 1887
SEE NUSBUMMER, Rosa

CHASE, Charlie Local Oct 11, 1888
Charlie Chase did not come all the way back to Clayton from Reno County Kansas with no purpose. Last week he went to LaHarpe where he quietly married Miss Maggie Hoke, daughter of Mr and Mrs Craven Hoke northeast of town. They departed for Kansas where Charlie has a claim which he calls his own.

CHATMAN, Miss Bell Feb 2, 1882
SEE LOHR, Jas.

CHATMAN, Florence Feb 28, 1889
SEE TRIPLETT, Elick

CHENEY, Miss Nerva J. Mar 24, 1881
SEE EASLEY, Ralph M.

CHILDS, Alice Apr 22, 1880
SEE STIVERS, Richard

CHRISTIE, Gerome Local Feb 16, 1882
Mr Gerome Christie and Miss Addie Farlow will be married this afternoon (Wednesday) at 4 PM by Rev L.F. Walden. They are among the best society people of the Point.

CHRISTIE, J.O. Camp Point Mar 17, 1881
The report was current Saturday that J.O. Christie and one of our society belles were married in St Louis last week. If so will go into details next week.

CHRISTIE, Jo Camp Point Feb 23, 1882
Jo Christie and Miss Addie Farlow were married last Wednesday afternoon and left for a trip east to visit Chicago, New York, Philadelphia and Washington.

CLAPP, Josie Jan 6, 1887
SEE GABLE, Gotleib

CLARE, Miss Frankie Mar 22, 1883
SEE LAWS, James B.

CLARK, Mr Ben Oakwood Dec 6, 1888
Mr Ben Clark of Mt Sterling, son of our friend Dick Clark and Miss Nannie Logue were married Thursday of last week at the home of brides parents.

CLARK, Ed Elm Grove Jan 20, 1887
Invitations are out for the wedding of Ed Clark and Miss Ritchey of Mt Sterling for next Thursday.

CLARK, Edward Neighborhood News Nov 29, 1888
Mr Edward Clark of Versailles, a bookeeper for J.R. & W.M. Reid was married Thursday eve at the home of brides parents in Versailles to Miss Mabel Hariman by Rev Wm McFifresh.

CLARK, Mr and Mrs George Neighborhood News May 8, 1884
Warsaw "Bulletin" Last Thursday, May 1st Mr and Mrs George Clark celebrated their 60th wedding anniversary. They were married by Rev Bayle in Antrim, Ireland, within a 20 minute walk of the Giant's Causeway. Living children are Mrs Simpson, Keokuk; Mrs Price, Hannibal; Mrs Wm Ayers, of Warsaw; Mrs R.A. Stansberry, Rich Hill, Missouri; David of Kansas; George of Portland, Oregon. Also have 45 grandchildren and 9 great grandchildren.

CLARK, Henry Pea Ridge Jan 24, 1884
Mr Henry Clark and Miss Minnie Bouker, all of Schuyler County were married last week.

CLARK, J.T. Local Jan 19, 1882
Mr J.T. Clark and Miss Anna E. Bower were married at the home of the brides parents last Wednesday by R.N. Asher. Mr Clark is one of Newton's most exemplary young men they will live Newton. Jimmie is a former Clayton boy. Newton Republican.

CLARK, Sophronia Oct 4, 1883
SEE CAMPBELL, Mr Chas.

CLARKE, Rev John Neighborhood News Nov 25, 1886
The Rev John Clarke and wife celebrated their 60th wedding anniversary at their home in Rushville last Tuesday.

CLARKE, Miss Nancy C. Apr 8, 1880
SEE MCCASKILL, Daniel M.

CLARY, James Dec 27, 1888
Married on Xmas eve at the home of Amos West, father of the bride in Concord township, Mr James Clary and Miss Annie West by Rev McKown.

CLEEVES, Mr Hardin Mound Station Jan 13, 1881
Married Mr Hardin Cleeves to Miss Nettie Rabb.

COATS, Rev H.C. Mounds Oct 6, 1881
Married at the home of the brides father in Adams County Sept 29th by Rev S. Coats, Rev H.C. Coats and Miss Addie B. Burke. Returned to Mounds same evening.

COHENOR, Mr J.N. Mounds Oct 15, 1881
Married at the home of the brides father Oct 7th by Rev H.C. Coats, Mr J.N. Cohenor and Miss Mollie Lester all of Mounds and vicinity.

COLBURN, Mrs Josephine Feb 3, 1881
SEE HACKNEY, Mr W.D.

COLBURN, Miss Nora "Supplement Sheet" May 10, 1888
Golden Miss Nora Colburn of this town was married in April in Kansas to James Schwartz formerly of Hancock County.

COLEGATE, Mr G.E. Married Aug 5, 1886
Married on Tuesday July 27th Mr G.E. Colegate of Clayton, Illinois and Miss Nellie Griffin of Marchfield, Indiana. Married in Lafavette, Ind.

COLEMAN, H.M. Neighborhood News Sep 13, 1883
Last week H.M. Coleman and Miss Lizzie Sanderson were married at Jacksonville and left for Chicagp on their way to Tocoma, W.T. While in Chicago Mrs Coleman gave all her money about $900 and he disappeared and not seen since. Mr Coleman came from New York and was well recommened, was a teacher in Jacksonville two years and Miss Sanderson moved in the best society in Jacksonville.

COLLIER, Miss Viola Local Jan 26, 1888
Married, in Mt Sterling, Tuesday Jan 24th 1888 Miss Viola Collier to Mr J.E. Anderson, both of Clayton by Rev S.R. Patten pastor of the Christian Church at Mt Sterling. Couple returned to Mr Anderson's brother's home, Mr J.B. Anderson Jr. where a supper was served to 25 or 30 guests.

COLPITT, Joseph Local Oct 13, 1887
Married at the Baptist parsonage in Clayton Sept 29th by Rev G.D. Kent, Mr Joseph Colpitt and Miss Cornelia O'conner all of Clayton, Adams Co.

COLPITTS, Mr James Married Dec 21, 1882
At the home of brides father in Concord township, on Thursday eve December 14th by Rev E.J. Rice Mr James Colpitts and Miss Louisa L. Kesting.

COMSTOCK, Rosa Jun 10, 1886
SEE WILLAGE, Franklin

CONN, Miss Minnie   Married   Apr 18, 1889
Married at the home of Hon and Mrs Ham Wash in Mt Sterling on Tuesday eve, Miss Minnie Conn to Mr John W. McCoy. Miss Conn lived in the family of the Enterprise man for several months, but has been absent for a visit to her parents in Missouri about two months. They have bought the home of John C. Lackey in south part of town which will be their home.

CONNER, Miss Mattie   Jun 1, 1882
SEE STRICKLER, Mr Roll

CONNER, William   Camp Point   Sep 29, 1881
William Conner and Sarah A. Moorley were married last Sunday at her home.

CONNOR, Charles C.   Sep 27, 1888
Married at the Baptist parsonage in Clayton, Adams County Illinois by Rev G.D. Kent, Mr Charles C. Connor of Clayton and Miss Mary Forstmeyer of Decatur.

CONNOR, C.H.   Local   May 2, 1889
Mr C.H. Connor and Miss Mary West, of Keokuk will be married at Helena, Montana next Sunday. That will be their future home.

CONNOR, Miss Effie   5 Years Ago   May 12, 1887
Miss Effie Connor was married to Mr A.M. Gibson by Rev Bruner.

CONNOR, Mrs Sarah E. and Charles   Local   Nov 29, 1883
Deposition to be read in the case of Mrs Sarah E. Connor vs Charles Connor, now pending in the Davis County Iowa circuit court were taken by J.L. Staker last week. When completed they made quite a book.
Mrs Connor has sued for support and possession and control of their children.

CONNORS, W.J.   Jun 3, 1886
SEE WILSON, Miss Allie

COOVERT, Isaac W.   Married   Aug 23, 1883
Married by P.D. Vermillion on Sunday August 19th at the home of John Jimison of Clayton, Illinois, Isaac W. Coovert of Concord township and Mary E. Mowen of McKee township, Adams County Illinois.

COVERT, Thomas   Elm Grove   Mar 12, 1885
Thomas Covert and Miss Mary Kettingring were married.

COVEY, Mr and Mrs Daniel   Neighborhood News   Jan 20, 1887
The 50th wedding anniversary of Mr Daniel Covey and wife was celebrated at Griggsville last Wednesday.

COX, Miss Effie   5 Years Ago   Feb 24, 1887
Miss Effie Cox was married to Wm Bradley at Bowen. They now live at Denver, Colorado.

COX, Miss Mary L.   Married   Jul 24, 1884
Married at the house of the brides step father, Mr J.B. Harlser, of Concord township on the eve of the 17th inst., by Rev J.V. Pringle, Mr Oliver Baker and Miss Mary L. Cox.

CRAIG, Miss Jennie   Mar 8, 1883
SEE HAM, George W.

CRAIG, Warren T.   Married   Dec 1, 1881
Married on Thursday November 24th at 2 PM at the home of the brides parents by Rev J.V. Pringle, Mr Warren T. Carig and Miss Lizzie A. Sargent.

CRAWFORD, Mr C.S.   Nov 11, 1886
SEE STROTHER, Miss Homie

CRAWFORD, Charles   Oct 21, 1886
SEE HOKE, Miss Ella

CRAWFORD, Miss Emma   Feb 21, 1889
SEE BRADLEY, Mr E.

CRAWFORD, Miss Fanny L. Local Oct 3, 1889
"Constitution Democrat" Last eve was wedding of Miss Fanny L. Crawford of Warsaw, having many friends in Keokuk and Leon W. Berry of Carthage at the home of brides mother, Mrs S.J. Crawford near Warsaw by Rev E.J. Lampton of Clarksville, Missouri and Rev Cromer of Carthage, Illinois. Will live Carthage where groom is in business. Card reads: Leon W. Berry Fanny L. Crawford married Sep 24, 1889 at home Carthage, Illinois Sept. 25th.

CRAWFORD, Henry C. Gölden Mar 29, 1888
Henry C. Crawford, of Bowen and Miss Margaret Cain were married in Quincy last Thursday. On Friday they went to Bowen and Mr and Mrs Laban Cain went with the latter returning home Saturday.

CREEKMUR, Mr J.W. Neighborhood News Jul 5, 1888
Married at the home of the brides parents, Burnside, Illinois June 20th Mr J.W. Creekmur and Miss Florence R. Bray. Will be at home after July 20th in Camp Point. Groom is principal of Maplewood High School and the bride, last year was teacher of the preparatory department.

CROFT, Mr M.T. Pea Ridge Jan 18, 1883
Mr M.T. Croft, of Virginia and Miss Minnie Shelley were married last Friday.

CROMWELL, Miss Mollie Jan 13, 1881
SEE MINTLE, Mr Morris

CROQUART, Mr Eugene Dec 29, 1887
SEE SHEPHERD, Miss Mary F.

CROSS, Miss Rhoda Feb 14, 1884
SEE SELLS, Lewis

CULLENAN, Miss Ella 5 Years Ago May 19, 1887
SEE NOLAN, Louis

CULLINAN, Miss Ella May 18, 1882
SEE NOLAN, Louis

CUNNINGHAM, Miss Phenicia Aug 23, 1888
SEE VAN ARSDELL, Sidney.

CURRY, Mr and Mrs B.A. Local Apr 1, 1880
Mr and Mrs B.A. Curry celebrated their crystal wedding anniversary Saturday eve.

CURRY, Charles Local Oct 25, 1883
Charles Curry was married to a Miss Garret at Camp Point Thursday eve last.

CURRY, Charlie Local Nov 1, 1883
Mr Charlie Curry and Miss Angie Garrett were married at the home of the brides father, Mr Robt. W. Garrett of Camp Point Thursday October 18th by Rev E.J. Lampton. Will live Clayton.

CURRY, Chris Oakwood Jun 5, 1884
Mr Zack Bennett, wife and daughter attended the silver wedding at Chris Curry's on Friday eve.

CURRY, "Dick" Local Dec 27, 1883
"Dick" Curry went to Camp Point last week and brought back a bride in the person of Miss Louis.

CURRY, Estey Local Jun 30, 1881
Estey Curry, well known to many of the boys here, was married in Griggsville June 22nd to Mrs Gussie Husbands, a young widow, good looking and had some "rocks".

CURRY, Mr Geo. Local Dec 5, 1889
Mr Geo. Curry, son of H.H. and Mrs Curry, and Miss Mary Curry, of Stronghurst, Henderson County were married on the 27th inst.

CURRY, Miss Laura Married Oct 3, 1889
Miss Laura, daughter of Mr and Mrs C.S. Curry was married to Mr Stewart T. Shank at the home of brides parents in Concord on eve of Thursday the 26th by Elder T.M. Johnson of the Christian Church. Both born and raised in this community.
CURRY, Miss Mary Dec 5, 1889
SEE CURRY, Mr Geo.
CURRY, Miss May G. Sep 13, 1883
SEE MUNFORD, Mr Wm
CURRY, Miss Nellie G. May 25, 1882
SEE POTTER, J. Will Jr.
CURRY, Samuel W. Dexterious Knot Nov 25, 1880
Married at the home of J.M. Earel, Columbus township, his daughter, Miss Jennie W. to Samuel W. Curry, Clayton township by Rev R.A. Omer.
CURRY, Miss Sarah E. Nov 8, 1883
SEE RHEA, James W.
CURRY, Thomas S. Mar 18, 1880
Married by S.J. Morey, esq. on the 10th inst at the home of Wiley Boran, Mr Thomas S. Curry, to Mrs Marsalete Gardner, both of Clayton.
CURTIS, Miss Apr 28, 1887
SEE BELLMEYER, David
CUSHENBERRY, Dr J.T. Additional Locals Dec 9, 1880
Dr J.T. Cushenberry of La Prairie and Miss Lizzie Thayer of Paloma were married at the brides parents home November 25th.
CUTLER, Mr Clinton Personal May 3, 1883
Miss Olive Howes attended the marriage of Mr Clinton Cutler of East Carthage and Miss Olive Ruhrbough at her parents home in Bently last Thursday.
CUTTER, Thomas Jan 20, 1887
SEE HALEY, Miss Ina
CUTTER, Wm May 24, 1883
SEE WELSH, Miss Annie
DAGGETT, Miss Ida Local May 19, 1887
Miss Ida Daggett, of Siloam, was married to Mr George Gilbert of Galesburg, Monday and passed thru this city Tuesday eve for their future home at Galesburg.
DANIELS, William Pearidge Feb 9, 1882
Married in Pearidge last Thursday eve Miss Amanda Johnson and William Daniels.
DAUGHERTY, Charles S. Local Jul 21, 1887
A marriage license has been issued to Charles S. Daugherty of Beverly and Maggie T. Bellimeyer of Clayton.
DAUGHERTY, Mr Jacob Married Feb 3, 1881
In Clayton January 27th at the bride, by C. Ballow, Mr Jacob Daugherty to Mrs Helen A. Wigle. Mr Daugherty is of the mineral springs at Liberty, but now lives here.
DAVIDSON, Miss Emma 5 Years Ago Jan 31, 1889
Miss Emma Davidson, was married to Mr Neal Hughes at Kellerville.
DAVIDSON, Miss Emma Lou Feb 7, 1884
SEE HUGHES, Mr Cornelius
DAVIDSON, Miss Minnie May 26, 1887
SEE PARKER, Horace
DAVIS, Chas. W. Neighborhood News Sep 15, 1887
Chas. W. Davis of the Meredosia commercial was married to Miss Anna Rausch, of Meredosia last Wednesday eve.

DAVIS, David | Married | Jan 3, 1884
At the home of John Jimison Esq. in Clayton, Adams County Illinois December 26th 1883 by Rev G.D. Kent Mr David Davis and Miss Sarah E. Jimison, all of Clayton.

DAVIS, Miss Ella | Personal | Feb 3, 1887
Miss Ella, daughter of James M. Davis formerly of this place was married to G.H. Allen of Buffalo, New York on the 17th inst.

DAVIS, Miss Emma | 5 Years Ago | May 31, 1888
Miss Emma E. Davis was wed to Lincoln Gore.

DAVIS, Miss Emma E. | May 24, 1883
SEE GORE, Mr Everett L.

DAVIS, Fannie E. | Jun 3, 1886
SEE KIRKPATRICK, Mr Orville F.

DAVIS, J.C. | Feb 24, 1881
Mr J.C. Davis and Miss Delia Lester were married at the Methodist Church last Sunday eve by Rev F.C. Bruner.

DAVIS, Miss Lona | Nov 6, 1884
SEE BISSELL, Mr F.I.

DAVIS, W.B. | Sep 27, 1888
Marriage of Mr W.B. Davis, editor Democrat Message, and Miss Laura Givens at the home of brides parents, Mr and Mrs John Givens in Mt Sterling Tuesday by Rev S.H. Whitlock elder of Quincy district. Left for east on a wedding trip.

DAVISON, Mr J. Ham | Married | Feb 3, 1881
In Kellerville last week, Mr J. Ham Davison to Amanda L. Hughes.

DAY, Miss Mary Idella | Jun 9, 1881
SEE ADAMS, Mr Kit

DECKER, Christina | Dec 18, 1884
SEE HUBER, Lambert

DEGROOT, Adelle | Jul 19, 1883
SEE ROBBINS, Henry C. and Adelle

DEHART, Duglas | Pea Ridge | Dec 9, 1886
Duglas Dehart took himself a wife.

DELANEY, John L. | Neighborhood News | Sep 12, 1889
Old John L. Delaney who was sent to the pen from Hancock County for bigamy has sued for divorce from his 7th wife, Mrs Mariah Fields Delaney, of Clinton, Iowa. It is said he wished to remarry his 8th wife, Sarah Atwater.

DELANY, Judge James R. | Elm Grove | Jan 3, 1884
Married in the township during the past week Judge James R. Delany of Henderson, Kentucky and Ella D. Powell, daughter of Rev Curtis Powell.

DEMENT, R.M. | Local | Jun 2, 1887
A license has been issued to R.M. Dement and Mrs Louisa Furgeson. They were married Sunday by Justice Kendrick.

DEMOSS, James E. | Married | Feb 17, 1881
Married at the home of E. Jimison, Esq. in Clayton, Illinois Feb 10th by Rev G.D. Kent Mr James E. Demoss and Miss Ida Whittaker, all of Adams County.

DENNIS, Mr Elmer | Mar 30, 1882
SEE BRIDGES, Miss Ella

DERRINGER, Miss Rhoda | Mar 7, 1889
SEE MAY, Mr Sam

DETMERS, Helka | Mar 1, 1883
SEE FRANZEN, Geo.

DEVER, Frank L. | Apr 23, 1885
SEE WARNER, Miss Aggie L.

DEWEY, Al A. Local Mar 2, 1882
Al A. Dewey, who made hosts of friends here while engaged in the Casco Mills, was married Tuesday of last week to Miss Eva Bagley of Kirksville, Missouri.
DIKES, Fred J. Jun 14, 1883
SEE MONTGOMERY, Miss Elva
DILL, H.H. Jan 18, 1883
SEE PYLE, Miss Hettie
DILLINGHAM, Mr and Mrs Almond Neighborhood News Nov 25, 1886
Mr and Mrs Almond Dillingham of Pittsfield celebrated their 62nd wedding anniversary last week.
DINGHAM, Mr Douglas Local Oct 4, 1883
On Thursday at Decatur, Illinois occurred the marriage of Mr Douglas Dingham freight agent of the Wabash and Miss Nettie Seehorn, daughter of Coroner Seehorn.
DISLER, Miss Mary Mar 10, 1887
SEE ARNTZEN, Mr Leopold
DISSLER, Mary Mar 3, 1887
SEE ARNTZEN, Leopold
DODD, Mr Benj Dec 16, 1880
SEE BELL, Miss Ann E.
DOKE, John Local Jun 28, 1888
A license has been issued to Mr John Doke and Miss Nora Myers to marry. Later: They were married by Rev H.R. Peairs at the home of the bride parents in Concord Tuesday eve.
DOOCY, Judge Edward Neighborhood News Jan 6, 1887
Tuesday eve December 28th Judge Edward Doocy of Pike County was married to Miss Clara L. Buttler of Griggsville.
DOOLITTLE, George H. Local May 4, 1882
Married at the home of James M. Walker in Concord township April 20th by Rev G.D. Kent, George H. Doolittle of Lincoln, Illinois and Miss Ethel G. Walker.
DORON, Rev Hugh Supplement Sep 20, 1888
Probably married Trinity Church last Thursday, their pastor Rev Hugh Doron to Miss Helena Knudson by Rev Blegar of Iowa a God Bless You was received from Germany.
DORSET, Mr Francis Local Jan 22, 1880
Married Jan 14th in Schuyler County at the home of the brides father, Mr Francis Dorset and Miss Ticia Simmons by Rev T. Ausmus.
DORSETT, Miss Ollie Jan 3, 1884
SEE WILSON, Lem
DORSETT, Miss Pet Oct 18, 1883
SEE BURNS, James and Ed
DOWNING, Charlie Golden Mar 3, 1887
Charlie Downing, of Houston and Fanny Whitford of Clayton were married Wednesday.
DOWNING, George Y. Neighborhood News Apr 10, 1884
Quincy "Whig" Married George Y. Downing of the firm of Downing Bros. Camp Point and Hattie B. Weir, daughter of J.S. Kelley of this city at the home of brides parents 175 N. 2nd St. Thursday afternoon by Rev J.G. Bonnell.
DOWNING, Joseph Cupid and His Work Jul 15, 1880
Married in the County during the past week: Joseph Downing of Camp Point to Anna Tipton of Keokuk Junction.
DOWNING, R.A. Camp Point Jan 29, 1880
Married Sunday eve by Rev W.A. Crawford, R.A. Downing to Miss Laura Underwood.

DOWNING, Robert Golden Mar 10, 1887
Robert Downing was married on Wednesday to Miss Anna Smith, daughter of Daniel Smith of Houston.
DOWNING, Wm Golden Feb 10, 1881
Mr Wm Downing and Miss Effie Kern were married Thursday eve at the home of Mr G.M. Kern, brother of the bride, 3 miles west of town.
DRAKE, Mr Feb 7, 1889
SEE NEATON, Eva
DUFF, Miss Etta Siloam Apr 28, 1889
Mr Green and wife will leave for Quincy this week. Mrs Green was formerly Miss Etta Duff. She has been married about a month.
DUNBAR, Mr Local Jan 29, 1880
Mr Dunbar of Ripley, Brown County and Miss Dora Swisher of Concord were married recently.
DUNCAN, Lew Siloam Nov 8, 1888
Married Sunday November 4th Mr Lew Duncan and Miss Sadie Vance.
DUNKLEBURG, John H. Apr 21, 1887
SEE WILSON, Miss Clara E.
DURBIN, Miss Sarah Dec 2, 1880
SEE BISSELL, Myron
DURFEE, Mr C.S. Sep 5, 1889
SEE BABB, Mrs Mary E.
DURMINE, Joseph Neighborhood News Sep 27, 1883
Married last week at the court house on Tuesday, Mr Joseph Durmine and Miss Emma L. Smyers by Elder S.R. Patton. Mount Sterling Message
DUSE, Miss Mattie Jan 3, 1889
SEE CARLIN, George
DYKE, Miss Ella Dec 1, 1881
SEE STEAD, Geo.
EAGER, John Local Jan 27, 1881
Marriage license returned to County Clerk and recorded last week, John Eager of Richfield and Eliza Johnson of McKee.
EAREL, Mr and Mrs A.B. Camp Point Aug 12, 1880
The most business like way of seperation we ever heard of , took place last week between Mr and Mrs A.B. Earel. They agreed to disagree and made a settlement satisfactory to both and they "Quit". She left for Iowa and he returned to his father's.
EAREL, Miss Jennie W. Dexterious Knot Nov 25, 1880
SEE CURRY, Samuel W.
EASLEY, Ralph M. Local Mar 24, 1881
We are invited to the wedding of Ralph M. Easley, editor of the Hutchinson (Kansas) News and Miss Nerva J. Cheney of Mechanicsburg, Ohio on the 23rd inst. Ralph is an old Clayton boy.
EASOM, Mr and Mrs John Jan 10, 1884
December 31st was the 15th wedding anniversary of Mr and Mrs John Easom.
EASUM, Mr and Mrs John Local Jan 10, 1889
5 Years Ago John and Mrs Easum celebrated their 15th wedding anniversary January 3rd.
EDMONDS, Jennie R. and Charles W. Local Jun 6, 1889
A divorce case in circuit court last week, Jennie R. Edmonds is complainant and Charles W. Edmonds is defendant. Cause-desertion.
EDMONDS, Jennie R. and Chas W. Local Jul 11, 1889
Decree in divorce signed in the cause of Jennie R. Edmonds vs Chas. W. Edmonds by the circuit judge and custody of son Roe was awarded to Mrs Edmonds.
EDMONSTON, Miss Lizzie Sep 8, 1881
SEE RIGG, Mr J.

EILERS, Ehure and Miss Golden Oct 20, 1881
Ehure Eilers and Miss Eilers both of this town were married a few days since and are living on the Clayton side of our village.

EILERT, Mrs Tompke May 24, 1883
SEE JURGENS, John J.

EINMAN, Mary Jul 15, 1880
SEE SYRKIL, John J.

ELIOT, Mr Vinton Newtown Feb 21, 1884
Mr Vinton Eliot and Miss Fronie Tandy were married at the home of brides father, Mr H.L. Tandy, Thursday eve February 14th by Rev King.

ELLERBROCK, Mr J.H. Matched Aug 25, 1887
At an early hour Thursday, Mr J.H. Ellerbrock and Mrs Belle Smith went to Mt Sterling and were married at 11 AM by Rev Robert Chapman. It was a surprise to Henry and brides friends. Will live in this city. Mr Ellerbrock has lived Clayton several years.

ELLIOT, Mrs Mary Local Oct 7, 1886
The marriage of Mrs Mary Elliot to Mr John Furgeson took place at Kellerville last week. Mr Furgeson is a farmer near Kellerville.

ELLIOTT, Miss Julia Jan 13, 1881
SEE GOOLEY, Mr R.

ELLIS, Georgia Feb 1, 1883
SEE LINDSEY, John

ELLUMIRA, Lena Feb 22, 1883
SEE BURKE, Henry

ELLUMIRE, Harmke Mar 1, 1883
SEE FREDERICK, Harm

ELSON, John Kellerville Oct 12, 1882
Married, Mr John Elson to Miss May Amen.

EMERY, Thomas E. Local May 29, 1884
Thomas E. Emery and Mrs Alpha B. Collier were married Wednesday May 21st by Squire Loyd.

ENNIS, Miss Ellis Oct 6, 1887
SEE PUGH, Mr Werter D.

ESHUM, Miss Hattie Local Mar 24, 1887
Married at Lima, this county on the 18th inst, Miss Hattie Eshum, of Lima to Mr Tuck Omer of this place.. Will live with Mr and Mrs A.F. Swope.

ETTINGER, J.W. Camp Point Apr 8, 1880
J.W. Ettinger, eloped to Mt Sterling, Illinois one night last week with Miss Georgia A. Roberts and were married there Tuesday AM. Returned Thursday.

EVANS, Miss Mary B. Mar 24, 1887
SEE WELLS, Mr and Mrs Edward

EVANS, Wm Elm Grove Dec 20, 1883
Wm Evans, the red head, and Sarah Hern were married last week. They are visiting at Grandpa McPherson's, Birmingham at present.

EVERETT, Rev W.P. Neighborhood News Oct 9, 1884
Barry Adage A wedding at Minneapolis, Minn Sept 25th, Rev W.P. Everett, of Quincy and Mrs H.C. Angle formerly of this city. Rev Everett is pastor of a Baptist Society at Quincy and it is said they will live in that city.

EWING, Miss Libbie Jan 3, 1884
SEE CHAMBERS, Rice

EYMAN, Daniel Pea Ridge Jan 17, 1884
The northwest winds brought the news that Mrs Emily Alexander and Daniel Eyman all of Adams County were married in Quincy last week.

FARLOW, Miss Addie Feb 16, 1882
SEE CHRISTIE, Gerome

FARLOW, Miss Caddie Jul 1, 1880
SEE STONE, Billie

FARMER, Mr Geo. Nov 25, 1886
SEE BENNETT, Miss Fredonia L.

FARRER, Mrs Jennie May 17, 1888
SEE BUSH, Mr E.J.

FEATHERINGILL, George T. Married Feb 21, 1884
At the home of the brides father, W.S. May in Concord township, Feb 16th 1884 by William Kendrick, J.P., Mr George T. Featheringill, of Philadelphia, Missouri to Miss Mary Ellen May of Concord, Adams County, Illinois.

FERGUSON, Lemuel Kellerville Oct 12, 1882
Married, Mr Lemuel Ferguson to Miss Nora Grady.

FERRIS, Miss Ellen Jul 4, 1889
SEE SCOFIELD, Ralph E.

FERRIS, Mrs J.J. Neighborhood News May 2, 1888
SEE MCGEHEE, Stephen

FERRIS, Miss Nettie Mar 23, 1882
SEE ROSS, Mr William

FIELDS, Mrs Mariah Neighborhood News Sep 12, 1889
SEE DELANEY, John L.

FINKHAUS, Miss Lena Nov 22, 1888
SEE LINK, John

FITZPATRICK, Joe Kellerville Jan 11, 1883
Married, Joe Fitzpatrick to Miss Maggie McNeff, who is a very amiable lady.

FLACK, Miss Hattie Local Sep 20, 1888
On Sunday night at Jacksonville, Miss Hattie Flack, age 18, eloped with her father's coachman, Preston Sands, a colored man and a married man.

FLAGG, Miss M. Frances Local Jun 9, 1887
Married at the home of brides parents, Mr and Mrs Geo. C. Flagg of Columbus on the 1st inst, Miss M. Frances Flagg to Mr E.T. Guymon of McPherson, Kansas. Will live after June 4th at McPherson, Kansas.

FLANDERS, Herbert 5 Years Ago Nov 4, 1886
SEE ROBISON, Miss Flora

FLANDERS, Herbert Mounds Nov 3, 1881
Mr Herbert Flanders returned last Tuesday AM from Sedalia with his bride, Miss Flora Robinson.

FLASSNER, Miss Christina Married Feb 28, 1889
Married at the home of groom's mother, Friday eve, Miss Christina Flassner to Mr Pete Matthews, both of this city by Wm Kendrick, esq.

FLATTERY, Mr John Personal Dec 22, 1881
Mr John Flattery of Versailles was lately married to Miss Maggie Glaze, also of that place.

FLEMING, Miss Mattie Local Dec 18, 1884
Miss Mattie Fleming of Clayton and a Mr Pullum of Camp Point were married last Friday at Camp Point.

FLEMING, Miss Mattie 5 Years Ago Dec 19, 1889
Married--Miss Mattie Fleming to Pink Pullam.

FLESNER, Henry H. Jr Mar 16, 1882
SEE HERRON, Sarah

FLYNN, Mrs Ida Local Apr 12, 1888
It is announced that Mrs Ida Flynn will be married to Mr Johnnie Rodems, the Wabash engineer on the branch at Camp Point next Sunday.

FOOTE, Miss Anna Neighborhood News Nov 22, 1883
Pike County "Democrat" Tuesday eve, Miss Anna Foote, daughter of the late George D. Foote and Mr John Rainwater were married at the home of the brides mother.

FORD, Calendonia J. Mar 8, 1883
SEE HAM, George W.
FOREMAN, Joseph I. Mar 28, 1889
SEE SWOPE, Miss Lottie
FORSTMEYER, Miss Mary Sep 27, 1888
SEE CONNOR, Charles C.
FOX, James B. Local Apr 21, 1887
Invitations are out for marriage of Mr James B. Fox to Miss Mamie McDade at the home of the brides mother on York St., Quincy this afternoon. (Wednesday)
FOX, Miss Lida M. May 24, 1883
SEE TOOF, Elder J.T.
FRANK, Miss Rosa Sep 15, 1881
SEE STERN, Chas.
FRANKLIN, Walter Married Feb 21, 1884
At the home of the parents of the bride, February 18th 1884 by Eli Loyd, Esq., Mr Walter Franklin to Miss Martha Stiffy.
FRANKS, Miss Lizzie Feb 8, 1883
SEE BELLOMY, Mac
FRANKS, Miss Sarah E. Apr 14, 1881
SEE BROWN, Virgil A.
FRANLIN, Walter 5 Years Ago Feb 21, 1889
SEE STIFFY, Miss Martha
FRANZEN, Geo. Golden Mar 1, 1883
Geo. Franzen of Basco and Helka Detmers of this town were married today.
FREDERICK, Harm Golden Mar 1, 1883
Harm Frederick of this town and Harmke Ellumire, daughter of Frederick Ellumire of Houston were married Thursday.
FRICKE, Caroline Arp 19, 1883
SEE VONHOLT, Henry
FRICKE, Caroline 5 Years Ago Apr 19, 1888
SEE VONHOLDT, Henry
FRISBIE, Mr and Mrs M.E. Mendon Dec 6, 1883
A family reunion at Mr M.E. Frisbie's in honor of their 25th wedding anniversary.
FRY, Miss Mary Feb 12, 1880
SEE GROFF, Mr Walter
FULLEN, Charles D. Local Dec 15, 1881
Mr Charles D. Fullen, of Agency City and Miss Anna B. Julian of Mt Pleasant, Iowa were married Monday eve December 5th, will go to San Antonio, Texas for the winter. Miss Anna was raised in Clayton.
FURGESON, Mr John Oct 7, 1886
SEE ELLIOT, Mrs Mary
FURGESON, Mrs Louisa Jun 2, 1887
SEE DEMENT, R.M.
GABLE, Gotleib Siloam Itemses Jan 6, 1887
Gotleib Gable and Josie Clapp were married last Sunday eve. Will live on his farm south of the one he lives on at present.
GABREL, Mr Chestline Jan 6, 1887
Married last Thursday eve, Mr Gabrel and Miss Boss by Esq. Peacock.
GARDNER, Lieut. J. Harry Quincy Nov 20, 1884
Liuet, J. Harry Gardner, of the 9th Cavalry is to be married at Pittsfield Wednesday to Miss Kitty Scandland of that place.
GARDNER, Mrs Marsalete Mar 18, 1880
SEE CURRY, Thomas S.
GARNER, Hattie G. and Dr W.A. Local Apr 4, 1889
Divorce case heard in Adams County Court this term, Hattie G. Garner vs Dr W.A. Garner.

GARNER, John Local Mar 10, 1881
Mr John Garner and Julia Campbell were married Sunday eve by Rev Bruner - at the ME parsonage.
GARNER, John Dec 5, 1889
SEE KNIGHT, Miss Josie
GARNER, Dr W.A. Local Oct 9, 1884
Dr W.A. Garner and Miss Hattie G. Staker were married Tuesday AM at the home of Wm Staker and left for Keokuk on the early train where Dr will continue his studies at medical college.
GARNER, Dr William A. Married Oct 9, 1884
Married at the home of William Staker, father of the bride Oct 7th at 7:30 AM by Rev M.M. Davidson of Carrolton, uncle of the bride, Dr William A. Garner to Miss Hattie G. Staker, both of Clayton.
GARRET, Miss Oct 25, 1883
SEE CURRY, Charles
GARRETT, Miss Local Oct 25, 1888
5 Years Ago Chas. Curry and Miss Garrett were married.
GARRETT, Miss Angie Nov 1, 1883
SEE CURRY, Charlie
GARVER, Jas. L. Local Apr 4, 1889
Jas. L. Garver and Ora Hamilton, both of Attica were married at the brides parents Mr and Mrs J.E. Hamilton in Attica Tueday. Mr Garver is a farmer. Attica, Kansas "Enterprise"
GATZ, Miss Frances Oct 17, 1889
SEE LAAGE, George F. (or E.)
GAY, Miss Lillie Local Nov 8, 1888
The marriage of Miss Lillie Gay to Mr Lute Wyatt occurred in Cass County Sunday.
GAY, Miss Lillie Cass County Nov 8, 1888
Letter to the Editor Clayton Enterprise contains marriage of Miss Lillie Gay to Mr Luther Wyatt at the Methodist Oregon Church near her sisters, Mattie Easum after the morning services. Retired for dinner at the home of grooms mother with 25 friends.
GERDES, John May 24, 1883
SEE JURGENS, John J.
GHORMLEY, E.D. Local Sep 19, 1889
First anniversary of the marriage of Miss Lizzie Wallace to E.D. Ghormley was celebrated at the home of brides mother, Mrs Martha A. Wallace Tuesday.
GHROMLEY, David E. Sep 20, 1888
SEE WALLACE, Miss Lizzie
GIBSON, Mr Alden M. Local May 11, 1882
Married after a long courtship, Mr Alden M. Gibson and Miss Effie Connor at the ME parsonage last Saturday eve by Rev F.C. Bruner.
GIBSON, Mr Collins Local May 31, 1888
Mr Collins Gibson was married at Centerville, Iowa to one of the popular young ladies of that city on the 25th ult.
GIDDINGS, Genevieve C. Locals Nov 21, 1889
Mr and Mrs I.H. Cannon sends a card announcing marriage of Genevieve C. Giddings to Mr Frank M. Richmond, Nov 28, 1889 at 12 o'clock at their home in Ogalalla, Nebraska. Bride elect is sister of Mrs Cannon.
GIDDINGS, Miss Mary Ann M. Aug 5, 1880
SEE MCPHERSON, Benj. G.
GIDDINGS, Miss Mittie Pearidge Aug 5, 1880
SEE MCPHERSON, Mr
GIDDINGS, Mr Terry Pea Ridge Dec 4, 1879
Married at the home of Mr ____ Arnold, near Mound Station, by Rev Smith Mr Terry Giddings to Miss Jennie Moore, both of Pea Ridge.

GILBERT, George May 19, 1887
SEE DAGGETT, Miss Ida

GILBIRDS, Mrs Jennie Local Sep 23, 1886
From the "Silver State" at Winnemucca, Nevada we learn of the marriage of Mrs Jennie Gilbirds, late of this city, to Mr Edward Howard which occurred at the above named place on the 8th inst by Rev T.E. Sisson of that place.

GILBIRDS, Miss Lulu F. Sep 20, 1883
SEE BADGLEY, Edward L.

GIVENS, Miss Laura Sep 27, 1888
SEE DAVIS, W.B.

GLASER, Miss Lizzie Local Feb 3, 1887
Miss Lizzie, daughter of Henry Glaser, 3rd St between Maine and Hampshire left home two weeks ago to visit friends in Clayton. Instead she was married to ____ an agent for a clothes wringer machine. The family knew nothing about the marriage until receipt of a letter from her. "Quincy Herald"

GLAZE, Miss Maggie Dec 22, 1881
SEE FLATTERY, Mr John

GLENN, Miss Tillie May 27, 1880
SEE MILLER, J.W.

GOEBEE, Henry Local Jan 27, 1881
Marriage license returned to County Clerk office and recorded last week: Henry Goebee of St Louis to Rose Grady of Kellerville.

GOLDEN, Mr Golden Nov 17, 1887
A son of Mr Golden, landlord of the American House, was married away on Thursday and came home to an infair dinner on Friday. This brought together a large collection of Schuyler County friends.

GOLDEN, Mr James Nov 17, 1887
SEE LONG, Ella

GOODRICH, Miss Ada Sep 16, 1886
SEE WEIR, Dr Wm A.

GOOLEY, Mr R. Mound Station Jan 13, 1881
Married, Mr R. Gooley to Miss Julia Elliott.

GOOST, George Golden Apr 14, 1887
George Goost, of Hannibal, Missouri, a former teacher of Trinity Parish school was married last Monday to Miss Katie, daughter of Ehnne Aden of this town.

GORDON, Mr Edwin and lady Elm Grove Dec 6, 1883
Mr Edwin Gordon and lady celebrated their Golden wedding anniversary last week.

GORDON, Rev and Mrs L.H. Quincy Aug 28, 1884
Last Thursday Rev and Mrs L.H. Gordon celebrated their 50th wedding anniversary at the home of their son O.B. Gordon, Rev Gordon is not well.

GORE, Mr Everett L. Local May 24, 1883
Married on the eve of the 17th inst, Mr Everett L. Gore and Miss Emma E. Davis by Rev J.V. Pringle at his home.

GORE, Lincoln 5 Years Ago May 31, 1888
SEE DAVIS, Miss Emma

GORE, Sadie L. Dec 18, 1884
SEE PARKER, John L.

GORHAM, Miss Edna Jun 30, 1881
SEE HARRINGTON, Lewis

GORIS, Kate Jan 11, 1883
SEE RIMER, William

GRABEL, Mr Chestline Jan 13, 1887
Squire Peacock was very happy Sunday a week ago, simply because he married Mr Grabel and Miss Bass.

GRADY, Alfred Siloam Jan 12, 1888
Alfred Grady and Miss Grey of Versailles were married at Versailles last Monday.
GRADY, Miss Nora Oct 12, 1882
SEE FERGUSON, Lemuel
GRADY, Rose Jan 27, 1881
SEE GOEBEE, Henry
GRAVES, Jimmie Sep 8, 1881
SEE MAY, Miss Sina
GRAY, Mrs Aug 4, 1881
SEE MAYFIELD, Cebron
GRAY, Mr Jas. Sep 19, 1889
SEE LOWRY, Miss Mattie
GRAY, Miss Jennie Mar 2, 1882
SEE SISSON, Mr A.E.
GREEN, Miss Etta Siloam Apr 28, 1889
SEE Duff, Miss Etta
GREEN, J. Milton Oct 17, 1889
SEE RUGG, Miss Dora
GREEN, John Kellerville Dec 2, 1880
Married during the week in the neighborhood: John Green to Miss Lizzie McNeff.
GREGG, Frank Nov 10, 1881
SEE HAMPTON, Miss Ella
GREGG, Mr and Mrs Thomas Neighborhood News Nov 11, 1886
The golden wedding of Mr and Mrs Thomas Gregg of _____ was announced for Wednesday the 10th inst.
GREY, Miss Jan 12, 1888
SEE GRADY, Alfred
GRIFFIN, Miss Nellie Aug 5, 1886
SEE COLEGATE, Mr G.E.
GRIFFITH, Miss Lottie Mar 2, 1882
SEE MILLER, S.D.
GRIMM, Mr and Mrs Henry Sr. Local Feb 21, 1884
Herald--Thursday was the 50th anniversary of the marriage of Mr and Mrs Henry Grimm Sr. They have been residents of Quincy since 1835. Came to this country from France in 1634, the years of their marriage. They are parents of six living children.
GROFF, Mr Walter Newtown Feb 12, 1880
Married, Sunday Feb 1st by Rev Linker, Mr Walter Groff to Miss Mary Fry.
GROOVER, Mr J.L. Local Oct 10, 1889
SEE PRETTYMAN, Miss Anna
GROSS, Miss Amelia Married Feb 3, 1881
Married in Mt Sterling (Wednesday) Miss Amelia Gross to Mr Frank Boehm.
GROVER, Mr M.D. Local Feb 12, 1880
Married, Mr M.D. Grover, of Clayton and Miss Lulu Buchanan of Kirkville, Missouri by C. Ballow, Esq. on last Friday eve at the home of Mrs Graham in this city.
GROVES, Anna Aug 8, 1889
SEE LEAPLEY, John
GROVES, Emma C. Feb 1, 1883
SEE STRICKLER, Wilbur
GUNN, Emma Jan 27, 1881
SEE HUNTER, Charles S.
GUNN, Johnny Siloam Mov 25, 1886
Johnny Gunn and Miss Bennett, were married on Sunday eve, November 14th at the home of the brides parents.

GUYMON, Mr E.T. Jun 9, 1887
SEE FLAGG, Miss M. Frances

HACKER, W.T. Romantic Marriage Feb 2, 1888
Two parties never seeing one another, but writing each other two months were married Mr W.T. Hacker of Benkleman, Nebraska and Miss Gertie Reath of this city. Mr Hacker is County Treasurer of Dundy County Nebraska and went west as a child and one of the early settlers of Dundy County. Miss Gertie has spent several years in Clayton. They were married by Rev H.R. Peairs Thursday eve and Mr Hacker left for Nebraska to ready a house and will come back soon for his bride.

HACKNEY, Joe Bryant Elm Grove Mar 5, 1885
Cards are out for wedding of the eldest son of Joe Bryant Hackney to only daughter of R.F. Burke.

HACKNEY, Mr W.D. Married Feb 3, 1881
In Elvaston, Jan. 30th by Rev G.I. Bailey, Mr W.D. Hackney of Golden to Mrs Josephine Colburn. Mr Hackney will continue his popular wagon shop in Golden.

HACKNEY, W.R. Golden Nov 23, 1882
W.R. Hackney and Miss Millie McClintock, youngest daughter of the late Wm McClintock of this vicinity were married in Quincy on Tuesday.

HAINSFURTHER, Miss Millie Notice Jun 7, 1883
A fashionable wedding took place at Griggsville Wednesday eve May 30th, Joseph Lesem, of Hannibal and Miss Millie Hainsfurther, an accomplished Jewess of Griggsville.

HALEY, Mr A.T. Local Aug 5, 1886
Married, Mr A.T. Haley of Creston and Miss Lizzie A. Miller at the brides parents home in Glenwood Thursday eve July 15th by Rev F.M. Parsons. Brides a daughter of Mr M. Miller. Will live Creston.

HALEY, Miss Ina Local Jan 20, 1887
Miss Ina Haley, youngest daughter of the judge, was married to Mr Thomas Cutter of Camp Point at the home of the brides relatives in Creston, Iowa last week.

HAM, George W. Local Mar 8, 1883
Married, George W. Ham of Camp Point and Miss Jennie Craig of Liberty and George Y. Lee and Caledonia J. Ford, both of Ursa, took place on February 28th.

HAMILTON, Miss Anna Oakwood Dec 12, 1889
A wedding in Oakwood, Miss Anna Hamilton to Mr Hembrough of Jacksonville on Thanksgiving day at 3 PM. Will live Jacksonville where groom has a beautiful home for his bride.

HAMILTON, Miss Annie P. Local Dec 12, 1889
Married, Hembrough-Hamilton at the home of brides parents near Clayton, Illinois by Rev E.W. Souders Wednesday November 27th 1889, Thomas S. Hembrough of Jacksonville and Miss Annie P. Hamilton, of Clayton, Ill.

HAMMOND, Mr Bowen Jun 24, 1880
G.W. Nash attended the marriage of Mr Hammond, of Wythe township last week.

HAMPTON, Miss Ella Local Nov 10, 1881
Marriage this Wednesday night at Mt Pleasant, Iowa, Miss Ella Hampton well known to many here to Mr Frank Gregg, a rising and popular attorney of that place. Dr E.T. Black left to be present.

HARBESTS, Mrs Frintzi May 24, 1883
SEE JURGENS, John J.

HARBISON, Mr A. Local May 11, 1882
Mr A. Harbison and Miss Mattie Hedenberg who were married in New York City on the 4th inst have arrived at Clayton. Will be at home here after June 1st.

HARBISON, Miss Hattie Nov 13, 1884
SEE TEACHENOR, Ike

HARBISON, John | Locals | Oct 6, 1887
Last week was the 60th wedding anniversary for John Harbison's. He has been in bed about five months and surprised the family by getting out of bed and walking to the door.

HARBISON, Capt and Mrs W.H. | Local | Aug 31, 1882
Capt and Mrs W.H. Harbison celebrated their 25th wedding anniversary Friday night August 25th at their home at the east end of Lafayette St. at 8 PM.

HARBISON, Mrs W.H. and Capt | 5 Years Ago | Sep 13, 1888
Capt and Mrs W.H. Harbison celebrated the 25th anniversary of their marriage.

HARDIN, Mr and Mrs W.C. | Neighborhood News | Dec 18, 1884
Mt Sterling Democrat Our old friend, W.C. Hardin and wife celebrated their 50th wedding anniversary at their home in Ripley Thursday December 4th. Mr Hardin lived this county over 54 years. Married at age 18 years. His wife is same age.

HARIMAN, Miss Mabel | | Nov 29, 1888
SEE CLARK, Edward

HARMON, Nancy J. | Neighborhood News | Oct 11, 1888
Nancy J. Harmon last Thursday procured divorce from her late liege lord, Charles W. Harmon and before the ink was dry James W. White rushed into the county clerks office and got a license to marry Nancy.
Mt Sterling Examiner

HARNEY, Miss Maymie | Locals | Sep 19, 1889
The marriage of Miss Mattie Lowry to Mr Jas. Gray and Miss Maymie Harney to Mr George Givens occurs at Mt Sterling today. (Wednesday)

HARRINGTON, Lewis | Camp Point | Jun 30, 1881
Mr Lewis Harrington, of Minnesota, and Miss Edna Gorham, of La Prairie were married at the home of the brides father last Thursday. Will live Minnesota. Left Tuesday AM.

HART, Mrs | Neighborhood News | Sep 1, 1887
Mr C.W. Self, formerly owner of the Hampton House, was married to Mrs Hart, of Keokuk on Tuesday of last week.

HARTLEY, J.M. | Elm Grove | Mar 29, 1883
News for some of our readers: Married on the 25th inst at the Lindell hotel, Springfield, Illinois, Mr J.M. Hartley and Miss Jennie Holmes by Rev T. Clark.

HARTLEY, J.M. | Local | Sep 16, 1886
J.M. Hartley of Elm Grove the popular teacher, was married some time ago to Miss Simms.

HASTINGS, John C. | Local | Oct 4, 1883
A double wedding took place at Gilmer on the 25th ult, at the home of the brides parents, John C. Hastings and Mercy A. Holmes and John E. Wagerly and Margarette A. Holmes.

HAYS, Miss Nora | Locals | Sep 15, 1887
Married at the home of John Hays, on Central City, Nebraska last week, Miss Nora Hays, to Mr Nichols, both of Central City.

HAZLETT, Mr and Mrs Jacob | Local | Dec 15, 1887
On the 8th Mr and Mrs Jacob Hazlett celebrated their 23rd wedding anniversary.

HAZLETT, John | Hazlett-Putman | Oct 14, 1886
Married at 8 PM at the home of brides parents, Mr and Mrs John Putman, 307 N. 5th St, Mr John Hazlett of Clayton and Miss Eva Putman, by Rev A.C. Byerly, of the Vermont St. ME Church, groom is son of Mr James Hazlett of Clayton.

HEMBROUGH, Thomas S. | | Dec 5, 1889
SEE HAMILTON, Miss Annie P.

HENDERSON, Mr Harvey B. Dec 16, 1886
SEE CAMP, Miss Maymie L.
HENLEY, Miss Clara Jan 5, 1882
SEE BLACK, Will
HENRY, Geo. N. Local Dec 21, 1882
Geo. N. Henry, ex. county clerk of Brown County, and Mrs Lydia Marshall were married at Rushville, Thursday December 14th.
HERMAN, Miss Sarah Jan 18, 1883
SEE BICKERS, Mr N.
HERMATET, Frank Local May 12, 1881
Frank Hermatet, of Clayton, and Miss Nellie Lyman of Camp Point were married in Quincy last Monday AM.
HERN, Sarah Dec 20, 1883
SEE EVANS, Wm
HERRN, Miss Johanna Sep 6, 1888
SEE PETERS, Folkers
HERRON, Miss Elm Grove Mar 30, 1882
Married, Frank Lanes and Miss Herron, also Henry Flesner and a Miss Herron.
HERRON, Miss Ankie Aug 18, 1887
SEE REPKE, Mr Frederick
HERRON, Sarah and Etje Golden Mar 16, 1882
Henry H. Flesner Jr and Sarah Herron, daughter of Leonard Herron were married Friday eve and Hiram P. Lenerts and Etje Herron, daughter of Harvey Herron, on Saturday afternoon, both were married by Rev Helbig at the Trinity parsonage.
HERSMAN, Mr and Mrs M.M. Neighborhood News Oct 25, 1888
Mr and Mrs M.M. Hersman celebrated their golden wedding at Mt Sterling, Thursday of last week.
HESS, Mr and Mrs Raleigh Local Aug 23, 1888
Mr and Mrs Raleigh Hess, at their home on Jos. Jefferson's farm celebrated their 10th wedding anniversary Saturday.
HILL, Geo. 5 Years Ago Sep 22, 1887
SEE BENNETT, Miss Maggie
HILL, Mr Henry Mounds Sep 21, 1882
Married September 7th at the home of Mr George Bennett, by Rev John Lee, Miss Maggie Brewster to Mr Henry Hill, all of Mounds.
HILL, J.A. Mar 10, 1887
SEE SCOTT, Miss Nancy
HILL, J.R. Locals Mar 3, 1887
Marriage license issued to J.R. Hill and Miss Nancy Scott, both of this vicinity.
HILL, Miss Mollie Local Apr 7, 1887
License was issued for marriage of Miss Mollie Hill age 30 and Mr Henry Brierton, age 46. Both of this city.
HILLMAN, Addie Jan 10, 1889
SEE JONES, Seth
HINCHMAN, James L. Local Oct 4, 1888
James L. Hinchman and Miss Katie Blood will be married at the home of brides parents in Camp Point the 10th inst.
HINMAN, Miss Mamie Dec 11, 1884
SEE CAPEL, Mr
HINMAN, Miss Fannie Dec 11, 1884
SEE CAPEL, Mr
HODGSON, Harry Mounds Jan 3, 1889
Married, Mr Harry Hodgson to Miss Mary Bradney by Capt Wm Mumford at the brides home Wednesday eve December 26th.
HOELSELL, Miss Jun 28, 1888
SEE HOGAN, Jas.

HOFFMAN, Albert	Kellerville	Nov 4, 1880
Married, Albert Hoffman and Miss Nannie Lierly.
HOFFMAN, Miss Emma	Sep 6, 1888
SEE HOUGH, Charles R.
HOGAN, Miss Annie P.	Local	Mar 24, 1887
Miss Annie P. Hogan, daughter of Frank and Mrs Hogan of Concord was married to Mr Jonah F. Sites of Camp Point in Quincy by Elder F.M. Calvin last Thursday. Will live Hays City, Kansas.
HOGAN, Jas.	Local	Jun 28, 1888
Jas. Hogan was married at Springfield Thuesday 26th inst to Miss Hoelsell.
HOGWOOD, Miss Julia	Apr 24, 1887
SEE BLAIR, Richard G.
HOKE, Alice	Feb 9, 1888
SEE BERRIER, David
HOKE, Miss Anna	Mar 2, 1882
SEE MORRIS, Mr Dayton
HOKE, Miss Ella	Crawford-Hoke	Oct 21, 1886
Married at the home of Mr and Mrs Craven Hoke, 1½ miles east of this city on, Wednesday eve, their daughter, Miss Ella, to Mr Charles Crawford, of Mt Sterling by Rev John Lee of Mounds. Will live Mt Sterling where Mr Crawford is engaged in business.
HOKE, James	Sep 15, 1887
SEE ROBINSON, Miss Mattie
HOKE, James	Married	Sep 14, 1882
Mr James Hoke to Miss Mattie Robinson by Rev Frank C. Bruner at Clayton, Illinois September 7th at the brides home.
HOKE, Miss Maggie	Oct 11, 1888
SEE CHASE, Charlie
HOLLIS, W.H. and wife	Local	Oct 20, 1881
W.H. Hollis and wife celebrated their wooden wedding anniversary Wednesday eve of last week.
HOLMES, Mrs Gabe	Local	Aug 19, 1886
About three weeks ago Mrs Gabe Holmes was married to George Washington who was porter at the Hampton House for many months. George fell from a ladder while working for Chris Curry some days ago and is laid up.
HOLMES, Miss Jennie	Mar 29, 1883
SEE HARTLEY, J.M.
HOLMES, Mercy A. and Margarette A.	Oct 4, 1883
SEE HASTINGS, John C.
HOPPER, Mrs Laura	Nov 8, 1888
SEE KETCHUM, George E.
HORNEY, Johnathon	Elm Grove	Jan 10, 1884
Cyrus Horney of Brooklyn has been visiting his brother William. He tells us that his son Johnathon is married.
HORNEY, Miss Mattie	Elm Grove	Jun 15, 1882
Miss Mattie Horney of La Prairie, who has a host of relatives and friends here, was married to S. Rigdon of the CB & Q. They will live Galesburg.
HOSKINS, Miss Lyde	1864-89	Sep 12, 1889
SEE MCCOY, John D. and wife
HOUGH, Charles R.	Local	Sep 6, 1888
Charles R. Hough was married at Enterprise, Kansas Sunday 2nd inst to Miss Emma Hoffman of that city.
HOUGH, Mr and Mrs G.R.	Local	Mar 29, 1883
Last Wednesday Mr and Mrs G.R. Hough celebrated their 25th wedding anniversary.
HOUGH, John E.	Sep 29, 1887
SEE LESTER, Miss Julia

HOUGH, Miss Laura E. Married Nov 1, 1889
Married at the Masonic Temple on Thursday eve Oct 24th Miss Laura E. daughter of Mr and Mrs Geo. R. Hough of this city and Mr Chas. E. Shute of River Bend, Colorado. Brides father and mother appeared first then the Rev Mr Souders of the First Presbyterian Church and then the bride and groom. At 10:30 bride and groom left for their drive to Camp Point where about 1 AM they took the "Eli" train on CB & Q for the West. After making a few stops in Kansas they then left for Colorado where the Clayton girl will reign queen of his extensive ranch.

HOUKE, Miss Louise Jan 8, 1880
SEE ZEIGLER, Henry

HOUKE, Miss Mary Dec 25, 1879
SEE MAY, Benjamin

HOWARD, Mr Edward Sep 23, 1886
SEE GILBIRDS, Mrs Jennie

HOWER, Miss Anna E. Jan 19, 1882
SEE CLARK, Mr J.T.

HOWES, Miss Olive May 3, 1883
SEE CUTLER, Mr Clinton

HOYT, Miss Grace Jan 3, 1884
SEE ROBBINS, Wm N.

HOYT, Miss Maggie C. Sep 9, 1886
SEE THOMAS, John B.

HUBER, Lambert Dec 18, 1884
Marriage license issued Saturday to Lambert Huber and Christina Decker of Camp Point.

HUDDLESTON, Clemens H. Local Oct 27, 1887
Clemens H. Huddleston and Miss Emma Bowers, of McKee township were wedded a few days ago by Justice Huddleston.

HUDDLESTON, Mrs Rose Sep 15, 1887
SEE SEVIER, Mr Valentine

HUGHES, Miss Captolia May 12, 1881
SEE MORLEY, F.A.

HUGHES, Mr Cornelius Married Feb 7, 1884
At the home of Dr J. Ham Davidson, brother of the bride, Kellerville, Illinois January 29th by Rev M.M. Davidson also a brother of the bride of Carrollton, Illinois assisted by Rev M.P. Wilkins of Clayton, Illinois. Mr Cornelius Hughes to Miss Emma Lou Davidson. Will live in Iowa.

HUGHES, George Local Apr 21, 1887
Wedding at the home of Prof John Jimison Sunday at 9 AM by Elder Calvin George Hughes and Miss Nora Barker. Mr Hughes is son of Mr George Hughes of McKee and Miss Barker is the daughter of she who was Mrs Baker, now Mrs Hughes, wife of the grooms father.

HUGHES, Mr J.W. Local Feb 9, 1882
Married, near Kellerville, Illinois February 5th Mr J.W. Hughes and Miss Mary A. Womelsdorff by Elder Chas. B. Newman.

HUGHES, Miss Lida Mar 6, 1884
SEE WELLS, Mr Otis

HUGHES, Mattie Feb 21, 1884
SEE HUNSAKER, Charlie

HUGHES, Sanford Hazel Dell Feb 26, 1885
Married this week, Mr Sanford Hughes to Miss Rebecca Yates.

HULEN, Thomas T. Golden Jul 26, 1888
Thomas T. Hulen and Mrs Skelley were married at Able Cain's last eve by Rev Middleton.

HUMPHREY, Miss Angie Married Feb 24, 1887
Married at the home of Mr and Mrs E.C. Cain, one mile west of this city at 4 PM Sunday, Miss Angie Humphrey to Mr Elmore D. Anderson by Elder F.M. Calvin of the Christian Church. Both well known to Clayton folks. Elmore was raised here.

HUNSAKER, Charlie Newtown Feb 21, 1884
Charlie Hunsaker and Mattie Hughes were married last week.

HUNT, Miss Amanda Neighborhood News Feb 19, 1888
A wedding Wednesday of last week in the parlors of the Union Hotel, at Galesburg. The porters had not seen each other until about one hour before the ceremony. The bride was Miss Amanda Hunt of Columbus, Ohio and the groom, Allen Thurman of Atwood, Kansas where he is in the drug business. They struck up a acquaintance about two years ago through a visitor of the bride living in Atwood and since been writing. The couple left for their new home at Atwood.

HUNTER, Charles S. Local Jan 27, 1881
Marriage license returned to county clerk and recorded last week. Charles S. Hunter to Emma Gunn of McKee.

HURST, Mr J. Pea Ridge Mar 25, 1880
At the home of the brides father, Mr J.H. Long, Mr J. Hurst of Hersman and Miss Belle Long of this place were married March 14th.

HUSBANDS, Mrs Gussie Jun 30, 1881
SEE CURRY, Estey

HUXTABLE, Thomas Mt Sterling Dec 18, 1879
Thomas Huxtable of Peoria and Miss Calista Price of this city, daughter of Leonidas Price were married at Christian Church on Tuesday eve of last week.by Elder Stewart.

IHNEN, Miss Apr 19, 1888
SEE BUSS, Gerd G.

IHNEN, Miss Wubke Mar 1, 1883
SEE BUSS, John G.

INGRAM, Mr and Mrs Henry Neighborhood News Jan 12, 1888
Mr and Mrs Henry Ingram celebrated their 50th anniversary of their wedding on the 31st.

INGRAM, Will Local Feb 21, 1884
Will Ingram and Miss Henrietta Herrel, the former from Chambersburg and the latter from Perry Springs, Pike County Illinois were married Wednesday in a Wabash train which was going at 40 miles per hour by Rev Drake of Versailles. They got on at Perry Springs Station. Married in the ladies coach.

JACKSON, Elvera Nov 8, 1888
SEE MASTERSON, James

JACOBS, Miss Anna Jan 22, 1880
SEE BURKINSHA, Geo. W.

JEFFERSON, Mr Taylor Married Sep 30, 1880
At the home of the brides parents, Wednesday September 22nd by Rev E.J. Rice, Mr Taylor Jefferson of Concord township and Miss Lissa Marshall of Lee township, Brown County.

JIMISON, Miss Sarah Locals Jan 3, 1889
5th wedding anniversary of Miss Sarah Jimison and Mr D.A. Davis which occurred at the home of Mr and Mrs Davis in south part of town on Wednesday eve last week.

JOHNSON, Miss Amanda Feb 9, 1882
SEE DANIELS, William

JOHNSON, Eliza Jan 27, 1881
SEE EAGER, John

JOHNSON, Miss Hilda Local Dec 13, 1883
Quincy "Herald" Miss Hilda Johnson, only daughter of Capt J.G. Johnson of Pittsfield was married at her fathers house Thursday to Chas. E. Battershell of Milton, Pike County Illinois.

JOHNSON, Katorah Nov 6, 1884
SEE WORLEY, Luther

JOHNSON, Mary Neighborhood News Sep 26, 1889
A few years ago at Cairo, Illinois, Mary Johnson married George Wilson, a few days ago it was discovered they were ½ brother and sister. The father of both had left his wife many years ago, gone to a distant country and married again. The couple have seperated.

JOHNSTON, Alex E. Neighborhood News Nov 10, 1887
The marriage of Mr Alex E. Johnston of Keokuk and Miss Clara E. Knox of Warsaw, was an elegant social event.

JONES, Miss Carrie Married Aug 26, 1886
Married, Miss Carrie Jones of this city to Mr Edwin Maxfield of Macoupin County at the home of brides parents, Mr and Mrs Thos. P. Flagg on eve of Tuesday 8 PM by Rev Peairs. Attendents were Miss Fannie Flagg, a relative of the bride and Eugene Cooper. Will live Macoupin County.

JONES, Mr and Mrs James E. Neighborhood News Sep 29, 1887
Friends assembled at the home of Mr and Mrs James E. Jones at Hamilton to celebrate the wedding of the aged couple who have been residents there for 20 years. They have two children, Miss Lotta, now one of the teachers in the schools and Alva, baggage master on the Clayton branch of the Wabash.

JONES, Miss Lucy Aug 5, 1880
SEE VANDORAN, Mr A.

JONES, Mr and Mrs N.W. Neighborhood News Aug 25, 1887
Today is the 64th wedding anniversary of Mr and Mrs N.W. Jones. Mr Jones was builder of the first log house built in Griggsville in 1833 and named the town. His wife is three years his senior and he is 85. Sons were present.

JONES, Mr and Mrs Nathaniel W. Neighborhood News May 5, 1887
Mr Nathaniel W. Jones and wife now residing in Griggsville have been married 63 years.

JONES, Seth Siloam Jan 10, 1889
Seth Jones and Addie Hillman were married at Mt Sterling on New Years Day. We understand they will live in Hancock County.

JULIAN, Miss Anna B. Dec 15, 1881
SEE FULLEN, Charles D.

JULIAN, Miss Annie 5 Years Ago Dec 16, 1886
Miss Annie Julian was married to Mr Chas. D. Fullen, a promising young lawyer at Fairfield, Iowa.

JURGENS, John J. Golden May 24, 1883
Married last week, John J. Jurgens and Mrs Tompke Eilerts. Also, John Gerdes and Mrs Frintzi Harbests.

KAISOR, Mrs Katharine Apr 7, 1887
SEE LAUGHLIN, Theodore

KAYLOR, Miss Josie Personal Jan 20, 1881
SEE MILBY, Will

KEARBY, Samuel G. Local Apr 13, 1882
Married at the home of the bride in Clayton, April 9th by Rev G.D. Kent, Mr Samuel G. Kearby to Miss Frances K. McQuown, all of Clayton.

KEE, Mr William Married May 8, 1884
At the home of brides father, Mr S.N. Black, on Wednesday afternoon May 7, 1884, Mr William Kee of Sedalia and Miss Mary Caroline Black of Clayton, Illinois by Rev E.J. Rice. Will live Sedalia.

KELLEY, J.S. Neighborhood News Apr 10, 1884
SEE DOWNING, George Y.

KELLEY, Miss Nora Jan 27, 1887
SEE O'HARA, Mr Batriek Jr.

KELLY, Edward Jan 17, 1889
SEE BOSTICK, Miss Nellie

KENDALL, Miss Carrie Jan 13, 1881
SEE ANDERSON, Will

KENDRICK, Mr H.B. Personal Oct 15, 1881
Rev Bruner will leave in a few days so he will be in Lima, Illinois on Thursday the 20th to marry Mr H.B. Kendrick and Miss Emma Bolt.

KENDRICK, Wm Esq. Dec 23, 1886
SEE WARD, Miss Bell

KERBY, Sam'l 5 Years Ago Apr 14, 1887
SEE MCQUOWN, Miss Kate

KERLEY, Edgar K. Married May 31, 1883
At the home of brides parents, Mr Robert Wright, Esq. in Kellerville, Adams County, by Rev G.D. Kent, Edgar K. Kerley, of Mounds, Brown County to Miss Anna Wright of Kellerville.

KERLEY, John Feb 17, 1887
SEE WRIGHT, Miss Dela

KERN, Miss Effie Feb 10, 1881
SEE DOWNING, Wm

KERN, Mr Samuel Golden May 19, 1881
Married Thursday eve in Houston by Squire Hanna, Mr Samuel Kern to Miss Sallie Bottorff, 3rd daughter of the late John S. Bottorff.

KERN, W. Everett Jan 3, 1889
SEE LIGGETT, Kittie

KESTING, Lewis Married Sep 28, 1882
At the home of brides father in Concord township on the eve of September 21st by Rev E.J. Rice, Mr Lewis Kesting and Miss Minerva Poland, all of Concord.

KESTING, Louis 5 Years Ago Oct 6, 1887
Louis Kesting and Miss Minerva Poland were married in Concord.

KESTING, Miss Louisa L. Dec 21, 1882
SEE COLPITTS, Mr James

KESTING, Theo. F. Local Dec 16, 1880
Married at the home of brides parents Wednesday eve, December 15th at 6 by Rev Wm Steffen, Mr Theo. F. Kesting and Miss Ellen Sharpe, all of Concord township.

KETCHUM, George E. Neighborhood News Nov 8, 1888
Married at the ME parsonage, Augusta, Illinois Wednesday October 31st "88", 4 PM Mr George E. Ketchum of Augusta and Mrs Laura Hopper of North East township Adams County by Rev T.W. Greeg. Mr Ketchum has lived at this place all his life and Mrs Hopper has been making her home with Mr W.B. Ketchum for past year. Couple will go to grooms home to live. "Augusta Eagle"

KETTINGRING, Miss Mary Mar 12, 1885
SEE COVERT, Thomas

KILE, Mr John Golden Oct 27, 1887
The Versailles Enterprise clips an article from a Kansas paper which tell of the marriage of Mr John Kile and Mrs Lucy Wyatt. We presume this is the former old hotel keeper here in the days of the old Clayton House.

KILE, Mr John Golden Oct 27, 1887
The Versailles Enterprise clips an article from a Kansas paper which tells of the marriage of Mr John Kile and Mrs Lucy Wyatt. We presume this is the former old hotel keeper here in the days of the old Clayton House.

KINNE, Rev and Mrs Niles Neighborhood News Sep 8, 1887
Saturday was the 50th wedding anniversary of Rev and Mrs Niles Kinne, of Barry. Reception at the Baptist Church.

KINNEAR, Mrs C.L. Jun 16, 1881
SEE BALLOW, Hon C.

KIRKPATRICK, James W. Sep 16, 1886
SEE MCMURRAY, Miss Nora

KIRKPATRICK, Miss Lillie M. Local May 10, 1888
Married, at the family home in Clayton, Illinois, Miss Lillie M. Kirkpatrick to Dr James R. Phelps May 9, 1888 by Rev McKown and left same evening for their future home in Topeka, Kansas.

KIRKPATRICK, M.W. Jan 13, 1887
SEE ANDERSON, Maude

KIRKPATRICK, Mrs Maude and Webb Little Brindle
Mrs Maude Kirkpatrick was granted a decree of divorce at Fargo, N.D. from her husband, Webb Kirkpatrick. Both were formerly of this city.

KIRKPATRICK, Mr Orville F. Local Jun 3, 1886
Married at the home of officiating clergyman, in this city May 31st 1886 by Rev G.D. Kent, Mr Orville F. Kirkpatrick and Miss Fannie E. Davis, all of Clayton, Illinois. Will live Bowen.

KLINE, Miss Feb 3, 1887
SEE MCFARLAND, Silas

KNIGHT, Miss Josie Locals Dec 25, 1889
Married, at the home of brides parents, Mr and Mrs Wm Knight of Pea Ridge, Miss Josie Knight to Mr John Garner on Thursday December 19th at 3 PM by Rev Jacob Crawford.

KNOX, Miss Clara E. Nov 10, 1887
SEE JOHNSTON, Alex E.

KNUDSON, Miss Helena Sep 20, 1888
SEE DORON, Rev Hugh

KOLLMAN, Herman Golden Mar 1, 1888
Herman Kollman and Miss Kate Buss were married last Tuesday at the home of her parents, Mr and Mrs Rolf Buss a mile southeast of town.

KOLLMANN, Herman Feb 23, 1888
SEE BUSS, Miss Kate

KONRAD, Mr and Mrs A. Local Aug 17, 1882
Monday Mr and Mrs A. Konrad celebrated their 10th wedding anniversary (August 14th).

KONRAD, Fred Local Jun 2, 1881
Mr Fred Konrad and wife, who were recently married are visiting at Conductor A. Konrad Monday.

KROLL, Miss Crissie Aug 12, 1880
SEE BURNS, Nick

KUNTZ, Frederick Married Nov 2, 1882
Married at the home of the bride's mother, Mrs L. Bartlett, in Clayton, Illinois October 26th by Rev G.D. Kent, Mr Frederick Kuntz and Miss Laura Bartlett, all of Adams County.

KUNTZ, Mr Will Dec 12, 1889
SEE MCMURRAY, Miss Bertis

LAAGE, George (F. or E.) Oct 17, 1889
Our best wishes to our friend Mr George F. Laage and his bride of Quincy.
The Optic says: At St Peters Roman Catholic Church last Tuesday AM occurred the marriage of George E. Laage and Miss Frances Gatz by Father McGirr groom is son of Mr and Mrs Geo. J. Laage and a member of Laage and Heine firm. Bride is daughter of Mr Alois Gatz an old resident of the city. Will live at 1007 Hampshire.

LACKEY, Mr Grant Local May 10, 1888
Mr Grant Lackey and Miss Kate Reath drove over to Mt Sterling Wednesday of last week, and were married by Rev Hann, of the Christian Church.

LACKEY, John C. Married Dec 27, 1883
Married at the Presbyterian parsonage, Thursday evening December 20th by Rev E.J. Rice, Mr John C. Lackey and Sadie J. Wright, all of Clayton, Illinois.

LAKIN, Mr Neighborhood News Mar 14, 1889
Mr Lakin, of the Barry Sun, was married the 6th inst.

LANCASTER, L.C. Neighborhood News Oct 25, 1888
L.C. Lancaster and Mrs Sue McDaniel were married at Mt Sterling recently.

LANES, Frank Mar 30, 1882
SEE HERRON, Miss

LANES, Miss Mary Dec 21, 1882
SEE BLOCK, Mr Alfred

LARIMORE, Miss Ida May 19, 1881
SEE BLAKE, Leander

LAUGHLIN, Theodore Neighborhood News Apr 7, 1887
Theodore Laughlin of Macomb aged 80 years and Mrs Katharine Kaisor, about 55 years were married.

LAUGHLIN, Wm Local Apr 28, 1881
Wm Laughlin and Miss Ida Tibbetts were married at the ME parsonage, Wednesday eve April 20th.

LAWLER, Mr Melvin Local Aug 24, 1882
Married, at the home of Mr James Gillenwater, in Concord township, Sunday the 13th, Mr Melvin Lawler and Miss Anna Baker by Rev Lee, of Mound Station. They are thinking of settling in Kansas.

LAWS, James B. Local Mar 22, 1883
Received to late for last weeks issue: Married in Mt Sterling, Thursday the 9th inst, Mr James B. Laws of Ripon, Kansas and Miss Frankie Clare of Brown County. Will live Kansas.

LEAPLEY, John Mound Station Aug 8, 1889
Married Wednesday (today) John Leapley and Anna Groves by Rev Crawford at the Rev's home.

LEE, George H. Jul 21, 1887
SEE ALLEN, Miss Hattie

LEE, George Y. Mar 8, 1883
SEE HAM, George W.

LEE, Henry Mound Station Jan 19, 1888
Mr Henry Lee and Miss Minnie Lucas were married at the brides home last Wednesday by Rev Steed.

LEMON, S.P. Locals Sep 15, 1887
S.P. Lemon and Miss Alice M. Atkins were married at Loraine this week. Mr Lemon is a business man in Loraine.

LENERTS, Hiram P. Mar 16, 1882
SEE HERRON, Sarah and Etje

LENNING, Miss Ann M. Jan 19, 1882
SEE WILLARD, Rev James

LESAGE, Miss Joeann Apr 29, 1880
SEE BRYANT, EVERETT P.

LESEM, Joseph Jun 7, 1883
SEE HAINSFURTHER, Miss Millie

LESTER, Miss Cora Apr 30, 1885
SEE WESTBROOK, Mr Chas. L.

LESTER, Miss Delia Feb 24, 1881
SEE DAVIS, J.C.

LESTER, Miss Julia Married Sep 29, 1887
Married, in Clayton, Adams County Illinois Sept 25, 1887 at the home of the brides father, G.W. Lester, Esq. by Rev G.D. Kent, Mr John E. Hough and Miss Julia Lester, all of Clayton.

LESTER, Miss Mollie Oct 15, 1881
SEE COHENOR, Mr J.N.

LEWIS, Miss Local Dec 27, 1888
December 21st 1883 Miss Lewis of Camp Point was married to Mr R.S. Curry. They celebrated the 5th anniversary of that event Friday night at their home in Camp Point.

LEWIS, Abraham Local Aug 16, 1883
Abraham Lewis and Miss Eliza Smith, both of Versailles were married at the Lambert House, Mt Sterling on last Thursday.

LEWIS, Mr Daily C. Married Jan 26, 1882
At the homeof the brides father, near Anderson station on the eve of January 19th at 6 PM Rev E.J. Eice, Mr Daily C. Lewis of Camp Point and Miss Lizzie L. Beckett, daughter of Mr James A. Beckett of Clayton.

LIBON, Frowkie Mar 18, 1880
SEE PETERS, Henry

LIERLE, Miss Adella Feb 3, 1887
SEE LUCAS, James E.

LIERLY, Miss Lettie Oct 12, 1882
SEE WEST, Mr Lafayett

LIERLY, Miss Nannie Nov 4, 1880
SEE HOFFMAN, Albert

LIGGETT, Kittie Married Jan 3, 1889
Married at the home of Mr and Mrs David Liggett on Xmas eve, their daughter Kittie, to W. Everett Kern at 6 PM. Wedding march played by Miss Vadie Greenhalgh and the happy couple took their places attended by Mr W.A. Zimmerman of Galesburg and Miss Lucy Thomas of this place. Marriage performed by brides uncle, Rev Orin Covert.

LIKES, James Chestline Jan 6, 1887
James Likes and Nanny Austin were married last Thursday eve.

LINDSEY, Henry Siloam Feb 7, 1889
Mr Henry Lindsey and Miss Libbie Miller, both of Pike County were married Friday night at the home of brides father, George Miller.

LINDSEY, John Local Feb 1, 1883
John Lindsey of Livingston County Missouri and Georgia Ellis, of Lima township were married by Justice Hutton last Thursday eve.

LINK, John Local Nov 22, 1888
A marriage license was issued to John Link and Miss Lena Finkhaus of Quincy Saturday. John is the man who gave Clayton the reputation for superior bread. He is in business on his own in Carthage.

LINN, Miss Minnie Married May 30, 1889
Married at Jacksonville, Saturday, Miss Minnie Linn, daughter of Mr and Mrs J.A. Linn of Concord to Mr Grant Hainline of Fairberry, Ill. They met at Jacksonville and were quietly married and returned to Clayton by evening train. Mr Hainline is a druggist at Fairberry.

LINTZ, Mr Frank Nov 17, 1887
SEE SMITH, Miss Lizzie

LISDELE, Miss Dora Oct 7, 1880
SEE ROY, John

LLOYD, John Locals Apr 14, 1887
Following appears in the Clark County (Dakota) Democrat of the 9th inst: Married at the home of brides parents Wednesday eve, Apr 6, 1887 by Rev W.A. Echols, of Raymond, Mr John Lloyd, of Clark and Miss Rosella Wiltse of the vicinity of Raymond. This is our John Lloyd, son of Eli Lloyd, Esq. now a prosperous young businessman of Clark, Dakota.

LOCK, Nancy and Nelson E. Quincy Dec 27, 1883
Divorce suit: Nancy Lock is plaintiff and Nelson E. Lock defendant, Nancy alledges drunkenness, adultery, abusive and obscene language and threats against her life. Asks property and custody of two children ages 18 and 13 years.

LOGUE, Miss Nannie Local Nov 29, 1888
Marriage of Miss Nannie Logue to Mr Benj. Clark of Brown County will be at the home of brides parents Wednesday eve. Groom is son of Mr Dick Clark, the extensive farm and stock man living north of Mt Sterling.

LOGUE, Miss Nannie Marriage Dec 6, 1888
At 12 noon Thursday November 29th at the home of brides parents, Mr and Mrs W.M. Logue, 3 miles northeast of this city, Miss Nannie Logue was married to Mr B.F. Clark, son of Mr and Mrs Dick Clark, north of Mt Sterling by Rev Abner Clark, brother of the groom.

LOHR, Jas. Columbus Feb 2, 1882
Married on Thursday eve January 19th by Rev A.M. Danely, Mr Jas. Lohr and Miss Bell Chatman.

LONEY, Mrs Nov 9, 1882
Mrs Loney, nee Tutt, known to Clayton people, and who has been living in Quincy for some time, eloped last week with James Patton, one of the policemen of that city.

LONEY, Mrs Local Nov 30, 1882
Mrs Loney who eloped with Detective Patten about a month ago returned to the city yesterday AM on the St Louis train. The money she took from her husband had all been spent and in order to get to Quincy she boarded the train and told the conductor she had been in St Louis buying goods and that her husband was an employee of the Wabash and hoped he would let her ride, which he did. Upon arriving here she at once sought her husband, but he would have nothing to do with her and she took rooms at a hotel on the levee.

LONG, Miss Belle Mar 25, 1880
SEE HURST, Mr J.

LONG, Ella Mound Station Nov 17, 1887
Thursday, at the home of the brides parents, Mr and Mrs J. Long, occurred the marriage of their daughter, Ella, to Mr James Golden of Schuyler County. They visited grooms parents in Golden Friday.

LONG, Miss Emma Wedded Aug 26, 1886
Married, Miss Emma Long of Mounds to Mr Louis Cass Marrett at the home of brides parents, Mr and Mrs R.D. Long in Mounds Thursday afternoon 3:30 PM on the 19th inst by Elder F.M. Calvin of the Christian Church in this city. Took a short train trip to Chicago on the evening train. Will return Monday night and live on East Washington Street.

LOUIS, Miss Dec 27, 1883
SEE CURRY, "Dick"

LOVEITT, Miss Lucy Local Nov 10, 1881
Miss Lucy Loveitt of Mt Sterling and Mr Edward Marnell of Hannibal, Missouri were married in Mt Sterling Wednesday eve November 2nd.

LOWRY, Miss Mattie Locals Sep 19, 1889
The marriage of Miss Mattie Lowry to Mr Jas. Gray and Miss Maymie Harney to Mr George Givens occurs at Mt Sterling today (Wednesday).

LUBBEN, Mr L.H. Locals Jul 4, 1889
From Creston, Iowa "Advertiser" Married Wednesday June 26th on North Cherry Street, Mr L.H. Lubben and Miss Augusta Peterson, both of Creston by Rev H. Wirth of the Evangelical Church. Ex-Fireman L.H. Lubben and his bride departed on #3 yesterday for a short visit to Omaha. "Mr Lubben is known to quite a number of our readers here."

LUCAS, D.W. Local Oct 18, 1883
Married at the home of the brides parents October 16th by Rev J.V. Pringle, Mr D.W. Lucas and Miss Hattie M., daughter of Mr John Ratcliff.

LUCAS, Frank Concord Mar 1, 1883
We learn that our friend, Frank Lucas, of Brown County and Miss Lola Oldenburg were married last week.

LUCAS, Miss Ida M. Aug 18, 1887
SEE ROY, Mr James L.

LUCAS, James E. Local Feb 3, 1887
Mr James E. Lucas of Mounds age 25, and Miss Adella Lierle of Barnard age 20, were on Saturday licensed to marry by our county clerk.

LUCAS, Miss Minnie Jan 19, 1888
SEE LEE, Henry

LUKER, Joe H. Jun 21, 1888
SEE MONTGOMERY, Miss Addie

LYKES, Mr Jan 13, 1887
SEE AUSTIN, Miss Nanny

LYMAN, Miss Nellie May 12, 1881
SEE HERMATET, Frank

LYON, Miss Etta Sep 9, 1886
SEE ROY, David

MACOMBER, Mary E. Jan 26, 1888
SEE CAMP, Samuel

MACOMBER, Miss Mary E. Jan 26, 1888
SEE CAMP, Samuel

MAGNER, Miss Maggie Married Oct 25, 1888
Married at Camp Point 10 AM Sunday October 21st Miss Maggie Magner to Mr John T. Sullivan both of this city by Father Johannes. She is daughter of John Magner. Will live Clayton. Mr Sullivan has been fireman on the branch for some time.

MANKER, John Chestline Sep 27, 1888
John Manker and Miss Edna Mixer went to Hannibal last week and were married.

MANLOVE, Miss Mollie Feb 23, 1888
SEE THOMPSON, Lewis

MARKSBERY, Perry Local Mar 24, 1881
Married in Clayton on the 17th inst, by Rev O.D. Gibson, Mr Perry Marksbery to Miss Annie E. Roland. The parties have lately come from Kentucky and settled in town.

MARNELL, Edward Nov 10, 1881
SEE LOVEITT, Miss Lucy

MARRETT, Mr Louis Cass Aug 26, 1886
SEE LONG, Miss Emma

MARSH, Maj. Asbury C. and Mary E. Neighborhood News Jan 6, 1887
After having been seperated for several months by a family disagreement, Major Asbury C. Marsh and Mrs Mary E. Marsh of Louisiana, Missouri were remarried on last Tuesday.

MARSHALL, Mr Abraham L. Married Jan 10, 1889
Married in Clayton, Adams County Illinois January 3, 1889 at the home of the brides father, Thomas Williams, by Rev G.D. Kent of Tolono, Mr Abraham L. Marshall, of Mounds and Miss Mary B. Williams of Clayton.

MARSHALL, Miss Alice Aug 22, 1889
SEE STEED, Rebert L.

MARSHALL, Miss Lissa Sep 30, 1880
SEE JEFFERSON, Mr Taylor

MARSHALL, Mrs Lydia Dec 21, 1882
SEE HENRY, Geo. N.

MARTIN, Charles Dec 2, 1886
SEE REID, Miss Dean

MARTIN, Grant — Neighborhood News — Feb 16, 1888
Grant Martin, age 15 years and Gracie Silvers age 13 years were married in Fairmont, this state, last Friday. They are the youngest couple ever married in the state.

MARTIN, Wm B. — Golden — Jun 15, 1882
Papers of Atlantic City, Iowa, last week, reported the marriage of Wm B. Martin of that city (son of Dr Martin of this town) to Miss R.A. Reeves of Norwalk, Iowa.

MASON, Rev and Mrs Chas. — Neighborhood News — Oct 6, 1887
The golden wedding of Rev and Mrs Chas. Mason, took place Monday eve of last week at their home in Barry.

MASTERSON, James — Chestline — Nov 8, 1888
James Masterson and Elvera Jackson were married last week by Squire Peacock.

MATTHEWS, Mr Pete Feb 28, 1889
SEE FLASSNER, Miss Christina

MAXFIELD, Mr Edwin Aug 26, 1886
SEE JONES, Miss Carrie

MAY, Benjamin — Pea Ridge — Dec 25, 1879
Married December 9th at the home of Mr John Long, Benjamin May to Miss Mary Houke, all of Pea Ridge.

MAY, Benj. Sr. — Pearidge — Aug 26, 1886
On Thursday of last week, the marriage of Uncle Benj. May Sr. to Mrs Simpkins both of this (Brown) county. We wish the aged couple happiness.

MAY, Miss Elizabeth Feb 5, 1885
SEE SCROGGAN, Lyman T.

MAY, Geo. W. Oct 28, 1886
SEE STAPLETON, Miss Iva

MAY, George T. and Ellen — Local — Nov 22, 1888
George T. May of this place has brought suit for divorce from his wife, Ellen May. Says they were married July 6, 1879 and lived together until December 1887 when she left to lead a life of shame in Kansas City. Since her departure he had discovered that Ellen was not true to her marriage vows while she lived with him.

MAY, George T. and Ellen — Local — Apr 4, 1889
Divorce case heard at this term of Adams County circuit court from this vicinity: George T. May vs Ellen May.

MAY, John T. — Local — Apr 5, 1883
Married at the home of the brides parents in Mound Station on the eve of March 29th by Rev J.V. Pringle, Mr John T. May and Miss Laura Belle Williams.

MAY, Miss Mary Ellen Feb 21, 1884
SEE FEATHERINGILL, George T.

MAY, Mr Sam — Local — Mar 7, 1889
The Adams House was the scene of a wedding Thursday. Mr Sam May and Miss Rhoda Derringer were wed.

MAY, Miss Sena Sep 22,1887
SEE RAWSON, Thomas

MAY, Miss Sina | Pea Ridge | Sep 8, 1881
Married in our vicinity, Miss Sina May to Jimmie Graves.

MAYFIELD, Cebron | Mounds | Aug 4, 1881
Cebron Mayfield was married Tuesday eve at the home of Mr Glenn to Mrs Gray by Rev H.C. Coats.

MEATS, Mr Frank | Local | Sep 29, 1881
Married in Clayton Wednesday eve, September 21st by Rev E.J. Rice, Mr Frank Meats to Miss Cenith Miller, took the train at 9:30 for Golden where they will live. Frank has a restaurant here. Parents visited them Thursday.

MEISSER, W.D. | Local | Apr 13, 1882
W.D. Meisser of the firm of Burgesser and Meisser started for Peoria Monday AM. Married on Tuesday AM April 11th W.D. Meisser son of Mr and Mrs Henry Meisser of Quincy to Miss Etta, daughter of exMayor Warner of Peoria. Couple will arrive in Clayton Thursday.

MEISSER, Will D. | Apr 14, 1887
SEE WARNER, Miss Etta

MERRILL, Miss Kate | Dec 9, 1886
SEE MILLER, Mr W.H.

MERRILL, Miss Katie | Jun 9, 1887
SEE MCMURRAY, Mr J.E.

MEYERS, Mr J.S. | Local | Oct 26, 1882
Married in Clayton, Wednesday eve October 18th at the home of Mr Samuel McBratney by Rev O.D. Gibson, Mr J.S. Meyers and Mrs Lucy C. Smith. Will live Stonington, Illinois.

MILBY, Will | Personal | Jan 20, 1881
Will Milby tells us that he was married to Miss Josie Kaylor of Quincy December 28th.

MILEHAM, Dr | Local | Apr 6, 1882
A decree of divorce has been filed in the Dr Mileham case of Camp Point.

MILEHAM, Dr Samuel | Camp Point | Nov 9, 1882
Dr Samuel Mileham and Miss Mattie J. Castle were married Sunday eve at the home of the brides mother by Rev Geo. W. Cyrus.

MILLER, Miss Cenith | 5 Years Ago | Sep 30, 1886
Miss Cenith Miller was married to Mr Frank Meats.

MILLER, Miss Emma A. | Nov 23, 1882
SEE BENNETT, Mr Josiah

MILLER, Miss Florence | Apr 27, 1882
SEE RIDINGS, Mills

MILLER, Henry | Elm Grove | Mar 13, 1884
Henry Miller was married last week. Happy Henry.

MILLER, J.W. | Mound Station | May 27, 1880
J.W. Miller went to county clerk office at Mt Sterling last week where he and Miss Tillie Glenn got a license to wed. Went to M.E. Church and were married by Rev R. Chapman Wednesday. Returned home Thursday.

MILLER, J.W. | Dec 23, 1886
SEE STEWART, Mrs Lillei

MILLER, Mr Joseph | Sep 9, 1886
SEE BAKERBOWER, Miss Caroline

MILLER, L.J. | Camp Point | Jan 8, 1880
L.J. Miller and Julia Roberts were married Saturday eve by W.A. Crawford.

MILLER, Miss Libbie | Feb 7, 1889
SEE LINDSEY, Henry

MILLER, Miss Lizzie A. | Aug 5, 1886
SEE HALEY, Mr A.T.

MILLER, Oliver C. Married Feb 23, 1888
Married at the home of brides parents in Clayton township, Adams County Illinois February 15th 1888 by Rev G.D. Kent, Mr Oliver C. Miller and Mrs Sarah E. Allen of Adams County.

MILLER, Mr Philip Locals Jul 4, 1889
Marriage of Mr Philip Miller and Miss Alma A. Selby, both of Golden occurred at the home of the brides father, Mr Seneca Selby on Saturday eve by Rev C.F. McKown, uncle of the bride.

MILLER, S.D. Mounds Mar 2, 1882
Latest by telegraph: Married yesterday eve, S.D. Miller and Miss Lottie Griffith.

MILLER, Mr W.H. Local Dec 9, 1886
The wedding of Mr W.H. Miller of Camp Point and Miss Kate Merrill of Abingdon was celebrated at the brides home on Thursday ar 5 PM November 25th 1886 by Rev D.B. Spencer of the Cong'l Church.

MILLER, Will E. Dec 8, 1881
Will E. Miller and Miss Ella R. Peyton, the step daughter of N.W. Wright, were married in Cheyenne, Wyoming Nov 23, 1881. It will be remembered that last summer Mr Wright and family and Will Miller went out to Wyoming together. Will is doing business with Craig and Gardner in the furniture line in Cheyenne.

MILLER, Miss Zura Sep 20, 1883
SEE ORR, Lewis

MINTLE, Mr Morris Local Jan 13, 1881
Mr Morris Mintle, of Bowen and Miss Mollie, oldest daughter of Jos. Cromwell, were married at the brides parents home December 29th at 2:30 PM by Rev F.C. Bruner.

MITCHELL, Miss Emma Neighborhood News Nov 15, 1888
Stout, the mute artist and bicycle rider of Ripley, lately married Miss Emma Mitchell of St Louis, who is and expert with indian clubs.

MIXER, Miss Edna Sep 27, 1888
SEE MANKER, John

MOFFETT, Miss Julia Married Aug 21, 1884
Married on the eve of August 13th 1884 at the home of Mr C.H. Moffett, in Clayton, Illinois, his daughter, Miss Julia and Mr John R. Wallace. Will live Chicago where Mr Wallace has been in business about 2 years.

MOFFETT, Miss Julia F. 5 Years Ago Sep 5, 1889
Miss Julia F. Moffett was married to Mr John R. Wallace on August 13th.

MONTGOMERY, Miss Addie Local Jun 21, 1888
Cards are out for marriage of Miss Addie, daughter of Major and Mrs W. Montgomery, to Mr Joe H. Luker at their home in this city, Wednesday eve June 27th at 6:30. Mr Luker will arrive from the west that day.

MONTGOMERY, Miss Addie Local Jul 12, 1888
The marriage of Joseph Luker, Treas. of the Selo Bros. Circus and Miss Addie Montgomery, daughter of Major Montgomery, of Clayton in this occurred in Kansas City, the past week. "Quincy Sunday Herald" We have a letter from Miss Montgomery saying They were NOT married.

MONTGOMERY, Miss Edith Local Jan 1, 1885
Miss Edith Montgomery was married to Mr Mark Wheeler of Georgetown, Colorado at that place on the 18th inst at the home of Mr A.R. Forbes.

MONTGOMERY, Miss Elva Wedding Bells Jun 14, 1883
Married last Tuesday eve at the home of Maj. Wm Montgomery at 7 PM, Miss Elva Montgomery daughter of Mr and Mrs Wm Montgomery to Mr Fred J. Dikes a railroad agent at Liberty, Missouri formerly of Mt Sterling Illinois by Rev F.M. Hayes.

MONTGOMERY, Ewing 5 Years Ago Oct 17, 1889
Ewing Montgomery was married at Grand Junction, Colorado.

MONTGOMERY, Major Wm and wife 25th Anniversary Sep 23, 1880
Last Saturday, Major and Mrs Wm Montgomery celebrated their 25th wedding anniversary at Clayton.

MONTGOMERY, Wm Aug 11, 1887
SEE STROAD, Mrs

MOORE, Mr Nov 28, 1889
SEE SLEBY, Miss Kittie

MOORE, Mr Local Dec 5, 1889
The Enterprises of last week got Mr Moore, of Kingston, marridd to the wrong lady. In fact the lady given by us, is a myth, so to speak, and has no real existence. It was his good fortune to get Miss Hittie Beckett, daughter of Capt and Mrs J.A. Beckett. She will make him a good wife

MOORE, J.W. Mound Station Aug 8, 1889
Married, May 15th by Rev L.A. Powell, Mr J.W. Moore and Mrs Lottie Thompson.

MOORE, Miss Jennie Dec 4, 1879
SEE GIDDINGS, Mr Terry

MOORLEY, Sarah A. Sep 29, 1881
SEE CONNER, William

MORLEY, F.A. Camp Point May 12, 1881
Married, at the home of the groom's father Sunday eve, May 8th F.A. Morley and Miss Captolia Hughes.

MORRIS, Mr Dayton Wedded Mar 2, 1882
Married, Mr Dayton Morris and Miss Anna Hoke at the home of Mr George Smith, near Dallas, Illinois Thursday February 23rd bride has many friends in Clayton.

MORRIS, Wm Neighborhood News Aug 22, 1889
Wm Morris' wife died at Canton Sunday July 7th on Monday she was buried and that eve he attended the circus. Tuesday he cused the undertaker for not furnishing a better coffin at counties expense and Wednesday he went to Lewiston and got a marriage license. Thursday he was married to an inmate of the county house.

MOTTER, L.H. Local Mar 9, 1882
Married, L.H. (Link) Motter and Miss Anna Bellow last Wednesday eve March 1st at the parsonage by Rev F.C. Bruner.

MOTTER, Mr L.H. 5 Years Ago Mar 10, 1887
SEE BLUE, Miss Annie

MOWEN, Mary E. Aug 23, 1883
SEE COOVERT, Isaac W.

MULKEY, Horace B. Cupid and His Work Jul 15, 1880
Married in the county during the past week: Horace B. Mulkey of Bannock City, M.T. to Flora J. Brown of Quincy.

MUNFORD, Mr Wm Local Sep 13, 1883
At the Presbyterian Church in Mt Sterling last Tuesday a double wedding Mr Wm Munford, a young attorney, to Miss Katie L. Barry and Mr Louis D. Bell, cashier of the First National Bank to Miss May G. Curry, all of Mt Sterling.

MYERS, Miss Fannie Local Nov 29, 1888
Miss Fannie Myers, daughter of Mr and Mrs Tom Myers of Concord was married last Sunday to Mr James Taylor of Mounds.

MYERS, Miss Fannie Mound Station Nov 29, 1888
Married, Mr Taylor to Miss Fannie Myers, by Rev Van Wey Sunday eve.

MYERS, Miss Fannie Oakwood Nov 29, 1888
Miss Fannie Myers and Jas. Taylor were married Sunday. Will live Missouri.

MYERS, Mr J.S. 5 Years Ago Oct 27, 1887
SEE SMITH, Mrs Lou

MYERS, Miss Nora Jun 28, 1888
SEE DOKE, John

MCANULTY, Samuel Camp Point Oct 25, 1883
Samuel McAnulty, formerly of this place, but now of Augusta and Mrs Margaret Thompson were married last week.

MCBRATNEY, Maude L. Sep 13, 1883
SEE BLACK, Dr Joseph N.

MCCASKILL, Daniel M. Pea Ridge Apr 8, 1880
Married at the home of the brides father, March 29th Mr Daniel M. McCaskill of Pea Ridge and Miss Nancy C. Clarke of Schuyler County by Elder T.P. Ausmus. Will live in a farm in Bates County Missouri where Mr McCaskill's father is a most worthy citizen and who bought and presented the farm to the groom.

MCCLAIN, Joseph Neighborhood News Sep 27, 1883
Mt Sterling "Message" Double wedding on Thursday afternoon at the courthouse, Joseph L. McClain and Susan Bowman of Adams County and Wm Sutton of Brown and Flora Adkinson of Schuyler by Elder S.R.Patton.

MCCLINTOCK, Miss Millie Nov 23, 1882
SEE HACKNEY, W.R.

MCCOY, F.A. Mar 3, 1881
Married, F.A. McCoy at 4 PM Thursday the 24th ult to Miss Libbie Thomas at the home of the brides mother in this city by Rev E.J. Rice.

MCCOY, James A. Married May 31, 1883
On Wednesday eve May 23rd at the home of the brides mother in Clayton, Illinois by Rev Edwin J. Rice, Mr James A. McCoy of Eureka, Kansas and Miss Julia A. Williams of this place. Will live in Eureka. Mr McCoy lived Clayton greater part of his life as did Miss Julia. They left on AM train for Kansas.

MCCOY, John D. and wife 1864-89 Sep 12, 1889
Surprise party for John D. McCoy and wife's wedding anniversary. They were married 5th September 1864. John D. McCoy and Miss Lyde Hoskins in the Methodist Church. Had two daughters, Miss Pearl and Miss May.

MCCOY, John W. Apr 18, 1889
SEE CONN, Miss Minnie

MCCRAY, Laura Jun 17, 1886
SEE ADAIR, Arthur P,

MCCRAY, Miss Laura Jun 17, 1886
SEE ADAIR, Mr Ad

MCCULLUM, H.E. Elm Grove Sep 15, 1887
Married, at the brides fathers, Mr H.E. McCullum to Miss Hattie M. Cameron.

MCDADE, Miss Mamie Apr 21, 1887
SEE FOX, James B.

MCDANIEL, Mrs Sue Oct 25, 1888
SEE LANCASTER, L.C.

MCDANNOLD, Mr S. Burns Married Sep 5, 1889
Married at the home of Mr E. Bennett in Clayton September by Rev E.W. Souders, Mr S. Burns McDannold, of St Louis and Miss Sadie Wiley of Clayton. He is a resident engineer of Frisco Railroad. Will live St Louis.

MCDANOLD, Wm 5 Years Ago Jun 7, 1888
Wm McDanold and Miss Bettie Wallace were married.

MCDONALD, Mr William Married Jun 7, 1883
At the home of the brides father on the 5th inst by Rev J.V. Pringle, Miss Elizabeth A. Wallace, eldest daughter of Mr C.I. Wallace and Mr William McDonald of Terre Haute, Indiana.

MCDONNAL, Mrs Sallie Mar 5, 1885
SEE SEALS, Chris

MCDOWELL, Capt and Mrs | 5 Years Ago | Dec 22, 1887
Friends surprised Capt and Mrs McDowell on their 25th wedding anniversary.
MCDOWELL, Mrs Nancy | 5 Years Ago | Jul 12, 1888
SEE VAUGHAN, John
SEE VAUGHN, John | | Jul 12, 1883
MCDOWELL, S.K. | 5 Years Ago | Mar 21, 1889
S.K. McDowell and Addie Caldwell were married at Helena, Montana.
MCDOWELL, Sam | Local | Mar 20, 1884
Sam McDowell was married on the 10th inst at Helena, Montana to Miss M. Caldwell. Since he heard the news Capt McDowell felt sufficiently elated to brevet himself.
MCDOWELL, Will | Local | Feb 3, 1887
Will McDowell will be married on the 9th inst at Shelbyville, Illinois to Miss Mattie Webster. We have a invitation.
MCDOWELL, Will H. | Married | Feb 17, 1887
"Shelbyville Daily Union of the 19th inst" Married Miss Mattie Webster to Mr W.H. McDowell at Shelbyville, her nuptials were celebrated at the home of her mother, Mrs Ella Webster last eve. Married at 8 PM by Rev W.J. Frazer in the parlor. Present was, Mr. H.W. Webster of Mattoon, W.A. Flowers of Pana, A.S. and Ed C. McDowell of Clayton, TH.W. McDowell of Anthony, Kansas and Miss Margaret Veeders of Boston, Mr and Mrs J.S. Veeders of Pana. Will live Salina, Kansas where a new home awaits them. Mr McDowell is proprietor of a drug store in Saline and with his brothers has long simce identified himself with the properity of that booming state.
MCFARLAND, Silas | Golden | Feb 3, 1887
Silas McFarland and his new bride once Miss Kline, of Camp Point, were on our streets, Monday.
MCGEHEE, Stephen | Neighborhood News | May 2, 1888
Stephen McGehee had recently married the divorced wife of J.J. Ferris a dissolute character, who went to the farm four miles south of Canton and shot McGehee. Ferris was arrested and taken to Lewistown and then to Peoria.
MCKINNEY, Mrs Evaline L. | | Sep 8, 1887
SEE BARTHOLOMEW, Mr James
MCLAIN, James | Pea Ridge | May 8, 1884
Married at the home of Wm McLain's, by Esq. Pevehouse, James McLain to Miss Yakely.
MCLAUGHLIN, Miss Bessie | | Jun 13, 1889
SEE BLACK, Dr C.E.
MCMINIMY, Mr and Mrs Richard | Neighborhood News | Aug 26, 1886
Golden wedding of Mr and Mrs Richard McMinimy was celebrated at Carthage recently.
MCMULLEN, Wm | Local | May 12, 1881
Old Mr Wm McMullen and Mrs Jane Scott were married Saturday eve April 30th.
MCMURRAY, Miss Bertie | Local | Dec 12, 1889
A wedding at the home of W.F. and Mrs McMurray Thursday eve December 2nd by Rev W.M. Reed, their daughter, Miss Bertie and Mr Will Kuntz.
MCMURRAY, Mr J.E. | Local | Jun 9, 1887
Mr J.E. McMurray, of Quincy was at 8:30 Thursday eve married to Miss Katie Merrill at the home of the brides mother, at Perry Pike County by Rev Stevenson.
MCMURRAY, Miss Nora | | Sep 16, 1886
Miss Nora, daughter of Mr and Mrs J.H. McMurray was married to Mr James W. Kirkpatrick on Tuesday of last week. Will live at Mr Kirkpatrick's home in Banner, Johnson County Wyoming.

MCNEFF, Miss Lizzie — Dec 2, 1880
SEE GREEN, John

MCNEFF, Miss Maggie — Jan 11, 1883
SEE FITZPATRICK, Joe

MCPHERSON, Mr — Pearidge — Aug 5, 1880
Married Wednesday at the home of brides father, Miss Mittie Giddings and Mr McPherson, all of Brown County by Rev Turner of Clayton.

MCPHERSON, Benj. G. — Local — Aug 5, 1880
Married at the home of brides parents in Pea Ridge township, Brown County Wednesday July 28th by Rev P.L. Turner, Mr Benj. G. McPherson of Cooperstown to Miss Mary Ann M. Giddings.

MCQUOWN, Miss Frances K. — Apr 13, 1882
SEE KEARBY, Samuel G.

MCQUOWN, Miss Kate — 5 Years Ago — Apr 14, 1887
Miss Kate McQuown was married to Sam'l Kerby.

MCREA, Edward — Newtown — Dec 1, 1881
Married on Thursday in Quincy: Edward McRea to Mrs Dora Wisenburg.

MCVEY, Frank — Neighborhood News — Jan 10, 1884
Pittsfield "Herald" Mr Frank McVey and Miss Jennie Sweetingy both from Perry were married in the parlor of the Pittsfield House Wednesday afternoon by his honor C.W. Patterson.

MCVEY, Wm — Local — Sep 8, 1881
Wm McVey living near Kingston, eloped Monday of last week with the hired girl, leaving his wife in almost a dying condition with consumption.

NEATON, Eva — Feb 7, 1889
"Pill School House, East Pea Ridge" Eva Neaton was married to Mr Drake on New Years day at Mr Stull's.

NEVINS, John — Aug 1, 1889
SEE BAUGHMAN, Miss Cora

NEWHOUSE, Miss Ollie — Oct 4, 1883
SEE BAIRD, John

NEWLAND, Mr and Mrs Abram — Local — Feb 21, 1884
Mr and Mrs Abram Newland celebrated their golden wedding in Colchester last week. Four children and 20 grand children were present and this is first time the family has been together since the children married and left home.

NICHOLS, Mr — Sep 15, 1887
SEE HAYS, Miss Nora

NIECE, Miss Rose — Apr 4, 1889
SEE SLAGLE, Wm J.

NOAKES, Mrs Ellen — Jul 5, 1883
SEE BERKETT, Alden S.

NOAKES, Miss Geneva — Nov 27, 1879
SEE CAMPBELL, Thomas A.

NOKES, Mrs Ellen — 5 Years Ago — Jul 5, 1888
Mrs Ellen Nokes was married to A.S. Berkitt.

NOKES, Miss Geneva — 10 Years Ago — Nov 28, 1889
SEE CAMPBELL, Mr Thos. A.

NOLAN, Louis — Persohal — May 18, 1882
Mr Louis Nolan and Miss Ella Cullinan were married at the Catholic Church in Mt Sterling last Sunday. Louis is well known to Clayton people. We do not know Mrs Nolan.

NOLAN, Louis — 5 Years Ago — May 19, 1887
Louis Nolan and Miss Ella Cullenan were married at Mt Sterling.

NORRIS, Miss Anna B. — Local — Jun 3, 1886
The marriage of Miss Anna B. Norris to Dr H.L. Salthouse took place at Columbus on the 20th inst.

NOYES, Dr T.C. Local Apr 11, 1889
Dr T.C. Noyes, who is known to our citizens, having practiced his profession here, and Mrs Lizzie Shields were married at Mt Sterling Wednesday last.

NUSBUMMER, Rosa Golden Mar 3, 1887
Rosa Nusbummer, of this town, and William Chambers of Augusta, went to Carthage Tuesday and were married.

OCONNER, Miss Cornelia Oct 13, 1887
SEE COLPITT, Joseph

OERTLE, Miss Anna Nov 1, 1883
SEE REIDINGER, David

O'HARA, Mr Batriek Jr. Neighborhood News Jan 27, 1887
At the home of the bride in Liberty township, Mr Batriek O'Hara Jr. of Liberty and Miss Nora Kelley, the daughter of Hon. Maurice Kelley, of Quincy were married.

OLDENBURG, Miss Lola Mar 1, 1883
SEE LUCAS, Frank

OMER, Mr and Mrs Jake Neighborhood News Dec 11, 1884
Camp Point Journal: Mr and Mrs Jake Omer celebrated their wooden wedding Thursday.

OMER, Lizzie Dec 18, 1879
SEE SEATON, James

OMER, Tuck Mar 24, 1887
SEE ESHUM, Miss Hattie

OMER, Warren Local Sep 9, 1880
Mr Warren Omer of Camp Point on September 1st married Miss Belle Smith of Clayton in Camp Point by Rev Crawford.

ORR, Lewis Neighborhood News Sep 20, 1883
Brown County Gazette Married in the past week in this city (Thursday eve) Mr Lewis Orr of Lee township and Miss Zura Miller, eldest daughter of Mr and Mrs D.W. Miller of this city by Rev L. Osborn, grandfather of the groom.

ORTON, Mr and Mrs Alias Local Nov 30, 1882
Mr and Mrs Clark Orton and their son in law and daughter, Mr and Mrs May have received invitations to the silver wedding of Mr and Mrs Alias Norton at their home in Willow Dale, Colorado November 18th. Sorry they can not go.

ORTON, Miss Berintha Nov 3, 1881
SEE BLACK, John

ORTON, Miss Berinthia Nov 3, 1881
SEE BLACK, John D.

OSBORN, Robert Neighborhood News Jun 7, 1888
Elopement of Robert Osborn and Miss Letha Burke, of Barry last Sunday caused the girl's mother to go into a fit of insanity, by a previous marriage to a member of the family Mr Osborn had incured displeasure of his wifes parents. They were married at Pittsfield next day and the daughter went home to comfort her mother, Mr Osborn also returned and it is probably the relatives will accept him and make the best of it.

OWEN, C.J. Local Sep 8, 1887
C.J. Owen, of Camp Point, formerly of this place, was recently married to Pauline Ward, of Galesburg.

PACKARDS, Miss Lizzie Sep 6, 1888
SEE SMITH, James A. "Allie"

PAGE, Mrs Lou Jan 17, 1884
SEE SCOTT, Miss Lou

PAPE, Mr Wm H. Married Dec 8, 1881
On Sunday, December 4th at the home of the brides father, A.L. Reeder, 3½ miles southeast of Clayton by Rev F.C. Bruner, Mr Wm H. Pape of Melrose and Miss Emma Reeder, Miss Alice Kirkpatrick and Mr Quinn Reeder attended the bride and groom as bridesmaid and groomsman.

PARKER, Horace Pea Ridge May 26, 1887
A quiet wedding in this vicinity a few days ago, the parties were, Mr Horace Parker and Miss Minnie Davidson, Jay Brown Esq. officiating.

PARKER, John L. Dec 18, 1884
Marriage license issued Saturday to John L. Parker and Sadie L. Gore of Clayton.

PARSONS, Miss Hattie A. Sep 23, 1886
See TEACHENOR, Monkey

PATTEN, Detective Local Nov 30, 1882
SEE LONEY, Mrs

PATTON, James Nov 9, 1882
SEE LONEY, Mrs

PAUGHBURN, Mrs Josephine May 8, 1884
SEE CARTER, Lawson G.

PAXON, Miss Lou Oct 13, 1887
SEE ALEXANDER, Mr John

PENDLETON, Chas. 5 Years Ago Mar 10, 1887
Mr Chas. Pendleton, of Kansas and Miss Rachael Walker of Elm Grove, were married.

PENNINGTON, Mr and Mrs Joel Neighborhood News Jan 13, 1887
Mr and Mrs Joel Pennington celebrated their 15th wedding anniversary at Pittsfield New Years Day.

PERKINS, Jackson Hazel Dell Jun 23, 1881
Jackson Perkins and Sarah Atchinson were married last Monday in Mt Sterling he being about 55 years old and her 17 years.

PETERS, Folkers Golden Sep 6, 1888
Folkers Peters and Miss Johanna Herrn, a daughter of John Herrn were married Friday.

PETERS, Henry Pea Ridge Mar 18, 1880
Mr Henry Peters and Miss Frowkie Libon were married at the brides fathers home by H.H. Holtcamp not long ago.

PETERS, Miss Lucinda Nov 8, 1883
SEE WALKER, Roswell

PETERS, Miss Sophia A. Nov 1, 1888
SEE SMITH, Andrew J.

PETERSON, Miss Augusta Jul 4, 1889
SEE LUBBEN, Mr L.H.

PEVEHOUSE, Miss Charlotte Married Sep 6, 1888
Married at the home of brides parents in this city about 9 AM Wednesday morn, Miss Charlotte Pevehouse, daughter of Mr and Mrs Jos. Pevehouse to Mr Geo. L. Anderson by R.H. Peairs. Immediately after ceremony Mr and Mrs Anderson drove over to the fair.

PEYTON, Miss Ella R. 5 Years Ago Dec 9, 1886
Miss Ella R. Peyton was married to Will E. Miller at Cheyenne, Wyo.

PHELPS, Dr James R. May 10, 1888
SEE KIRKPATRICK, Miss Lillie M.

PICKEN, Mr and Mrs Geo. L. Neighborhood News Apr 11, 1889
Thursday March 28th was celebrated by Mr and Mrs Geo. L. Pickens at Carthage as the 50th anniversary of their marriage.

PICKLER, Mr Jonas Dec 16, 1880
SEE BOOTHE, Miss Ella

PIERCE, Mr Nathaniel Jun 30, 1881
SEE TIPTON, Miss Nellie

PLATTENBURG, Perry and wife Neighborhood News Dec 6, 1888
Perry Plattenburg and wife of Canton celebrated their 64th wedding anniversary a few days ago.

PLEW, Dr E.J. Jun 3, 1886
Married, Dr E.J. Plew came down from Chicago and married Miss Nettie Raymond of Clayton by Elder Calvin at the home of brides mother, Mrs Julia Raymond at 5 AM Sunday and took the morning train for Chicago where he had a cottage ready for his bride at 216 S. Chaton St.

POLAND, Miss Minerva Sep 28, 1882
SEE KESTING, Lewis

POMROY, Mr and Mrs Caleb Quincy Oct 16, 1884
Last Wednesday was the 50th wedding anniversary of Mr and Mrs Caleb Pomroy, her illness prevented any formal celebration. They were married in Cincinnati in 1834 and came to Quincy 1837.

POOL, Miss Carrie Dec 15, 1887
SEE BALDWIN, Mr T.S.

PORT, Catherine F. Dec 18, 1884
SEE BUSS, John J.

POST, Catherine F. 5 Years Ago Dec 19, 1889
Married, Catherine F. Post to John J. Buss

POTTER, Edgar S. May 25, 1882
Invitations printed at this office marriage of Edgar S. Potter and Miss Puss Sims will take place at Virden, Illinois this eve (Wednesday) at 8:30. Clayton claims Ed as one of her boys. Miss Puss is of one of the best families in Virden. Will live Quincy.

POTTER, J. Will Jr. Married May 25, 1882
At the home of Benj. A. Curry, father of the bride by Elder Toof of Quincy, Mr J.W. Potter Jr. and Miss Nellie G. Curry Monday May 23rd at 8 PM. Mr Potter now lives Quincy, but was formerly of Clayton he is in the U.S. Railway mail service. Left Wednesday for Virden to attend marriage of Edgar S. Potter and Miss Puss Sims at 8:30 Wednesday.

POWELL, Ella D. Jan 3, 1884
SEE DELANY, Judge James R.

POWELL, Miss Susie A. Mar 20, 1884
SEE CATE, Mr Horatio W.

PRANTE, August and Miss Julia Ursa Mar 6, 1884
Married, at the home of the groom near Ursa, Thursday eve by Rev Reader of Quincy, Mr August <u>Prante</u> and Miss Julia <u>Prante</u>.

PRETTYMAN, Miss Anna Local Oct 10, 1889
Married, Wednesday at 8 PM at the home of brides brother J.W. Prettyman, Mr J.L. Groover of Canton, Illinois to Miss Anna Prettyman of Burlington. Will live Bushnell, Ill. "Burlington Daily Gazette"

PRICE, Miss Calista Dec 18, 1879
SEE HUXTABLE, Thomas

PRICE, Mr Chas. A. Jan 17, 1889
SEE BOSTICK, Miss Nellie

PRIGMORE, Mr Dec 6, 1888
SEE BLANK, Miss Nettie

PUGH, Mr Werter D. Locals Oct 6, 1887
Married at the home of Mr William Rutledge at 9 o'clock October 4th Mr Werter D. Pugh and Miss Ellis Ennis, both of Edina, Missouri. Mr Pugh is one of Edina, Missouri business man and Miss Ennis is a niece of Mr and Mrs Rutledge. Married by Dr West. Will live Edina.

PULLAM, Pink 5 Years Ago Dec 19, 1889
SEE FLEMING, Miss Mattie

PULLIS, Miss Lou Jun 28, 1883
SEE BALLOW, Charles B.

PULLUM, Mr Dec 18, 1884
SEE FLEMING, Miss Mattie

PUTMAN, Miss Eva Local Oct 7, 1886
The marriage of Miss Eva Putman to Mr John Hazlett is to take place on the 12th inst.

PUTMAN, Miss Mattie G. Jun 12, 1884
SEE TURNER, Mr C.B.

PYLE, David Neighborhood News Aug 16, 1888
August 2nd 1838, David Pyle and Miss Martha A. Willstree were married by Rev John Smith in Pike County Illinois at a house ½ mile south of their present home. They celebrated their 50th anniversary lately.

PYLE, Miss Hettie Mulberry, Ark. Jan 18, 1883
Married in Mulberry, Arkansas on December 25, 1882 H.H. Dill to Miss Hettie Pyle. (Letter from E.D. Pyle)

RABB, Miss Nettie Jan 13, 1881
SEE CLEEVES. Mr Hardin

RAE, Miss Emma T. Sep 27, 1883
SEE STUBLEFIELD, Jeff

RAINWATER, John Nov 22, 1883
SEE FOOTE, Miss Anna

RANDALL, J. Jul 26, 1888
SEE WOGON, Maria

RANDOLPH, David Neighborhood News Oct 18, 1883
Jacksonville "Journal" On last Sunday at the home of A.C. Armentrot, of Lincoln, Mr David Randolph, a worthy, well to fo widower who has passed his 72nd milestone was married to Miss Eva Whitehorst a highly esteemed lady of this city, age 40 years.

RATCLIFF, Miss Hattie M. Oct 18, 1883
SEE LUCAS, D.W.

RAUSCH, Miss Anna Sep 15, 1887
SEE DAVIS, Chas. W.

RAWLINS, R.W. Local Sep 28, 1882
We learn that R.W. Rawlins of the Wabash at Bowen was married Thursday at 1 P.M. We failed to get brides name. They left on the evening train for a visit to the home of Mr Rawlins, at Milmine.

RAWSON, Thomas Pea Ridge Sep 22, 1887
Wednesday the 14th at Mt Sterling court house, Thomas Rawson of Schuyler County and Miss Sena May of this vicinity were married. Will live Phillips County Nebraska.

RAWSON, Thomas Local Sep 22, 1887
Mr Thomas Rawson, of Huntsville, Schuyler County and Miss Sena May of Pea Ridge township Brown County were married at the court house in Mt Sterling, Wednesday by M. Brooks, Esq.

RAYMOND, Miss Nettie Jun 3, 1886
SEE PLEW, Dr E.J.

REATH, Miss Gertie Feb 2, 1888
SEE HACKER, W.T.

REATH, Miss Kate May 10, 1888
SEE LACKEY, Mr Grant

REED, Henry F. Local Oct 17, 1889
Henry F. Reed, son of our ME minister and Ruth H. Anderson, of Camp Point were married at the home of the bride Sunday at 3 PM by Rev W.M. Reed.

REEDER, Miss Connie Local Sep 1, 1887
Mr and Mrs Reeder of Melrose have sent out invitations of the marriage of their daughter, Miss Connie, to Mr Chas. F. Bernsen which will be this Wednesday eve at 8 in the Melrose Chapel.

REEDER, Miss Emma Dec 8, 1881
SEE PAPE, Mr Wm H.

REEVES, Miss R.A. Jun 15, 1882
SEE MARTIN, Wm B.

REID, Miss Dean Local Dec 2, 1886
Miss Dean Reid is no longer Dean Reid, but Mrs Charles Martin, of Belle Mead, Meade County Kansas. They were married at Dodge City on November 11th. Versailles Enterprise.

REIDINGER, David Local Nov 1, 1883
Quincy News: The marriage of David Reidinger and Miss Anna Oertle took place Thursday afternoon at the home of the brides father.

REPKE, Mr Frederick Golden Aug 18, 1887
Wedding Bells Mr Frederick Repke teacher of the Trinity Parish School and Miss Ankie Herron, daughter of Henry Herron of Houston (formerly of Clayton) were married yesterday AM at Trinity Church by the pastor.

RHEA, James W. Local Nov 8, 1883
Mr James W. Rhea and Miss Sarah E. Curry were married last Thursday eve by Rev A.P. Stewart of Mt Sterling at the home of R.S. Curry.

RICE, Rev E.J. Nov 9, 1882
Next Tuesday friends will help Rev and Mrs E.J. Rice celebrate their tin (10th) wedding anniversary.

RICE, Miss Mary Oct 13, 1881
SEE BRUPHY, Wm

RICHARDSON, Jos. Nov 7, 1889
SEE ANDERSON, Miss Clara

RICHMOND, Frank M. Nov 21, 1889
SEE GIDDINGS, Genevieve C.

RIDINGS, Mills Local Apr 27, 1882
Married, at the ME parsonage on Wednesday eve 19th inst, by Rev F.C. Bruner Mr Mills Ridings to Miss Florence Miller, both of Clayton.

RIGDON, S. Jun 15, 1882
SEE HORNEY, Miss Mattie

RIGG, Mr J. Personal Sep 8, 1881
Mr J. Rigg and wife, nee Lizzie Edmonston who were lately made one of Mt Sterling, Ky are on a wedding visit to Mr A.P. Keith. Mrs Rigg was formerly a resident of this vicinity.

RIMER, William Jan 11, 1883
William Rimer, 60 years old was married Wednesday of last week in Independence, Missouri to Kate Goris, 14 years old, he gained her consent by giving her $5,000 out right and settling $26,000 on her at his death.

RIPPETOE, Miss Nellie Married Feb 7, 1889
Married at the residence of the brides father, Mr A.F. Rippetoe at 6 PM Monday, Miss Nellie Rippetoe to Mr W. Edward Camp of this city by Justice Kendrick.

RITCHEY, Miss Jan 20, 1887
SEE CLARK, Ed

ROBBINS, Henry C. and Adelle DeGroot Jul 19, 1883
On Saturday at Quincy, Henry C. Robbins, of North East, commenced suit for divorce from Adele DeGroot Robbins, aleging cruelty as the cause.

ROBBINS, Miss Mary O. Oct 11, 1888
SEE CAIN, James Harvey

ROBBINS, W.N. Jan 10, 1889
SEE ALEXANDER, Miss Olive

ROBBINS, Wm N. Elm Grove Jan 3, 1884
Married in the township during the past week Wm N. Robbins and Miss Grace Hoyt daughter of Ed G. Hoyt of Houston township.

ROBERTS, Miss Georgia A. Apr 8, 1880
SEE ETTINGER, J.W.

ROBERTS, Julia Jan 8, 1880
SEE MILLER, L.J.

ROBERTSON, Mr and Mrs J.F. Camp Point Jan 19, 1882
Mr and Mrs J.F. Robertson celebrated their 9th wedding anniversary last Thursday.

ROBERTSON, Mr Jas. F. Personal Dec 20, 1888
Mr Jas. F. Robertson, popular Wabash agent at Camp Point and Miss Lillie M. Work of Bloomfield O. were married recently.

ROBINSON, Miss Flora Nov 3, 1881
SEE FLANDERS, Herbert

ROBINSON, Miss Mattie Sep 14, 1882
SEE HOKE, James

ROBINSON, Miss Mattie 5 Years Ago Sep 15, 1887
Miss Mattie Robinson was married to James Hoke they now live at Hutchinson, Kansas and they say Jim is getting rich.

ROBISON, Miss Flora 5 Years Ago Nov 4, 1886
Miss Flora Robison was married to Mr Herbert Flanders, of Mounds.

RODEMS, John Local Apr 19, 1888
Mr John Rodems the Wabash engineer on the Keokuk branch has claimed one of Clayton's ladies for a wife at 11 AM Sunday he and Mrs Ida Flynn of this city were married at the Catholic Church in Camp Point. Will live in Keokuk.

RODEMS, Johnnie Apr 12, 1888
SEE FLYNN, Mrs Ida

ROE, Dr G.L. Local Sep 7, 1882
Married at Odell, Nebraska Thursday August 31st, Dr G.L. Roe and Miss Ida L. Thompson the groom is a Clayton boy and Miss Ida is the daughter of one of the prominent families of Odell. They came to Clayton Saturday to visit his father for a week.

ROLAND, Miss Annie E. Mar 24, 1881
SEE MARKSBERY, Perry

ROSS, Will Golden Nov 24, 1887
Will Ross will be married on Wednesday to Miss Emma Seward, of Augusta.

ROSS, Mr William Local Mar 23, 1882
Married, at the Parker House in Clayton, Illinois March 15th by Rev E.J. Rice, Mr William Ross of Clayton and Miss Nettie Ferris of Pike County Missouri. Both colored.

ROUTH, Miss Etta V. Nov 24, 1881
SEE YOUNG, Mr Calville

ROY, David Local Sep 9, 1886
Mr David Roy, son of Mr Jno. Roy of Concord, was married to Miss Etta Lyon of Springfield at Mt Sterling Saturday AM by Rev Harper. Will live with his father.

ROY, Mr James L. Local Aug 18, 1887
A marriage license has been issued to Mr James L. Roy of Concord and Miss Ida M. Lucas of Mounds.

ROY, John Oct 7, 1880
Clip from Hot Springs, Arkansas, "Daily Gazette" Mr John Roy returned from Memphis this Am with his fair young bride. She was Miss Dora Lisdele of Memphis and they were married Wednesday eve.

ROY, Miss Mary Local Apr 4, 1889
Miss Mary Roy was married to Mr T.T. Burke at the grooms home, near Elm Grove, at 7 PM March 21st by Rev Middleton. She is daughter to Mr and Mrs Jno. Roy of Concord. She will make a good patient and affectionate mother for the children of Mr Burke.

RUGG, Miss Dora | Local | Oct 17, 1889
Marriage of a former Clayton boy: Married at the home of M.J. Rugg 319 Ave. B. east yesterday noon, J. Milton Green and Miss Dora Rugg at 12 noon. Attended by Mr King and Miss Hettie Rugg by Rev Joe Waldrop. From Hutchinson, Kansas "News" of the 10th inst.

RUHRBOUGH, Miss Olive | May 3, 1883
SEE CUTLER, Mr Clinton

RUNTE, Miss Louisa R. | Apr 12, 1883
SEE ZEIGER, Albert

RUTLEDGE, Mr and Mrs Wm | Local | Apr 12, 1883
Last Sunday the 8th was the 25th wedding anniversary of Mr and Mrs Wm Rutledge.

SALTHOUSE, Dr H.L. | Jun 3, 1886
SEE NORRIS, Miss Anna B.

SANDERSON, Miss Lizzie | Sep 13, 1883
SEE COLEMAN, H.M.

SANDS, Preston | Sep 20, 1888
SEE FLACK, Miss Hattie

SARGENT, Miss Lizzie A. | Dec 1, 1881
SEE CRAIG, Warren T.

SCANDLAND, Miss Kitty | Nov 20, 1884
SEE GARDNER, Lieut. J. Harry

SCANLAND, Miss Lotta W. | Feb 2, 1888
SEE TURNER, F.G.

SCHWARTZ, James | May 10, 1888
SEE COLBURN, Miss Nora

SCOFIELD, Ralph E. | Neighborhood News | Jul 4, 1889
Ralph E. Scofield, an attorney of Kansas City was married at Carthage Thursday to Ellen, daughter of Hon. H.G. Ferris President of the Hancock County National Bank.

SCOTT, Mrs Jane | Local | May 12, 1881
SEE MCMULLEN, Wm

SCOTT, Miss Lou | Elm Grove | Jan 17, 1884
Miss Lou Scott, formerly of the Grove, but now of Osceola, Iowa answers to the name of Mrs Page.

SCOTT, Miss Nancy | Married | Mar 10, 1887
Miss Nancy Scott was married to Mr J.A. Hill at the home of Mr Thos. Jamison in this city by Elder F.N. Calvin Sunday afternoon. Bride has grown up here, groom has made his home with Mr P.S. Williams for a considerable time. Mr and Mrs Hill were called by a telegram to Osceola, Iowa to attend the bedside of the brides sick sister, Mrs Alexander and they departed Wednesday AM.

SCOTT, Miss Nancy | Mar 3, 1887
SEE HILL, J.R.

SCROGGAN, Lyman T. | Married | Feb 5, 1885
Married on the eve of January 29th 1885 by Rev J.V. Pringle, at the home of the same, Mr Lyman T. Scroggan and Miss Elizabeth May, all of Adams County Illinois.

SCRUGGS, Miss Jessie | May 10, 1888
SEE THOMPSON, Jas. N.

SEALS, Chris | Loraine | Mar 5, 1885
Mr Chris Seals, of this place and Mrs Sallie McDonnal, also of Loraine but for some time visiting in Indiana were married in Quincy Thursday. by Judge Allen.

SEATON, James | Camp Point | Dec 18, 1879
James Seaton and Lizzie Omer were married by W.A. Crawford last Thursday eve.

SEEDS, Mr H.E. Jan 13, 1887
SEE STROTHER, Miss Cora

SEEHORN, Miss Nettie Oct 4, 1883
SEE DINGHAM, Mr Douglas

SELBY, Miss Alma A. Jul 4, 1889
SEE MILLER, Mr Philip

SELBY, Miss Kittie Locals Nov 28, 1889
Miss Kittie, daughter of Mr H.E. Selby, Golden, will be married to Mr Moore of Kingston, this eve (Thursday).

SELF, Mr C.W. Neighborhood News Sep 1, 1887
Mr C.W. Self, formerly owner of the Hampton House, was married to Mrs Hart, of Keokuk on Tuesday of last week.

SELLS, Lewis Local Feb 14, 1884
A dispatch from Topeka to the "Globe Democrat" announces the marriage in February 6th of Lewis Sells of Columbus, Ohio to Miss Rhoda Cross of Topeka.

SENSENEY, Frank Local Mar 27, 1884
Frank Senseney and Miss Ollie Smith were married at Camp Point last Thursday AM.

SEVIER, Mr Valentine Local Sep 15, 1887
Married, in Clayton, Adams County Illinois September 7th 1887, Mr Valentine Sevier and Mrs Rose Huddleston, all of Clayton.

SEWARD, Miss Emma Nov 24, 1887
SEE ROSS, Will

SEWARD, Miss Mary Golden Dec 23, 1886
Married, Miss Mary Seward, the oldest daughter of our hotel landlady to Mr J.F. Weathers of Augusta. Will live Augusta.

SEWARD, Mrs Mary F. Golden Jul 19, 1888
Mrs Mary F. Seward formerly landlady of the American House, but at present landlady of a hotel in Augusta was married last week to one of her boarders.

SEYMOUR, Prof. Arthur Camp Point Jul 1, 1886
Prof Arthur Seymour, of State University of Madison, Wisc. a former Camp Point lad, has arrived home with his bride for a visit with friends and relatives.

SHANK, Mr Chas. E. May 23, 1889
SEE BATES, Miss Mamie

SHANK, Daniel Valentines Day 1887 Feb 17, 1887
Last Monday was Valentines day and Dan'l shank that day brought home his second bride for family and friends. Married at the home of the brides father, Allen Smith, Esq. of Mounds by Elder G.D. Kent and Rev Crawford, Mr Daniel Shank of Pea Ridge and Miss Amanda J. Smith, all of Brown County Illinois.

SHANK, Mr Jacob Local Aug 24, 1881
Mr Jacob Shank and Miss Minnie E. Bobbitt were married last week, all of Pea Ridge.

SHANK, Maggie Pearidge Apr 2, 1885
Married last week, Maggie Shank of this vicinity to Philip Alexander by Rev Palmer.

SHANK, Mr Stewart T. Oct 3, 1889
SEE CURRY, Miss Laura

SHANK, Rev Wm R. Dec 25, 1884
SEE BURT, Miss Mary

SHARPE, Miss Ellen Dec 16, 1880
SEE KESTING, Tho. F.

SHELLEY, Miss Minnie Jan 18, 1883
SEE CROFT, Mr M.T.

SHEPHERD, Miss Mary F. Locals Dec 29, 1887
Judge Ball had a wedding Sunday afternoon at the home of Mr and Mrs Stephen Shepherd, their daughter Miss Mary F. was married to Mr Eugene Croquart.

SHIELDS, Mrs Lizzie Apr 11, 1889
SEE NOYES, Dr T.C.

SHIRLEY, Mrs Mary Local Dec 21, 1882
Mrs Mary Shirley, nee Williams, sister of our artist, writes for the Enterprise from Denver, Colorado she tells us she and Mr Shirley were married in Hannibal, Missouri over a year ago.

SHULTZ, Mr and Mrs Jackson Neighborhood News Mar 3, 1887
Mr and Mrs Jackson Shultz will soon celebrate their golden wedding at Carthage.

SHUTE, Mr Chas. E. Nov 1, 1889
SEE HOUGH, Miss Laura E.

SILVERS, Gracie Feb 16, 1888
SEE MARTIN, Grant

SIMMONS, Mrs Linnie Sep 21, 1882
SEE BOREN, James A.

SIMMONS, Mrs Linnie A. Sep 19, 1889
SEE WILSON, David B.

SIMMONS, Miss Ticia Jan 22, 1880
SEE DORSET, Mr Francis

SIMMS, Miss Sep 16, 1886
SEE HARTLEY, J.M.

SIMONS, Mr Geo. Married Mar 1, 1888
Married in Clayton, Adams County Illinois at the home of brides mother, Mrs M. Wever, February 26th 1888 by Rev G.D. Kent, Mr Geo. Simons, of Sonora, Hancock County Illinois to Miss Dora Viola Wever of this place.

SIMPKINS, Mrs Aug 26, 1886
SEE MAY, Benj. Sr.

SIMS, Miss Puss May 25, 1882
SEE POTTER, Edgar S.

SISSON, Mr A.E. Local Mar 2, 1882
Married, January 26, 1882 at the M.E. parsonage in Haysville, Kansas Mr A.E. Sisson of Bunker Hill, Illinois to Miss Jennie E. Gray of Sedgewick County Kansas.

SITES, Mr Jonah F. Mar 24, 1887
SEE HOGAN, Miss Annie P.

SKELLEY, Mrs Jul 26, 1888
SEE HULEN, Thomas T.

SLAGLE, Wm J. Local Apr 4, 1889
A license has been issued for the marriage of Wm J. Slagle and Miss Rose Niece, both of McKee township.

SMITH, Mr Elm Grove Nov 15, 1883
Married, last Thursday eve at the home of Wm Bagby, Mrs Wade and Mr Smith. Don't know whether the groom's name was John or Jim.

SMITH, Miss Amanda J. Feb 17, 1887
SEE SHANK, Daniel

SMITH, Andrew J. Local Nov 1, 1888
A license has been issued to Andrew J. Smith, of Huntsville and Miss Sophia A. Peters, of Elm Grove to marry.

SMITH, Andrew J. Married Nov 8, 1888
Married at the home of Mr R. Walker, Oct 31, 1888 by Rev S. Middleton, Andrew J. Smith of Huntsville township, Schuyler County to Miss Sophia Peters of Northeast township Adams County. Present, the parents and brother of the groom with his lady, mother of the bride and many others.

SMITH, Miss Anna Mar 10, 1887
SEE DOWNING, Robert

SMITH, Mr and Mrs B.W. Local Jan 20, 1881
Mr and Mrs B.W. Smith will celebrate their 20th wedding anniversary on the 26th inst.

SMITH, Miss Belle Sep 9, 1880
SEE OMER, Warren

SMITH, Mrs Belle Aug 25, 1887
SEE ELLERBROCK, Mr J.H.

SMITH, Charles E. Local Oct 13, 1887
Married, at the Presbyterian parsonage at Mt Sterling Thursday AM October 6th by Rev W.D. Smith, Mr Charles E. Smith and Miss Anna B. Bolton, both of this city. Mr Smith was born and raised in Clayton. Miss Bolton came here from the south several years ago as a child.

SMITH, Miss Eliza Aug 16, 1883
SEE LEWIS, Abraham

SMITH, Mr and Mrs F.C. Local Dec 9, 1880
Mr and Mrs F.C. Smith celebrated their 15th wedding anniversary at their home 2½ miles west of town December 14th.

SMITH, Miss Ida E. Jun 1, 1882
SEE BERRY, Mr Leon W.

SMITH, James A. "Allie" Local Sep 6, 1888
Miss Sallie Smith left a card at the office which reads: "Married Aug 28, 1888 at Pittsburg, Penn., Miss Lizzie Packards to Mr James A. Smith". No details only that Allie is married to a pleasant little Penn. lady and is happy.

SMITH, Miss Lizzie Nov 17, 1887
Married at Canton, Illinois on Thursday November 19th 1887, Miss Lizzie Smith, daughter of R.M. Smith of this city to Mr Frank Lintz of Canton at the home of groom's mother and witnessed by Mr Smith and sister, Miss Sallie, father and aunt to the bride as well as relatives of the groom.

SMITH, Mrs Lou 5 Years Ago Oct 27, 1887
Mrs Lou Smith was married to Mr J.S. Myers.

SMITH, Mrs Lucy C. Oct 26, 1882
SEE MEYERS, Mr J.S.

SMITH, M.W. Nov 18, 1880
M.W. Smith of Illinois and Mrs Francis Wommack of Lincoln County Missouri were married at the Laclede hotel in St Louis Tuesday October 24th. Bride is 74 years old and groom is 78 years. Both are wealthy.

SMITH, Miss Mary J. Feb 1, 1883
SEE BROWN, Mr Alonzo

SMITH, Miss Nora Jun 10, 1886
SEE BRYANT, Mr O.E.

SMITH, Miss Ollie Mar 27, 1884
SEE SENSENEY, Frank

SMITH, Mr Rankin Married Oct 4, 1883
Married at the home of the bride's father on the 25th ult by Rev J.V. Pringle, Mr Rankin Smith and Miss Adda Bennett, daughter of Mr Alvin Bennett.

SMITH, Mr and Mrs T.C. 15th Anniversary Dec 23, 1880
Mr and Mrs T.C. Smith celebrated their 15th wedding anniversary on the 14th inst.

SMITH, Miss Tracy Dec 21, 1882
SEE BENNETT, Mr Robert

SMITH, W. Local Mar 6, 1884
W. Smith and Emma Burke of Elm Grove were married last week.

SMITH, Mr and Mrs W.B. China Wedding Feb 3, 1881
Mr and Mrs W.B. Smith celebrated their 20th wedding anniversary January 26th at their home.

SMYERS, Miss Emma L. Sep 27, 1883
SEE DURMINE, Joseph

SOLE, Miss Mary J. May 23, 1889
SEE WILLIAMS, Mr Amos W.

SPILLARDS, Mr Spencer Local Aug 30, 1883
Mr Spencer Spillards and Miss Tillie Wiley of this place were married at the Diamond House in Quincy, Thursday last, will live in Clayton.

SPILLARS, John Married Mar 13, 1884
At the home of the parents of the bride, March 6th 1884 by Wm Kendrick, J.P. Mr John Spillars to Miss Maggie Brooks all of Clayton, Illinois.

STAKER, Miss Adda Mar 29, 1883
SEE BURGESSER, John Q.

STAKER, Miss Addie 5 Years Ago Mar 29, 1888
Miss Addie Staker was married to Mr J.Q. Burgesser.

STAKER, Miss Hattie G. Oct 9, 1884
SEE GARNER, Dr William A.

STAKER, Miss Hattie G. Aug 8, 1889
SEE WOOSTER, Benjamin F.

STAKER, Mr and Mrs Wm 25th Anniversary Jun 9, 1881
Mr and Mrs Wm Staker celebrated their 25th last Thursday eve at their home. About 80 persons were there.

STAPLETON, Miss Iva Local Oct 28, 1886
Married, at the home of brides parents in Buckhorn township Brown County Illinois on Sunday eve the 24th inst by Rev David Orr, Miss Iva Stapleton to Mr Geo. W. May of Pea Ridge township. Mr May is a farmer of Pea Ridge.

STEAD, Geo. Local Dec 1, 1881
Geo. Stead of Griggsville and Miss Ella Dyke of Quincy were married Wednesday night of last week.

STEED, Rebert L. Local Aug 22, 1889
Invitations are out announcing the marriage of Rebert L. Steed to Miss Alice Marshall, of Girggsville on the 4th prox. Rev Steed is a missionary to Utah under appointment from the Illinois Conference last fall. He will be home for conference September 11 and they will return to Utah immediately after.

STEINBACK, Mr and Mrs Wm Local Dec 6, 1888
Mr and Mrs Wm Steinback of Columbus celebrated their golden wedding last week.

STERN, Chas. Sep 15, 1881
Marriage of Mr Chas. Stern of the extensive clothing house of Stern and Sons, Quincy to Miss Rosa Frank of New York City was solemnized in that city last Wednesday eve.

STEUTEMANN, Wm M. Neighborhood News Mar 17, 1887
Yesterday afternoon license was granted by deputy county clerk head for the marriage of Wm M. Steutemann, 18 years old and Ida May Stratten 14 years old. Consent of mother of Wm was a Mrs Josephine and father of the girl, Wm H. Stratten, was given over their x marks, being unable to sign their names.

STEVENS, James Local Dec 23, 1880
A marriage certificate was found at the depot last week bearing the names of James Stevens, Johnson County Nebraska to Celestie Beckman at Tecumseh. Dated Nov 18, 1880. Parties can have it by applying at this office.

STEVENS, James A. Kellerville Dec 2, 1880
Married during the week in the neighborhood James A. Stevens to Miss Celeste Beckmon.

STEWART, Mrs Lillei Local Dec 23, 1886
A Quincy woman, Mrs Lillei Stewart conducted a correspondence with J.W. Miller of EauCalire, Wisconsin whom she has never seen and became engaged to him. She recently went there and married him. The couple will come to Quincy on their wedding trip to get the brides two children. Miller is a lumberman of some means.

STIFFY, Miss Nov 20, 1884
SEE WOODWORTH, John

STIFFY, Miss Martha Feb 21, 1884
SEE FRANKLIN, Walter

STIFFY, Miss Martha 5 Years Ago Feb 21, 1889
Miss Martha Stiffy was married to Mr Walter Franlin.

STIVERS, Richard Camp Point Apr 22, 1880
Richard Stivers and Alice Childs were married by Squire Cyrus Sunday afternoon. Moved Monday to the farm to settle down.

STONE, Billie Camp Point Jul 1, 1880
Billie Stone and Miss Caddie Farlow were married last Tuesday eve by Rev W.A. Crawford.

STOUT, Mr Nov 15, 1888
SEE MITCHELL, Miss Emma

STOUT, Miss Flora Local Jun 9, 1887
Married, Miss Flora Stout, youngest daughter of Mrs C. Stout to Mr W.E. Anderson by Rev R. Chapman at Mt Sterling Wednesday at 3 PM.

STRATTEN, Ida May Mar 17, 1887
SEE STEUTEMANN, Wm M.

STRICKLER, Mr Roll Camp Point Jun 1, 1882
Mr Roll Strickler and Miss Mattie Conner were married last Thursday AM by Squire Geo. W. Cyrus.

STRICKLER, Wilbur Local Feb 1, 1883
Wilbur Strickler and Emma C. Groves, of Houston, were married by Justice Cyrus, at Camp Point last Thursday.

STROAD, Mrs Local Aug 11, 1887
It is reported that Mrs Stroad, who has been living near the Soldiers Home, eloped on Saturday with a married man named Wm Montgomery. Both leave children.

STROTHER, Mr and Mrs B.L. 5 Years Ago Jun 21, 1888
Mr and Mrs B.L. Strother celebrated their 10th wedding anniversary.

STROTHER, Miss Cora Local Jan 13, 1887
Cards are out announcing the marriage of Miss Cora, daughter of F.K. and Mrs Strother, to Mr H.E. Seeds at the Baptist Church in Abiline, Kansas on the 15th inst.

STROTHER, F.K. and B.V. Linen Wedding Jan 27, 1881
It was our pleasure to attend the 30th anniversary of our parents F.K. and B.V. Strothers at Griggsville last Thursday eve. Six loving children and three grand children.

STROTHER, Frank Local Aug 15, 1889
Frank Strother, youngest son of F.K. Strother, of Abiline, Kansas was recently married to Miss Blanche Burgiss. They have gone to Tacoma, Washington where Frank will take charge of a leading paper.

STROTHER, Miss Homie Local Nov 11, 1886
A card received announcing the marriage of Miss Homie Strother to Mr C.S. Crawford, at the Baptist Church in Abilene, Kansas on Tuesday eve the 23rd inst.

STROTHER, Mr S.K. Dec 11, 1884
SEE CAPEL, Mr

STUBLEFIELD, Jeff Neighborhood News Sep 27, 1883
Mt Sterling "Message" Married Thursday 9 AM Mr Jeff Stublefield and Miss Emma T. Rae at the homeeof brides parents, this city, by Rev J.G. Lowrie. Expect to live at LaCross, Wisconsin.

STULL, Miss Sarah L. Feb 19, 1880
SEE VEACH, Mr Miles

SULLIVAN, John T. Oct 25, 1888
SEE MAGNER, Miss Maggie

SUTTON, Wm Sep 27, 1883
SEE MCCLAIN, Joseph L.

SWEET, Miss Cora Jun 17, 1886
SEE ANDERSON, George A.

SWEETING, Miss Jennie Jan 10, 1884
SEE MCVEY, Frank

SWISHER, Miss Dora Jan 29, 1880
SEE DUNBAR, Mr

SWOPE, Mr Homer Local May 26, 1887
Mr Homer Swope and Miss Hallie Bradley were married Tuesday eve at the home of Mr and Mrs W.T. Dwire, on E. Vermont by Rev Byerly. They are now at home on Broadway.

SWOPE, Homer M. Personal May 19, 1887
A.F. and Mrs Swope and daughter, Miss Lottie, attended the wedding of Homer M. Swope, Esq. to Miss Hattie Bradley in Quincy Tuesday eve.

SWOPE, Dr J.M. Additional Locals Dec 9, 1880
Dr J.M. Swope of Arenzville, Illinois, but formerly of Clayton was married last Tuesday to Miss M. Julia Yeck.

SWOPE, Miss Lottie Married Mar 28, 1889
Married at the home of Mr and Mrs A.F. Swope by Rev H.R. Peairs, their daughter Miss Lottie and Mr Joseph I. Foreman of Butte City, Montana at 7 PM Wednesday the 20th inst. They met at Chaddock College. Mr Foreman then lived in Missouri and is now a successful business man in that western town, being a carpenter and contractor. Will live Butte City.

SYRCLE, Daniel Siloam Mar 14, 1889
Daniel Syrcle and Lydia Veatch were married Sunday at Mr Veatch's. Dan's father is very low.

SYRCLE, Dan'l Siloam Apr 4, 1889
Dan'l Syrcle was not married as we reported a couple of weeks ago, but we are informed that he was married last Sunday.

SYRKIL, John J. Cupid and his work Jul 15, 1880
Married in the county during the past week: John J. Syrkil to Mary Einman of Beverly.

TANDY, Fronie Newtown Feb 21, 1884
SEE ELIOT, Mr Vinton

TAUSMAN, Miss Bertha Jan 27, 1887
SEE BUSS, W.J.

TAYLOR, Mr James Nov 29, 1888
SEE MYERS, Miss Fannie

TEACHENOR, Ike Local Nov 13, 1884
Ike Teachenor was quietly married to Miss Hattie Harbison on October 22nd but his chums did not learn of it until Sunday last.

TEACHENOR, Mr and Mrs Ike L. Local Oct 24, 1889
Ike L. Teachenor and wife celebrated their 5th wedding anniversary Tuesday night.

TEACHENOR, Monkey Personal Sep 23, 1886
Mrs Hattie Teachenor went to Shelbyville, Missouri today (Wednesday) to attend the wedding of Monkey Teachenor to Miss Hattie A. Parsons daughter of a wealthy citizen of that place, which takes place Thursday.

THACKWRAY, Mr and Mrs Sam	Neighborhood News	Apr 7, 1887
Mr and Mrs Sam Thackwray celebrated their golden wedding recently at Griggsville.

THAYER, Miss Lizzie	Additional Locals	Dec 9, 1880
SEE CUSHENBERRY, Dr J.T.

THOMAS, Mr Charles	Feb 24, 1887
SEE WRIGHT, Miss Ida M.

THOMAS, John B.	Local	Sep 9, 1886
Married at LaPrairie Wednesday night at the home of E.G. Hoyt, Mr John B. Thomas and Miss Maggie C. Hoyt daughter of Edwon and Ellen Hoyt. Groom is son of Evan and Lucy Thomas.

THOMAS, Miss Laura	Feb 24, 1887
Miss Laura Thomas will be married to Mr Will C. Chambers at the home of the bride's mother this eve at 7 (Wednesday).

THOMAS, Miss Laura A.	Married	Mar 3, 1887
Married Wednesday eve, the 23rd inst Miss Laura A. Thomas to Mr Will C. Chambers, both of this city by Rev H.R.Peairs. Will has lived here two or three years. Will live on East Washington St where Mr Chambers had a home ready for his bride.

THOMAS, Luther	Elm Grove	Jan 3, 1884
Married in the township during the past week Luther Thomas and Miss Lily Bacon, daughter of R.N. Bacon.

THOMPSON, Edward	10 Years Ago	Dec 26, 1889
Mr Edward Thompson and Mrs Lottie Yarnell were married.

THOMPSON, Mr Elsworth	Married at Elm Grove	Oct 25, 1888
Married October 18th at the home of Mr D.F. Eyman by Rev H.R. Peairs, Mr Elsworth Thompson and Miss Della M. Alexander, a daughter of Mrs Eyman by a former husband. Gifts from Mr and Mrs Wilson Alexander, Mr and Mrs L. Thompson, Mr and Mrs Charles Alexander, Mary F. Alexander, Mrs L.A. Shank, Miss S.A. Petey, Elijah Eyman, Mrs Roberts and S.T. Shank.

THOMPSON, Miss Ida L.	5 Years Ago	Sep 1, 1887
SEE ROE, Dr G.L.

THOMPSON, Jas. N.	Neighborhood News	May 10, 1888
Jas. N. Thompson and Miss Jessie Scruggs, deaf mutes, were married at Macomb, last week.

THOMPSON, Lewis	Personal	Feb 23, 1888
Lewis Thompson and Miss Mollie Manlove of Elm Grove were married in this city yesterday. While in the city they registered at the New Windson. "Friday Quincy Herald"

THOMPSON, Mr Lewis	Elm Grove	Feb 23, 1888
Married at the home of Brock Alexander, Miss Mollie Manlove to Mr Lewis Thompson on Friday of last week.

THOMPSON, Mrs Lottie	Aug 8, 1889
SEE MOORE, J.W.

THOMPSON, Mrs Margaret	Camp Point	Oct 25, 1883
SEE MCANULTY, Samuel

THURMAN, Allen	Feb 9, 1888
SEE HUNT, Miss Amanda

TIBBETTS, Miss Ida	Apr 28, 1881
SEE LAUGHLIN, Wm

TIPTON, Anna	Cupid and his work	Jul 15, 1880
SEE DOWNING, Joseph

TIPTON, Charles H.	Golden	Oct 13, 1881
Married in Houston Wednesday afternoon at the home of brides parents, Charles H. Tipton, oldest son of Samuel and Amanda Tipton of this place to Amanda, youngest daughter of Samuel and Amanda Woods.

TIPTON, Miss Nellie Golden Jun 30, 1881
Married last Saturday, Miss Nellie, second daughter of Samuel Tipton of this place was married in Quincy to Mr Nathaniel Pierce of Camp Point township by Rev Smyth of the Presbyterian Church.

TOUENCE, Dr John and wife Neighborhood News Dec 2, 1886
Dr John Touence and wife celebrated their "Golden Wedding" Wednesday November 10th at the home of their youngest daughter, Mr J.H. Crump at Pleasant Hill, Pike County.

TRIPLETT, Elick Siloam Springs Feb 28, 1889
Elick Triplett and Florence Chatman were married last week. Will live in McKee township.

TURNER, Mr C.B. Neighborhood News Jun 12, 1884
Mr C.B. Turner, the editor of the "Old Flag" was married at Beardstown at the home of brides parents May 28th to Miss Mattie G. Putman.

TURNER, F.G. Neighborhood News Feb 2, 1888
F.G. Turner of the Pittsfield Old Flag was married to Miss Lotta W. Scanland, daughter of R.C. Scanland of that place Tuesday eve.

UNDERWOOD, Miss Laura Jan 29, 1880
SEE DOWNING, R.A.

UNDERWOOD, Mr and Mrs Peter Camp Point Jul 10, 1884
Mr and Mrs Peter Underwood celebrated their silver wedding Friday eve, June 27th.

VAIL, Mrs A.J. Neighborhood News Jun 28, 1888
Mrs A.J. Vail, of Bennett, Kansas former a resident of Industry, recently left her home to visit relatives in McDonough County Illinois since which time all trace of her has been lost. It seems however, that Mrs Vail was not lost, as she had eloped with a methodist minister of Bennett, who had a wife and several children.

VANARSDELL, Sidney Golden Aug 23, 1888
Sidney VanArsdell and Miss Phenicia Cunningham were married Thursday eve in Houston by Parson Hanna.

VANCE, Miss Sadie Nov 8, 1888
SEE DUNCAN, Lew

VANDORAN, Mr A. Camp Point Aug 5, 1880
Married, at the home of Jas. Robertson, Esq. on the 31st ult by Rev W.A. Crawford, Mr A. VanDoran and Miss Lucy Jones of Quincy.

VAUGHAN, John 5 Years Ago Jul 12, 1888
John Vaughan and Mrs Nancy McDowell were married.

VAUGHAN, Lucinda Sep 19, 1889
SEE BULLEIN, Lugwig

VAUGHN, John Married Jul 12, 1883
At the parsonage, Clayton, Illinois July 6th 1883 by Rev F.M. Hayes Mr John Vaughn, to Mrs Nancy McDowell.

VEACH, Mr Miles Local Feb 19, 1880
Married, February 12th by Rev Snyder, Mr Miles Veach of Adams County to Miss Sarah L. Stull of Hancock County Illinois.

VEATCH, Lydia Mar 14, 1889
SEE SYRCLE, Daniel

VERMILLION, Elbert Jan 22, 1885
SEE ALEXANDER, Alice

VONHOLDT, Henry 5 Years Ago Apr 19, 1888
Henry Vonholdt and Caroline Fricke were married.

VONHOLT, Henry Local Apr 19, 1883
Henry Vonholt of Concord and Caroline Fricke have been licensed to marry. Henry is a good judge of wood and is considered a square German by all; no doubt he is an equally good judge of a wife.

WADE. Mrs Nov 15, 1883
SEE SMITH, Mr

WAGERLY, John E. Local Oct 4, 1883
SEE HASTINGS, John C.
WALDECK, Dr D.D. Sep 9, 1886
SEE ARTZ, Miss Helen
WALKER, Chas. Elm Grove Jan 26, 1882
Chas. Walker was married, but we don't know to who.
WALKER, Miss Ethel G. May 4, 1882
SEE DOOLITTLE, George H.
WALKER, Miss Mary Elm Grove Apr 10, 1884
Married, Miss Mary Walker and George Burke.
WALKER, Miss Ollie Sep 28, 1882
SEE BURKE, Mr Thadeus
WALKER, Miss Rachael 5 Years Ago Mar 10, 1887
SEE PENDLETON, Chas.
WALKER, Miss Racheal Elm Grove Mar 9, 1882
Married on the 22nd ult Mr Charles Pendleton, of Wellington, Kansas to Miss Racheal Walker of Elm Grove at Quincy. Will live Kansas.
WALKER, Roswell Elm Grove Nov 8, 1883
Married at Quincy October 31st Mr Roswell Walker and Miss Lucinda Peters, both have lived at the Grove all their lives. Mr Walker is our tax collector for the season. She is daughter of our Squire Peters.
WALLACE, Miss Bettie 5 Years Ago Jun 7, 1888
SEE MCDANOLD, Wm
WALLACE, Miss Elizabeth Jun 7, 1883
SEE MCDONALD, Mr William
WALLACE, James A. Jr. Golden Mar 29, 1888
James A. Wallace Jr and wife celebrated today their silver wedding at their home northwest of town.
WALLACE, John R. Aug 31, 1884
SEE MOFFETT, Miss Julia A.
WALLACE, Mr John R. 5 Years Ago Sep 5, 1889
SEE MOFFETT, Miss Julia F.
WALLACE, John S. Married Oct 23, 1884
Married October 19th 1884 at the home of brides father, Mr Henry S. Whitford, Golden, Illinois by Rev Edwin J. Rice of Clayton. Mr John S. Wallace and Miss Alice E. Whitford will live Harlem, Shelby County, Iowa.
WALLACE, Mr Lincoln Sep 2, 1886
SEE WREATH, Miss Ida
WALLACE, Miss Lizzie Sep 20, 1888
"Another Flower Plucked" Married at the home of brides mother in this city afternoon of September 17th Mr David E. Ghormley, of New Haven, Conn. and Miss Lizzie Wallace of this place by Rev C.F. McKown. Left for the east on the train in evening. Mr Ghromley is a student of the divinity school at Yale. His home is in Reno County Kansas. After the school year they will live Kansas.
WALLACE, Samuel A. Locals Oct 18, 1888
Mr and Mrs O. Wallace returned Tuesday night from their visit of friends in Colorado and various points. He tells us of the marriage of his son Samuel A. Wallace and Miss Jennie Wilson of Hastings, Nebraska at Hastings about three weeks ago.
WALLACE, Mr Samuel R. Local Nov 16, 1882
Married, Mr Samuel R. Wallace and Miss Mary F. Black last Thursday eve by Rev J.V. Pringle. Bride is daughter of J.H. Black.
WARD, Miss Bell Local Dec 23, 1886
The marriage of Miss Bell Ward to Wm Kendrick Esq. takes place today (Thursday).

WARD, Miss Belle Married Dec 30, 1886
Married on Thursday eve December 23rd, Miss Belle Ward and Wm Kendrick Esq. at the home of Miss O. Horves in this city which had been the home of Miss Ward the past few years, by Rev H.R. Peairs. Both church workers. Will remain here in this city.

WARD, Pauline Sep 8, 1887
SEE OWEN, C.J.

WARE, Mr Columbus Local Jan 29, 1880
Mr Columbus Ware and Miss Wilty were married recently.

WARNER, Miss Aggie L. Local Apr 23, 1885
Cards are out announcing wedding of Miss Aggie L. Warner, sister of Mrs W.D. Meisser, with Frank L. Dever at Peoria on the 30th. Miss Warner is known to many young folks of Clayton.

WARNER, Miss Etta Apr 13, 1882
SEE MEISSER, W.D.

WARNER, Miss Mollie E. Local Oct 18, 1888
The Editor received an invitation from Mr and Mrs John Warner of Peoria to attend marriage of their daughter, Miss Mollie E. to Mr Will E. Bryant of this city on the 25th inst. Will live Clayton.

WASH, Miss Prina Local Oct 4, 1888
A society wedding at Mt Sterling, Tuesday eve, Miss Prina Wash, daughter of Col. Ham Wash was married to Mr John Barry.

WASHINGTON, George Aug 19, 1886
SEE HOLMES, Mrs Gabe

WATSON, Robert Personal Dec 8, 1881
Mr Robert Watson and Miss Alice Bridges, daughter of W.C. Bridges were married at Hamilton, Illinois on Wednesday, the 30th ult.

WEAR, Miss Aug 23, 1888
SEE BENT, Fred

WEAR, Zeke Hazel Dell Feb 26, 1885
Married this week, Mr Zeke Wear to Miss Frona Amen.

WEATHERS, Mr J.F. Dec 23, 1886
SEE SEWARD, Miss Mary

WEBSTER, Miss Mattie Feb 17, 1887
SEE MCDOWELL, Will H.

WEENS, Mr Jesse E. Neighborhood News May 8, 1884
Quincy "Whig" Married, Mr Jesse E. Weens and Mrs Mary E. Brawner at 9 PM Wednesday at 614 Jersey St by Rev Dr Hays of the Presbyterian Church. Will live at 614 Jersey St.

WEIR, Hattie B. Apr 10, 1884
SEE DOWNING, George Y.

WEIR, Dr Wm A. Neighborhood News Sep 16, 1886
The wedding of Dr Wm A. Weir to Miss Ada Goodrich took place at Carthage last Wednesday.

WELBORN, Miss Margaret Local Mar 17, 1887
Mr H.H. Dodd tells us that Miss Margaret Welborn, who made her home many years with S.J. Morey, now deceased is married to Mr O.W. Ballagh and lives at West Fall Brook, Calif. Mr Dodd tells us that her claim against the Morey estate of $1,164 has been paid.

WELLS, Mr and Mrs Edward Local Mar 24, 1887
Mr and Mrs Edward Wells celebrated their golden wedding at the family home in Quincy on Saturday. March 19, 1837 Mr Edward Wells and Miss Mary B. Evans were married in that city and have resided there since. Mr Wells came to Quincy in 1834.

WELLS, Lee Married Dec 1, 1881
In Clayton Thursday eve, Nov. 24th at the home of the brides father, Dr T.G. Black, by Elder Stewart of Mt Sterling and Elder Newman of Clayton, Mr Lee Wells, of Creston, Iowa and Miss Mattie Black.

WELLS, Mr Otis Newtown Mar 6, 1884
Mr Otis Wells and Miss Lida Hughes were married last Monday at Quincy.
WELSH, Miss Annie Camp Point May 24, 1883
Married, Miss Annie Welsh and Wm Cutter at the home of the brides parents, Saturday at 7 PM.
WEST, Miss Annie Dec 27, 1888
SEE CLARY, James
WEST, Mr Lafayett Kellerville Oct 12, 1882
Married, Mr Lafayett West to Miss Lettie Lierly.
WEST, Miss Mary May 2, 1889
SEE CONNOR, C.H.
WEST, Milton Local Jan 29, 1880
Mr Milton West and Mary Amon of Concord were married recently.
WESTBROOK, Mr Chas. L. Local Apr 30, 1885
Married on eve of the 22nd inst at the home of Squire Brooks in this city, Mt Chas. L. Westbrook to Miss Cora Lester.
WEVER, Miss Dora Viola Mar 1, 1888
SEE SIMONS, Mr Geo.
WEVER, Miss Jennie Dec 29, 1887
SEE WILLIAMS, Mr Robert
WHEELER, Hiram N. Local Feb 2, 1888
Hiram N. Wheeler, editor of the Journal, and Mrs Bertha Brockman were married in Quincy last week.
WHEELER, Mr Mark Jan 1, 1885
SEE MONTGOMERY, Miss Edith
WHIPPLE, Rev W.W. Locals May 19, 1887
Rev W.W. Whipple was married at Yonkers, N.Y. on the eve of the 11th inst to Mrs Wiltsie of that city and will live that city. Bride is sister of Congressional Librarian Spafford at Washington.
WHITE, James W. Oct 11, 1888
SEE HARMON, Nancy J.
WHITEHORST, Miss Eva Oct 18, 1883
SEE RANDOLPH, David
WHITFORD, Miss Alice E. Oct 23, 1884
SEE WALLACE, John S.
WHITFORD, Fanny Mar 3, 1887
SEE DOWNING, Charlie
WHITSON, Laura A. Sep 30, 1880
SEE BASSET, Chas. R.
WHITTAKER, Miss Ida Feb 17, 1881
SEE DEMOSS, James E.
WIGLE, Mrs Helen A. Feb 3, 1881
SEE DAUGHERTY, Mr Jacob
WILEY, Miss Sadie Sep 5, 1889
SEE MCDANNOLD, Mr S. Burns
WILEY, Tille Aug 30, 1883
SEE SPILLARDS, Mr Spencer
WILKIN, Rev and Mrs M.P. Local Oct 30, 1884
30th wedding anniversary of Rev and Mrs M.P. Wilkin was celebrated October 23rd.
WILKINS, Rev and wife 5 Years Ago Nov 7, 1889
Rev Wilkins and wife celebrated their 13th wedding anniversary.
WILLAGE, Franklin Local Jun 10, 1886
A marriage license was issued to Franklin Willage to Rosa Comstock, both of Quincy, Ill. Tuesday. Frank lived in Clayton a few years ago.
WILLARD, Rev James Golden Jan 19, 1882
Married in Houston on Thurs. night, Rev James Willard, of the Baptist Church, and Miss Ann M. Lenning by Hon Wm Hanna, J.P.-P.M. It was a very cold night.

WILLIAMS, Mr Amos W. Married May 23, 1889
Married at Mt Sterling, May 14th by Rev Jacob Craford, Mr Amos W. Williams and Miss Mary J. Sole, both of Mounds. Couple left right away by train for their western home.
WILLIAMS, Billy Feb 24, 1881
Married, Billy Williams and Mrs Rhoda Boren on the eve of the 10th inst by Squire Ballow. The secret is out, Ha! Ha!! Ha!!!
WILLIAMS, Miss Julia A. May 31, 1883
SEE MCCOY, James A.
WILLIAMS, Miss Laura Belle Apr 5, 1883
SEE MAY, John T.
WILLIAMS, Miss Mary B. Jan 10, 1889
SEE MARSHALL, Mr Abraham L.
WILLIAMS, Mary Local Dec 21, 1882
SEE SHIRLEY, Mrs Mary
WILLIAMS, Mr Robert Married Dec 29, 1887
At the Baptist parsonage in Clayton Dec 25, 1887 by Rev G.D. Kent Mr Robert Williams and Miss Jennie E. Wever, all of Clayton.
WILLIAMS, Wm C. Local Feb 3, 1881
Quincy Herald says a marriage license was issued Monday to Wm C. Williams and Rhoda E. Boren of Clayton.
WILLSTREE, Miss Martha A. Aug 16, 1888
SEE PYLE, David
WILSON, Miss Allie Neighborhood News Jun 3, 1886
The marriage of Miss Allie Wilson to Mr W.J. Connors at Griggsville last week.
WILSON, Miss Clara E. Local Apr 21, 1887
A license to marry issued to Miss Clara E. Wilson to Mr John H. Dunkleburg. Mr Dunkleburg has been prospecting west and has decided to go there, taking a help-meet with him.
WILSON, David B. Married Sep 19, 1889
Married at home of B.A. Curry Esq. Sunday afternoon September 15th, Mr David B. Wilson of East Du Brique, Illinois and Mrs Linnie A. Simmons of Clayton by Elder T.M. Johnson. Bride is daughter of B.A. Curry. Groom is a fine looking man about 40 years and is in the railroad business will live E. Du Buque.
WILSON, George Sep 26, 1889
SEE JOHNSON, Mary
WILSON, Miss Jennie Oct 18, 1888
SEE WALLACE, Samuel A.
WILSON, Lem Elm Grove Jan 3, 1884
Married in the township during the past week: Lem Wilson and Miss Ollie Dorsett of Shiloh.
WILTSE, Miss Rosella Apr 14, 1887
SEE LLOYD, John
WILTY, Miss Jan 29, 1880
SEE WARE, Mr Columbus
WING, Theodore Local Sep 7, 1882
Married at Mt Sterling August 30th Mr Theodore Wing and Miss Rhoda Carter.
WISENBURG, Mrs Dora Dec 1, 1881
SEE MCREA, Edward
WOGON, Maria Crestline Jul 26, 1888
Maria Wogon, of Fish Hook and J. Randall, of Baylis were married last week.
WOMELSDORFF, Miss Mary A. Feb 9, 1882
SEE HUGHES, Mr J.W.

WOMMACK, Mrs Francis Nov 18, 1880
SEE SMITH, M.W.

WOOD, Miss Bertha Jul 18, 1889
SEE BINNEY, James Jr.

WOODS, Miss Amanda Oct 13, 1881
SEE TIPTON, Charles H.

WOODWORTH, John Local Nov 20, 1884
Squire Loyd had another wedding Friday: Mr John Woodworth married Miss Stiffy, daughter of John Stiffy all of Clayton.

WOOSTER, Benjamin F. Wooster-Staker Aug 8, 1889
Card announcing the marriage of Mr Benjamin F. Wooster and Miss Hattie G. youngest daughter of William Staker and wife and sister of the writer reads: Mr and Mrs Wm Staker request your presence at the marriage of their daughter Hattie G. to Benjamin F. Wooster Wednesday August 7th 12 o'clock, at their home, Clayton, Illinois. Guests included grooms parents, Mr and Mrs Dick Pyatt, she being a sister of groom besides several relatives of bride, including several from a broad. Married by Rev M.M. Davidson, uncle of the bride. Groom is a business man in Jacksonville where he has lived since childhood.

WORK, Miss Lillie M. Dec 20, 1888
SEE ROBERTSON, Mr Jas. F.

WORKING, Miss Ida M. Neighborhood News May 5, 1887
Miss Ida M. Working was married to Mr J.O. Balfour at Augusta on the 27th ult.

WORLEY, Mr Luther Ursa Nov 6, 1884
Mr Luther Worley and Miss Katorah Johnson were married October 23rd.

WREATH, Miss Ida Locals Sep 2, 1886
It is reported that Miss Ida Wreath was married to Mr Lincoln Wallace at Mt Sterling Sunday the 22nd inst. If this is true we wish them happiness.

WRIGHT, Miss Anna May 31, 1883
SEE KERLEY, Edgar K.

WRIGHT, Miss Dela Local Feb 17, 1887
Miss Dela Wright of Kellerville was married to Mr John Kerley of Lee township Brown County since our last issue.

WRIGHT, Miss Ida M. Married Feb 24, 1887
Married at the Presbyterian parsonage in this city 8 PM Tuesday by Rev H.R. Peairs, Miss Ida M. Wright, to Mr Charles M. Thomas. Both have spent most of their lives in this city. Miss Laura Thomas, sister of the groom, will be married to Mr Will C. Chambers at the home of the brides mother this eve at 7 (Wednesday) at which time a reception will be tendered Charlie and wife.

WRIGHT, N.W. Local Jul 21, 1881
Mr N.W. Wright and Mrs Emma Parker were married last Thursday eve by Rev F.C. Bruner. Wright thought it would be right to go to Wyoming with another Wright.

WRIGHT, Miss Ollie Kellerville Nov 2, 1882
Married, Mr Campbell and Miss Ollie Wright, daughter of our good neighbor, Mr Rob't Wright.

WRIGHT, Miss Ollie M. Nov 2, 1882
SEE CAMPBELL, Allen D.

WRIGHT, Sadie J. Dec 27, 1883
SEE LACKEY, John C.

WYATT, Mrs Lucy Oct 27, 1887
SEE KILE, Mr John

WYATT, Luther Nov 8, 1888
SEE GAY, Miss Lillie

WYATT, Mr Lute — Nov 8, 1888
SEE GAY, Miss Lillie

WYLIE, Miss Ida M. — 5 Years Ago — Aug 2, 1888
Miss Ida M. Wylie and Mr Edgar Bennett were married.

YAKELY, Miss — May 8, 1884
SEE MCLAIN, James

YARNELL, Mrs Lottie — 10 Years Ago — Dec 26, 1889
SEE THOMPSON, Edward

YATES, Elder and Mrs — Pleasant Event — Sep 16, 1880
Last Monday eve Elder and Mrs Yates celebrated their 20th wedding anniversary.

YATES, Miss Rebecca — Feb 26, 1885
SEE HUGHES, Sanford

YECK, Miss M. Julia — Dec 9, 1880
SEE SWOPE, Dr. J.M.

YOUNG, Calville — Local — Nov 24, 1881
Married at Carthage November 10th Mr Calville Young and Miss Etta V. only daughter of R.H. and O.A. Routh, all of Augusta.

YOUNG, Mr and Mrs Colville — Neighborhood News — Nov 18, 1886
Mr and Mrs Colville Young of Augusta celebrated their 5th wedding anniversary Wednesday November 10th.

YOUNG, Mr George L. — Sep 16, 1886
SEE BURGESSER, Miss Mae

YOUNG, Miss Maggie — Feb 28, 1884
SEE BRADSHAW, Mr and Mrs

ZEIGER, Albert — Local — Apr 12, 1883
Since our last issue Mr Albert Zeiger of Camp Point and Miss Louisa R. Runte, daughter of Mr Henry Runte, one of the most respected and influential Germans in Concord have been married.

ZEIGLER, Henry — Camp Point — Jan 8, 1880
Married, Saturday eve by Thos. Bailey, Henry Zeigler to Miss Louise Houke, all of Camp Point Bakery.

ZOLLER, Miss Phillie — Personal — Oct 3, 1889
Miss Julia Gross went to Palmyra Tuesday to attend the wedding of her friend, Miss Phillie Zoller this week. Miss Julia will be her first attendant at the wedding.

ABBEY, Miss Cora 5 Years Ago Jun 26, 1890
SEE SHOCKLEY, Shepherd
ABBOTT, Rev H.S. Dec 2, 1897
SEE SCOGGAN, Miss America
ABEL, Ewald G. Ill Brevities May 31, 1894
Ewald G. Abel and Miss Catherine Vandenboom were married at Quincy.
ACKLAM, Miss Jennie Local Jan 12, 1893
Cards are out announcing the marriage of Miss Jennie Acklam, daughter of Mr and Mrs Benj. Acklam to Mr Wm L. Hirons on Jan. 18th .
ACKLAM, Miss Jennie E. Married Jan 26, 1893
Married at the home of Mr Benj. Acklam near Camp Point Wednesday of this week, his daughter, Miss Jennie E. and Mr William L. Hirons of near Clayton at 12 oclock. They were accompanied by Mr John Stahl of Quincy and Miss Ola VanDervoort of Clayton. Married by Rev Stahl of Augusta. Will live near Mound Station.
ADAIR, H.L. 5 Years Ago Dec 18, 1890
SEE PEVEHOUSE, Miss Emma
ADAMS, Miss Hattie Little Brindle Feb 21, 1895
Ed Purcell, the county clerk of Brown County was married to Miss Hattie daughter of J.Q. Adams in Mt Sterling last Thursday.
ADAMS, Isaac City Brevities Dec 22, 1898
Mrs John Swope attended wedding of Mr Isaac Adams and Miss Mollie Hudson at Camp Point Thursday of last week.
ADAMS, Mr Jno. Q. Little Brindle News Jul 5, 1894
Married, Mr Jno. Q. Adams and Mrs Anna M. Gordley, Tuesday June 26th.
ADAMS, W.H.H. Jul 13, 1893
SEE BOOTH, Mrs Mary E.
ADEN, George Feb 20, 1896
SEE BUSS, Mamie
ADEN, Ranke H. Local Feb 6, 1896
Marriage license issued Tuesday--Ranke H. Aden of Golden age 24 and Chistina Schoene of Golden age 19.
ALBERS, Menne Our Own Bailiwick Feb 21, 1895
Menne Albers age 24 and Catherina Gembler age 17 were permitted to marry, girls mother gave her consent.
ALEXANDER, Miss Emma Sep 24, 1891
SEE STRAUB, Edward
ALEXANDER, Miss Mary F. Elm Grove Dec 21, 1893
Daniel Alexander and family will attend wedding of his niece, Miss Mary F., daughter of S.S. Alexander near LaPrairie which ocurs this week. She was born in this neighborhood and spent her childhood here..
ALEXANDER, Miss Pearl Oct 20, 1898
SEE UNDERWOOD, George
ALEXANDER, Miss Stella Mar 7, 1895
SEE DUTTON, John
ALEXANDER, Wm Adams County Sep 8, 1898
Wm Alexander and Miss Carrie Walker were married at Quincy Tuesday. Both are known in Elm Grove neighborhood.
ALLARD, Cad Neighbors Jan 2, 1896
Cad Allard, editor of the Beardstown Daily Star and Miss Bernice Sexton well known socially at Virginia were married the 8th.
ALLEN, Cora Sep 30, 1897
SEE EDMUNDS, James
ALLEN, Mrs Ella Jul 21, 1898
SEE CLARK, Thomas M.

ALLEN, Frank | Camp Point | Aug 22, 1895
Frank Allen and Hattie Blood were married at the home of the brides last Thursday eve. Left same eve for southern part of the state where Frank has a school.

ALLEN, Miss Hattie | 5 Years Ago | Jul 21, 1892
Miss Hattie Allen married Feo. F. Lee in Mt Sterling.

ALLEN, Miss Lula | | Jan 20, 1898
SEE HORNECKER, Edwin

ALLEN, Wm | 5 Years Ago | Oct 30, 1890
Wm Allen and Miss Mary J. Bolton were married.

ALSPAUGH, Frank | | Sep 1, 1892
SEE HALEY, Miss Lou

AMEN, Albert | Local | Dec 5, 1895
Married Albert Amen and Miss Annie Blaschok at Mt Sterling Wednesday AM. Will live Bowen.

AMEN, Emily | | Nov 26, 1896
SEE DAUGHERTY, Thomas J.

AMEN, Philip | Our Own Bailiwick | May 3, 1894
Philip Amen of Columbus and Miss Allie Kelly of Liberty were married last week. Will live Columbus where Mr Amen is a merchant.

AMEN, Philip | Local | May 31, 1894
By an exchange we learn Philip Amen, of Columbus, son of our old friend Francis, and Miss Allie Kelley of Liberty were married at the home of the brides parents, Mr and Mrs Maurice Kelley, near Liberty, Wednesday, the 11th inst.

AMRINE, Miss Bertha | | Jun 11, 1896
SEE LUCAS, Chas.

ANDERSON, Miss Annie S. | Married | Jan 5, 1893
Married at the home of brides mother, Mrs John Anderson, near Buckhorn in Brown County by Rev J.J. Thompson, Miss Annie S. Anderson and Mr Clement L. Hawkins. Mr Hawkins is one of leading educators in county at present teaching at Colpitts school in Concord. He lived here three years. Will live Clayton.

ANDERSON, C.N. | Local | Aug 25, 1892
We learn from the Abingdon Enterprise that C.N. Anderson and Miss Lizzie V. Wigle were married at the brides home in Abingdon Wednesday eve the 10th inst by Dr White. Groom is professor in the Math department of Normal College and has been elected principal of Yates City school. Bride is one of our Camp Point girls. "Camp Point Journal"

ANDERSON, Mr C.S. | 10 Years Ago | Dec 21, 1893
Mr C.S. Anderson and Miss Jane Brierton were married.

ANDERSON, Miss Elizabeth | | Feb 6, 1896
SEE WHITE, James

ANDERSON, Miss Ella | | Dec 4, 1890
SEE HUFFMAN, Mr Albert

ANDERSON, George L. | Sept 1888 | Sep 15, 1898
Married, George L. Anderson and Miss Charlotte Pevehouse.

ANDERSON, Mr H.C. | | Jan 16, 1896
SEE ELDER, Miss Laura

ANDERSON, Henry S. | Married | Nov 10, 1898
Married in Clayton Thursday eve November 3rd, Mr Henry S. Anderson, foreman of the Enterprise and Miss Ella B. Stiffey, daughter of Mrs Mary Stiffey at 7:30 PM in home of brides mother by Rev Edwin J. Rice.

ANDERSON, Miss Mary | Local | Feb 12, 1891
Married at the home of brides father, Mr C.S. Anderson of this city on Thursday eve February 5th, Miss Mary Anderson to Mr Ezra Wing by Rev. W.M. Reed.

ANDERSON, Maude | Ancient History | Feb 25, 1897
SEE KIRKPATRICK, Web

ANDERSON, Robert L. | Orange Blossoms | Jun 11, 1891
From Huntingburg (Ind.) "News" Marriage of Mr Robert L. Anderson to Miss Amelia K. Woelker was last Thursday eve at 7 at home of brides father on corner of Main and Second Streets by Rev W.P. Wallace of the English ME Church. Groom is employed by the "News" past seven months. Bride is only daughter of Dr Carl Woelker of Huntingburg.

ANDERSON, Miss Ruth A. | October 1889 | Oct 5, 1899
SEE REED, Henry T.

ANDERSON, Sarah A. and James W. | Local | Feb 21, 1895
Quincy Journal Sarah A. Anderson began suit for separate maintenance against James W. Anderson. They married in 1866 in this county and on Jan 2, 1895 they seperated. Had one child born to them 27 years ago. She says she left him in 1884 on account of cruelty also. Says he has $1900 property and a pension of $12 a month.

ANDERSON, Sarah A. and Jas. W. | Local | Mar 28, 1895
In circuit court Monday the seperate maintainance case of Mrs Sarah A. Anderson against Jas. W. Anderson was dismissed. It is understood the case has been compromised.

ANDERSON, Sarah E. | | Feb 6, 1896
SEE WHITE, James H.

ANDREWS, Fred | Marriage | May 7, 1896
Married, Mr Fred Andrews of the Gem City and Miss Carrie Eva Curry at the home of Mr B.A. Curry Thursday eve April 28th. Miss Jessie Givler was bridesmaid and Sam Curry, brother of bride, was best man. Will live at 2005 Hampshire St. Quincy.

ANGEL, Mr and Mrs Robert | Little Brindle | May 27, 1897
Rushville paper reports celebration Monday eve of silver wedding of Mr and Mrs Robert Angel, for years residents of that place. They were married May 17, 1872. Attending was Mrs Thomas Clemmons, mother of Mrs Angel.

ANSTIN, Geogo H. | Local | Nov 28, 1895
Geoge H. Anstin and Myrtle Flynn of McKee were licensed to marry.

APSLEY, Lee W. | Local | Oct 25, 1894
Mr Lee W. Apsley of Chestline and Miss Lottie E. Covert, of Beverly were married Saturday at the home of grooms cousin in Quincy by Justice Avise.

ARENZ, Miss Kate | | Jun 26, 1890
SEE LESTER, Sam H.

ARNOLD, Fred | News from Little Brindle | Nov 2, 1893
Fred Arnold of Mt Sterling and Miss Nettie M. Cleaves of Fargo were married at ME parsonage in that city at 4 PM Thursday by Rev E.H. Lugg.

ARNTZEN, Ed | | Dec 29, 1892
SEE DISSLER, Miss Dora

ARNTZEN, Mr Henry | 5 Years Ago | Dec 11, 1890
SEE WHITE, Miss Addie

ARNTZEN, Lee | | Mar 17, 1892
SEE DISSLER, Miss Mary

ARNTZEN, Oscar | Married | Mar 4, 1897
Married at the home of brides father, Mr John Padgett, Wednesday eve February 24th, Oscar Arntzen and Miss Carrie M. Padgett, both of Kellerville. Groom is only son of Mr and Mrs Henry Arntzen and a young teacher. Both born and raised in this vicinity.

ASHLEY, Mr Fred | News from Little Brindle | Nov 9, 1893
Mr Fred Ashley of Siloam and Miss Christina Hetzell of Clayton were married last Sunday by Police Magistrate Thos. E. Davis of Mound Station. "Examiner"

ASHTON, Mrs Lou "Pike" Sep 16, 1897
Pike County Republican The Griggsville Press reports wedding of Mrs Lou Ashton, of that place, to a man calling himself Dr J.M. Baker of Seattle, Washington. He had been in Griggsville 4 or 5 days until they were married. After she sold her property that had been 20 years in the making they left on a wedding trip. In a day or 2 the Doctor deserted his new bride at Detroit with one dress and a postage stamp, he having the money.

ATKINSON, Miss Laura E. Pike County Oct 10, 1895
Editor Donohue of the Pike County Republican will be married today to Miss Laura E. Atkinson, of New Canton.

ATKINSON, Mary Ellen Jan 3, 1895
SEE MOFFETT, Grant L.

ATKINSON, William E. Little Brindle Nov 24, 1898
Married at Hersman Thursday eve, William E. Atkinson and Miss Lena Means both of Bloomington at home of Charles Hersman whose wife is a sister of the bride.

AUSMUS, Miss Alma Local Feb 16, 1893
Marriage of Miss Alma Ausmus to Mr William Curry occurred at the home of Mr and Mrs George W. Ausmus, parents of the bride on West Washington Street in this city Sunday eve by Elder H.G. VanDervoort. Atttended only by family of bride and Mr James Curry, brother of groom.

AUSMUS, Miss Blanche Local Jul 14, 1892
Married today at the Vermont Street ME Church Quincy, Miss Blanche Ausmus to Mr J.A. Roy by Rev C. Galeener. Groom has taught school this county several years.

AUSMUS, Miss Emma Aug 9, 1894
SEE WEAR, Mr

AUSMUS, Geo. F. Local Oct 24, 1895
Wedding at the home of Mr John Harper in tis city last night, Geo. F. Ausmus and Lucy B. Parker, both of Clayton by Rev F.B. Madden. Will live with his mother who recently lost her husband.

AUSMUS, Mrs Jennie D. Apr 21, 1898
SEE ORR, Matthew

AUSTIN, Miss Emma May 15, 1890
SEE SHIELDS, Rev Parker

BABB, Mrs Mary E. September 1889 Sep 7, 1899
Married at Grand Marias, Minn., Mrs Mary E. Babb and Mr C.S. Durfee.

BACON, R.H. All Over the County Sep 16, 1897
R.H. Bacon and wife, of LaPrairie last Thursday, Sept. 2nd, celebrated their 50th wedding anniversary.

BADGELY, Mr Ed 10 Years Ago Sep 28, 1893
SEE GILBIRDS, Miss Lulu

BADGETT, Mrs Isabella Brown County Nov 9, 1899
Bushrod H. Glasscock of Dewitt County Arkansas and Mrs Isabella Badgett of Mt Sterling were married by Elder A.D. Veatch at 5 PM last Sunday at home of bride three miles east of this city. (More than a quarter of a century ago when she was a school girl he was her "beau". Each married and raised children and fate brought them together again.) Will live Dewitt, Arkansas.

BADGLEY, Mr Edd 15 Years Ago Sep 15, 1898
Married--Mr Edd Badgley and Miss Lulu Gilbirds.

BAGBY, Joseph N. Brown County Mar 29, 1900
Joseph N. Bagby of Fargo and Miss Lillie M. McDonnell, of Mound, were married in the latter place Tuesday by Rev Alex Orr.

BAILEY, Thomas Wedding Apr 16, 1896
Squire Thomas Bailey of Camp Point was down today getting a license to marry Mrs Pamelia Rhea a middle aged widow of same town. Squire is over 70 years old and worth about $70,000. Quincy Herald. Married by Col. Wm Hanna of Golden Friday eve. Mrs Hanna and Mrs Bailey are sisters and will live Camp Point.

BAILEY, William Taylor Little Brindle Dec 1, 1898-
William Taylor Bailey, son of Alex Bailey, of this city, and Miss Olive Pearl Scott, daughter of Mr and Mrs James Scott were married by Rev Alex McGaffin, pastor of Presbyterian Church in this city at 8 PM Tuesday at home of brides parents in East Galesburg.

BAILY, Alex Brown County May 10, 1900
Republican Alex Baily of this city and Miss Eva Joseph of Camp Point were married Monday afternoon at home of Rev Beadles 223 N. 4th St. Quincy. Witnessed by Mr Baily's son, Mark. Will live Quincy. Left for Winfield, Kansas to spend several weeks with Mr Baily's brother.

BAKER, Mr Albert Local Apr 9, 1891
Mr Albert Baker of Liberty and Miss Belle Smith of Kellerville were married Sunday Apr 5th by Rev H. Denning at his home in Clayton.

BAKER, Miss Anna Local Dec 4, 1890
Miss Anna Baker and Mr Preston Hughes were married by Rev F.N. Calvin in Quincy on Sunday and returned on evening train.

BAKER, Bert Local Feb 7, 1895
Bert Baker and Miss Margaret Rumple of Clayton township were married at Mt Sterling Thursday. Bert is 20 years old and lady is 18 years old.

BAKER, Conrad Local Apr 19, 1894
Wednesday Whig says under head of "Never to Old to Love" Conrad Baker 73 years old and Nancy Hendricks, a blushing widow, 63 years old were licensed to marry yesterday. Both are from Kellerville.

BAKER, Conrad Little Brindle Jun 24, 1897
Brown County Republican Mr Conrad Baker age 76 and Mrs Comelia Harwood both of Concord, Adams County were married in the courthouse in this city yesterday afternoon by Squire John McCabe.

BAKER, Conrad and Nancy Local Sep 13, 1894
To whom it may concern, my wife, Nancy Baker, having without cause, left my bed and board I hereby give notice that I will not be responsible for any debts she may contract. Conrad Baker.

BAKER, Conrad and Nancy Local Nov 12, 1896
Divorce case of Conrad Baker against Nancy Baker was tried in circuit court Friday. Mr Baker is an old resident of Concord township. Mrs Baker's previous name was Hendricks. She lives with her son at Kellerville.

BAKER, Emma L. Little Brindle News Jul 5, 1894
Emma L. Baker, age 15 of Clayton was married to John S. Johnson age 28 of Pea Ridge Thursday by Esq. Mart Brooks. "Democrat Message"

BAKER, Miss Ida Sep 6, 1894
SEE BINKLEY, Lewis E.

BAKER, Dr J.M. Sep 16, 1897
SEE ASHTON, Mrs Lou

BAKER, James V. Little Brindle Jun 24, 1897
Brown County Republican James V. Baker age 26 of Kellerville and Miss Sophia Shelly age 23 of Mound, were married Sunday eve at Methodist parsonage by Rev F.B. Madden, accompanied by Mr Ira Bowen and Miss Rose Baker.

BAKER, Mrs Lilly Belle Mar 4, 1897
SEE HUGHES, Geo. W.

BAKER, Mrs Mary L. Brown County Oct 17, 1895
Mrs Mary L. Baker of Clayton and Jesse Huddleston of Exeter, Illinois were married last Tuesday afternoon by Rev G.A. Little. "Demo. Mess"

BAKER, Miss Minnie Dec 13, 1894
SEE FERRE'L Henry D.

BAKER, Miss Nora 5 Years Ago Apr 28, 1892
Miss Nora Baker and Mr Hughes were married at the home of Prof. Jimison.

BAKER, Oliver 10 Years Ago Aug 2, 1894
Mr Oliver Baker and Miss Mary Harper were married. Ol. died about two years ago.

BAKER, Wm Mar 16, 1893
SEE SHEPPARD, Alice

BAKERBOWER, Miss Rosa Jan 25, 1900
SEE MILLER, Mr Jos. S.

BAKERBOWER, Will Local Sep 25, 1890
Will Bakerbower came in Friday eve on his return trip home to Kansas City, where he nowhad a home of his own and a wife awaits him. His marriage occurred about a month ago.

BALFOUR, Miss Nettie Oct 22, 1891
SEE HUGHES, Wm

BALL, Fred Jr. Adams County Jun 15, 1899
Capt Fred Ball Jr and Miss Emily C. Brent were married 8 PM Thursday at home of the bride. Capt. Ball is a rising young colored attorney. He went through the late Spanish War as Capt of Co. 1 8th Ill. Vol.

BALL, John Dec 15, 1892
SEE ROBINSON, Miss Myrtle

BALLARD, Rev. Local Dec 7, 1893
Rev Ballard, formerly publisher of the Messenger at this place has taken unto himself a wife, Mary C. Berrin, of Fowler.

BALLARD, Elder Chas. Camp Point Nov 30, 1893
Elder Chas. Ballard and Miss Mary Berrian, both of Ursa, were married at the Christian parsonage by Elder Dilley.

BALLARD, Chas. S. Local Nov 23, 1893
A marriage license has been issued to Chas. S. Ballard of Ursa and Mary C. Berrian of Fowler.

BALSAR, Lewis A. Our Own Bailiwick Oct 29, 1896
A marriage license has been issued to Lewis A. Balsar of Camp Point and Amelia C. Scheiferdecker of Clayton.

BANGOR, Fredrick Jan 15, 1891
SEE KRAMER, Miss Kate

BANKER, Edward Local Feb 6, 1896
Marriage license issued Tuesday Edward Banker of Quincy age 26 and Ora McVey, Clayton age 21.

BANKS, Ed Little Brindle Oct 21, 1897
Republican of the 14th Ed Banks and Miss Belle Swisher, so it is reported were married recently, the first of last week or the last of the week previous, at Decatur. They left here on the 1st to go to Springfield fair, from which place they went to Decatur and were married. Came home last Thursday night and Friday went to bride's parents home near Kellerville.

BARKLEY, Mr A.H. Feb 6, 1890
SEE BOWER, Miss Alice

BARLEY, Mary J. May 30, 1895
SEE WADE, Edward

BARLOW, Miss Belle Sep 14, 1893
SEE MILLER, Frank A.

BARNES, Miss Ida Personal Feb 13, 1896
Mrs Dr Black returned from Good Hope where she attended the wedding Friday of her cousin, Miss Ida Barnes and Mrs Frank Harden at 7:30 PM Wednesday. Groom is business man in Good Hope, being engaged in lumber, furniture and undertaking business.

BARNES, John A. City Brevities Jan 5, 1899
Marriage of John A. Barnes of Chicago and Miss Emma A. Hughes, youngest daughter of Mr Geo. Hughes, of Kellerville, occurred last week.

BARNET, Fred Neighborhood News Nov 1, 1894
The Bowen Chronicle says--Married, Miss Eva, daughter of our friends Mr and Mrs David Kemp of Maple Grove farm near Bowen to Fred Barnet, also of Bowen.

BARNETT, Aggie Sep 23, 1892
SEE BRUEGGER, Peter

BARNETT, Mr and Mrs John Neighborhood News Jul 25, 1895
Mr John Barnett and wife celebrated their golden wedding at Bowen July 10th.

BARR, William P. Sep 26, 1896
SEE SAMUELS, Mary L.

BARROWS, Bushrod W. and Mary A. Locals Nov 12, 1891
Circuit court Barrows vs Barrows briefly states: On July 10, 1889 Bushrod W. Barrows married Mrs Mary A. Buttofff in Quincy and brought her home to this city and on July 12th Mr Barrows gave his wife a warrenty deed of date July 10, 1889 conveying his property in this city to her, shortly afterwards estrangement of affection and seperation followed. Mrs Barrows failed to record the deed and on Oct 8, 1891 B.W. Barrows delivered a deed for same premises to Arthur H. Barrows, a son by a former wife, which deed was recorded Nov 11th following, one month prior to recording of the one given his wife. Upon the facts Mrs Barrows sued her husband in Brown county circuit court for title, alleging conspiracy on part of father and son to defraud her. Case tried February term 1891. Premise title given to Mrs Barrow now the case is pending in Adams County circuit court where Mrs Barrows sues for seperate maintenance. Mt Sterling Examiner.

BARROWS, Fred May 8, 1890
SEE STAHL, Miss

BARROWS, Miss Margaret G.. Brown County Dec 21, 1899
Democrat Message Married at the home of M.M. McKenney, Keokuk, Iowa, Tuesday afternoon, Miss Margaret G. Barrows, daughter of Mr and Mrs A.H. Barrows of this city and W.J. Goodwin of Keokuk. Some months the bride has been living at Lapote City, Iowa employed as a trimmer in a millinery est. Groom is with a wholesale furniture store at keokuk.

BARROWS, Mary A. and Bushrod W. Local Nov 13, 1890
Quincy Herald Case in circuit court yesterday AM, Judge Marsh signed a decree in the case of Mary A. Barrows vs Bushrod W. Barrows, suit for seperate maintenance allowing $100 alimony for attorney fees and $140 for her immediate expenses. Will be of interest to this city and people of Brown County.

BARTELLS, Miss Lottie Sep 23, 1897
SEE SHELLY, Walter

BARTOLDOS, John 5 Years Ago Dec 25, 1890
SEE PARKER, Miss Eliza

BATES, Mr Henson E. Jun 5, 1890
SEE SAWYER, Miss Hattie E.

BATES, Dr Lee   Camp Point   Sep 21, 1899
A very pretty wedding took place at the home of Dr and Mrs Henry, Thursday eve at 7:30 when their daughter, Miss Fannie, was married to Dr Lee Bates by Rev T.M. Dillon on the lawn.

BATES, Dr Lee   Camp Point   Sep 21, 1899
Mrs Mary Anderson of Martinsburg, Iowa, Mrs Anna McFarland of Atlanta, Iowa, Dr's Walter and Ed Henry of Omaha, were here to attend marriage of their sister, Miss Fannie, to Dr Lee Bates.

BATES, Orville Lee   County News   Sep 21, 1899
Marriage license issued last week by county clerk to Orville Lee Bates and Fannie Birdenia Henry. Both of Camp Point.

BATES, Will   Camp Point   Oct 5, 1899
Wedding of Will Bates and Miss Lillie Mensendike will take place at the home of the bride Thursday eve this week.

BAUGHMAN, Miss Cora A.   Jan 1, 1891
SEE NEVINS, John A. and Cora A.

BEACOCK, George   Neighborhood News   Aug 18, 1892
George Beacock, a rich farmer of Rush township JoDaviess County and Julia Dean a grand daughter of Mr Beacock's former wife were married on the 11th. When Mr Beacock was 21 he married Mrs Elizabeth Benjour, a widow more than twice his age who had a numerous family. There were 21 children several of whom were older than their stepfather and they lived together 20 years. Last March Mrs Beacock died and the widower married his late wife's granddaughter.

BEADLES, James   Brown County   Nov 23, 1899
Rev Browne performed marriage of James Beadles of Winchester and Miss May Harper of Clayton, yesterday.

BEADLES, Wm J.   Nov 23, 1899
SEE HARPER, Miss May

BEALL,   Personal   Mar 5, 1896
Mr Stegall of Stewartsville, Missouri a relative of the bride came to attend the Beall-Hopper wedding last week. He is the son in law of Mrs Litzenburg, now deceased, who lived here several years ago.

BEALL, Frankie   Local   Feb 20, 1896
Wedding invitation of two Claytonians: Mrs E.J. Beall invites you to be present at the marriage of her daughter, Frankie to Howard Merriam Hopper Thursday, Feb 27th, 1896 at 8 PM Clayton, Illinois.

BEALL, Miss Frankie   Married   Mar 5, 1896
Married Thursday eve last week at home of Mrs E.J. Beall their daughter, Miss Frankie and Mr Howard M. Hopper by Rev A.C. Hodgson. Bride attended by Miss Adah Hiles and Greta Coe as flower girl.

BEALL, Lina and Wm   Neighbors   Sep 9, 1897
Herald Attorneys Akers and Babcock docket a divorce case of Lina Beall vs Wm Beall, they were married in Clayton in 1883 and have two children. Husband deserted her in 1893 and is now supposed to be in LaSalle County.

BEALL, Mrs Lina   Adams County   Oct 20, 1898
Camp Point Journal Walter S. Ward and Mrs Lina Beall were married in Springfield September 30th.

BEAN, Addie E.   Mar 4, 1897
SEE COLPITTS, Joseph A.

BEAN, Miss Belle   Local   Oct 13, 1892
The home of C.C. Connor was the wedding on Wednesday of Miss Belle Bean to Mr Edward Crawford of Mt Sterling by Elder Van Dervoort.

BEAN, Fannie   Mar 30, 1893
SEE CANNON, John H.

BEAN, Miss Martha J. Oct 10, 1895
SEE SYRCLE, John W.
BEAN, Mrs Rebecca Sep 12, 1895
SEE SHATZER, Jacob
BEARD, Miss Maud A. Feb 17, 1898
SEE LONG, Chas. V.
BECHTEL, Samuel Dec 30, 1897
SEE BLACK, Miss Minnie V.
BECKETT, Clarence Camp Point Feb 9, 1899
Invitations are out for wedding of Clarence Beckett to Miss Lizzie McFarland, Feb 15th at 6 o'clock.
BECKETT, Clarence E. Adams County Feb 16, 1899
Invitations are out for marriage of Miss Lizzie McFarland to Clarence E. Beckett. Mis McFarland is daughter of Albert McFarland, who lives midway between Camp Point and Golden.
BECKETT, Miss Della Adams County News Nov 9, 1893
Invitations are out announcing the marriage of Mr C.W. Stinson of Bowen and Miss Della Beckett of Golden. Will occur at home of brides' parents, Mr and Mrs James A. Beckett Wednesday November 15th. "New Era"
BECKETT, Della Local Nov 23, 1893
The home of Capt. J.A. Beckett and wife was the scene of the social event of Golden, Wednesday last their daughter, Della was married to Mr Charles S. Stinson by Rev W.D. Atkinson. Charlie is a compositor on this paper.
BECKETT, Harry I. Local Nov 17, 1892
Golden New Era Last Thursday Harry I. Beckett and Miss Dora Duis, both of this city were married by Rev Smith at the brides parents home.
BECKETT, Mr and Mrs Harry I. Our Own Bailiwick Nov 21, 1895
Monday was the third anniversary of marriage of Harry I. Beckett and wife. "Golden New Era"
BECKETT, John Camp Point Mar 12, 1896
Mr John Beckett and Miss Electa Selby of Golden were married at Christian parsonage last Wednesday eve.
BECKMAN, Miss Anna Feb 1, 1894
SEE FLOATMAN, John
BECKMAN, Charles Married Mar 18, 1897
Two young people of Concord went over to Mt Sterling and were married by Mart Brooks, Esq. they are, Charles Beckman son of Henry Beckman and Miss Hylas Sharp, daughter of Mrs Sharp, all of Concord. Brides brother Amos accompanied them.
BECKMAN, Miss Electa May 10, 1900
SEE GIBSON, Alden M.
BECKWITH, Lillian Jan 25, 1894
SEE WEAKLY, P.E.
BEHRENS, Miss Ricka Local Apr 22, 1897
Wedding at the home of Mr Herman Behrens, four miles north of the city Wednesday their daughter, Miss Ricka to Mr Albert Totsch, son of Jacob Totsch north of town.
BEHRENS, Ulfert Jr. Our Own Bailiwick Oct 1, 1896
A license to marry was issued to Ulfert Behrens Jr of Golden and Grace Meints of Golden.
BEHRENS, Ulfert Local Apr 8, 1897
A marriage license issued to Ulfert Behrens and Anna Lubben, both of Golden.
BELL, Amanda Pea Ridge Jan 8, 1891
Married at the home of brides parents in Missouri township, Amanda Bell to Mr Putman of that place.

BELL, Chas. | Pea Ridge | Dec 22, 1892
Chas. Bell and Miss Lizzie Howe were married Wednesday eve. Will live in the place he bought of Mr Pevehouse.

BELL, Miss Eliza L. | Nov 24, 1892
SEE CAMPBELL, John S.

BELL, John | Local | Feb 13, 1896
To be married in town this eve, John Bell and Miss Mary Howe at home of Mr and Mrs James Howe in east part of town. Miss Mary has made her home at the Bell home several months where she has been nursing Mrs Bell who is an invalid.

BELLOMY, Miss Hattie C. | Local | Aug 13, 1896
Marriage of Miss Hattie C. Bellomy, daughter of Mr and Mrs Bellomy of Brown county to Mr Ray Campbell of Morgan county occurred at Baptist Church in Mt Sterling by Rev F.P. Douglass. Will live on the farm in Morgan county.

BELLOMY, Dr W.T. | 5 Years Ago | Sep 4, 1890
Dr W.T. Bellomy and Miss Hattie Knight were married, they now live in Schuyler county where Dr Bellomy has a good practice.

BELMEYER, Miss Eva | Jul 12, 1894
SEE WATSON, William C.

BELMEYER, Miss Gertie | Local | Jun 18, 1891
Marriage of Miss Gertie Belmeyer to Mr Orville Douglas was at Mt Sterling Thursday AM of last week. Mr Douglas is an industrious young farmer living near Hazel Dell school house in Concord. His wife is daughter of Mrs Bellmeyer who with her family moved to town from Chestline some months ago. The ladys father is Sol Belmeyer of Quincy, the deputy county clerk. Since the death of Mrs Douglas the mother to the groom, the groom and father had been housekeeping alone.

BELTS, John | Oct 24, 1895
SEE SCOTT, John and Fannie

BEMIS, Henry R. | Local | May 22, 1890
A marriage license has been issued to Henry R. Bemis, of Siloam age 24 and Bertha May Duff, of Burton age 18.

BEMIS, Henry R. | Other Days | May 24, 1900
Married, Henry R. Bemis and Mary Duff of Siloam.

BENJOUR, Mrs Elizabeth | Aug 18, 1892
SEE BEACOCK. George

BENNETT, Mrs Addie | Supplement | Oct 19, 1893
10 Years Ago Mrs Addie Bennett married Rankin Smith.

BENNETT, Mr Edgar | Aug 1883 | Aug 11, 1898
SEE WILEY, Miss Ada

BENNETT, Mr Edgar | Decade Ago | Aug 10, 1893
SEE WILEY, Miss Ida

BENNETT, J.A. | 5 Years Ago | Apr 16, 1891
SEE NORTON, Miss Alice

BENNETT, S.C. | Little Brindle | Jun 29, 1899
S.C. Bennett, our photographer and barber and Miss Mary A. Blansett of Pea Ridge by Rev Rigg at the parsonage in Mt Sterling Tuesday. Mr Bennett is son of Mr and Mrs Maurice Bennett of Mound and Miss Blansett's parents are well to do people of Pea Ridge.

BENNETT, Sam S. | Little Brindle | Jun 29, 1899
Married Sam S. Bennett of Mounds age 29 and Mary A. Blansett of Pea Ridge age 21.

BENNETT, Mr Walter Henry | Jun 3, 1897
SEE INCE, Miss Nellie Caroline

BENSON, Miss Belle | Neighborhood News | Dec 5, 1895
SEE DAVIS, Charles H.

BENT, Effie Jan 17, 1895
SEE FRANKS, Oscar
BENT, George H. Little Brindle Aug 2, 1898
Democrat Message of the 27th Last Saturday PM Esq. McCabe was called to marry George H. Bent and Miss Martha Webb, both of Kellerville.
BENT, Martha O. May 6, 1897
SEE CAMP, William E.
BENTLY, James O. Neighborhood News Dec 24, 1891
Cards are out announcing the marriage of Mr James O. Bently, one of the editors of the Baylis Guide, and Miss May L. Wilson at the home of Mr and Mrs R.L. Wilson in Hadley township December 24th.
BENTON, Mrs Lavina Feb 1884 Feb 2, 1899
SEE CURRY, B.A.
BERRIAN, Miss Hannah Neighborhood News May 4, 1893
Miss Hannah Berrian, daughter of Judge B.F. Berrian was married Tuesday eve last week to Lyman McCarl, master of chancery.
BERRIAN, John S. Our Own Bailiwick Jun 11, 1896
Miss Harriett E. Sewery, formerly matron of Blessing hospital and John S. Berrian of this city were married Wednesday at the home of the bride in Barrie, Ontario. The engagement of Miss Sewery to Mr B.F. Berrian Jr was announced in Optic two years ago but seems a change of heart somewhere, the prospective groom is an elder brother of the gentleman then named for the office "Optic".
BERRIAN, Miss Mary Nov 30, 1893
SEE BALLARD, Elder Chas.
BERRIAN, Mary C. Nov 23, 1893
SEE BALLARD, Chas. S.
BERRIN, Mary C. Dec 7, 1893
SEE BALLARD, Rev.
BERTHOLF, Mr and Mrs Edward Supplement Dec 14, 1899
Exchanges Mr and Mrs Edward Bertholf of Rushville cleebrated their 61st wedding anniversary.
BETZER, Soloa Local Oct 22, 1896
Justice Allen this afternoon married Soloa Betzer of Hazelwood and Josephine Keltz of Clayton, Illinois.
BEUTEL, Frank Local Dec 21, 1899
Marriage license granted at Quincy Monday to: Frank Beutel and Mary A. Hocamp, both of Columbus.
BILLINGS, Albert and Mary A. Kingdom Of Pike Jan 25, 1894
Mrs Mary A. Billings feeling that her husband, Albert Billings, was not entitled to have two wives, caused his arrest last week on charge of bigamy.
BINKLEY, Lewis E. Little Brindle News Sep 6, 1894
Wednesday, Lewis E. Binkley, of Kellerville, secured a license to marry Miss Ida Baker of the same place.
BIRKEE, Miss Addie Aug 24, 1899
SEE HOUK, John
BIRKETT, Alden S. July 1883 Jul 7, 1898
Married, Alden S. Birkett and Mrs Ellen Noakes.
BIRKETT, Miss Flora Sep 2, 1897
SEE HODGSON, Rev Arthur C.
BLACK, Miss Frances Jun 21, 1894
SEE SNIVELY, Rev George L.
BLACK, Mr Iyin Local Dec 22, 1892
Mr Iyin Black, son of S.N. Black and wife and Miss Rosa S. Bottorff of La Prairie will be married today.

BLACK, Mr Ivan Dec 29, 1892
SEE BOTTORFF, Miss Rosa

BLACK, Miss Minnie V. Supplement Dec 30, 1897
EXAMINER, Samuel Bechtel of Camden, Schuyler County was in town Tuesday extracting himself from a dilemma, Miss Minnie V. Black married a man named Nodson that afterward she applied for and obtained a divorce from Nodson in Schuyler County, but the decree was not signed, a fact she was probably not aware of at time of her second marriage shortly after rendering the decree, viz: Nov 26, 1896 Mrs Nodson and Mr Bechtel were married and Mr Bechtel did not learn of the true situation until sometime after he married her. Mr Bechtel is not regretting his marriage, only that it should be straightened out.

BLACK, Mr R.S. 5 Years Ago Nov 26, 1891
SEE MCBRATNEY, Miss Mary

BLACK, Miss Rosa Married Nov 2, 1899
Married last Thursday eve October 26th, Miss Rosa, daughter of Mr and Mrs Samuel N. Black to Mr Christian J. Hollock at the home some four miles north of town at 6:30 PM. Groom's former home was in McDonough County but now of Memphis, Tenn. where he has been in business for years. Married by Rev Edwin J. Rice.

BLANSETT, Miss Cora Local Nov 14, 1895
Married at brides parents home, Mr and Mrs L.H. Blansett in Pea Ridge Thursday eve last week (October 31st) their daughter, Miss Cora and Mr George Williams, a son of Mr Steven Williams of Mounds by Elder Joseph Crawford of Mounds. Will live on farm near Mounds.

BLANSETT, Mary A. Jun 29, 1899
SEE BENNETT, Sam S.

BLANSETT, Miss Mary A. Jun 29, 1899
SEE BENNETT, S.C.

BLASCHOK, Miss Annie Dec 5, 1895
SEE AMEN, Alebert

BLISS, Alfred P. Little Brindle May 11, 1899
Records of County Clerk office show but one marriage license issued during the week, Alfred P. Bliss and Irene Click, both of Clayton.

BLOOD, Charles Local Sep 7, 1899
Married in Chicago last week Tuesday, Mr Charles Blood and Miss Grace Rhea, both of Camp Point. Bride is sister of Mrs Dr Boothe of this city.

BLOOD, Miss Harriet J. Our Own Bailiwick Aug 22, 1895
Camp Point Items Quiet wedding on north side Thursday eve when Miss Harriet J. Blood was married to Mr Frank N. Allen by Rev A.N. Simmons. Left on 8:40 train for Martinsville, Clark county where they will live. Groom is high school principal there.

BLOOD, Miss Katherine S. Adams County Jun 8, 1899
Marriage of Miss Katherine S. Blood of Camp Point, daughter of the dry goods man to Mr Herbert C. Summey of Omaha occurred this week.

BLOOMBERG, Mr Nov 9, 1899
SEE HUGHES, Miss Mary

BLOOMFIELD, Mrs Ada and C. Melville Little Brindle Jun 18, 1896
Mrs Ada Bloomfield of Mt Sterling filed for divorce from her husband, C. Melville Bloomfield for desertion. Asks custody of there child.

BLOOMFIELD, Ada and C.M. Little Brindle Sep 24, 1896
Divorce was granted to Ada Bloomfield from C.M. Bloomfield.

BOBBITT, Miss Anna Camp Point Oct 7, 1897
At the close of Sunday school convention at Christian Church Sunday eve, Mr James Brown of Iowa and Miss Anna Bobbitt were married by Elder Dilley.

BOBBITT, Miss Ollie Camp Point Oct 29, 1891
Miss Ollie Bobbitt was married Monday eve to a gentleman from White Hall.

BOGER, Fred J. Camp Point Feb 27, 1896
Wednesday eve this week occurs the marriage of Fred J. Boger and Miss Effie Rhea at the brides home.

BOGER, J. Fred Feb 27, 1896
SEE RHEA, Miss Effie

BOGER, Lawrence Camp Point Apr 29, 1897
Lawrence Boger and Gertrude Jewell were married at the home of the bride last Wednesday eve by Rev Simmons.

BOLDIN, Mrs Feb 8, 1894
SEE SEATON, G.K.

BOLING, Miss Hattie Local Jan 15, 1891
Miss Hattie Boling, daughter of Mr and Mrs Wm Boling of Concord township will be married at noon today (Wednesday) to Mr Fred W. Vering, also of Concord. Will live on a farm recently bought by Mr Verring from Mr Boling.

BOLINGER, Miss Blanche City Brevities May 11, 1899
Married, daughter of Mr R. Bolinger who as a little girl was known in this vicinity in Pueblo, Colorado Monday May 1st 1899, John Vay of Pueblo and Miss Blanche Bolinger of Eads, Colorado by Rev A.A. Hoskin.

BOLINGER, Miss Clara Local Mar 15, 1900
Miss Clara Bolinger was chaperoned to Mt Sterling last week by Mr and Mrs Henry Hickman of Quincy where she married Mr Leon W. Huddleston who has been a student in one of the colleges of that city, He hails from the southwest. Will live Quincy.

BOLINGER, Miss Emma Married Oct 15, 1891
Married at the home of Mr and Mrs John R. Wallace Wednesday eve last week, Miss Emma Bolinger to Mr Thos. Moore, both of this city. Mr Moore is member of one of our leading business firms. Bride has lived Clayton several years. Married by Rev J.J. Thomson.

BOLTON, Miss Ann E. 5 Years Ago Oct 13, 1892
Miss Ann E. Bolton was married to Mr C.E. Smith at Mt Sterling.

BOLTON, Miss Mary J. 5 Years Ago Oct 30, 1890
SEE ALLEN, Wm

BOND, Sidney J. Ill Brevities Sep 6, 1894
Sidney J. Bond and Miss Estelle M. Tunis were married at Jacksonville.

BONNELL, Miss Lizzie 10 Years Ago Dec 3, 1891
Miss Lizzie Bonnell became Mrs D. Burleigh.

BONSER, Mr Edward Little Brindle Feb 22, 1894
Married at the court house in this city this AM by police magistrate T.M. Wallace, Mr Edward Bonser of Nebraska to Miss Lillian Gedding of this county. Republican

BOOKMAN, Richard Mt Sterling Mar 30, 1893
Richard Bookman, the poultry dealer and Miss Della Jennings, second daughter of David Jennings were married in Macomb last Monday and returned home Thursday AM.

BOOTH, Charles Adams County Jul 6, 1899
Camp Point Examiner Charles Booth, a Clayton dentist and Mary Katherine Rhea, the Camp Point Milliner were married by Rev R.A. Omer at his home Wednesday 8 PM. Present was Charles Blood and Grace Rhea. After July 5th will be at home in Clayton.

BOOTH, Frank Camp Point Feb 15, 1894
Frank Booth and Miss Bertha Kline were married Wednesday eve by Elder O. Dilley.

BOOTH, Rev and Mrs J.R. Ill Brevities Apr 12, 1894
Silver wedding at La Harpe of Rev and Mrs J.R. Booth, their friends gave them a bucket containing 102 silver dollars.

BOOTH, Mrs Mary E. Neighborhood News Jul 13, 1893
Barry had a wedding recently that savors of romance. W.H.H. Adams, a well to do farmer of Clay County desired the companionship of a help-mate and sought, through an advertisement and it caught eye of Mrs Mary E. Booth, a widow of Barry. She answered and it ended in their marriage. Both are over 50.

BOOTHE, Dr J.C. City Brevities Jun 29, 1899
Marriage of Dr J.C. Boothe of this city and Miss Mollie Rhea of Camp Point is to occur at the family home of the bride, Mr and Mrs Thos. Bailey, Wednesday at 8 PM will live Clayton.

BOOTHE, Dr John C. Adams County Jul 13, 1899
Dr John C. Boothe of Clayton and Miss Mary K. Rhea were married Wednesday eve at home of Elder R.A. Omer, who performed the ceremony.

BORDERICK, Jennie May 3, 1900
SEE RENAKER, W.G.

BOREN, Mr D.B. Apr 9, 1891
SEE ROYER, Miss Nellie

BOREN, James A. Jan 3, 1895
SEE CHASE, Mrs Emma

BOSTIC, Mrs Carrie Aug 6, 1891
SEE KELLER, Mrs Carrie

BOSTIC, Frank Aug 6, 1891
SEE KELLER, Mrs Carrie

BOSTICK, Henry Occurrences of Dec 1885 Dec 11, 1890
Henry Bostick, the colored barber married Mrs McFadon. She fired the vesatile and handsome Henry soon after.

BOSTICK, Miss Nellie Local Dec 31, 1891
Mr J.R. Kern tells us that Nellie Bostick and Jas. W. Heirs are married. By some complication these lovers became estranged and she married Mr Price, which was unhappy and Mrs Price was divorced from him. This is probably as it should have been and we hope Mr and Mrs Heirs to be happy and contented. Jim is on the Globe Democrat and his a pleasant position.

BOSWELL, Mr L.B. Our Own Bailiwick Feb 6, 1896
Married a popular young Quincyite, Mr L.B. Boswell and Miss Elizabeth F. Roland at Kansas City Feb 12th.

BOSWELL, Louis B. Local Nov 14, 1895
Louis B. Boswell of Quincy is receiving congratulations on his engagement to Miss Nora J. Roland of Kansas City.

BOTTORFF, Miss Rosa Married Dec 29, 1892
Married at the home of brides parents, Mr and Mrs James Bottorff, one mile north of La Prairie, Miss Rosa Bottorff to Mr Ivan Black of Black Station at 12 o'clock Wednesday December 21st by Rev Hartrick of the ME Church of La Prairie.

BOTTORFF, Miss Rosa S. Dec 22, 1892
SEE BLACK, Mr Iyin

BOUCHELL, Miss Julia Oct 20, 1898
SEE SAXER, Fred B.

BOUNCER, Mr Ed Feb 22, 1894
SEE GIDDINGS, Miss Lillian

BOWEN, Caspar Little Brindle Feb 1, 1894
Mr Caspar Bowen, of Buckhorn and Miss Nellie DeWitt of Siloam Springs were married Monday eve last.

BOWEN, Mr Dora Hazel Dell Mar 12, 1896
Mr Dora Bowen and Miss Hattie Davis were married at Mound last Sunday eve by Rev Jonas VanWey. Will live Quincy where groom has a nice home.

BOWEN, Mr Nova Apr 16, 1896
SEE SHIELDS, Miss Zuda
BOWEN, Sylva Jan 4, 1900
SEE WHITESIDE, Chas. R.
BOWEN, William Local Mar 7, 1895
Marriage of Mr William Bowen and Miss Edith Stevens occurred at home of brides parents, Mr and Mrs B.C. Stevens in this city 6 PM Monday by Rev J. Terrill. Mr Bowen is a barber at Columbus. Will live Columbus.
BOWER, Miss Alice Married Feb 6, 1890
At the parsonage of First ME Church at 12 noon January 30th, Miss Alice Bower of Mt Sterling to Mr A.H. Barkley of Springfield. Will live Springfield. She is the daughter of Mr and Mrs Dr W.W. Bower of this city.
BOWERS, Lettie Camp Point Jan 3, 1895
Miss Sherrick and Miss Emma Lyon went to Mt Sterling Thursday to attend wedding of Lettie Bowers.
BOWLES, L.W. Dec 11, 1890
SEE WALLACE, Miss Etta
BOWLING, Albert Local May 6, 1897
Licensed to wed, Albert Bowling, Kellerville and Effie Hutchinson, Williamsville.
BOWMAN, Bertha Nov 4, 1897
SEE PILLING, William H.
BOWMAN, Sennie Neighbors Jun 29, 1899
Sennie Bowman, a Plymouth Lassie and Homer Hough of Galesburg eloped recently and were married.
BOYLAN, Miss Jul 18, 1895
SEE NOLAN, Peter
BRADFORD, John M. Married Feb 11, 1897
Heralds Correspondent writing from Clayton says: Married at the home of Joseph W. Marrett in this city on Thursday AM February 15th at 5 AM, Mrs Jennie Gilbirds Howard, of Clayton and John M. Bradford of Milton, Illinois by J.P. bride has lived here many years. Was wife of the late Col. C.A. Gilbirds, the popular Wabash Railmaster. After Mr Gilbirds death she moved to Colorado for several years and returned to Clayton to live with her daughter, Mrs Ed Badgley. Will live Milton.
BRADFORD, John M. John & Jennie Joined Feb 11, 1897
Marriage license issued to John M. Bradford of Milton 66 years old and Jennie Howard of Clayton 62 years old.
BRADFORD, John M. All Over the County Aug 26, 1897
John M. Bradford, a member of the Home who married sometime since and located in Milton, Pike county has returned to the Home. Uncle John found that all was not gold that glittered and that even amidst the flowers and sweet toned marriage bells there were many thorns and hard knots.
BRADLEY, Henry T. "Tip" Locals Dec 27, 1894
City Newspaper announced the issueing of a marriage license to Henry T. Bradley and Miss Maymie Hamilton a few days ago. They were married by a Methodist clergyman in Quincy Thursday. Will live Denver. Tip will go now and Mrs Bradley will join him there.
BRADNEY, Miss Belle City Brevities Jun 16, 1898
Cards have bben received announcing marriage of Miss Belle Bradney to Charles W. Maxwell at Delta, Colorado Thursday June 2, 1898.
BRADNEY, Miss Kate Wedding Mar 1, 1894
Delta, Colo. "Independent" in reference to a former Clayton girl; John A. Curtis and Miss Kate Bradney were married Tuesday 2:30 PM by Rev J.H. Gill. Miss Bradney had been in Delta 3 years and Mr Curtis lived there about 6 years and is county surveyor. Wedding at home of brides uncle and aunt, Mr and Mrs H. Hammond.

BRADSHAW, Rev Arthur Neighborhood News Aug 2, 1894
Rev Arthur Bradshaw, of Champaign County has commenced proceedings for divorce. Mr Bradshaw is an aged divine of the Methodist Church. A year ago he took a wife of 16 or 18 years. The young girl soon tired of her octogenarian husband and deserted him.

BRADSHAW, Mrs Charles May 3, 1900
SEE WALTERS, Mrs Anna

BRADY, Bernard AM Wedding Nov 24, 1898
Married at St Thomas Church, Camp Point, Illinois Thursday November 22nd, Mr Bernard Brady, son of Mr and Mrs James Brady of Damon, Ill. and Miss May Agnes Flynn, daughter of Mr and Mrs John Flynn, of this city by Rev Costello. Attended by Mr James Brady and Miss Margaret Flynn.

BRADY, John Little Brindle Feb 16, 1899
Married, Sunday 5th inst at 12:30 John Brady and Miss Esther Redmond, both of Pea Ridge at St Mary's Church. Wedding dinner at home of Mrs Charles Schneider, sister of bride.

BRATTON, Robert May 17, 1900
SEE GRAY, Rebecca (Mrs Capt K.H.)

BRECKENRIDGE, Kitty and Husband County News Feb 1, 1900
The husband of the notorious Kitty Breckenridge has finally decided to get rid of her and has petitioned the court in Adams county to untie the knot that still binds him to her.

BRECKENRIDGE, Mrs Nora May 7, 1896
SEE GILLIS, Mr O.M.

BREED, Mr Camp Point Oct 10, 1895
Mr Breed of Cedar Falls, Iowa and Mrs Amanda Smith of La Harpe were married at the home of Mrs B.'s daughter, Mrs Hez Henry last Wednesday AM.

BREMER, Bertie Jan 29, 1891
SEE COLLIN, William

BRENT, Miss Emily C. Jun 15, 1899
SEE BALL, Fred Jr.

BRENTS, Miss Eunice D. Dec 3, 1896
SEE HUNSAKER, Columbus C.

BRENTS, T.H. Local Jan 25, 1894
Marriage of Mr T.H. Brents to Miss Emma Kohl daughter of Mr Nich Kohl the wholesale grocer, will occur at the Kohl home in Quincy Thursday. They will go to Chickasaw, IT where he has been transferred in the railroad employ.

BRESTER, Mr Oct 20, 1898
SEE ZIMMERMAN, Miss

BREWSTER, Mr Haley Mound Station Apr 3, 1890
Married by April 30th by Rev VanWey, Mr Haley Brewster and Miss Nettie Shields.

BRICKER, Mrs Kate 5 Years Ago Sep 4, 1890
SEE HUGHES, Geo.

BRIDGEMAN, Miss Jennie Aug 10, 1899
While Mr Simmons of Burlington was "doing time" in the city prison at La Harpe recently he was married to Miss Jennie Bridgeman. City officers got a marriage license, paid the minister and gave the newly married couple 48 hours to leave town.

BRIDGEMAN, Margaret Kingdom Aug 27, 1896
Pike County Democrat A Mrs Sherwood whose maiden name was Margaret Bridgeman was examined on a charge of bigamy, she having married Sherwood knowing him to be a married man. Sheriff went to Kentucky to get him and he is in jail.

BRIDGES, Miss Alace   10 Years Ago   Dec 10, 1891
Miss Alace Bridges, daughter of our worthy friend "Old Boody" was married to Mr Robt Watson.

BRIERTON, Miss Emma   Local   Dec 26, 1895
Miss Emma Brierton of Versailles, known to Clayton people when she was a child was married to Dr F.C. Noyey, of Mt Sterling on Xmas eve.

BRIERTON, Miss Jane   10 Years Ago   Dec 21, 1893
SEE ANDERSON, Mr C.S.

BRIERTON, Miss Lena A.   Mar 15, 1894
SEE HARTMAN, Dan A.

BRIGGS, Mrs Catherine and B.F.   Brown County   Sep 12, 1895
Monday afternoon Mrs Catherine Briggs was granted a divorce from B.F. Briggs and with in 8 minutes after the divorce she remarried to John Maddox. The couple hail from north of Versailles township.

BRIGGS, Miss Laura   10 Years Ago   Oct 16, 1890
SEE CAMPBELL, Allen

BRIGGS, Loren M.   Feb 13, 1896
SEE VERMILLION, Miss Nellie F.

BRIGGS, Richard M.   Brown County   Feb 15, 1900
Democrat Message Just 50 years ago Jan 31, 1850 Richard M. Briggs and Theresa Morgan were married. The event was celebrated last week.

BROCKMAN, Clarence Eugene   May 30, 1895
SEE SOHM, Miss Teresa H.

BROOKS, Mrs L.W. and Arthur   Personal   Aug 31, 1893
Mrs L.W. Brooks was here to visit old friends. She is living at Centerville, Iowa with her son Arthur who was married about two months ago. Art is railroading there.

BROPHY, Miss Mary   Dec 6, 1894
SEE SCHROER, Duke

BROWN, Alonzo   10 Years Ago   Feb 9, 1893
Mr Alonzo Brown and Miss May Smith were married in Mt Sterling.

BROWN, Mrs Cora   Sep 6, 1894
SEE SMITH, Henry M.

BROWN, Effie   Oct 24, 1895
SEE SCOTT, John and Fannie

BROWN, Miss Fannie   Little Brindle   Apr 29, 1897
Democrat Message Miss Fannie Brown of Mound and E.E. Ratliff of Lewistown were married at the Curry hotel, Mt Sterling Thursday by Rev F.B. Madden. Miss Brown is a school teacher.

BROWN, James   Oct 7, 1897
SEE BOBBITT, Miss Anna

BROWN, Mary I. and Alonzo   Local   Jul 2, 1896
Monday Judge Bonney signed the decree in divorce in the the case of Mary I. Brown vs Alonzo Brown.

BROWN, Miss Maude and Jno. L.   Local   Jan 11, 1900
Clayton friends of Miss Maude Brown daughter of Jno. L. Brown, who moved from here to Hannibal about two years ago, will be surprised to learn that she will be married today. Her cousin Miss Maude Brown of this city has gone to Hannibal to attend the wedding.

BROWN, Miss Maude   Mar 8, 1900
SEE HAZLETT, James

BROWN, Ray   Little Brindle   Nov 18, 1897
Mound Correspondent to Democrat Message Ray Brown of near Mound, and Miss Cora Stevens, of Clayton, were married at Springfield during the fair at that city and are living with Ma Brown.

BROWN, Riley | County News | Jan 25, 1900
Marriage license issued yesterday to Riley Brown and Dora May Whitaker, both of Chestline.

BRUEGGER, Peter | Neighborhood News | Sep 23, 1892
Peter Bruegger of Nauvoo and Aggie Barnett of Blandinsville, deaf mutes, were married in Blandinsville last week.

BRUNER, Mr and Mrs | Little Brindle | Oct 13, 1898
Brown County Republican Judge Hegbee made his final ruling on the Bruner case Friday. Mrs Bruner was given $600 and Mr Bruner a divorce. Mr Bruner will leave for Florida as soon as he can get things arranged.

BRYANT, Amelia | Married | Oct 16, 1890
In Los Angeles, at the First Congregational Church, Amelia Bryant of Camp Point and Frank Reeves of Amodor City, California.

BRYANT, B.W. | Local | Feb 7, 1895
Today is 25th anniversary of the marriage of B.W. Bryant and Miss Anna E. Edwards.

BRYANT, Mr and Mrs Ben W. | 10 Years Ago | Feb 13, 1890
Ben W. and Mrs Bryant celebrated their thirtieth wedding anniversary.

BRYANT, E.P. | Local | Sep 28, 1893
E.P. Bryant was married the 20th inst to an Ohio lady at Cleveland.

BRYANT, E.P. | 15 Years Ago | May 30, 1895
May 1--E.P. Bryant and Joann LeSage were married.

BRYANT, Mrs Ella | City Brevities | Sep 29, 1898
Mrs Ella Bryant his applied for divorce in the county alleging as a ground for divorce desertion and drunkeness. Set of Oct. term.

BRYANT, Ella B. and Wm E. | City Brevities | Jan 19, 1899
Court signed decree of divorce in the case of Ella B. Bryant vs Wm E. Bryant. Custody of the child was awarded the mother.

BRYANT, Frederick Edward | | Oct 14, 1897
SEE PARKER, Minnie Adelle

BRYANT, Mr and Mrs O.E. | Local | Jun 15, 1893
Mr and Mrs O.E. Bryant celebrated their 7th wedding anniversay last week.

BRYANT, W.E. | Local | Apr 23, 1896
Married, W.E. Bryant and Miss Ella Hough by Justice J.W. Marrett Thursday eve of last week.

BUCKER, Mrs Kate | 10 Years Ago | Sep 12, 1895
SEE HUGHES, Geo.

BUCKNER, Miss Hattie | | Jan 1, 1891
SEE NOFTZ, Theodore

BUETEL, Frank | Camp Point | Dec 28, 1899
Frank Buetel and Miss Mary Hocamp were married at the home of the bride last Thursday.

BUGBEE, Miss Edith | Our Own Bailiwick | Apr 12, 1894
Marriage of Miss Edith Bugbee and Mr John Wood drew a large assembly of friends to the Cathedral in Quincy Tuesday eve. Groom is a popular traveling man who visits Clayton frequently.

BULMAN, Frank R. | Local | Nov 9, 1899
Marriage license issued in this county to Mr Frank R. Bulman, the young business man of Mounds and Miss Mollie, daughter of Samuel A. and Mrs Moore of that place.

BUNDA, James | | Sep 7, 1893
SEE SWEETRING, Miss Nellie

BURGESS, Emma Francis | | Sep 9, 1897
Rev William Burgess, formerly of Mendon announces the marriage of his daughter, Emma Francis, to Rev Wm L. Byers, on Tuesday August 31st at DesPlaines, Illinois.

BURGESSER, Clara Blanch | Local | Sep 29, 1892
Card received that reads: Mr and Mrs Q. Burgesser requests your presence at the marriage of their daughter, Clara Blanch to Edward W. Rockwell, Thursday eve October 11th 1892 at 7:30 PM at 1256 North Lawrence Ave. Wichita, Kansas. At home after October 17th at 724 W. State St. Jacksonville, Illinois. Groom is a commercial man traveling out of Jacksonville.

BURGESSER, Miss Clara Blanch | Married | Oct 21, 1892
Last Thursday eve at home of Mr and Mrs Q. Burgesser, 1256 N. Lawrence Ave, Miss Clara Blanch Burgesser and Mr Edward Rockwell of Jacksonville, Illinois by Rev J.M. Martindale at 7:30 PM. Miss Carrie Dubois was bridesmaid and Mr J.L. Hall of Jacksonville was groomsman. Will live Jacksonville. Wichita Kansas "Daily Beacon" October 15th.

BURGESSER, Mr and Mrs G.W. | Little Brindle News | Oct 18, 1894
Mr and Mrs G.W. Burgesser celebrated their golden wedding at Versailles with a household full of descendents to the fourth generation.

BURGESSER, John Q. | April 1883 | Apr 28, 1898
Married, John Q. Burgesser and Addie Staker, March 22nd.

BURGESSER, Miss May | 5 Years Ago | Oct 15, 1891
Miss May Burgesser married Geo. L. Young. They live in Wichita.

BURGESSER, Mr and Mrs Q. | 10 Years Ago | Dec 25, 1890
The 21st wedding anniversary of Q and Mrs Burgesser was observed.

BURKE, C.H. | 5 Years Ago | Nov 21, 1890
C.H. Burke and Mrs Butler were married at Elm Grove.

BURKE, C.H. | Elm Grove | Oct 15, 1896
Married Wednesday Sept. 30th at Carbondale, Illinois C.H. Burke of Elm Grove and Miss Annie Hamilton of Carbondale. They met in Kansas where both resided for some years.

BURKE, Thad T. | 5 Years Ago | May 3, 1894
SEE ROY, Miss Mary

BURLEIGH, Mrs D. | 10 Years Ago | Dec 3, 1891
SEE BONNELL, Miss Lizzie

BURNES, Mr | Camp Point | Mar 11, 1897
Mr Burnes and Miss Cora Newmann were married at the Francis Hotel, the home of the bride, last Thursday eve. Only the family witnessed the ceremony. Left Friday AM for their home in Chicago.

BURNETT, Miss Carrie | Local | Apr 27, 1893
Miss Carrie Burnett and Mr Mark Judy of Camp Point were married in Quincy Saturday.

BURNETT, Frank T. | Jan 5, 1893
SEE SOUDERS, Miss Ella

BURNETT, J.M. | Little Brindle | May 19, 1898
Democrat Message of the 14th J.M. Burnett and bride arrived in this city Thursday from Fairfield, Iowa, where they were married Tuesday will go to housekeeping on E. Chestnut St.

BURNETT, Mulford | City Brevities | May 5, 1898
Mr Mulford Burnett will be married at Fairfield, Iowa, next week to Miss May Fordyce.

BURROUGHS, Miss Alice | Local | Oct 15, 1896
Mrs S.H. Treog is in Quincy to attend the wedding of her sister, Miss Alice Burroughs to Mr Thomas Sterne a wealthy farmer of Ellington township at 4 PM Wednesday.

BURROUGHS, Miss Eva | Jul 28, 1892
SEE TREGO, Prof. S.H.

BURTON, Mrs Malissa | Dec 8, 1898
SEE SWISHER, Absolem B.

BURTRIDGE, Bert | Exchanges | Nov 16, 1899
Bert Burtridge, a son of farmer living south of Pittsfield and Emily Carey, 17 year old daughter of Dr A.B. Carey of Pittsfield, eloped on Wednesday and were married in Bowling Green, Missouri both of prominent families and attended high school in Pittsfield.

BUSBOM, Heye | 10 Years Ago | May 21, 1891
SEE SARTORIUS, Hannah

BUSBY, Mr Aldridge | May 28, 1891
SEE RICE, Miss Maggie

BUSH, Ralph Edward | Aug 31, 1899
SEE SWAIN, Miss Gertrude.

BUSS, Miss Hattie | 5 Years Ago | Feb 12, 1891
Miss Hattie Buss of Pea Ridge married Mr Heye Wertz.

BUSS, Mrs Ikke | Mar 18, 1897
SEE FLASNER, Henry M.

BUSS, Kate J. | Feb 16, 1899
SEE FRITZEN, George

BUSS, Mamie | Golden | Feb 20, 1896
Married, Mamie, daughter of Mr and Mrs Buss last Thursday to George Aden of Chatten by Rev Darrow. Will live on Mr Buss's farm near Elm Grove after March 1st.

BUTLER, Mr | May 12, 1892
SEE GRIMES, Miss Neva

BUTLER, Mrs | 5 Years Ago | Nov 21, 1890
SEE BURKE, C.H.

BUTLER, William J. | Jan 8, 1891
SEE HALEY, Mrs Susan

BUTTOFF, Mrs Mary A. | Nov 12, 1891
SEE BARROWS, Bushrod W. and Mary A.

BYERS, Rev Wm L. | Sep 9, 1897
SEE BURGESS, Emma Francis

BYRD, Mrs Isabella | Oct 16, 1890
SEE WALKER, George H.

BYRNES, Marguerite A. | Married | Jan 5, 1893
Over in Brown County ten miles north of Mt Sterling lives Mr Frank Byrnes. He lived for a time in Clayton after his return from the war. Later he married and settled in area he now lives. Mr John T. Chapman became acquainted with Miss Marguerite A., one of his daughters some years ago and they were married Wednesday December 28 at home of her father by Rev Abner Clarke of Chaddock College. Rev Clarke was a former instructor of Miss Byrnes when she was a student at Chaddock. Friday the couple went to home of grooms parents, John and Mrs Chapman one mile north of town for reception. They will live in D.A. Davis property on Morgan St.

BYRNES, Miss Hattie | Sep 15, 1892
SEE SHANK, George

BYRNS, Miss Kate | Local | Jun 16, 1892
Little bird tells us that Miss Kate Byrns of Mt Sterling and Mr S.M. Ross of this city were married by Elder H.G. VanDervoort at home of brides parents. We welcome Mr and Mrs Ross to Clayton as residents.

BYRNS, Katie Mae | Married | Jun 23, 1892
Married at the home of Dr G.A. Byrns and wife at 7 PM last Wednesday their daughter, Katie Mae and Samuel M. Ross of Clayton by Elder H.G. VanDervoort. Left to visit grooms relatives and friends in Pike and Morgan counties. Will live Clayton.

BYRNS, Miss Maggie A. | Jan 12, 1893
SEE CHAPMAN, John T.

BYRNS, Mr Sharon   Little Brindle News   Apr 25, 1895
Cards are out announcing marriage of Mr Sharon Byrns and Miss Della Ward at the family home near Scott Mill May 1st.
CAGLE, Wesley   Neighbors   Nov 11, 1897
Wesley Cagle was convicted of forgery in Schuyler county and was issued a license to wed Miss Tennessee Moore. Miss Tennessee Moore and Wesley Cagle were married by Judge Mourning. Groom is 22 years old and previous to this trouble bore a good reputation.
CAIN, Calvin L.   Neighbors   Jun 16, 1898
Cards are out announcing the marriage of Calvin L. Cain and Miss Blanche Dunn at the home of brides parents, Mr and Mrs W.T. Dunn of Pulaski Wednesday. "Augusta Eagle"
CAIN, Catherine   "Old Pike"   Feb 4, 1897
Indictment was found against Wesley R. Williams and Catherine Cain, (of Loraine) for adultery. Bail in each case was $100. Both parties have left for parts unknown. (Williams was divorced from his wife at last term of court)
CAIN, Mr and Mrs Emery   Local   Mar 19, 1896
Mr and Mrs Emery Cain celebrated their 10th wedding anniversary with a dinner for friends on March 15th.
CAIN, Harvey   5 Years Ago   Oct 19, 1893
Mr Harvey Cain and Miss Mary Robbins were married.
CAIN, Jos. H. .   Little Brindle News   Nov 8, 1894
Mr Jos. H. Cain of Missouri township and Miss Eulalia J. McCormick of Kellerville, were married at the courthouse Monday afternoon of this week by Squire Brooks. "Republican"
CAIN, Miss Josephine   Mar 16, 1899
SEE SHANK, John M.
CAIN, Miss Nora   Locals   Jun 11, 1891
SEE CONNOR, S.M. "Selbert"
CAIN, Miss Norr   Apr 30, 1891
Miss Norr Cain and Mr S.N. Connor were married at ME parsonage Wednesday eve by Rev Reed.
CAIN, Miss Orphie   City Brevities   Apr 27, 1899
A Golden Correspondent writes: Miss Orphie Cain and Warren Hillyer were married at home of brides parents, Mr and Mrs Philip Cain, one mile southwest of Pulaski Sunday eve April 23rd. Miss Rena Hopper was bridesmaid and Charlie Cain brother of bride was best man. Groom attended school in Quincy and studied medicine and now practices in Huntsville. Will live Huntsville.
CALDWELL, Miss Susie   Camp Point   Apr 29, 1897
Married since last week, Miss Susie Caldwell and Chas. Getts at Christian parsonage.
CALEY, Miss Alta   Oct 26, 1899
SEE VONHOLT, John W.
CALEY, Edward   Exchanges   Dec 6, 1899
Edward Caley of Bowen and Anna Dievert of Concord were married at county clerks office by Police magistrate Wallace this AM.
CALEY, Nola M.   Jul 13, 1899
SEE HOBBS, William H.
CALLAHAN, Albert   Dec 20, 1894
SEE CHILDS, Misses Nellis and Lura
CAMERON, John   Pea Ridge   Jun 27, 1895
John Cameron, who recently married one of Pea Ridges fairest daughters is now residing with his father near Pine Grove.
CAMERON, Miss Sallie   Elm Grove   Aug 28, 1890
The announcement some time since that a Mr Moss and Miss Sallie Cameron were married by Cyke Burke, was premature. Sallie "flewd" the track.

CAMP, Edward and Nellie Local Oct 15, 1896
Edward Camp filed for divorce against Nellie Camp last week. He is represented by J.A. Roy, "Whig".

CAMP, Samuel 5 Years Ago Jan 26, 1893
SEE MALCOMBER, Mary E.

CAMP, William E. Local May 6, 1897
Licensed to wed: William E. Camp, of Quincy and Martha O. Bent, of Quincy.

CAMPBELL, Allen 10 Years Ago Oct 16, 1890
Mr Allen Campbell and Miss Laura Briggs were married.

CAMPBELL, Charles O. Married Jan 4, 1900
At 6:30 PM New Years Day at home of Jas. B. Hirons and wife northwest of town, Mr Charles O. Campbell and their daughter Miss Saidee were married by Rev Peter Slagle of the ME Church of this place. Miss Mary Deege of Columbus played wedding march on the organ. Groom is youngest son of the pioneer farmer, James Campbell of this township. He is also a farmer. Bride is eldest daughter of Jas. B. Hirons.

CAMPBELL, Miss Ella Local Jun 20, 1895
SEE WALLACE, Samuel

CAMPBELL, Mr George A. City Brevities Oct 6, 1898
Rev Peter Slagel went to Denver Sunday to marry Mr George A. Campbell of this community to Mrs Louisa A. Herring of Denver at high noon at home of brides parents, Mr and Mrs A.J. Clark. Will live Clayton on the farm, a mile north of town. Clarks lived this community 40 years ago.

CAMPBELL, J. Emery Local Dec 7, 1893
Marriage of Mr J. Emery Campbell and Miss May Harris who has lived with relatives on the Rosson place northeast of town a year or more occurred Wednesday eve at Quincy by Elder English. They are now at home of Mr and Mrs James Campbell north west of town. They think of going to Missouri to live.

CAMPBELL, Mr and Mrs James Married 50 Years Jan 26, 1899
The 50th anniversary of the marriage of Mr and Mrs James Campbell was celebrated Jan. 18th at their beautiful home by their children and grandchildren.

CAMPBELL, Jimmie City Brevities Jun 22, 1899
Uncle Jimmie Campbell was a caller Monday PM. He is oldest settler in Clayton township having come here in April 1831 when 5 years old with parents from Kentucky. Family settled the ¼ section now owned by Samuel Newhouse. Mr Campbell is now past 73 years old. Mr and Mrs Campbell celebrated their 50th wedding anniversary last January.

CAMPBELL, John S. Local Nov 24, 1892
Mr John S. Campbell of Clayton and Miss Eliza L. Bell of this city were married at 7:30 PM last Wednesday by Elder M.D. Sharples at the home of Mr and Mrs James McMurray just north of town. Mrs Campbell is a sister of Mrs McMurray. Mt Sterling Examiner

CAMPBELL, Miss Julia 10 Years Ago Mar 12, 1891
Miss Julia Campbell wed John Garner. They live at Bowen.

CAMPBELL, Miss Minnie 5 Years Ago Oct 16, 1890
Miss Minnie Campbell married J.H. Smith.

CAMPBELL, Mr Orie Local Dec 28, 1899
Cards are out announcing marriage of Mr Orie Campbell and Miss Sadie Hirons on New Years eve at 7:30 at the Hirons home a mile west of town.

CAMPBELL, Mr Ray Aug 13, 1896
SEE BELLOMY, Miss Hattie C.

CAMPBELL, W.D. Neighborhood News Jun 6, 1895
W.D. Campbell, editor of the Good Hope Reflector, and Miss Bird Harden of that village eloped to Monmouth and were married.

CANNON, Mr Clarence H. City Bervities May 18, 1899
The Keith County News of Ogallallo, Nebraska contains this item of a young man well known in this vicinity. Married Thursday May 11, 1899 at the home of Mr and Mrs J.H. Cannon, Mr Clarence Cannon and Miss Emma Reed. Bride is daughter of Fred Reed formerly of Keystone and was a teacher several years. Groom lived Keith County over 10 years. He has rented his fathers farm and will farm this year. Marriage at 3 PM by Rev Allen Chamberlain.

CANNON, John H. Local Mar 30, 1893
John H. Cannon, of St Clair, Ill. age 29, Fannie Bean of Quincy 26 were licensed to marry Saturday.

CANNON, Miss Pearl Local Dec 7, 1899
Miss Pearl Cannon well known to Clayton people was married to Mr Fritz Hostetter at Jacksonville last week.

CAREY, Emily Nov 16, 1899
SEE BURTRIDGE, Bert

CARLEY, Mr and Mrs F.J. Adams County News Nov 9, 1893
Golden wedding of Mr and Mrs F.J. Carley of Quincy was celebrated.

CARNAHAN, Miss Millie Jan 6, 1898
SEE WILLIAMS, W.L.

CARPENTER, Miss Ada M. Jun 29, 1893
SEE DAVIS, Wm F.

CARROLL. Mrs Josephine Local Mar 10, 1898
Mrs Josephine Carroll, who lives near Meyer, Illinois was the other day married to Charles Mayhew a Spaniard, by Justice Allen of Meyer. This makes the brides third husband within a year. The other two are under the sod.

CARTER, Lewis Little Brindle Nov 11, 1897
Examiner of the 6th Mr Lewis Carter of Clayton, and Mrs Maria Wheeler of this city (colored) were married at the brides home at 8 PM Thursday last by Mart Brooks, Esq.

CARVER, Miss Katie Neighborhood News Jun 14, 1894
Wedding at Jackssonville right after brides graduation from Illinois Conservatory of Music. Graduation exercises were held at State St. Presbyterian Church and right after the bride and groom to be entered a carriage and was taken to the college to be married. Persons were Miss Katie Carver and M.D. Schroll, both of Meredosia.

CARVER, Miss Katie Sep 17, 1896
SEE ROSSON, Geo. A.

CARVER, Lucile City Brevities Apr 6, 1899
Cards read--You are invited to marriage of Lucile Carver to Mr J. Walter Christian Wednesday eve April 12th at Asbury ME Church Webster St. Cincinnati at home after April 24th at Seneca, Illinois. Mr Christian is a railroad locomotive engineer.

CASTLE, Harry Camp Point Mar 15, 1900
Harry Castle and Miss Emma Kickehofel were married Thursday eve at their own home.

CASTLE, Joe Camp Point Oct 5, 1899
Joe Castle and Miss Kate Sawin were married last Thursday eve at their home in the north end of town. The home is a gift from Mrs Mileham, sister of the groom.

CASTLE, Miss Mabel H. Jul 29, 1897
SEE HUDSON, Elmer

CASTLE, Polly Oct 13, 1892
SEE WYSONG, Joseph

CATE, Miss Nona Jan 26, 1899
SEE CHILDS, Arthur

CAUGHLAN, Charles W. Local Oct 30, 1890
Charles W. Caughlan, the junior member of the firm of Chubback and Caughlan was married last Friday to Miss Anna M. Long of Payson. She is daughter of Henry Long of Payson. Mr Caughlan is one of the publishers of the Plainsville Observer.

CAVABAUGH, Miss Maggie Neighborhood News Feb 23, 1893
A chinese laundryman and Miss Maggie Cavanaugh, both of Mason City, were married, the chinaman wears American clothes and has sacrificed his "pig tail".

CECIL, Mrs Sarah Jane Our Own Bailiwick Aug 20, 1896
Mrs Sarah Jane Cecil started proceedings for divorce from James Cecil. They were married in Quincy Aug 20, 1892 and lived together one day when he deserted her. She asks custody of her 3 year old daughter, Stella.

CHADSEY, Mr Harvey A. Nov 5, 1891
SEE CRASKE, Miss Mamie

CHAMBERLAIN, Jas W. Personal Jan 29, 1891
Jos. Laughlin and wife attended the wooden wedding of brother Jas. W. Chamberlain and wife south of Mounds Tuesday.

CHAMPION, Otto Local Jan 18, 1894
From Tom Jamison we learn of marriage of Otto Champion to daughter of Mr and Mrs Stratton, of Hutchinson, Kansas which took place at home of brides parents December 31st 7 PM.

CHAPMAN, Miss Anna Local Aug 31, 1893
Married this week, Miss Anna, daughter of John and Mrs Chapman to Mr Joseph V. De Less at the home of Mr and Mrs Chapman north of the city 4 PM Sunday by Rev J. Glick pastor of the family. Sister of groom, Miss Carrie De Less of Jacksonville attended. Will live Clayton.

CHAPMAN, Chas. E. Little Brindle Apr 23, 1896
Republican: Chas. E. Chapman, age 25 and Laura E. McPhail age 22 both of Mound, have been granted a license to marry.

CHAPMAN, Henderson S. Local Dec 21, 1899
Marriage license granted at Quincy Monday to Henderson S. Chapman of Lee, Brown County and Amanda E. Jewett of Concord.

CHAPMAN, Henderson S. Married Dec 28, 1899
Married at the home of brides parents near Clayton at noon Dec 20th Henderson S. Chapman and Amanda E. Juett by Rev Jas. H. Davis of Mound, Illinois. Both members of Mounds Baptist Church.

CHAPMAN, John T. Local Jan 12, 1893
Married, John T. Chapman of Clayton and Miss Maggie A. daughter of Frank Byrns of Missouri township by Rev Abner Clarke at home of brides father on Wednesday Decmeber 28th ulst. Mr Chapman is the Clayton Eneterprise typographic force.

CHASE, Miss Alpha Mar 18, 1897
SEE WRIGHT, Gus

CHASE, Mrs Emma Locals Jan 3, 1895
Married at the Methodist parsonage Xmas eve Mrs Emma Chase and Mr James A. Boren, both of this city, by Rev J. Glick.

CHASE, Miss Etta Jan 24, 1895
SEE HAZLETT, Chas. H.

CHASE, Miss Libby Married Aug 17, 1899
Married last Wednesday in Chicago, a Clayton lady, Miss Libby Chase and Mr Harlan H. Haskett. Mr Haskett was for some time secretary of the Feebleminded institute where Miss Chase taught and it was there they met. He is now in the offices of the Northwestern Railroad at Chicago. Married Wednesday afternoon of last week.

CHENOWETH, Ida Sep 10, 1896
SEE REID, Ralph

CHILDS, Arthur Camp Point Jan 26, 1899
Arthur Childs and Miss Nona Cate were married at the brides home Thursday eve January 19th by Rev Porter.

CHILDS, Mr Lewis Nov 29, 1894
SEE SHARP, Miss Eliza

CHILDS, Misses Nellie and Lura Camp Point News Dec 20, 1894
Thursday will occur the double wedding of Misses Nellie and Lura Childs to Mr Porter and Albert Callahan.

CHITTENDEN, Samuel F. Neighborhood News Jun 29, 1893
Mr Samuel Chittenden, Mendon's leading young merchant, was recently married to Miss Anna E. McCormick.

CHRISTIAN, J. Walter Apr 6, 1899
SEE CARVER, Lucile

CHRISTIE, Jerome O. Ancient History Mar 18, 1897
February 1882 Married Jerome O. Christie and Addie Farlow, Camp Point.

CLAIR, Mr and Mrs John Our Own Bailiwick Feb 21, 1895
At Mendon, Mr and Mrs John Clair celebrated their golden wedding, no less than 28 children and grandchildren were present.

CLAIRE, Moses H. Married at Pittsfield Dec 17, 1896
Married at Pittsfield Sunday a week ago, Mr Moses H. Claire, of Pittsfield and Mrs Nettie Stevens of this place. Will live Pittsfield.

CLARE, Mrs Moses H. Old Pike Feb 11, 1897
Divorced Saturday, Mrs Moses H. Clare from her husband, been married not many weeks.

CLARK, Rev Abner Ill State News Aug 27, 1896
Rev Abner Clark of Quincy and Miss Julia A. Toot of Bloomington, were married the other day. Bride is member of faculty of the Wesleyan College of Music at Bloomington. Mr Clark is member of Illinois Conference of ME Church. Both were members of faculty of Chaddock College, Quincy for some years.

CLARK, Miss Alta Aug 16, 1894
SEE TOLAND, Chas.

CLARK, Miss Anna Local Jun 27, 1895
Marriage of Miss Anna Clark and Mr Chester Folkemer was announced to be solemized at Camp Point Wednesday eve.

CLARK, Benjamin November 1888 Nov 3, 1898
Married: Benjamin Clark and Nannie Lague.

CLARK, Emma A. Mar 15, 1894
SEE REID, Joseph

CLARK, Miss Helen Little Brindle Mar 25, 1897
Brown County Republican Invitations are out for wedding Thursday March 25th at 7:30 PM of Miss Helen Clark, daughter of Mr and Mrs T.J. Clark of Pea Ridge township, to Mr Wm H. McCaskill, also of that township at the brides parents home by Rev J.M. Bell of this city.

CLARK, James W. Apr 18, 1895
SEE SKINNER, Miss Fannie L.

CLARK, Lilly E. Little Brindle Nov 23, 1893
SEE KNOWLES, George and Lilly E.

CLARK, Thomas M. City Brevities Jul 21, 1898
A card received from our former Clayton citizen reads: "Mr Thomas M. Clark and Mrs Ella Allen announce their marriage on Thursday, July 14th 1898, Niagara Falls, N.Y. at home after August 1st at 142 Woodbridge Ave. Buffalo, N.Y." Good wishes Tom.

CLARK, W.E. 5 Years Ago Nov 2, 1893
W.E. Clark and Miss Mollie Dain were married in San Diego, California.

CLARK, W.E. November 1888 Nov 3, 1898
Married at San Diego, California W.E. Clark and Mollie E. Dain.

CLARKSON, Daniel Personal Jul 30, 1896
Mrs Susan Pevehouse, Mrs S.D. Rosson, Mrs H.L. Adair by invitation have gone to Brasher, Missouri to attend golden wedding of Daniel Clarkson which will be celebrated July 30th.

CLARKSON, Josie Jun 30, 1898
SEE KNIGHT, L.H.

CLEAVES, Gilbert O. Local Nov 30, 1893
"Democrat Message" Gilbert O. Cleaver of Mounds and Miss Lana Ruth Davis were married at home of brides parents, Mr and Mrs C.J. Davis, two miles north of Mounds 7 PM Thursday by Rev F.P. Douglas of Mounds.

CLEAVES, Hobert A. Little Brindle Mar 17, 1898
Democrat Message of the 12th: Hobert A. Cleaves and Miss Lizzie Ada Preece were married at home of brides mother, Mrs Lucinda Preece, in Pea Ridge township at 7 PM March 9th.

CLEAVES, Miss Nettie M. Nov 2, 1893
SEE ARNOLD, Fred

CLEEK, Miss Victoria Jun 1, 1899
SEE MOORE, James T.

CLEMENTS, A.W. Jan 1, 1891
SEE SHEPHERD, Miss Emma

CLEMMONS, Mr and Mrs Thomas Little Brindle Jun 22, 1899
The 50th anniversary of Mr and Mrs Thomas Clemmons occurred this week. They were married in Missouri in 1849 and lived in this section over 30 years.

CLEMONS, Eugene Neighborhood News Mar 26, 1891
Eugene Clemons of Warsaw went to Carthage and got license to marry Miss Mary O. Mairs. The couple were married in Tioga next day. Afterward question as to its legality arose as license was issued in Hancock County and marriage was in Adams. To ease their minds Mr Clemons went to Carthage and got a duplicate license and they were remarried at Warsaw on the 15th inst.

CLICK, Irene May 11, 1899
SEE BLISS, Alfred P.

CLICK, Miss Victoria Jun 1, 1899
SEE MOORE, J.T.

CLINE, Joseph Dec 4, 1890
SEE MIKESELL, Miss Addie

COAKE, Walter May 24, 1894
SEE FANSCHMIDT, Miss Ida P.

COBB, Arhcibald Little Brindle Dec 8, 1898
Examiner: Marriage license issued since Friday of last week, Archibald Cobb of Morellville and Miss Anna Kallash of Elkhorn.

COE, Ed Married Nov 22, 1894
The Examiner, published at Mt Sterling has this; Mr Ed Coe and Miss Retta Watkins, all of Clayton were married in this city by Rev G.A. Little last Thursday eve. It was attended by her sister, Mrs Bert Hough and other Clayton folks.

COE, Henry P. 25 Years Mar 26, 1896
Mr and Mrs Henry P. Coe celebrated their 25th wedding anniversary 8 PM Saturday. Greta Coe, little grandaughter presented them with their gifts.
COE, Jas. B. 10 Years Ago Jun 27, 1895
SEE SMITH, Miss Maymie
COE, James Bissel and wife Jun 27, 1895
Mrs Coe surprises Postmaster Jim Surprise birthday party in honor of her husband, James Bissel and their 10th wedding anniversary at the Masonic Hall at Mt Sterling (150 guests).
COGBURN, John Local Dec 7, 1893
Andy Phillips has been married over 40 years and had never been charivaried until Friday night. John Cogburn who has lived all his life with Mr Phillips and Miss Fróna Inman were married Wednesday eve and the boys thinking them at Phillips went to pay their respects but the young couple were not there.
COGBURN, John N. Local Dec 7, 1893
Married at Baptist Parsonage in Clayton, Illinois Wednesday Nov 29th 1893, Mr John N. Cogburn and Miss Sophronia E. Inman, both of Concord by Rev J.H. Terrill.
COLE, Mrs Kate Oct 16, 1890
SEE FUGATE, Moses
COLEMAN, Gabe Apr 20, 1899
SEE HOWE, Miss Mattie
COLEMAN, Ida Mar 9, 1899
SEE HARDIN, Mat
COLGATE, Dick 10 Years Ago Jul 4, 1895
SEE LOYD, Miss Helen
COLGATE, Mr John Married Jan 15, 1891
Sunday December 28, 1891, Mr John Colgate, brother of Mr O.W. Colgate of this city, and Miss Helen Loyd, daughter of Mr and Mrs E. Loyd at the home of brides parents, near Clark, Dakota.
COLLIER, Miss Alpha B. 10 Years Ago May 24, 1894
SEE EMERY Thos. E.
COLLIER, Miss Belle Nov 19, 1891
SEE OMER, Wm
COLLIER, Eliza J. and Joseph N. Local Mar 9, 1893
Notice is hereby given that I will not be responsible for any debts of Eliza J. Collier hereafter contracted. Dated Feb 18, 1893
Signed Joseph N. Collier
COLLIER, Mrs Eilza Jane & Jos. N. Local Aug 2, 1894
Mrs Eliza Jane Collier, of this city has applied for divorce from her husband Jos. N. Collier to whom she was married at Maywood, Missouri in 1882. She charges him with being an habitual drunkard since 1880 and when under influence of liquor is cruel and abusive. Also that in 1892 he committed adultry. They have 5 children, ages 3, 5, 7, 9 and 11 years. She desires to have the care and custody of these given to her by the court.
COLLIER, G.S. All Over the County Jul 1, 1897
Trumpet, Camp Point Married last eve, G.S. Collier to Miss Ella Honnold at home of Mrs Mary Honnold by Rev A.N. Simmons.
COLLIER, Mrs Jennie City Brevities Feb 16, 1899
Mrs Jennie Collier was married to Mr Perry W. Monroe on the 16th of January. Mr Monroe is a well to do farmer of Richland,Missouri. Mrs Collier formerly lived here.

COLLIER, Joe and wife | Local | Nov 12, 1896
Joe Collier returned to town Saturday. He had been at Beardstown lately. Mrs Collier filed for divorce here and found out he had already filed and received a divorce some time ago in Oklahoma. Mrs Collier is now working to support their little children.

COLLIN, William | Black Station | Jan 29, 1891
William Collin of this place and Bertis Bremer of Golden were married on Thursday.

COLLINS, Mr | Local | Nov 29, 1896
SEE CROMWELL, Oliver

COLPITT, Arthur | 5 Years Ago | Oct 23, 1890
Arthur Colpitt and Alice M. Gollaway were married.

COLPITTS, Mr Jos. | 5 Years Ago | Oct 13, 1892
SEE O'CONNOR, Miss Cornelia

COLPITTS, Joseph A. | Little Brindle | Mar 4, 1897
Mt Sterling Examiner Mr Joseph A. Colpitts and Mrs Addie E. McClain, nee Bean, of Clayton quietly went to this city Monday last and were married by Mart Brooks Esq. at the home of Ed Crawford. Mrs Crawford and the bride are sisters.

CONDEE, H.M. and wife | Nov 2, 1899
SEE FOLEY, Mr and Mrs W.B.

CONLEY, Miss Belle | Oct 12, 1899
SEE WALL, John E.

CONNOR, Miss Hattie M. | Jul 3, 1890
SEE NEWHOUSE, Fred

CONNOR, S.M. "Selbert" | Locals | Jun 11, 1891
S.M. Connor has lately taken himself a life partner in the person of Miss Nora Cain. He has purchased a dynamo and fixed up an engine and other appurtenances for the purpose of doing electro plating in nickle, silver and gold. Selbert can do the work if given a chance.

CONNOR, S.N. | Apr 30, 1891
SEE CAIN, Miss Norr

COOK, Miss Inez A. | Personal | Jan 11, 1894
Mrs Hartman attended the wedding of Miss Inez A. Cook on New Years Day to Dr D.D. Neece.

COOPER, Anna | May 3, 1900
SEE WALTERS, Mrs Anna

COPPAGE, Miss Mattie B. | Supplement | Jun 18, 1891
Neighborhood News Wedding at home of James Coppage in this city at 3 PM Sunday says the Mt Sterling Democrat Message George W. Harker of Jackson County Kansas and Miss Mattie B. Coppage. About 8 or 9 years ago Miss Coppage answered an ad in the National Tribune that Mr Harker solicited a lady correspondent and from then on they kept steady correspondence, neither having seen the other until a day or two before the marriage. Mr Harker is a farmer in comfortable circumstances 33 years old. Bride was reared in this city.

CORBIN, Miss Alta | Mar 14, 1895
SEE CURRY, Mr Guy L.

CORBY, Mrs Josephine | 10 Years Ago | Feb 12, 1891
Mrs Josephine Corby married W.D. Hackney of Golden.

CORFIELD, Miss Emma | Nov 5, 1896
SEE GIDDINGS, George

CORNICLE, Della | Jun 27, 1895
SEE FRIDAY, Wm

CORRIGAN, David A. | Our Own Bailiwick | May 30, 1895
David A. Corrigan, of Liberty, age 40, was licensed to marry Eva Corrigan age 26. Bride is the widow of grooms deceased brother.

CORTNEY, Mrs Matilda Feb 9, 1899
SEE LANTICE, William
COVERT, Miss Lottie E. Oct 25, 1894
SEE APSLEY, Lee W.
COX, Miss Daisy Little Brindle Dec 23, 1897
Republican--Married, Miss Daisy Cox and Dr L.H. Neville of Cooperstown by Rev Alex McGaffin at the home of brides father, Mr Stephen Cox.
COX, Mrs Elizabeth Nov 23, 1893
SEE THOMPSON, Mr Edward Sr.
COX, Miss Inez Brown County Oct 19, 1899
On Thursday eve at the home of brides mother, 2 of Mt Sterlings young people were married, Dr Charles B. Dearborn and Miss Inez Cox.
COX, Miss Inez Brown County Oct 12, 1899
SEE DEARBON, Dr C.B.
COX, Miles Ill Brevities Sep 6, 1894
Miles Cox and Miss Dolly Mitchell, both of Cooperstown, Brown County eloped and were married.
COX, Miss Nellie Little Brindle Oct 7, 1897
Republican of the 30th Cards are out announcing the wedding of Miss Nellie, daughter of Dr and Mrs Wm Cox of this city, to Mr Eugene Walker of Jacksonville, Illinois at 12 Wednesday October 6th.
CRAIG, Belle Feb 9, 1893
SEE DERRINGER, Lewis
CRAIG, Mrs Cina 5 Years Ago Mar 12, 1891
Mrs Cina Craig married J.M. Overstreet. Mrs Craig died.
CRAIN, Fred Pine Grove Jun 11, 1896
We understand that Mr Fred Crain and Miss Mattie Newcomb are to be married in about a week.
CRAMER, Miss Effie Local May 11, 1893
Mendon Dispatch Miss Effie Cramer our assistant Postmistress is to be married this AM lucky groom is our genial townsman, Mr A.H. Taft at the Congregation parsonage by Rev Wm Burgess.
CRANE, Ezra Married Oct 19, 1899
Married at the home of Mr and Mrs S. Johnson at 528 York St. in Quincy Monday at 8:30 PM, Mr Ezra Crane and Miss Adah, daughter of Mr and Mrs Johnson by Rev Edwin J. Rice of this city. Attended by her sister, Miss May and their friend Miss Beatrice Sanftlenben. Will live with Miss Beall at the South Side of the Park in this city.
CRANE, F.W. Little Brindle News Sep 27, 1894
Cards are out announcing marriage of Mr F.W. Crane, assistant cashier of the First National bank of this city to Miss Augusta Miner of Louisville, Kentucky. This happy event will take place in the above named place next Thursday. "Republican"
CRANE, Rev L. Burton Brown County Oct 19, 1899
Democrat Message Cards reached this city of approaching marriage of Rev L. Burton Crane of Buffalo, New York son of Fred D. Crane of this city and Miss Josephine Hopkinson of Baltimore at 5 PM October 25th at Brown Memorial Church, Baltimore. Groom was reared in this city. He is pastor of the Second Presbyterian Church at Buffalo.
CRANE, William E. Little Brindle Nov 18, 1897
Examiner Married, Mr William E. Crane, of this city, and Mrs Addie Stewart, of San Francisco, California; relict of Elder A.P. Stewart at the home of ex senator John M. Palmer in Springfield at 3:30 PM Wednesday by Rev U.B. Rogers of Baptist Church. Arrived at their home in this city tonight. Mr Crane lived this city nearly 40 years and Mrs Crane formerly lived here, her husband being pastor of Christian Church at the time.

CRANSTON, Miss Anna 5 Years Ago Mar 20, 1890
Miss Anna Cranston was married to Jas. Busby of Eldorado Springs, Missouri.

CRASKE, Miss Geneva Marriage Bells Nov 5, 1891
A two line personal last week saying that John W. Tebo had gone to Rushville to attend a wedding was true, it being his own. Marriage bells at the home of one of our best citizens, Mr Henry Craske, Wednesday eve October 28th and will sound again at same place today. At 8 PM Rev W.F. Cellars married Miss Mamie Craske to Mr Harry A. Chadsey and at 11 AM today Rev W.F. Cellars married Mr John W. Tebo and Miss Geneva Craske. Mr Tebo is a well to do merchant of Clayton and will start housekeeping here in a new house about ready for them.

CRASKE, Miss Mamie Marriage Bells Nov 5, 1891
Marriage bells at the home of one of our best citizens, Mr Henry Craske, Wednesday eve October 28th 1891 and will sound again at the same place today. At 8 PM Rev W.F. Cellars married Miss Mamie Craske and Mr Harry A. Chadsey and at 11 AM today Rev Cellars married Mr John W. Tebo and Miss Geneva Craske.

CRAWFORD, Ed May 14, 1891
SEE MCBRATNEY, Miss Jennie

CRAWFORD, Mr Edward Oct 13, 1892
SEE BEAN, Miss Belle

CRAWFORD, Miss Eva Mounds Sep 15, 1898
Miss Eva Crawford, daughter of Elder Jacob Crawford, formerly of this place, but now of Lewistown, Illinois was married to Mr Kelley Peppinger of Pea Ridge at noon Tuesday of this week at home of Elder Crawford.

CRAWFORD, Miss Jennie Oct 17, 1895
SEE DAVIS, Wm H.

CRAWFORD, John Jul 15, 1897
SEE FOOTE, Miss Miranda

CRAWFORD, Miss Pearl Sep 28, 1899
SEE JOHNSON, Mr Pink

CRAWFORD, Miss Rose L. Married Jan 21, 1897
Marriage of a young lady known to Clayton people, having lived here in the family of Mr W.T. Hedenberg and wife some years. Miss Rose L. Crawford to John Henry Looman at 12:30 PM Sunday Jan 10, 1897 at the home of Mr and Mrs Will T. Hedenberg, the latter being a sister of the bride by Rev W.M. Hailey. Groom has been in general merchandising until recently under the firm of Looman Bros,, but having sold out this business he is clerking for Mr Edward Geiss in the same business. Will live here. Bride has been connected with the news office as a compositor.

CREEKMUR, Prof. J.W. Dec 31, 1891
SEE CYRUS, Miss Jessie

CREW, Miss Mamie Blanch Local Dec 8, 1892
The marriage of Miss Mamie Blanch Crew to Mr Robert Currier will be at the home of brides parents in Quincy on the 14th inst. Mr Currier has been connected for some years with the shoe house of Upham & Gordon.

CROMWELL, Joseph F. Little Brindle Nov 11, 1897
Rev McCoy married Joseph F. Cromwell and Miss Dora Lowery, both of Clayton this afternoon at the parsonage.

CROMWELL, Oliver Local Nov 26, 1896
News from Kansas concerning a former Clayton man, Oliver Comwell was convicted of criminal assault upon his daughter Dec. term 1894 in Kingman Co. Kan. and sent to prison 5 years. Since then he has been proven innocent. Cromwell was a widower and daughter was his housekeeper. She had a suitor named Collins who was forbidden to see her and she gave birth to a child. Which she charged her father with paternity of, they since have married and was guilty of her downfall. Ollie's punishment comes from liquor. Father cleared of charges.

CROMWELL, Will | Personal | Jan 11, 1900
Will Cromwell was here from LaPrairie. He is going to be married and will move to the E.M. Marsh farm north of town.
CROMWELL, William T. | | Feb 22, 1900
SEE PEARCE, Miss Saidee
CROMWELL, Wm T. | Local | Feb 22, 1900
Wm T. Cromwell and his new bride have moved to the farm two miles northeast of town.
CROQUART, Eugene and Florence | Local | Aug 31, 1893
In circuit court Tuesday, Eugene Croquart filed for divorce from his wife Florence Croquart, nee Shepherd. They were married at Clayton on Xmas 1887 and lived together till last February 6th when he found she had been unfaithful to him and left her. He charges her with adultry in Quincy. He asks custody of their two children, Benny age 5 and Berthol age 3.
CROQUART, Eugene and Florence | Local | Dec 14, 1893
A decree of divorce was signed by Judge Bonney Friday in the case of Eugene Croquart from Florence Croquart, for adultery. He was also given the custody of their two children.
CROSBY, Mr | | Apr 16, 1896
SEE MCCULLOM, Miss Angie
CROSS, Mrs | | Mar 25, 1897
SEE MCCLINTOCK, Thomas J.
CROWDER, David M. | | Aug 15, 1895
SEE SHANK, Miss Lydia
CRUMBACKER, Mr and Mrs J.M. | Ill State News | Jan 11, 1894
Mr and Mrs J.M. Crumbacker celebrated their golden wedding in Galena the other eve. Have lived Galena their whole married life.
CRUSE, Miss Florence Alice | Brown County | Dec 5, 1895
At the brides home three miles south of Mounds, Miss Florence Alice Cruse and Mr G.F. Taylor of Henry County were married.
CULVER, Miss Emma | | Apr 1, 1897
SEE FRICKE, Chas.
CURLESS, Flora | | Feb 8, 1900
SEE LIKES, Robert
CURRIER, Robert | | Dec 8, 1892
SEE CREW, Miss Mamie Blanch
CURRY, B.A. | Feb 1884 | Feb 2, 1899
Married: B.A. Curry and Mrs Lavina Benton, of Schuyler County.
CURRY, Miss Bertha M. | | May 7, 1896
SEE WATSON, Elmer A.
CURRY, C.S. and wife | 10 Years Ago | Jun 14, 1894
C.S. Curry and wife celebrated their silver anniversary.
CURRY, Miss Carrie Eva | | May 7, 1896
SEE ANDREWS, Fred
CURRY, Charles A. | Brown County News | Jun 15, 1893
Marriage of Mr Charles A. Curry and Miss Effie Larkin occurred Thursday afternoon at the home of brides mother, Mrs Mary Larkin, in Mt Sterling. The happy couple left for Chicago.
CURRY, Chas. | 10 Years Ago | Oct 26, 1893
Supplement Mr Chas. Curry and Miss Mollie Garrett were married at Camp Point.
CURRY, Clarence H. | Local | Dec 8, 1892
By Mr C.S. Curry who returned from Kirksville, Missouri a few days ago we learn of marriage of Mr Clarence H. Curry at Caldwell, Kansas, son of Mr and Mrs W.H. Curry to Miss Blanch Stern of Arkansas City, Kansas on November 20th.

CURRY, Edgar T. "Tommie" Cupids Net Apr 30, 1896
Mr Edgar T. Curry has been snared in cupids net. None more popular than Tommie with the girls. Ceremony occurred at Jacksonville Thursday last week to Miss Vauna Holdren will live Clayton on Washington St.

CURRY, Florence Dec 14, 1899
SEE DEMOSS, James E.

CURRY, Mr F.C. Brown County News Oct 12, 1893
Coming marriage to Mr F.C. Curry and Miss Eugenia Rottger to be on the 19th of this month.

CURRY, Frank C. Little Brindle Oct 26, 1893
Married a couple of weeks ago, Mr Frank C. Curry, to young dry goods merchant of Mt Sterling and Miss Eugenia A. daughter of Hon Fred W. and Mrs Rottger. She is a leader of Mt Sterling society. He too is a native of Mt Sterling.

CURRY, Frank L. Brown County May 24, 1900
Yesterday afternoon in county clerks office Squire McCabe married Frank L. Curry of Clayton and Miss Rega Varner of Kellerville. Will live at Haselwood, Adams County where groom is farming.

CURRY, Mr Guy L. Local Mar 14, 1895
Marriage of Mr Guy L. Curry, son of Mr and Mrs H.H. Curry of Kirkville, Missouri to Miss Alta Corbin of that city at 9 AM Sunday March 3rd at home of Prof. Laughlin, a tutor of college where Guy is a student. Groom has a teachers certificate tip and Mrs Curry, son of George and his wife and the young daughter live on a farm near Kirksville..

CURRY, James S. Married Nov 26, 1896
James S. Curry went to Augusta, Kansas Wednesday to wed Miss Ola Van Dervoort, daughter of former Clayton people, Elder and Mrs Harry G. Van Dervoort on Thursday eve 19th inst. Mr Curry's father quit farming in summer leaving Jimmie in charge so the bride and groom will live on the farm.

CURRY, Miss Laura Nov 30, 1893
SEE SEATON, Tom

CURRY, Miss Nellie G. 15 Years Ago Jul 1, 1897
May 1882 Weddings Miss Nellie G. Curry and Mr J. Will Pottor, May 23rd.

CURRY, Miss Prathana E. Oct 1, 1891
SEE HAIR, Clement W.

CURRY, R.S. 10 Years Ago Jan 18, 1894
Mr R.S. Curry and Miss Lewis were married. They live at Camp Point.

CURRY, S.W. Take Notice May 28, 1891
All persons are hereby notified that I will not be responsible for any debts contracted by my wife, or any other person on my account.
S.W. Curry Clayton May 23, 1891

CURRY, Miss Sarah E. Nov 1882 Nov 3, 1898
SEE ROWE, Jas. W.

CURRY, William Feb 16, 1893
SEE AUSMUS, Miss Alma

CURRY, William B. Local Apr 26, 1900
William B. Curry and Miss Gertrude Deiterle went to Mt Sterling and were married last week. Will live Clayton, boarding with his father and sister on W. Washington.

CURRY, William B. Brown County Apr 26, 1900
William B. Curry of Clayton and Miss Gertrude T. Dieterle of Kellerville obtained a license to marry at court house this afternoon.

CURTIS, John A. Mar 1, 1894
SEE BRADNEY, Miss Kate

CYRUS, Miss Jessie Local Dec 31, 1891
Xmas eve Miss Jessie, daughter of Geo. W. Cyrus was married to Prof. J.W. Creekmur, principal of Maplewood school at home of Bro. Cyrus in Camp Point.

DAIN, Miss Mollie 5 Years Ago Nov 2, 1893
SEE CLARK, W.E.

DAUGHERTY, Helen A. Dec 1, 1892
SEE HERNDON, James R.

DAUGHERTY, Miss LaBert Married Sep 15, 1892
Married Thursday eve at the home of Mrs Martha Wallace, her niece, Miss LaBert Daugherty to Mr Harry Hough by Rev J.J. Thomson. Lunch served by Miss Maggie Hough. Tuesday eve Mr and Mrs Geo. Hough gave a reception in their home on Washington St. nearly opposite his father's home Harry is having a hew home fitted up for his bride. Mr Hough is a fireman on the Keokuk branch of the Wabash.

DAUGHERTY, Thomas J. Our Own Bailiwick Nov 26, 1896
Thomas J. Daugherty, of Fowler and Emily Amen of Columbus were licensed to marry Monday.

DAVIDSON, Earl Local Feb 4, 1897
Marriage license issued to Mr Earl Davidson and Miss Alice Lirely of McKee township.

DAVIDSON, Miss Emma Lou 10 Years Ago Feb 15, 1894
SEE HUGHES, Columbus

DAVIDSON, Guy L. Little Brindle Jun 18, 1896
Examiner: Guy L. Davidson and Miss Dorothy Hughes, both of Kellerville were married by Elder Chas. Laycock at his home in this city 9 PM last Saturday.

DAVIDSON, Dr Ham 10 Years Ago Feb 12, 1891
SEE HUGHES, Miss Amanda L.

DAVIDSON, Mr I.T. "Gube" Local Dec 25, 1890
At the Baptist Church, Monday eve by Rev H. Denning, Mr I.T. Davidson and Miss Eva Jackson were married. Gube is a pleasant man who has many friends in Clayton and among railroad men.

DAVIDSON, Jennie D. Apr 21, 1898
SEE ORR, Matthew

DAVIS, Charles H. Neighborhood News Dec 5, 1895
Mr Charles H. Davis and Miss Belle Benson of Huntsville township near Pine Grove were married in Quincy last Wednesday by Rev Miller at his home.

DAVIS, Miss Clara Locals Nov 6, 1890
Marriage of Miss Clara Davis, daughter of Mr D.A. Davis to Mr E.E. McDowell will be at the family home the evening (Wednesday). Groom was born in Clayton and came to manhood here. Bride has also grown up here.

DAVIS, Miss Clara S. Married Nov 13, 1890
On last Wednesday eve at 6 PM at the home of brides father, Miss Clara S. Davis to Mr Edgar McDowell, both of Clayton by Rev H. Denning pastor of Baptist Church here, will live here in town.

DAVIS, Miss Effie Feb 20, 1896
SEE THOMPSON, James

DAVIS, Miss Ella E. Dec 27, 1894
SEE GORE, Emory C.

DAVIS, Miss Ellen Oct 20, 1898
SEE LOGUE, Wm M.

DAVIS, Emmor O. Local Jan 5, 1893
Married at the Presbyterian parsonage in this city December 28th by Rev S.H. Hyde, Emmor O. Davis and Miss Eliza Rand, both of Prairie township. "Carthage Gazette"

DAVIS, F.M. Little Brindle News Feb 27, 1896
Democrat Message Married Sunday, Mr F.M. Davis and Miss McHenry of Clayton by Rev Jonas VanWey at his home.
DAVIS, Miss Hattie Mar 12, 1896
SEE BOWEN, Mr Dora
DAVIS, Mr Hiram 5 Years Ago Mar 12, 1891
SEE VARNER, Miss May
DAVIS, Hope S. Our Own Bailiwick May 23, 1895
Hon Hope S. Davis, one of Quincy's attorneys married Miss Melissa Ward Tuesday.
DAVIS, Miss Ina K. Oct 16, 1890
SEE RATCLIFF, Myron
DAVIS, Miss Lana Ruth Nov 30, 1893
SEE CLEAVES, Gilbert O.
DAVIS, Miss Lillie May 13, 1897
SEE TEGMEYER, Frank
DAVIS, Miss Maude Local Dec 28, 1899
Married at home of brides parents, Mr and Mrs J.W. Davis of this city at 8 AM Saturday, Miss Maude Davis to Mr Elmer Glaser by Rev R. Lierly will live with Mrs Glaser, mother of groom.
DAVIS, Miss Maymie Jan 14, 1897
SEE OMER, Roy
DAVIS, Mollie E. Nov 1888 Nov 3, 1898
SEE CLARK, W.E.
DAVIS, One May 31, 1894
SEE RIGGS, Miss Alice
DAVIS, Otis Oct 15, 1896
SEE HOPPER, Miss Pauline
DAVIS, Robert Camp Point Feb 6, 1896
Robert Davis and Miss Rebecca Jonson were married one eve last week.
DAVIS, Wm F. Brown County News Jun 29, 1893
Supplement Wm F. Davis of Mounds and Miss Ada M. Carpenter of Buckhorn were married at brides home in Buckhorn Sunday 18th by Rev W.S. Lowe.
DAVIS, Wm H. Local Oct 17, 1895
Wm H. Davis, of Clayton and Miss Jennie Crawford, daughter of Rob Crawford of this city, were licensed to marry at Quincy last Wednesday. Mr Davis formerly lived here and was kinfolk of the late R.R. Golden and family. "Brown County Republican"
DAVISON, Miss Emma Jan 1884 Jan 12, 1899
SEE HUGHES, Neal
SEE HUGHES, Cornelius Feb 1884 Feb 2, 1899
DEAN, Julia Aug 18, 1892
SEE BEACOCK, George
DEARBON, Dr C.B. Brown County Oct 12, 1899
Democrat Message Marriage of Dr C.B. Dearbon and Miss Inez Cox is to take place at the home of Mrs S.A. Cox at 8 PM October 12th.
DEARBORN, Dr Charles B. Oct 19, 1899
SEE COX, Miss Inez
DEARINGER, Sarah L. and James C. Local Apr 2, 1891
In divorce court news: Sarah L. Gray married James C. Dearinger Oct 5, 1871 at Clayton lived on and off in Illinois and Missouri until 1888 when they settled in Clayton, stayed two years or until complainant discovered her husband was unfaithful to marriage vows and had committed adultery when she left him Oct 1, 1890. Three children born to this union one dead, another married, with whom complainant is now living and a third daughter 13 years of age whom she asks to have custody.

DEARL, Miss Annie — Jun 16, 1892
SEE FLEMMING, A.E.

DECKER, Miss Hannah — Mar 1, 1900
SEE HERREN, Henry H.

DEEGE, Miss — Personal — Apr 21, 1898
Miss Sadie Hirons will attend wedding of her friend, Miss Deege, this week.

DEEGE, Philip J. — Apr 1, 1897
SEE KOCH, Elnora

DEETERLE, Fred — Little Brindle — Jun 29, 1899
Married, Fred Deeterle, Chestline, age 20 and Alta Mayfield, Siloam age 20.

DEGON, Joseph and Mrs — Ill State News — Mar 29, 1894
Joseph Degon, age 75 and Mrs Degon age 71 were married at Freeport. This is the second marriage of the couple. They had lived happily together for many years, raising a family of children. 20 years ago they were divorced, Mr Degon going west where he married another. His second wife died and he returned to Freeport and after a score of years, they were reunited.

DEGROOT, John B. — Elm Grove — Oct 31, 1895
John B. DeGroot and Mrs Sophronia Eeads were married a short time ago at LaPrairie by Squire Mock.

DEGROOT, Miss Phoebe — 5 Years Ago — Sep 12, 1895
SEE STARK, Elder J. Carroll.

DEHART, William — Aug 3, 1893
SEE WORDEN, Dora E.

DEHAVEN, Miss Hattie — Apr 12, 1900
SEE OMER, Pete

DEHAVEN, Miss Maggie — Sep 21, 1899
SEE OMER, Boon

DEHAVEN, Maggie L. — Sep 21, 1899
SEE OMER, Daniel B.

DEHAVEN, Will — Camp Point — Dec 1, 1898
Will Dehaven and Miss Florence Joseph were quietly married at brides home Thursday eve by Rev T.M. Dillen.

DEITERLE, Miss Gertrude — Apr 26, 1900
SEE CURRY, William B.

DEJEAN, C.B. — All Over the County — Oct 7, 1897
C.B. DeJean, formerly editor of the Coatsburg Review, and Miss Minnie Thompson, both of Coatsburg, have been licensed to wed.

DELESS, Jos. V. — August 1893 — Aug 11, 1898
Married, Mr Jos. V. DeLess and Miss Anna Chapman, by Rev Glick.

DELESS, Joseph V. — Aug 31, 1893
SEE CHAPMAN, Miss Anna

DEMOSS, Miss Birdie — Local — Dec 30, 1897
Mr Charles Peacock, son of our old friend Judge Peacock, of MeKee will tonight be married to Miss Birdie, daughter of John and Mrs DeMoss, living west of town.

DEMOSS, James E. — Local — Dec 14, 1899
Cards are out for wedding on the 21st inst of Florence, daughter of Mr and Mrs S.W. Curry, to James E. DeMoss of Clayton. "Camp Point Journal"

DEMOSS, Leroy — Ill Brevities — Dec 27, 1894
Leroy Demoss and Miss Gracie, daughter of Mr and Mrs Silas Sloan of Fairbury, were married the other day.

DERRINGER, Jim and Mrs Sarah — Locals — Mar 12, 1891
Mrs Sarah Derringer has brought suit for divorce. She alleges that Jim is cruel and an awful bad man generally. It will be hard for her to make people believe this kind of story.

DERRINGER, Lewis | Local | Feb 9, 1893
There will be a wedding Thursday in town, Lewis Derringer and Belle Craig, of Mt Sterling will be married.

DERRINGER, Miss Martha | | Sep 24, 1896
SEE HARBISON, Mr Clarance

DEVLIN, Stephen | Little Brindle | Dec 1, 1898
Married in St Mary's Church by Rev D.J. Ryan last Sunday at 4 PM, Mr Stephen Devlin of Jacksonville and Miss M. Adeline Smith, daughter of Mr and Mrs Andrew Smith of this city.

DEWITT, Mr Clinton | | Aug 11, 1892
SEE MORISON, Miss Ella

DEWITT, Miss Nellie | | Feb 1, 1894
SEE BOWEN, Caspar

DEXTER, Mr Frank | | Jul 12, 1894
SEE MOORE, Miss Lottie

DICKSON, Miss Sarah Isabelle | | Jan 25, 1900
SEE THOMPSON, Rev John J.

DIESTERIE, Miss Mary | Ill Brevities | Mar 7, 1895
Miss Mary Diesterie commenced breach of promise suit in Adams County against Albert Hoffman of Kellerville claiming $5,000 damages. Says Mr Hoffman courted her two or three years and wedding plans were made when Mr Hoffman went to Quincy and met Miss Harah Morgan of Meadville, Missouri and they were married.

DIETERLE, Miss Gertrude T. | Brown County | Apr 26, 1900
SEE CURRY, William B.

DIEVERT, Anna | | Dec 6, 1899
SEE CALEY, Edward

DIKES, Mr and Mrs Fred J. | Little Brindle | Jun 30, 1898
Republican: Mr and Mrs Fred J. Dikes, of Kansas City celebrated their crystal wedding June 15th Fred is an old Mt Sterling boy while his wife was a Clayton girl.

DIKES, Fred S. | Jan 1883 | Jun 30, 1898
SEE MONTGOMERY, Miss Elva

DISS, Frank | | Jan 12, 1899
SEE WATERS, Miss Agnes

DISSLER, Frank A. | | Mar 22, 1900
SEE ELLIOTT, Miss Nora

DISSLER, Miss Dora | Chestline | Dec 29, 1892
Married this Wednesday, Miss Dora Dissler and Ed Arntzen. Mr Arntzen lived this county for several years.

DISSLER, Miss Mary | 5 Years Ago | Mar 17, 1892
Miss Mary Dissler was married to Mr Lee Arntzen.

DISSLER, Philip E. | Local | Apr 26, 1900
At the home of John Elliott, a wealthy farmer near Quincy on the 17th inst occurred the marriage of Mr Philip E. Dissler and Miss Nora E. Elliott. Will live Kellerville where Philip has a business established that of a blacksmith.

DISSLER, Miss Rosa or Rose | All Over the County | Jan 14, 1897
Mrs Hatfield writes us from Quincy of the wedding of Miss Rosa Dissler formerly of this vicinity. The journal of Tuesday says: At 5 PM last eve in Lutheran Memorial Church Rev H.A. Ott, the pastor married Prof Carl A. Mundt and Miss Rose Dissler, both of Quincy. Bride is a music teacher and piano tuner who came to Quincy a year ago. Will live on North 6th Street.

DISTIN, Miss Eva | | Jan 7, 1897
SEE EMMONS, Lawrence E.

DOAK, Mr John June 1888 Jun 30, 1898
Married, Mr John Doak and Miss Nora Myers.

DOERR, Miss Thea Adams County May 4, 1899
Major-General Leo J. Kadeski of the Catholic Knights of America was married to Miss Thea Doerr of Quincy last Wednesday.

DONLEY, Anderson and Jack Adams County Mar 23, 1899
Married, at home of James L. Manard, Camp Point township Wednesday eve March 8th, Anderson Donley and Miss Nora E. Manard by Rev T.M. Dillion. Jack Donley and Miss Fairy Downing were married at the home of brides parents, Mr and Mrs W.O. Downing, Clayton township Wednesday eve March 8th by Rev C. Wehrman. The grooms are brothers and they were married about the same hour.

DONOHUE, Mr Oct 10, 1895
SEE ATKINSON, Miss Laura E.

DOUGLAS, Mr Orville Jun 18, 1891
SEE BELMEYER, Miss Gertie

DOWNEY, Mrs Belle and Uri O. City Brevities Mar 2, 1899
Mrs Belle Downey, daughter of Mr John Elwood of this place has filed for divorce in this county from her husband, Uri O. Downey. They married at Mt Sterling Mar 21, 1895 and have one child Vennie Downey age 3 years. Charges desertion. Uri picked up one winter day and went to Pike county where his people live and never returned.

DOWNEY, Belle and Uri Adams County Jul 13, 1899
The divorce case of Belle Downey vs Uri Downey was dismissed for want of prosecution.

DOWNING, Miss Bertha Sep 8, 1898
SEE EDMUNDS, Roe

DOWNING, Miss Fairy Mar 23, 1899
SEE DONLEY, Anderson and Jack

DOWNING, Miss Hattie B. Aug 20, 1896
SEE LANTZ, Joseph B.

DUFF, Bertha May Local May 22, 1890
A marriage license has been issued to Henry R. Bemis of Siloam, age 24 and Bertha May Duff of Burton age 18.

DUFF, Mary May 1890 May 24, 1900
BEMIS, Henry R.

DUIS, Miss Dora Nov 17, 1892
SEE BECKETT, Harry I.

DUISSAIR, Mr Local Feb 25, 1897
Mr Duissair and Miss Florence Thoroman, daughter of Mr Thoroman, east of town were married in Quincy last week.

DUKE, John 5 Years Ago Jun 29, 1893
SEE MEYERS, Miss Mary

DUKER, Miss Anna M. Oct 31, 1895
SEE ORDING, John C.

DUMPKIN, Mrs Mary A. Jun 23, 1898
SEE HUGHES, George

DUNBAR, Mr 20 Years Feb 15, 1900
Jan 1880 Married Mr Dunbar and Dora Swisher both of Concord.

DUNBAR, Miss Clara Aug 13, 1896
SEE EMBREE, Thomas

DUNBAR, George C. Oct 23, 1890
SEE MCDANNOLD, Miss Clara

DUNKLEBURK, J.H. 5 Years Ago Apr 28, 1892
SEE WILSON, Miss Clara

DUNLAP, Miss Mae Feb 4, 1897
SEE MOORE, Olen

DUNN, Miss Blanche Jun 16, 1898
SEE CAIN, Calvin L.
DUNN, Miss Mollie May 5, 1892
SEE THOMPSON, Mr R.W.
DURANT, Mr and Mrs Thomas Neighborhood News Nov 9, 1893
Thomas Durant and wife of Sonora celebrated their 50th wedding anniversary the other day.
DURFEE, Mr C.S. Sept 1889 Sep 7, 1899
SEE BABBS, Mrs Mary E.
DUTTON, John Elm Grove Mar 7, 1895
Invitations are out for marriage of Mr John Dutton to Miss Stella Alexander to take place Thursday eve March 7th.
DYKES, Fred J. Decade Ago Jun 15, 1893
SEE MONTGOMERY, Miss Elva
DYSON, O.E. Supplement Jun 11, 1891
Neighborhood News Schuyler "Citizen" Monday the first inst O.E. Dyson and Jesse M. McCorkle married Wednesday March 5th 1891 at Dixon, Illinois by Rev _____ A. Bunker. Bride is one of Rushvilles teachers. Groom is son of Edwin Dyson of the times who has finished a course and entered the practice of veterinary surgery.
EASUM, Mr Henry A. 5 Years Ago Feb 19, 1891
SEE GAY, Miss Mattie
EASUM, Mr and Mrs John Local Jan 4, 1894
Mr and Mrs John Easum celebrated their silver wedding on January 1st. Mr Ben Curry considered himself fortunate as he kissed the bride of 25 years ago.
EBERT, Miss Minnie 5 Years Ago Jul 4, 1895
Miss Minnie Ebert married Mr Harry Haley.
ECHLIN, Lena and William H. Local Oct 9, 1890
Suit was docketed in circuit court Tuesday in which Lena Echlin sues for a divorce from her husband, William H. Echlin, shows they were married at Springfield March 6, 1886 and lived together until May 26, 1890. It also says he earns $70 a month for the Wabash Railroad and she has no property, either real or personal to support herself. He has an adulterous, Laura Wear and other women. She asks support and divorce. Whig
ECHLIN, Lena and Wm H. Locals May 14, 1891
In circuit court this week in the case of Lena Echlin vs Wm H. Echlin, a decree of divorce was signed and filed.
ECKHOFF, Mattie Apr 5, 1900
SEE JURGEN, John J.
ECKHOFF, Miss Mattie Apr 12, 1900
SEE JURKENS, John
EDDINGS, Silas Local Aug 29, 1895
Silas Eddings, age 20 was married Sunday to May Ross of Clayton age 18 years. Silas's mother Mrs Alice Webb gave her consent to the union.
EDIE, Miss Hallie Local Dec 7, 1893
Former friends of Miss Hallie, daughter of Rev and Mrs J.A. Edie former pastor of the UP Church in this city learn of her marriage to Mr Louis A. Grim at the home of her parents in Beaver, Penn. a few days ago. Groom is an attorney at the Beaver Bar.
EDMUNDS, James Pea Green Apr 28, 1892
Mr James Edmunds and Miss Florence Renaker were married recently, they tried the elopement plan.

EDMUNDS, James Locals Sep 30, 1897
In March 1882 James Edmunds of Carthage and Cora Allen of Barry went to Jacksonville and were married. They lived afterwards at Carthage but kept marriage a secret. Both died about 3 years ago leaving a daughter. The other relatives alleged her parents were never married and therefore she was not heir to her grandfather who died recently at Carthage leaving estate valued at $80,000. Search was made in nearly every county in this state and Missouri for evidence of the marriage and the record was found at Jacksonville which proves that the couple were married there.

EDMUNDS, Roe City Brevities Sep 8, 1898
Mr Roe Edmunds of this city and Miss Bertha Downing, daughter of James E. Downing, deceased were married at the parental home in Camp Point township at 8 PM yesterday by Rev Dr Scott of Quincy. Will go to Keokuk for a brief time.

EDWARDS, Anna E. Local Feb 7, 1895
SEE BRYANT, B.W.

EDWARDS, Mary Dec 27, 1894
SEE SEWARD, Mahland

EEADS, Mrs Sophronia Oct 31, 1895
SEE DEGROOT, John B.

EGNOR, George N. Dec 30, 1897
SEE STIFFY, Miss Susan

EIGENBURG, Miss Minnie Jan 18, 1900
SEE HARBERTS, Jurgen H.

ELACE, Mrs Nancy Feb 27, 1890
SEE MANN, Mr

ELDER, Ethel Exchanges Oct 26, 1899
Mr and Mrs John Elder of Carthage has issued invitations for the marriage of their daughter, Ethel to Argyil J. McMahan, a young lawyer.of Carthage and partner of Judge C.J. Scofield. Wedding will be October 31st.

ELDER, Miss Laura Neighbors Jan 16, 1896
Married Xmas day at Green City, Missouri Miss Laura Elder, daughter of Capt J.M. Elder of Carthage and Mr H.C. Anderson of Green City, Missouri.

ELLERBROCK, City Brevities Nov 3, 1898
Divorce case of Ellerbrock vs Ellerbrock was dimissed Tuesday without prejudice to his cause.

ELLERBROCK, Mr and Mrs City Brevities Oct 27, 1898
Mrs Ellerbrock by her attorney Mr Vandeventer, has filed an answer to the bill for divorce of Mr Ellerbrock and asks court for alimony. Trial next Friday.

ELLERBROCK, Henry City Brevities Mar 9, 1899
Henry Ellerbrock has commenced another divorce against his wife, Mrs Ellerbrock came here recently from Kansas City and left again.

ELLERBROCK, J.H. and Florence Local Nov 23, 1899
Evidence was taken in circuit court Saturday in the divorce case of J.H. Ellerbrock vs Florence Ellerbrock. Henry filed for divorce in October term when it was contested, but no appearance by the defendant Saturday. Court has not passed upon the case, but it will probably be granted.

ELLERBROCK, J. Henry Married Oct 29, 1896
Married at the home of his honor J.W. Marrett in this city at noon Sunday October 25th 1896 Mr J. Henry Ellerbrock of Clayton and Miss Flora Gillispie of Kansas City, Missouri. Will live on the south part of this town.

ELLIOTT, J.B. Mound Station Oct 2, 1890
Sunday was the marriage of J.B. Elliott of this place and Miss Ida Hulette of Cooperstown.

ELLIOTT, Miss Nora | County News | Mar 22, 1900
Miss Nora Elliott of Burton and Frank A. Disseler, of Kellerville, will be married at home of brides parents, Mr and Mrs John Elliott of Burton April 17th. Quincy Whig

ELLIOTT, Miss Nora E. | Apr 26, 1900
SEE DISSLER, Philip E.

ELLIS, William H. | Nov 16, 1899
Examiner William H. Ellis of Griggsville age 67 and Mrs Dorothy Ann Grady of Versailles age 67 also, were married by police magistrate Wallace in County clerks office Tuesday afternoon. Groom threw down $1.50 as a marriage fee and walked out.

ELWOOD, Belle | Mar 2, 1899
SEE DOWNEY, Mrs Belle and Uri O.

EMBREE, Thomas | Little Brindle | Aug 13, 1896
Republican Married at count clerks office in this city Monday AM Mr Thomas Embree of Clayton and Miss Clara Dunbar of Cooperstown by Rev Geo. F. Davis.

EMERY, Thos. E. | 10 Years Ago | May 24, 1894
Thos. E. Emery and Miss Alpha B. Collier were married.

EMMONS, Lawrence E. | All Over the County | Jan 7, 1897
Quincy Herald announces the engagement of Mr Lawrence E. Emmons, a young lawyer of Quincy and Miss Eva Distin, daughter of Col. W.L. Distin.

ENGLAND, Warren | Aug 15, 1895
SEE WALLACE, Sarah M.

ENNEN, Miss Onney | Mar 23, 1899
SEE HIPPEN, John H.

ENSMINGER, Sam | 5 Years Ago | Jan 12, 1893
Sam Ensminger of Camp Point married at Galesburg.

EPSTEIN, Mr B.C. | Apr 27, 1893
SEE TEGMEYER, Miss Minnie

EUCKE, Miss Lilly | Nov 3, 1892
SEE SCHLAGENHAUF, Wm

EVANS, Miss Bertha | Elm Grove | Oct 15, 1896
Married Thursday eve October 1st at 6 PM at the home of grooms father in Plymouth, Miss Bertha Evans and Mr John Foller, both of Plymouth. Left on evening train for Golden to the home of brides parents.

EVANS, Frank W. | Oct 16, 1890
SEE LEASE, Miss Nora

EVARTS, Miss Minnie | Jul 3, 1890
SEE HALEY, Harry

EVERETT, Mrs Catherine W. | Feb 16, 1899
SEE MONTGOMERY, Dr Robert

EWING, Albert | Aug 24, 1899
SEE PARKS, Miss Lila

EYMAN, Miss Georgie | Local | Nov 13, 1890
The Loti (Kansas) Western Farmer contains the announcement of the marriage of Miss Georgie Eyman, a former Clayton girl to Rev P.G. Shanklin, a Baptist minister of Leoti. Rev Shanklin entertained 50 guests of bride and groom at her home.

FALER, Bert | Local | Aug 15, 1895
Married, at the family home in Concord township this county at 6 PM Sunday August 11th Mr Bert Faler and Miss Liola Swisher, daughter of Mr and Mrs A.S. Swisher of Concord. Groom has lived with William Staker much of his life. Married by Rev W.R. Lierle of Clayton.

FANSCHMIDT, Miss Ida P. | Ill Brevities | May 24, 1894
Miss Ida P. Fanschmidt of Quincy and Walter Coake of Edina, Missouri were married.

FARLOW, Addie | Ancient History | Mar 18, 1897
SEE CHRISTIE, Jerome O.
FARLOW, Mis Maggie | Dec 4, 1890
SEE THOMAS, Curt
FARLOW, Miss Mattie | Apr 29, 1897
SEE HENRY, Hez G.
FARLOW, Nellie | Jan 5, 1899
SEE POPE, Sam
FAVRHOW, Mr and Mrs Thomas | Our Own Bailiwick | Apr 23, 1896
An article in Quincy paper says: 14 years ago Thomas Favrhow and a lady were married at Louisiana, Missouri and lived together seven years. He took to drink and became a drunkard, a seperation and divorce followed and the wife came to Quincy. Three years ago Mr Favrhow decided to reform and took treatment at a Willow Bark institution and hasn't drank since. His wife satisfied he had reformed and always devoted and a christian lady gave her consent to a remarriage ceremony that was performed last Thursday.
FENSTERMAKER, Mr | Dec 7, 1893
SEE SHANK, Miss Emma
FENSTERMAKER, S.F. | Dec 14, 1893
SEE SHANK, Miss Emma
FERRE'L, Henry D. | Little Brindle News | Dec 13, 1894
Supplement Henry D. Ferre'l of Pea Ridge and Miss Minnie Baker of Adams County were married Thursday eve by Rev Crawford in Mt Sterling.
FERRIS, Elmer | Neighborhood News | Jun 25, 1891
Elmer Ferris, a young farmer married Ella Jones at Paris, Illinois. Early next AM he was met by Thomas Benson with whom he had been on bad terms for some time. Benson referred to Ferris's marriage and made an insulting allusion to his wife, a fight ensued in which Farris stabbed Benson in the heart killing him instantly.
FERRIS, Miss Phoebe | Oct 12, 1893
SEE WOOSTER, Wm
FIELDS, Miss Addie | Old Pike | Dec 10, 1896
Versailles Correspondent Mr and Mrs G.I. Fields have issued invitations to the marriage of their daughter, Miss Addie and Harvey Turner of Fish Hook which will take place Thursday eve December 10th at their home.
FIELDS, Miss Maggie | Little Brindle | Apr 1, 1897
Democrat Message: Married at the home of the brides parents in Versailles at 8 PM Sunday last, Miss Maggie Fields and John W. Webster, of Rushville. Groom is of Schuyler County, while bride is daughter of G.I. Fields of Versailles Enterprise.
FIELDS, Mrs Mary | Oct 20, 1898
SEE JOSLIN, Joseph
FIELDS, Miss Nannie | Little Brindle | Feb 23, 1899
Miss Nannie Fields, daughter of G.L. Fields of the Versailles Enterprise and A.J. Perkins of Jacksonville were married at the latter place Tuesday last week by Rev Preston Woods in the ME parsonage.
FINKHAUS, William F. | Ill Brevities | Sep 27, 1894
William F. Finkhaus age 70 and Mrs Eva Schwartzburn age 65 of Quincy were married recently.
FINLAY, Rev and Mrs W.B. | Neighbors | Apr 23, 1896
Rev and Mrs W.B. Finlay have been together as man and wife 61½ years.
FITZJOHN, Miss Alice | Local | Feb 4, 1892
We suspected Homer Flagg was here with some malicious intention. Read this clipped from the Pike County Banner: Mr Homer H. Flagg of Dorchester Nebraska and Miss Alice Fitzjohn were married at 3 PM Wednesday at the home of brides parents northeast of this place by Rev S.H. Huber. Will live Nebraska.

FLAGG, Mr Homer H. Feb 4, 1892
SEE FITZJOHN, Miss Alice

FLASNER, Mrs Anna Moore Nov 26, 1896
SEE SCOTT, Mr J.V.

FLASNER, Henry M. All Over the County Mar 18, 1897
Henry M. Flasner, of Golden, died Wednesday, age 81 years, deceased died after short illness. Came to this locality about 1876 a comparative stranger and married Mrs Ikke Buss, widow at that time of John Buss. Born in Slawerfelm, Hanover.

FLASNER, Miss Jennie May 10, 1894
SEE HILL, James

FLASSNER, Martin 5 Years Ago Oct 23, 1890
Martin Flassner and Miss Moore, of Mt Sterling were married.

FLEMING, Miss Mattie Mar 18, 1897
SEE GERRY, Mr Ollie

FLEMING, Theodore Married Feb 6, 1890
At Quincy, Illinois Jan 29th 1890 by F.N. Calvin, pastor of Christian Church, Mr Theodore Fleming, of Clayton and Miss Minnie Satoreous, of Golden, left for Denver, Colorado where Mr Fleming goes to deliver a temperance speech.

FLEMMING, A.E. Personal Jun 16, 1892
Mr and Mrs R.H. Meats went to Litchfield last week to attend wedding of her brother, A.E. Flemming to Miss Annie Dearl, a young lady of that city Sunday eve.

FLEMMING, Miss Florence Married Sep 18, 1890
Married, Miss Florence Flemming of Bowen and Mr Reuben Meats of this city at the home of Mrs Flemming, mother of the bride at noon last Sunday. Nuptials were attended by groom's mother, Mrs Meats, Mr and Mrs F.J. Meats, and Miss Ella Stiffy from this place. Will live Clayton.

FLEMMING, Wm Little Brindle Aug 26, 1897
A marriage license was issued tthis week to Wm Flemming and Mary Strahan, both of Clayton.

FLESNER, Miss Marie Feb 28, 1895
SEE TOTSCH, Charles

FLESSNER, Miss Helena Jan 21, 1897
SEE FRITZEN, Martin

FLESSNER, John W. Supplement Dec 16, 1897
All Over the County John W. Flessner and Antje J. Lerhoff, both of Golden were Saturday granted a license to wed.

FLETCHER, Fred Camp Point Apr 8, 1897
Fred Fletcher and Miss Dollie Welch were married at the home of the bride Sunday 4 PM.

FLIGHT, Charles Ill Brevities Dec 13, 1894
Charles Flight is wanted in Quincy at answer charges of bigamy. Warrent sworn out by his first wife and mother of his 16 year old son, second wife was formerly Anna Gaskill of Jacksonville and she is mother of a child a year old. Both wives live in Quincy, but whereabouts of Mr Flight is unknown.

FLOATMAN, John Local Feb 1, 1894
Married Wednesday of last week, Mr John Floatman and Miss Anna Beckman of southwest part of town. They will live near Camp Point.

FLOETMAN, John Camp Point Feb 1, 1894
Will Floetman of the East St Louis Journal came up to attend wedding of his brother John to Miss Anna Beckman last Wednesday at high noon.

FLYNN, John J. Our Own Bailiwick Sep 13, 1894
Our young friends Johnnie Flynn and Miss Minnie Rentschler went to Springfield and the Friday journal says: Married at 5 PM Wednesday Sept 5th at the church of Immaculate Conception the Father Timothy Hickey married John J. Flynn and Miss Minnie Rentschler, both of Clayton, Illinois. Groom is brakeman on the Wabash Railroad. 21 years old and son of John Flynn. Bride is daughter of Jacob Rentschler age 18 years. Attendents were Frank C. Murray and Miss Mary Foley both of Springfield. Will live in this city.

FLYNN, Miss May Agnes Nov 24, 1898
SEE BRADY, Bernard

FLYNN, Myrtle Nov 28, 1895
SEE ANSTIN, George H.

FOGGY, Rob't 5 Years Ago Apr 23, 1891
SEE HENDRICKS, Anna

FOLCKEMER, Paul Camp Point Jan 2, 1896
Paul Folckemer and Miss Mary Honnold were married at the home of the bride last Wednesday by Rev A.N. Simmonds.

FOLCKMER, Paul Camp Point Dec 26, 1895
Cards are out announcing marriage of Paul Folckmer to Miss Mamie Honnold Wednesday.

FOLEY, Mr and Mrs W.B. Brown County Nov 2, 1899
C.A. Weaver of the Feed Mill offered 25 pounds of meat to the couple who had been married the longest present at the Christian Church, dinner at the opera house Thursday. It was awarded to Mr and Mrs W.B. Foley who were married Oct 10, 1840, 59 years ago. Next oldest married couple was H.M. Condee and wife who were married Apr 12, 1846 and 10 pounds of flour to most recently married couple, Dr C.B. Dearborn and wife.

FOLKEMER, Chester Camp Point Jul 4, 1895
Chester Folkemer and Miss Anna Clark were married at home of brides mother last Wednesday eve by Rev A.N. Simmonds.

FOLLER, John Oct 15, 1896
SEE EVANS, Miss Bertha

FOOTE, Miss Miranda Neighbors Jul 15, 1897
Scandal in Stronghurst--Miss Miranda Foote, a village belle, eloped with John Crawford, a negro who groomed her fathers horses.

FORBES, A.R. 20 Years Ago Apr 19, 1894
Marriage of A.R. Forbes and <u>Mrs</u> Minnie M. Scott occurred at Georgetown, Colorado.

FORD, Ed Golden Mar 29, 1894
Ed Ford and Miss Kimball were married last Sunday by Justice Duis.

FORDYCE, Miss May May 5, 1898
SEE BURNETT, Mulford

FOSTER, Johnson and wife Local May 28, 1896
Mr and Mrs Johnson Foster will be married 56 years Saturday the 28th inst.

FOSTER, Mrs Johnston Local Dec 26, 1895
Mrs Johnston Foster has a cancer and is very low. Mr and Mrs Foster has been married 56 years.

FOVAL, Jesse and Mamie Apr 3, 1890
Calhoun County trial ended the 17th in which Jesse Foval was granted a divorce from his wife Mamie Foval he is a rich farmer in Calhoun County Illinois. Married Mamie Isdell in St Louis, Missouri Oct 30, 1889, she was housekeeper of his nephew, Isaac Foval of 4119 Pleasant St., St Louis.

FRANCIS, John T. Local Jun 19, 1890
Mr John T. Francis of Camp Point and Miss Lizzie T. O'Neil of Perry, Ill. were married last week. Mr Francis is a businessman of our neighboring city.

FRANCIS, Mrs Margaret Adams County Mar 30, 1899
Mrs Margaret Francis, widow of Mr V. Francis who died at Camp Point has resigned the position of matron of Y.W.C.H. at Quincy and will be married at home of Mr and Mrs Samuel Francis in Camp Point, April 3rd to Mr Housler, of Galesburg.

FRANK, Charlie City Brevities Mar 2, 1899
Mr Charlie Frank, living about 6 miles south of town, and Miss Sidney Poland, daughter of Mr and Mrs Bruce Poland were married in Mt Sterling last Saturday.

FRANKS, Martha A. and Preston M. Chancery Notice Apr 30, 1891
County of Adams County Illinois Preston M. Franks vs Martha A. Franks the defendant for divorce June term 1891.

FRANKS, Mrs Mattie Local Jun 4, 1896
Clipping from newspaper received tells of marriage of Mrs Mattie Franks, formerly of Clayton, now of Amarillo, Texas to Mr R.N. Smith in Gonzales, Texas April 14th.

FRANKS, Oscar Little Brindle Jan 17, 1895
From Siloam Herald: Oscar Franks and Effie Bent went to Mt Sterling and were married and returned to Jasper Franks where there was a grand dinner awaiting them.

FRANKS, Preston M. Local Mar 12, 1896
Licensed to wed: Preston M. Franks of Quincy age 55 and Mary E. Jones of Quincy age 47 years.

FRANKS, Miss Susie 5 Years Ago Feb 12, 1891
Miss Susie Franks married Mr John H. Smith in Concord.

FRAZIER, Miss Ada Adams County Jul 14, 1898
Golden New Era Miss Ada Frazier and John Wallace were married at the home of brides mother in this city Wednesday eve by Rev M.W. Lorimer, pastor of the United Presbyterian Church.

FREEMAN, Inez Ill State News Jan 11, 1894
Inez Freeman, age 14 eloped from Aurora, with a man named Gribble and they were married.

FRENCH, Jessie Jan 3, 1895
SEE WILSON, Charlie

FREY, William Married Mar 19, 1896
Mr William Frey and Miss Nellie Montgomery Wednesday eve at Methodist parsonage by Rev W.A. Reynolds. Quiet wedding owing to recent death of the brides father. Bride born and raised here and groom lived here since early boyhood. Will live with their parents for a time.

FRICKE, Caroline 10 Years Ago May 4, 1893
Caroline Fricke and Henry Vonholdt of Concord, were married.

FRICKE, Chas. Local Mar 25, 1897
Mr Chas. Fricke was married Wednesday to a school teacher living south of Camp Point. We did not learn the name of the bride.

FRICKE, Chas. Local Apr 1, 1897
From Quincy Whig Thursday AM A quiet wedding yesterday 4 PM at home of Rev H.A. Ott 1105 Jersey St. in which the Rev married Mr Chas. Fricke of Mt Sterling, Ill. and Miss Emma Culver of Freeport, Ill. Groom is in flour milling business in Mt Sterling. Bride is daughter of Mr and Mrs George Culver of Freeport and taught school near Camp Point 5 years. Will live Mt Sterling.

FRICKE, William F. Mar 10, 1892
SEE THORNHILL, Miss Kate

FRIDAY, Charley F. Apr 29, 1897
SEE LOGSDON, Lillie

FRIDAY, Wm | Supplement | Jun 27, 1895
Little Brindle News Wm Friday last May married Della Cornicle and a few days later deserted his wife and refused to live with her. Last Tuesday upon her complaint Wm was bound over to circuit court in $500 and in default now reposes within barb wire inclosure. "Examiner"

FRITZEN, George | Adams County | Feb 16, 1899
Marriage license issued to George Fritzen and Kate J. Buss, both of Golden.

FRITZEN, Martin | All Over the County | Jan 21, 1897
Martin Fritzen and Miss Helena Flessner, daughter of John Flessner and wife were married by Rev Oetting, pastor of the Prairie Church Sunday afternoon.

FROST, Mr and Mrs John | Camp Point | Jan 9, 1896
Mr and Mrs John Frost celebrated their 50th wedding anniversary last Wednesday.

FRUHLING, Anna | | Jun 9, 1892
SEE JONKIN, Henry Deis

FRY, Harvey | Little Brindle | Apr 15, 1897
Versailles Enterprise Married at the home of brides parents, Mr and Mrs G.W. Means of Hersman, Illinois April 8th, 1897 at 8 PM Mr Harvey Fry and Miss Florence Means by Rev E.C. Fulton. Groom is a farmer of this county.

Fugate, Moses | Neighborhood News | Oct 16, 1890
Moses Fugate and Mrs Kate Cole, of Bushnell, have been married. He is a giddy youth of 76 and his wife is over 75.

FUHRKEN, Miss Anna | Local | Dec 3, 1896
TIEKEN, Fred Jr.

FULLER, Mr and Mrs Charles H. | Neighborhood News | Apr 12, 1894
Macomb Bystander wants to know if you've seen Charlie or not seems Mrs Charles H. Fuller is looking for her husband. They were married recently and Charlie almost immediately forsook his bride and departed for some place unknown to wife.

FUNKHOUSER, Lida | | Nov 27, 1890
SEE SMITH, W. Lee

GABRIEL, Geo. G. | | Jun 2, 1892
SEE HALL, Miss Nina B.

GALLAHER, James | Local | Dec 22, 1892
James Gallaher, age 25 and Nora Whitaker, age 15, both of Chestline were licensed to wed.

GALLAHER, Miss Poline | | Feb 1, 1894
SEE WHITAKER, Philip

GARDNER, Miss Nellie | Local | Dec 9, 1897
Married Sunday 6 PM at Presbyterian parsonage in this city by Rev Paul Heiligman, Mr Charles W. Linn of Agricola, Kansas and Miss Nellie Gardner of this place. Groom is well to do farmer, known each other since childhood, both having lived in vicinity of Liberty, this county many years. Will live Kansas.

GARNER, Mr | Pea Ridge | Apr 25, 1895
Mr Garner and Miss Jettie Knight were married at home of brides parents Sunday at 11 by Elder J. Crawford of Mounds.

GARNER, Ella | | Mar 18, 1897
SEE KNIGHT, George J.

GARNER, Lew | Pea Ridge | Aug 10, 1899
Married in our neighborhood Thursday AM, Lew Garner and Miss Kindheart daughter of Conrad Kindheart by Squire Lambert.

GARNER, Dr W.A. | | Jun 28, 1894
Married, at the Hampton House, Thursday June 21st, Dr W.A. Garner and Mrs Ida B. Jones, both of this city by Rev Riley Lierly.

GARRETT, Miss Kate | Local | Dec 14, 1893
Miss Kate Garrett will be married to a prominent Quincy young gentleman today at Camp Point. It was a profound secret until Jim Al Smith heard of it ten days ago.
GARRETT, Miss Kate | | Dec 21, 1893
SEE WALTER, Frank
GARRETT, Miss Mollie | 10 Years Ago | Oct 26, 1893
SEE CURRY, Chas.
GASKILL, Anna | Ill Brevities | Dec 13, 1894
SEE FLIGHT, Charles
GAY, Miss Bertha | | Nov 2, 1899
SEE MCCARTY, James E.
GAY, Grant | Camp Point | Jun 13, 1895
Mr Grant Gay and Miss Ida Wilson were married at home of Mr Arthur Gay last Thursday eve.
GAY, Miss Mattie | 10 Years Ago | Mar 19, 1891
SEE EASUM, Henry A.
GAY, Miss Mattie | 5 Years Ago | Feb 19, 1891
Miss Mattie Gay was married to Mr Henry A. Easum. They now live on the Gay farm north of town.
GAY, Will | Personal | May 14, 1891
Miss Margaret Vandeventer of Versailles is here to attend wedding of her nephew, Will Gay.
GAY, Mr Wm E. | | May 14, 1891
SEE GRIFFITH, Miss Clenay
GEDDES, Col and Mrs | Neighborhood News | Jan 8, 1891
Col. and Mrs Geddes of Fountain Green celebrated their 60th wedding anniversary the 9th inst.
GEDDING, Miss Lillian | | Feb 22, 1894
SEE BONSER, Mr Edward
GEISS, Mr Henry | Neighborhood News | Sep 8, 1892
Meredosia News announces marriage of Mr Henry Geiss of that place to Miss Ida Rockwood, of Concord, Morgan County, at the home of brides parents at 5 PM Sunday by Rev Feree. Henry is known to many Clayton people.
GEMBLER, Catherina | | Feb 21, 1895
SEE ALBERS, Menne
GERRY, Mr Ollie | Married | Mar 18, 1897
Mr Ollie Gerry, of Quincy was married to Miss Mattie Fleming of Clayton on the 4th of March at Christ's Church St Louis, Missouri by Rev Allen K. Smith. Groom represents the Weider Paint Co. of St Louis. Mrs Gerry left Saturday for Decatur, her future home.
GETTS, Chas. | | Apr 29, 1897
SEE CALDWELL, Miss Susie
GHORMLEY, Mr D.E. | 15 Years Ago | Sep 15, 1898
Married, Mr D.E. Ghormley and Miss Lizzie Wallace.
GIBBS, Luther C. | | Dec 26, 1895
SEE MCGAUGHEY, Miss Jessie I.
GIBSON, Alden M. | Married | May 10, 1900
Married at Mt Sterling Thursday of last week, Mr Alden M. Gibson and Miss Electa Beckman both of this city for several months Miss Beckman has been housekeeper for Mr Gibson and her devotion to the children is indeed remarkable. Married at Mt Sterling Thursday and will continue to live in Clayton.
GIBSON, Collie | June 1888 | Jun 30, 1898
Collie Gibson married at Centerville, Iowa lady.
GIBSON, Miss Nellie | | Dec 29, 1898
SEE REED, Henry L.

GIDDINGS, George Little Brindle Nov 5, 1895
Beacon Light Married at the Baptist parsonage by Rev R.E. House at 4 PM Wednesday, Mr George Giddings of Pea Ridge to Miss Emma Corfield of Concord. He is a well to do farmer.

GIDDINGS, Mr and Mrs Homer A. Local Jun 6, 1895
The 50th wedding anniversary of Mr and Mrs Homer A. Giddings was celebrated by a few neighbors and relatives at their home on Pea Ridge Wednesday eve.

GIDDINGS, Miss Lillian Pea Ridge Feb 22, 1894
Married, Thursday Feb 15th, Miss Lillian, daughter of Homer Giddings of this vicinity and Mr Ed Bouncer of Nebraska. Will live Nebraska where Mr Bouncer owns a farm.

GIDDINGS, Miss Mary A. 10 Years Ago Aug 7, 1890
Miss Mary A. Giddings was married to Benj. G. McPherson July 28th.

GILBERT, Harry Little Brindle Nov 24, 1898
Last Saturday eve Justice McCabe married Harry Gilbert, the colored porter at the Curry House and Miss Lillie Ross, colored maiden of Clayton.

GILBIRDS, Miss Lulu 10 Years Ago Sep 28, 1893
Miss Lulu Gilbirds married Mr Ed Badgely.

GILLILAND, Jno. T. Other Days May 17, 1900
April 1890 Married Mr Jno. T. Gilliland and Miss Alice Harwood.

GILLILAND, John N. Apr 10, 1890
SEE Harwood, Miss Alice

GILLIS, Mr O.M. Married May 7, 1896
Married at Christian Church by Elder G.A. Hendrickson, Mr O.M. Gillis and Mrs Nora Breckenridge.

GILLISPIE, Miss Flora Oct 29, 1896
SEE ELLERBROCK, J. Henry

GITHENS, Dr and Mrs W.H. Neighbors Mar 16, 1899
At their home in Hamilton, Dr and Mrs W.H. Githens celebrated their 50th wedding anniversary.

GIVENS, Geo. Sept 1889 Sep 7, 1899
Married at Mt Sterling, Mr Geo. Givens and Miss Maymie Harney.

GIVLER, Hugh Local Dec 28, 1893
Mr and Mrs W.F. Givler and daughter, Miss Jessie, went to Decatur to attend wedding of Mr Hugh Givler to occur in that city in that day. Lady is a Presbyterian Minister's daughter in that city.

GIVLER, Miss Jessie Local May 6, 1897
Mr and Mrs W.F. Givler announce the engagement of their daughter, Miss Jessie Givler to Rev John Allen Mac Gaughey.

GIVLER, Miss Jessie Aug 19, 1897
SEE MCGAUGHEY, Rev John A.

GLASER, Elmer Dec 28, 1899
SEE DAVIS, Miss Maude

GLASER, Nellie Jan 7, 1892
SEE GREENHALGH, Edward W.

GLASS, Wiley M. Jun 23, 1892
SEE REA, Roberta Y.

GLASSCOCK, Bushrod H. Nov 9, 1899
SEE BADGETT, Mrs Isabella

GLINES, Miss Nevva Nov 4, 1897
SEE SEARS, William A.

GLINES, Miss Nora Supplement Dec 14, 1899
Exchanges Hamilton press says a young lady who was born and raised here was married Sunday at 11 AM at home of the bride on Elm St, Miss Nora Glines and Mr Harry Thornton of Keokuk. Brides parents prepared meal afterward. Groom is of Keokuk but came from St Joseph, Mo. and is a glass blower by trade. Will live Keokuk.

GOLDMAN, Mrs Mary April 1890 May 17, 1900
SEE SHANK, Wm
GOLLAWAY, Alice M. 5 Years Ago Oct 23, 1890
SEE COLPITT, Arthur
GOLLIER, James Dec 29, 1892
SEE WHITAKER, Miss Nora
GOODWIN, Elder Hardin and wife Kingdom News Apr 30, 1896
Elder Hardin and wife of Pittsfield were married Mar 15, 1835 and were joined together in the county in which they now live.
GOODWIN, Mary May 23, 1895
SEE WARD, Tommy (Pipestone)
GOODWIN, W.J. Dec 21, 1899
SEE BARROWS, Miss Margaret G.
GOODWIN, W.R. Nov 10, 1892
SEE HAZLETT, Miss Eva
GOOLEY, Miss Anne Jan 5, 1893
SEE STEVENS, Clarence
GOOLEY, Miss Ella Sep 25, 1890
SEE LONG, Albert
GORDLEY, Mrs Anna M. Jul 5, 1894
SEE ADAMS, Mr Jno. Q.
GORDON, Edward and wife 10 Years Ago Dec 14, 1893
Edward Gordon and wife celebrated their golden wedding at Elm Grove.
GORE, E.L. May 1883 Jun 23, 1898
Married, Mr E.L. Gore and Miss Emma E. Davis.
GORE, Mr and Mrs Emery Local Dec 21, 1899
Mr and Mrs Emery Gore celebrated their 5th wedding anniversary Tuesday night.
GORE, Emory C. Locals Dec 27, 1894
Married at the home of Mrs Susan Gore, Emory C. Gore and Ella E. Davis of Clayton, Illinois on December 19th. Lawrence, Kansas Gazette says: "What is Claytons loss is Lawrences gain". They will live at 1322 Tennessee Street.
GORE, John L. Hazel Dell Feb 27, 1896
Marriage of John L. Gore and Miss Mamie E. Wright will be celebrated at the home of brides parents near Augusta on Thursday afternoon. Will live Kansas.
GORE, John L. Mar 5, 1896
SEE WRIGHT, Maymie
GORHAM, Mr and Mrs John Ill State News May 12, 1896
Mr and Mrs John Gorham celebrated their 60th wedding anniversary at Jacksonville at the home of their daughter, Mrs John McAhan. Mrs Gore lived Jacksonville 74 years and is one of the oldest citizens. Large number of relatives present.
GORHAM, Mr and Mrs John Ill State News Mar 11, 1897
Mr and Mrs John Gorham celebrated their 61st wedding anniversary at Jacksonville. Married Jacksonville March 3, 1836.
GRADY, Mrs Dorothy Ann Nov 16, 1899
SEE ELLIS, William H.
GRADY, Miss Louise Feb 14, 1895
SEE WATKINS, Brock
GRADY, Miss Nellie Locals Mar 24, 1892
Miss Nellie Grady and Mr George Williams are married and Geo. is receiving the congratulations of friends.
GRAHAM, Miss Mary Mar 20, 1890
SEE SMITH, John H.

GRAHAM, Miss Nellie Mae Local May 27, 1890
Quincy Saturday Review The marriage of Mr E.A. Vosburgh of Wilkesbarre, Penn. and Miss Nellie Mae Graham, took place at the home of brides parents, Mr and Mrs James Graham Tuesday AM by Rev Graham, uncle of the bride. Mr and Mrs Vosburgh will be at home after July 1st at the home of Mr and Mrs Graham.

GRAY, Mr A.E. Local Sep 16, 1897
Mr and Mrs E.D. Frantz went to Bond County Illinois last week to attend wedding of Mrs Frantz's brother, Mr A.E. Gray, who chose for his life partner Miss Lolah Williams of his native town. They were married Wednesday eve last week and came here with Mr and Mrs Frantz for over Sunday. On Monday they left for LaHarpe, Illinois where Mr Gray is in the jewelry business and where they will live.

GRAY, Jas. Sept 1889 Sep 7, 1899
Married at Mt Sterling, Mrs Jas Gray and Miss Hattie Lowry.

GRAY, Rebecca Brown County May 17, 1900
County Clerk Purcell received a letter Wednesday from Rebecca Gray, of Barry, Illinois stating that in 1881 or 82 she was married to Robert Bratton and that she will give him $10 if the marriage license is not recorded. In fact she offers $25 if there is no record of the marriage she says "He sent a foolish boy for license, law don't allowed to send idiot after license" also "Bratton married soldier's widow, she never prommest to marry him, has straitigum ways to get her pension money; and worse than all, "the man that married him to soldiers widow had never married a person, he was so scared he never half married him to Major K.H. Gray's widow", after raising the reward to $25 she says, "Hope its not on record as it will be thousands in my pocket.

GRAY, Mrs S.L. Feb 2, 1893
SEE PEARL, Mr J.E.

GRAY, Sarah L. Apr 2, 1891
SEE DEARINGER, Sarah L. and James C.

GREEN, Mrs Sarah J. Apr 21, 1892
SEE WESTBROOK, Capt U.S.

GREENHALGH, Edward W. Married Jan 7, 1892
Married at the Presbyterian parsonage Tuesday eve, the 5th inst by Rev E.W. Souders, Edward W. Greenhalgh of Camp Point and Miss Nellie Glaser of Clayton, Illinois.

GREENHALGH, Vadie Adams County News Jan 4, 1894
SEE LIGGETT, Mrs Chas. S.

GREENWELL, Geo. Neighborhood News Jan 9, 1890
Geo. Greenwell, age 73 years and Rachel Ward age 64 were married in Lee township last week.

GREENWOOD, Miss Etta E. Apr 22, 1897
SEE MEANS, John H.

GREGG, Mr and Mrs Thomas Supplement Dec 3, 1891
Neighborhood News Mr and Mrs Thomas Gregg, of Hamilton, Illinois celebrated their 55th wedding anniversary last week.

GRIBBLE, Mr Jan 11, 1894
SEE FREEMAN, Inez

GRIFFIN, Miss Blanche Aug 4, 1892
SEE MCARTHUR, A.L.

GRIFFITH, Miss Clenay Marriage May 14, 1891
Miss Clenay, daughter of Capt and Mrs A.J. Griffith, of Concord was married to Mr Wm E. Gay at the family home Tuesday eve at 8 by Rev W.M. Reed. Reception held at home of Mrs Nancy Gay north of the city today. (Wed.)

GRIFFITH, Miss Hattie Feb 20, 1890
SEE KIRBY, Thomas J.

GRIFFITH, Miss Hester | Pea Ridge | Feb 27, 1890
Married at the brides parents on the 6th, Miss Hester Griffith and Thomas Kirby at 3 PM by Squire Pevehouse.
GRIFFITH, Miss Nadine | Oct 19, 1893
SEE ROBERTSON, William
GRIFFITH, Sarah E. | Aug 22, 1895
SEE MCFARLAND, Oliver
GRIFFITH, Miss Tillie | 5 Years Ago | Mar 12, 1891
Miss Tillie, daughter of Capt and Mrs Griffith married John Robinson, a prosperous Beverly farmer.
GRIGGS, George | Jun 30, 1898
SEE IRWIN, Miss Ora M.
GRIM, Louis A. | Dec 7, 1893
SEE EDIE, Miss Hallie
GRIMES, Miss | Oct 29, 1891
SEE HOPPER, Mr Jas. L.
GRIMES, Dr | City Brevities | Nov 17, 1898
Marriage of Dr Grimes and Miss Taylor occurred at Camp Point last week.
GRIMES, Miss Neva | Local | May 12, 1892
Married three weeks ago, the youngest daughter of Dr Grimes of Camp Point, Miss Neva and Mr Butler. Have gone to Butte, Montana to live. Was sick when she arrived there.
GRIMES, Wm B. | Sep 15, 1898
SEE WEISTER, Miss Kate
GRIMM, Wm H. | Adams County News | Dec 7, 1893
A fellow named Wm H. Grimm who once lived in Quincy worked for the railroad and kept a saloon is under arrest in Brooklyn, N.Y. He was married to five women which of course came to grief.
GROFF, Mr and Mrs Theo. | County News | Nov 2, 1899
Mr and Mrs Theo. Groff of Liberty celebrated their golden wedding anniversary Saturday.
GROOM, Miss Elizabeth | May 23, 1895
SEE ROTHGEB, Capt Frank.
GROSCHNER, Mr and Mrs Antone | Little Brindle | Jan 11, 1894
In State's attorney office Wednesday a compromise on the suit of seperate maintainance against Antone Groschner by Mrs Groschner was effected by the defendant signing two mortgages of $200 and $400 on his farm in Pea Ridge township and Mrs Groschner will not prosecute on the arson charge against him.
GROSS, Miss Alberta | Nov 10, 1892
SEE MEYER, Mr Frank D.
GROSS, Lieut. Fred | 5 Years Ago | Nov 21, 1890
Lieut. Fred Gross and Miss Georgie Petrie were married.
GROSS, George | Local | Sep 27, 1894
Mrs Hettie Wilson went to Louisiana, Missouri last week to attend wedding of her brother, George Gross to Miss Minnie Peiper. Owing to serious illness of brides father the nuptials were private. Geo. expects to quit the government service when his term expires this fall.and will engage in business, probably in Louisiana.
GROSS, John G. | Jun 2, 1892
SEE YAKLE, May

GROSS, Miss Julia Married Oct 26, 1899
Married at the home of Prof and Mrs John D. Gross in this city Thursday last week, October 19th, Miss Julia, the daughter of Prof and Mrs Gross and Mr John T. Little, formerly of Clayton, but now head miller for Model Mills at Mt Sterling at 4 PM by Rev P. Slagle, attended by her little niece, Ola Wilson, her sister Miss Lula played the wedding march. Cake was sent by Mr Boehm her brother-in-law of Louisiana, Missouri. Groom left on train for Louisiana, Missouri where they visited Mr and Mrs Boehm then visited Mr and Mrs Zoller at Palmyro, Missouri and her brother George Gross at St Louis. Will be at home in Mt Sterling after November 1st. Attending guests were: Mr and Mrs B. Zoller of Palmyra, Missouri (Mrs Zoller was god mother of bride).

GROSS, Julius Local Nov 25, 1897
Mr Julian Gross and Miss Anna Norton, accompanied by Misses Mary, Effie and Ada Norton and Mrssr Alfred Norton, Omer Baker, of Kellerville and Edgar Bowman of Fishhook, drove to Mounds Wednesday where they were married. Groom is son of Philip Gross of Pea Ridge, recently purchased a fine farm where they will live. Bride is daughter of Mr and Mrs John Norton of Concord.

GROSS, Matilda (Lillie) Apr 9, 1896
SEE HOPKA, Henry

GROVER, M.D. 10 Years Ago Feb 13, 1890
M.D. Grover and Miss Lulu Buchanan were married by C. Ballow, Esq. Grover acted badly and was afterward sent to the pen.

GROVER, Oscar A. Mar 2, 1899
SEE WASH, Miss Georgia May

GUNN, Mr John Nov 27, 1890
SEE PARKER, Miss Alice L.

GUSWELLER, Martin Ill Brevities Mar 29, 1894
Martin Gusweller was sentenced to penitentiary from Bloomington 13 months ago for bigamy his term expired the other day and he was welcomed home by wife #2. His first wife secured a divorce while he was in prison.

HACKNEY, W.D. 10 Years Ago Feb 12, 1891
SEE CORBY, Mrs Josephine.

HAINLINE, Grant June 1889 Jun 22, 1899
Married at Jacksonville, Mr Grant Hainline and Miss Minnie Linn.

HAINLINE, Mrs Minnie Local Jan 25, 1900
On Friday the 5th inst at Rosewood near Chicago, Mrs Minnie Hainline, daughter of Mr and Mrs J.A. Linn of Concord was married to Mr G.E. Hardin, formerly of Mason County, now of Chicago. The parents of Mr and Mrs Hardin lived on adjoining farms in Mason County when they were children and grew up together and were lovers. When family of Mr Linn moved to this vicinity they were seperated and recently met again. Will live Chicago where Mr Hardin is employed in some large manufacturing concern.

HAIR, Clement W. Local Oct 1, 1891
Married at the home of Elder H.G. VanDervort at 9 Thursday September 24, 1891, Clement W. Hair od Columbus, Illinois and Miss Prathana E. Curry of Clayton.

HALEY, Miss Alice Local Oct 30, 1890
SEE SMITH, Frank

HALEY, Harry Local Jul 3, 1890
Married, by Rev W.M. Reed, Mr Harry Haley and Miss Minnie Evarts at the ME parsonage at 7:30 PM Tuesday July 1st 1890.

HALEY, Mr Harry 5 Years Ago Jul 4, 1895
SEE EBERTS, Miss Minnie

HALEY, Ina — Ancient History — Feb 25, 1897
January 1886, Ina Haley married Thomas Cutter.

HALEY, Miss Lou — Local — Sep 1, 1892
Marriage of Miss Lou Haley to Mr Frank Alspaugh occurred at Burlington Monday of last week. Arrived in Clayton to visit her mother, Mrs Butler and family. Will live in Cedar Rapids. Mr Alspaugh is a railroad fireman who met and won Miss Haley during her two years residence in Burlington.

HALEY, Mrs Susan — Married — Jan 8, 1891
At the home of the bride in this city at 6 PM Sunday January 4th 1891, Mrs Susan Haley to Mr William J. Butler by C. Ballow, Esq. Mr Butler came here last spring from Missouri and had lived this vicinity before going to Missouri. Mrs Haley has lived here most of her life.

HALL, Calvin — Little Brindle — Nov 9, 1893
Thursday license to wed was issued by County clerk to Mr Calvin Hall and Miss Elva Moore, all of Elkhorn township. "Examiner"

HALL, Miss Frances — May 10, 1894
SEE WILSON, George H.

HALL, Miss Jessie — Dec 3, 1891
SEE SWAN, Mark E.

HALL, Miss Nina B. — Local — Jun 2, 1892
Married Tuesday eve May 24th at 8 PM at home of brides parents, Mr and Mrs S.F. Hall of Camp Point, Miss Nina B. to Mr Geo. G. Gabriel of Payson by Elder O. Dilley. Groom is a teacher.

HALL, Mrs Sarah — Oct 26, 1899
SEE REATH, Mr Henry

HALL, Sarah J. and Wm H. — Notice — Jul 16, 1891
To whom it may concern, notice is hereby given that my wife Sarah J. Hall has left me bed and board without any just cause or provacation and I will not be held responsible for any debts of her contracting beyond bare necessities. The public are warned not to harbor or trust her upon my account. Wm H. Hall Smithfield, Ill Jul 6, 1891

HALLE, August — Brown County News — Jun 22, 1893
August Halle and Miss Lottie Hatfield were married at Mt Sterling on Wednesday the 14th. "Whig"

HALLE, Miss Wilhelmina J. — May 31, 1894
SEE KLETTKE, William G.

HALSTEAD, Mr Jasper — Personal — Jul 31, 1890
Mr Jasper Halstead, of Breckenridge, Missouri is to be married this week. He is known to many of the young folks here. Ed Curry and Miss Ella Kirkpatrick have gone to attend the nuptials.

HALSTEAD, Olof — Apr 17, 1890
SEE HENRY, Miss Clara

HAMILTON, Miss Annie — Oct 15, 1896
SEE BURKE, C.H.

HAMILTON, Miss Ardell — Oct 15, 1891
SEE SHANK, William O.

HAMILTON, Miss Fredonia "Dona" — Local — Jan 15, 1891
Miss Fredonia Hamilton, daughter of E.H. and Mrs Hamilton was married to Mr Wilbourn Williams the photographer at Quincy, Thursday of last week. Miss Dona is a pleasant young lady.

HAMILTON, Miss Maymie — Dec 27, 1894
SEE BRADLEY, Henry T. "Tip"

HAMILTON, Miss Ora — 5 Years Ago — May 3, 1894
Miss Ora Hamilton maried Mr Garver in Kansas.

HAMMOND, Miss Phebe — Oct 13, 1898
SEE HUBBARD, S.A.

HANKE, John City Brevities Dec 29, 1898
Married at the German Lutheran Church in Concord township Wednesday eve, John Hanke, the youngest son of Mr Fred Hanke and Miss Emma Vollbracht, daughter of Mr and Mrs William Vollbracht of Concord by Rev George Blicvernicht.

HANKE, Miss Maude Mar 11, 1897
SEE VONHOLDT, Fred

HANNA, Jennie Nov 16, 1899
SEE LEE, William H.

HARBERTS, Jurgen H. County News Jan 18, 1900
Golden New Era Wednesday of last week, Jurgen H. Harberts and Miss Minnie Eigenburg, both of Golden, went to Quincy and were married that eve by Lutheran minister at his home on 9th and State Sts. Miss Eigenburg is daughter of John Eigenburg of this village. Will live north part of town.

HARBIN, George Little Brindle Apr 29, 1897
Mt Sterling Examiner George Harbin, who has been working for James Irwin on the farm, and Miss Mattie J. McFaddon, of Clayton, both colored were married by Mart Brooks, Esq. at the court house Wednesday eve.

HARBINS, Miss C.T. Little Brindle Oct 8, 1896
Democrat Message Squire Tom Wallace was called to the county clerks office to marry Miss C.T. Harbins and Richard Lewis, both colored, of Clayton. They were accompanied by James Harbin, brother of the event.

HARBISON, Abraham 15 Years Ago Jul 1, 1897
May, 1882 Wedding, Abraham Harbison and Mattie A. Hedenberg in New York, May 4th.

HARBISON, Charles Married Jan 8, 1891
Mr Charles Harbison arrived from Lancaster, Ohio Thursday AM with his bride at the home of Capt and Mrs Harbison of the marriage the Lancaster Daily Eagle of the 30th ult says: This morning marriage of Miss Lauretta Vorys and Mr Chas. Harbison was at the home of the bride on N. Broad St. by Rev McMillen of the First Presbyterian Church at 8 AM. Will live Chicago.

HARBISON, Mr Clarance Local Sep 24, 1896
Wednesday eve of last week Mr Clarance Harbison and Miss Martha Derringer were married by Rev J.H. Terrill at home of the clergyman. They will live with grooms'grandmother, Mrs Hughes and care for her in her declining years.

HARBISON, Miss Lizzie Local Dec 26, 1895
Married, December 9th at Chicago, Miss Lizzie Harbison, daughter of Capt and Mrs W.H. Harbison to Mr J.D. Murphy by Rev Wm F. Merrill of the 6th Presbyterian Church of Chicago. Will live Chicago where he works for the Chicago Herald.

HARBISON, Miss Puss 5 Years Ago Jun 12, 1890
Miss Puss Harbison married Mr O.L. Westbrook by Rev Rice.

HARDEN, Miss Bird Jun 6, 1895
SEE CAMPBELL, W.D.

HARDEN, Frank Feb 13, 1896
SEE BARNES, Miss Ida

HARDIN, Mr G.E. Jan 25, 1900
SEE HAINLINE, Mrs Minnie

HARDIN, Melvin T. Jul 4, 1895
SEE HORNECKER, Miss Josie

HARDIN, Nat Little Brindle Mar 9, 1899
Married, Nat Hardin and Ida Coleman of Clayton, both are colored. Bride is 16 years old and 6 ft. 1 in. tall. Married by Sq. McCabe.

HARDING, Miss Ella Nov 24, 1892
SEE REEDER, James

HARDING, Ernest City Brevities Oct 6, 1898
The nuptials of Mr Ernest Harding and Miss Allyene Norris, of Mt Sterling is set for Sunday the 16th inst at Quincy.

HARDING, Ernest E. Married Oct 20, 1898
Married at the home of brides uncle, Mr J.L. Hickman in Quincy on the afternoon of Tuesday October 16th 1898 occurred the marriage of Mr Ernest E. Harding of this city and Miss Allyne E. Norris of Mt Sterling Illinois by Rev Dr Ince, pastor of Baptist Church in Quincy. Groom is a member of the new firm of Shank and Harding Jr. Will live in cottage of Benn Curry Jr. on Washington St.

HARKER, George W. Jun 18, 1891
SEE COPPAGE, Miss Mattie B.

HARNEY, Don S. Nov 10, 1898
SEE PERRY, Miss Minnie

HARNLY, David H. Mar 16, 1899
SEE SLAGLE, Miss Nellie

HARPER, Mr Local Oct 18, 1894
SEE SMITH, Miss Nellie

HARPER, Carrie Local Nov 12, 1891
Married, at the brides home in Concord township Nov 4th 1891 at 6:30 by Elder VanDervoort, Carrie, daughter of Mr and Mrs Benjamin Harper, to Mr Chipman Ratcliff.

HARPER, Mrs Ella Apr 23, 1896
SEE THRELKELD, Alfred

HARPER, Frank Local Oct 28, 1897
Mr Frank Harper, son of Mr and Mrs B.F. Harper, of Concord, and Mrs Zooetta Penney of Kahoka, Missouri have recently been married. Will live Clayton with his parents.

HARPER, Gertrude Little Brindle Dec 1, 1898
Married at the home of brides parents, Mr and Mrs John Harper at 3 PM last Tuesday the 22nd inst their daughter, Gertrude and Mr Joseph G. Taylor of Chicago by Rev Joseph Browne, pastor of Fargo and Olive Presbyterian Churches.

HARPER, Miss Maggie Dec 27, 1894
SEE WILSON, Harve

HARPER, Miss Mary 10 Years Ago Aug 2, 1894
SEE BAKER, Oliver

HARPER, Miss May Local Nov 23, 1899
Marriage of Miss May Harper, daughter of Mr and Mrs J.B. Harper, of Concord to Mr Wm J. Beadles of Exeter, Scott County Illinois at Mt Sterling Wednesday afternoon of last week by Rev Browne. Will locate on a farm somewhere in the spring.

HARRIS, Miss Anna A. Local Nov 17, 1892
At the Christian parsonage Sunday eve at 6 PM Miss Anna A. Harris and Mr James A. Rowe were married by Elder H.G. VanDervoort. Bride had lived with Mr and Mrs C.M. Sloan to whom she was related for a year or so. Groom lived in Concord all his life. Will live Milard, Missouri.

HARRIS, Miss Lulu Feb 22, 1900
SEE KLEIN, Will

HARRIS, Miss May Dec 7, 1893
SEE CAMPBELL, J. Emery

HARRISON, Cyrus Brown County Jan 4, 1900
Licensed to wed since last issue of Examiner: Cyrus Harrison of Siloam and Hettie Johnson of Hazelwood.

HART, Charlie Camp Point Jun 13, 1895
Charlie Hart and Pearl Livingston were married last Tuesday eve at home of Elder O. Dilley officiating clergyman.

HART, Miss Laurissa Oct 16, 1890
SEE RANIER, Mr Hudson

HARTMAN, Dan A. Local Mar 15, 1894
Quincy paper tells of marriage license to Dan A. Hartman and Miss Lena A. Brierton, both of Versailles. They were married in Quincy Wednesday of last week and will live Versailles. Bride lived here as a girl, daughter of Henry Brierton and a cousin of Henry S. Anderson.

HARTMAN, Mr Jos. Local Nov 3, 1892
Married Thursday eve by Justice McDonnell, Mr Jos. Hartman, of Loraine and Miss Rosa McCormick of Quincy, formerly of Loraine. Was at one time a deputy sheriff, now is a veterinary surgeon at Loraine where they will live.

HARVEY, John Sr. Neighborhood News Nov 30, 1893
Married at Warsaw, John Harvey Sr. age 86 married his step grandaughter, Miss Lizzie Harvey age 20.

HARWOOD, Miss Alice Locals Apr 10, 1890
Married, Miss Alice Harwood to Mr John N. Gilliland at the home of brides parents in this city at 6:30 PM Thursday last April 3rd by Rev C.F. McKown of Paloma. Mr Gilliland has been in Adams County since childhood, an orphan boy.

HARWOOD, Miss Alice April 1890 May 17, 1900
SEE GILLILAND, Jno. T.

HARWOOD, Miss Bella Feb 13, 1896
SEE VEACH, Mr Miles

HARWOOD, Mrs Comelia Jun 24, 1897
SEE BAKER, Conrad

HASKETT, Harlan H. Aug 17, 1899
SEE CHASE, Miss Libby

HASSEN, Miss Jennie 5 Years Ago Sep 4, 1890
Miss Jennie Hassen was married to Mr Will E. Omer.

HATCH, Dr Local Sep 7, 1893
Dr Hatch of Quincy and Miss Emma Lyon, of Sedalia, Missouri were married Wednesday.

HATFIELD, Mr C.W. Local Jun 30, 1892
Mr C.W. Hatfield of Quincy was married to a Warsaw lady last Thursday.

HATFIELD, Miss Cora May 31, 1894
SEE SPEARS, Fred

HATFIELD, Miss Lottie Jun 22, 1893
SEE HALLE, August

HAWKINS, Clement L. Jan 5, 1893
SEE ANDERSON, Miss Annie S.

HAYES, Jessie Jan 3, 1895
SEE PEAIRS, Dr George M.

HAZLETT, Miss Anna Married Apr 23, 1891
Married at the home of Mr James Hazlett on East Washington St Tuesday eve, Miss Anna, their daughter, to Mr John Sweetring of Quincy. Attending from Quincy were: Mr and Mrs Sweetring, father and mother of groom and his sisters, Edith and Nellie and brother, Romey, attended by Charlie Hazlett, brother of bride and Miss Clara Harwood of Jerseyville a close friend, by Rev E.W. Souders of the First Presbyterian Church. Mr Sweetring has an elegant home ready for her in Quincy. Groom is a popular commercial man for a leading St Louis shoe house.

HAZLETT, Chas, H. | Local | Jan 24, 1895
Monday afternoon Mr and Mrs John Sweetring, Mr Chas. H. Hazlett and Miss Etta Chase drove over to Mt Sterling in a surrey. At Mounds they arranged for Rev J. VanWey to marry them and went on to Mt Sterling and got license, back to Mounds and were married. Groom, Charlie is son of Jas. Hazlett, mayor of Clayton. He is now engaged with F.W.Burgesser. Bride is eldest daughter of Mrs Jas. A. Boren.

HAZLETT, Miss Eva | Local | Nov 10, 1892
At Quincy, Wednesday of last week, Miss Eva Hazlett, of Lincoln, Nebraska, well known here, was married to Mr W.R. Goodwin of Chicago.

HAZLETT, James | Local | Mar 8, 1900
A marriage license issued to Mr James Hazlett and Miss Maude Brown, both of Clayton. No date has been set.

HAZLETT, Miss Lizzie | Local | Oct 21, 1892
At 4 PM Wednesday Rev E.W. Souders married, Miss Lizzie Hazlett, eldest daughter of Mr and Mrs Jacob Hazlett to Mr Frank Unglaub at the brides home. They met while Frank was telegraph operator in this city, Grooms people live at Woodson. Will live in the hotel Cutler, Carthage where he is wabash agent.

HEADEN, George H. | Ill Brevities | May 31, 1894
George H. Headen and Miss Mamie E. Holmes were married at Jacksonville.

HEAVENER, Miss Dove | | Mar 1, 1894
SEE STEPHENSON, Elder J.G.

HEAVENOR, Miss --ove | | Feb 22, 1894
SEE STEPHENSON, Rev J. Gilman

HEDENBERG, Mattie A. | May 1882 | Jul 1, 1897
SEE HARBISON, Abraham

HEDRICK, Miss Mabel | | Feb 10, 1898
SEE MARRETT, Ralph O.

HEDRICK, Will C. | City Brevities | Oct 6, 1898
Will C. Hedrick of Augusta and Miss Lora Strahan of near Clayton were married Wednesday Sept 21st in Mt Sterling. Will live Augusta. "Augusta Courier"

HEINECKE, August | Our Own Bailiwick | Feb 21, 1895
August Heinecke and Ida Werts of Golden were licensed to wed. Live Golden.

HEIRS, Jas. W. | | Dec 31, 1891
SEE BOSTICK, Nellie

HENDERSON, Miss Nellie | | Oct 8, 1896
SEE STONE, George

HENDRICKS, Anna | 5 Years Ago | Apr 23, 1891
Anna Hendricks married Rob't Foggy at Kellerville.

HENDRICKS, J.R. | Our Own Bailiwick | Sep 26, 1895
Last week a marriage license was issued to J.R. Hendricks of Fairweather, over 18 and Lou Likes of Plainville, over 17.

HENDRICKS, Nancy | | Apr 19, 1894
SEE BAKER, Conrad

HENDRICKS, Miss Sarah | | Nov 23, 1893
SEE LONG, A.C.

HENDRICKS, T.J. | Little Brindle News | May 10, 1894
T.J. Hendricks and Eva Hughes of Kellerville, were licensed to wed on Thursday, in Brown County.

HENRY, Annie | | Feb 14, 1895
SEE MCFARLAND, Isaac and Annie

HENRY, Miss Clara | Neighborhood News | Apr 17, 1890
The marriage of Miss Clara Henry to Mr Olof Halstead occurred at Cooperstown recently. They are both deaf mutes.

HENRY, Dr Ed C. All Over the County Aug 26, 1897
Invitations are out for wedding of Dr Ed C. Henry of Camp Point, to Miss Edith Stahl of Chicago at St Mark Church in the latter city.

HENRY, Miss Fannie Camp Point Sep 2, 1899
SEE BATES, Dr Lee

HENRY, Fannie Birdenia Sep 21, 1899
SEE BATES, Orville Lee

HENRY, Hez Camp Point Apr 29, 1897
Hez Henry and Mattie Farlow were married at Quincy Wednesday eve of last week.

HENRY, Hez G. All Over the County Apr 29, 1897
Hez G. Henry, cashier of the People's Bank, at Camp Point and Miss Mattie Farlow, ass't cashier were married at Quincy Thursday.

HENSON, Miss Mattie Mound Station Aug 14, 1890
SEE RATCLIFF, Horace G.

HERBIG, Thomas Supplement Jun 19, 1890
Locals Oxford, Kansas paper announces marriage of Miss Belle Lindsay to Mr Thomas Herbig. He was one of the family that lived in the brick house, now owned by E. Eyman north of town, years ago.

HERMAN, Mr William H. Local Jul 9, 1891
50 years ago last Wednesday, Miss Sarah Parvin married Mr William H. Herman near Quincy and soon after moved to Concord which since has been their home, where seven children were born, five still living. The family are scattered, none but Mrs A.S. Birkett of this city and Mrs Sullivan of Lee township being in this vicinity. On that day Mr and Mrs Birkett went down and surprised the old people, the old folks are in feeble health, but are able to be about.

HERMITETT, Frank 10 Years Ago May 14, 1891
Frank Hermitett and Nellie Lyman were married. He is now seeking a divorce.

HERNDON, James R. Local Dec 1, 1892
A Quincy paper carries the marriage of a Clayton lady, James R. Herndon of Camp Point and Helen A. Daugherty, of Clayton were married Thursday by Justice Moorehead.

HERREN, Henry H. Local Mar 1, 1900
Neighbors northeast of town in the German settlement are on tiptoe of expectation in anticipation of the marriage of Mr Henry H. Herron and Miss Hannah Decker, will occur this week. Mr Herren is son of a prosperous farmer living in northwest corner of Pea Ridge township. Bride is eldest daughter of Mr and Mrs John Decker living about four miles northeast of town.

HERRING, Mrs Louisa A. Oct 6, 1898
SEE CAMPBELL, Mr George A.

HERSMAN, Charles G. Brown County News Sep 21, 1893
Married at Bloomington Thursday eve, Mr Charles G. Hersman of Hersman to Miss Anna Means, of that city. Reception in home of grooms father Mr George Hersman.

HERSMAN, M.M. and wife Neighbors Jul 9, 1896
Examiner M.M. Hersman and wife are probably the oldest Brown County married couple residing in that county. They were married nearly 58 years ago, viz Oct 18, 1838. They were the first couple married after the county was taken from Schuyler under the new county organization.

HERZOG, Miss Sep 26, 1895
SEE SCHUHARDT, Charlie

HESS, Cora | Our Own Bailiwick | Apr 12, 1894
Cora Hess applied for divorce, case was heard in circuit court and Cora thought thats all there was to it and without waiting for a decree proposed to marry Mr Stotlar and they got their license, but she will have to wait.

HETZELL, Miss Christina | Nov 9, 1893
SEE ASHLEY, Mr Fred

HEUBNER, Miss Lena | Jan 20, 1898
SEE MARSH, Charles

HEWITT, Miss Emily H. | Sep 6, 1894
SEE WIDMAYER, Wm F.

HIBBARD, Mr and Mrs R.B. | Neighborhood News | Apr 25, 1895
The golden wedding of Mr and Mrs R.B. Hibbard was celebrated at Stone's Prairie April 3.

HIBBS, Miss Villa | Apr 20, 1899
SEE JARVIS, Leslie

HICKS, Col D.D. and wife | Neighborhood News | Jul 11, 1895
At Pittsfield, Col D.D. Hicks and wife celebrated their 50th wedding anniversary with children and grandchildren and friends.

HICKS, Miss Ollie V. | Dec 13, 1894
SEE MARSHALL, Jas H.

HILES, Tom | Local | Jul 24, 1890
Tom Hiles barber, went to Missouri ten days ago and got married. He has not sufficiently recovered to come back to work.

HILES, Thos. H. | 5 Years Ago | May 14, 1891
SEE WILLIAMS, Miss Alice

HILL, James | Golden | May 10, 1894
Mr James Hill of Golden and Miss Jennie Flasner of Clayton were married in Quincy Saturday last. Will live Golden.

HILL, Miss Marie | Sep 17, 1891
SEE SCHWENK, Mr and Mrs

HILLYER, Warren | Apr 27, 1899
SEE CAIN, Miss Orphie

HIPKINS, Miss Belle | Jan 31, 1895
SEE PETERS, Edward

HIPPEN, John H. | Married | Mar 23, 1899
Marriage of Mr John H. Hippen and Miss Onney Ennen occurred at home of parents of bride, Mr and Mrs Enne Ennen of Pea Ridge, Brown County Wednesday afernoon the 15th inst.

HIPPEN, Miss Trinkie | Apr 20, 1899
SEE PENDLETON, Christopher T.

HIRONS, Miss Sadie | Dec 28, 1899
SEE CAMPBELL, Mr Orie

HIRONS, Miss Saidee | Jan 4, 1900
SEE CAMPBELL, Charles O.

HIRONS, William L. | Jan 26, 1893
SEE ACKLAM, Miss Jennie E.

HIRSHEIMER, Miss Ida B. | Neighborhood News | Jan 7, 1892
Marriage of Mr Abraham L. Stone of Chicago to Miss Ida B. Hirsheimer of Pittsfield last Wednesday eve at Fishell's opera house at 7:30 PM.

HOBBS, D.C. | Camp Point | Nov 22, 1894
D.C Hobbs of Perry, while a marriage license was being written for him remarked: "this makes the fourth marriage license issued to me from this desk." as he is only 64 years old, he is probably good for one or two more.

HOBBS, Mr Jab | Local | Feb 18, 1897
Mr Jab Hobbs and Miss Hattie Jackson were licensed to wed by Clerk Haselwood and are enjoying all the pleasures that come to young married people.

HOBBS, Miss Ruth | | Feb 3, 1898
SEE WORSTER, Washington

HOBBS, William H. | Little Brindle | Jul 13, 1899
William H. Hobbs of Clayton and Nola M. Caley of Bowen were married last Sunday AM by Squire McCabe in the court house.

HOCAMP, Miss Lizzie | | Jan 20, 1898
SEE SHARP, Amos

HOCAMP, Miss Mary | Camp Point | Dec 28, 1899
SEE BUETEL, Frank

HOCAMP, Mary A. | | Dec 21, 1899
SEE BEUTEL, Frank

HODGSON, Rev Arthur C. | Married | Sep 2, 1897
Married at high noon, August 23rd 1897, Rev Arthur C. Hodgson, pastor of the First Baptist Church of LaSalle, Illinois and Miss Flora Birkett of Peoria, Illinois at the home of brides aunt, Mrs Laura Thompson, 213 Ellis St. Peoria, by Rev Geo. E. Nicholson, of Fairmont, Illinois a friend of the groom. Spent honeymoon in Chicago. Will live LaSalle.

HODSON, Miss Fannie | | Apr 6, 1899
SEE WHITEHEAD, Mr Alta

HOFFMAN, Albert | Ill. Brevities | Mar 7, 1895
SEE DIESTERIE, Miss Mary

HOFFMAN, Albert | Local | Feb 28, 1895
Married this afternoon by Justice Allen, Mr Albert Hoffman, of Kellerville, Illinois and Miss Sarah Morgan, of Meadville, Missouri. "Quincy Journal 22nd"

HOFFMAN, Miss Blanche | | Aug 17, 1899
SEE SMITH, Mr Alva

HOFFMAN, George | Local | Jan 23, 1896
Marriage license issued Tuesday to George Hoffman of Haselwood, age 23 and Ida M. Purpus of Kellerville, age 22.

HOFFMAN, Gertrude | | Mar 28, 1895
SEE HUGHES, Edward

HOFFMAN, Miss Jessie | | Nov 23, 1893
SEE HUGHES, Benjamin O.

HOFFMAN, John | Local | Sep 28, 1899
John Hoffman and Caroline E. Smith, both of Kellerville were married at the Occidental Hotel, Quincy, last Wednesday.

HOGAN, Edith | | Jan 25, 1900
SEE WILSON, Manford

HOGAN, Jas. | Supplement | Jun 29, 1893
5 Years Ago Jas. Hogan, now Wabash roadmaster, and Miss Hoelsell were married at Springfield.

HOGAN, Martin | Little Brindle News | Feb 6, 1896
Republican: Martin Hogan of Clayton, and Miss Annie Webster of Meredosta were married at city hotel yesterday eve by Rev B.F. Madden.

HOKE, Mr and Mrs Craven | Local | Nov 11, 1897
Uncle Craven Hoke and wife of Kirksville, Missouri (formerly of this place) had a family reunion yesterday that being their 50th anniversary. Relatives from Kentucky and Kansas and other places attended there were about 50 guests present. Quincy Journal.

HOKE, Mr Jas. | 10 Years Ago | Sep 15, 1892
SEE ROBISON, Miss Mattie

HOKE, Minnie | | Dec 2, 1897
SEE MEATHERINGHAM, John

HOKE, Miss Sarah E. Married Oct 16, 1890
At the home of Robert W. Hoke, Clayton township October 1st James W. Meatheringham and Miss Sarah E. Hoke by Elder F.N. Calvin of Quincy.
HOLDREN, Miss Vauna Apr 30, 1896
SEE CURRY, Edgar T. "Tommie"
HOLLOCK, Christian J. Nov 2, 1899
SEE BLACK, Miss Rosa
HOLMES, Charles Wedding Mar 30, 1893
Married at home of Capt James Kirkpatrick near Banner on March 9th Mr Charles Holmes and Lillie M. Phelps at 12 by Rev Bostwick. Bride is daughter of Capt James Kirkpatrick, a citizen of Sheridan County. Groom is one of Sheridan's business men. Will live Sheridan.
HOLMES, Miss Mamie E. May 31, 1894
SEE HEADEN, George H.
HOMER, Miss Nellie Mar 24, 1898
SEE MEYERS, Henry
HONNOLD, Miss Ella Jul 1, 1897
SEE COLLIER, G.S.
HONNOLD, Miss Mamie Dec 26, 1895
SEE FOLCKMER, Paul
HONNOLD, Miss Mary Jan 2, 1896
SEE FOLCKEMER, Paul
HOOTON, Prof J.E. Neighborhood News Jul 27, 1893
Prof J.E. Hooton, prin. of Mendon public schools is soon to be a married man, Miss Dora Ada May of Norton, Illinois will become Mrs Hooton at high 12 Wednesday July 26th.
HOPKA, Miss Annie Louise Feb 21, 1895
SEE MUSICK, George P.
HOPKA, Henry Elm Grove Apr 9, 1896
Marriage of Mr Henry Hopka to Miss Lillie Gross of Pea Ridge occurred Wednesday April 8th at high noon at home of bride by Rev Bell of Mt Sterling. Reception Thursday eve at grooms parents home.
HOPKA, Henry Elm Grove Apr 9, 1896
Invitations are out for the wedding of Henry Hopka, of Elm Grove and Matilda Gross of Pea Ridge on the 8th.
HOPKINSON, Miss Josephine Oct 19, 1899
SEE CRANE, Rev L. Burton
HOPPER, Personal Mar 5, 1896
SEE BEALL,
HOPPER, Mrs Ella Oct 15, 1896
SEE MCMURRAY, N.F.
HOPPER, Mr and Mrs Henry S.W. Pea Ridge Mar 3, 1892
Sunday was the 14th wedding anniversary of Mr and Mrs Henry Hopper.
HOPPER, Howard Merrian Feb 20, 1896
SEE BEALL, Frankie
HOPPER, Mr Jas L. Local Oct 29, 1891
A letter from Mrs T.C. Smith tells of marriage of Mr Jas L. Hopper, formerly of this vicinity to Miss Grimes an Iowa lady.
HOPPER, Miss Pauline Local Oct 15, 1896
Speaking of the marriage of her mother: Miss Pauline Hopper went to Mt Sterling with her lover, Mr Ptis Davis, a few days later where they were quietly married by Elder Laycock.

HORN, Frank Neighborhood News Mar 10, 1892
13 years ago, Frank Horn of Schuyler County came from Germany to the U.S. He left behind him Anna Warneske to whom he ahd plighted his love. He was a poor young man and promised to send for Anna as soon as he could make money enough to support a wife. He was industrious and saving and having earned a good farm recently sent word for her to come. She arrived in this country two months ago and last week the happy couple were married, and are now living on one of the finest and best improved farms in Bainbridge township. Ex.

HORNECKER, Miss Anna Oct 10, 1895
SEE ZOLLER, Mr

HORNECKER, Edwin Camp Point Jan 20, 1898
Edwin Hornecker and Miss Lula Allen were married last Wednesday.

HORNECKER, Josie Camp Point Jul 4, 1895
At the home of the bride, ½ mile south of town last Wednesday noon, the marriage of Miss Josie Hornecker and Melvin T. Hardin by Rev A.N. Simmonds.

HORNECKER, Miss Mary Elm Grove Feb 20, 1896
Mrs Herman Renschel went to Coatsburg last Tuesday to attend wedding of her niece, Miss Mary Hornecker.

HORNEY, Miss Kate Neighbors Oct 14, 1897
Dr William Six pleaded guilty in Sangamon Circuit Court to a charge of bigamy and sentenced to Chester Penitentiary, his latest wife was Miss Kate Horney, of near Barry, to whom he was married last spring. He had 10 or 12 wives located in Ind., Mo., Kan., Okla. and Texas.

HOSTETTER, Mr Fritz Dec 7, 1899
SEE CANNON, Miss Pearl

HOUGH, Mr Bert Feb 26, 1891
SEE WATKINS, Miss Lottie

HOUGH, Charles Sept 1888 Sep 15, 1898
Married at Emporia, Kansas, Charles Hough and Miss Emma Hoffman.

HOUGH, Miss Ella Apr 23, 1896
SEE BRYANT, W.E.

HOUGH, Mr Frank Jan 8, 1891
SEE RUTLEDGE, Miss Mollie

HOUGH, Frank E. Married Jan 8, 1891
At the home of brides parents, Mr and Mrs W.H. Rutledge, Jan 1st, 1891 by Rev E.W. Souders, Mr Frank E. Hough of Springfield and Mary S. Rutledge, of Clayton.

HOUGH, Harry Sep 15, 1892
SEE DAUGHERTY, Miss LaBert

HOUGH, Homer Jun 29, 1899
SEE BOWMAN, Sennie

HOUGH, Mr J.E. 5 Years Ago Sep 29, 1892
SEE LESTER, Miss Julia

HOUGH, J.E. Married May 6, 1897
Married at the home of brides father, Mr Jno. A. Smith of Pittsfield, Illinois at 4 PM Wednesday April 28th Mr J.E. Hough of Springfield and Miss Laura Smith, of Pittsfield by Rev George L. Snively. Groom is son of Mr and Mrs Geo. R. Hough of Clayton. Will live Springfield.

HOUGH, Miss Marguerite Locals Dec 13, 1894
Last Thursday eve about dusk at the Methodist parsonage, Rev J. Glick married, Miss Marguerite Hough, daughter of Mr and Mrs Geo. R. Hough and Jeptha E. Marrett.

HOUGH, Miss Nettie E. Local Oct 9, 1890
Cards are out announcing marriage of Miss Nettie E. Hough to Mr Sam S. Marrett at the home of brides father, Thursday eve.

HOUK, Miss Ida S. Brown County Dec 5, 1895
Squire Wallace married Miss Ida S. Houk of Schuyler County and Albert Knight of Pea Ridge at the court house last Wednesday.
HOUK, John Pea Ridge Aug 24, 1899
Married in our vicinity Sunday eve, John Houk and Miss Addie Birkee, will live with Mr Long.
HOUSE, Miss Maude May 6, 1897
SEE JOHNSON, Roy
HOUSLER, Mr Mar 30, 1899
SEE FRANCIS, Mrs Margaret
HOWARD, Jennie Gilbirds Feb 11, 1897
SEE BRADFORD, John M.
HOWE, Miss Ella B. Jun 24, 1897
SEE MCMURRAY, Fred M.
HOWE, Miss Lizzie Dec 22, 1892
SEE BELL, Chas.
HOWE, Miss Mary Feb 13, 1896
SEE BELL, John
HOWE, Miss Mattie Camp Point Apr 20, 1899
Gabe Coleman and Miss Mattie Howe were to have been married last Wednesday eve, but Mattie decided that she would not be married and so she wasn't.
HOWELL, Miss Nellie Nov 23, 1893
SEE OBRIEN, Mart
HOXIE, Miss Lucie B. Oct 16, 1890
SEE RUTLEDGE, J.F.
HUBBARD, S.A. Little Brindle Oct 13, 1898
Examiner, Mt Sterling Mr S.A. Hubbard left last night for Redfield, Iowa where at next Tuesday noon he will be married to Miss Phebe, daughter of Prof H.E. Hammond. Will live this city.
HUBER, Miss Ella Jan 26, 1893
SEE LANDON, Ed
HUBNER, Miss Lena Elm Grove Jan 6, 1898
Marriage license issued to Miss Lena Hubner and Chas. Marsh.
HUCKLEBURY, Miss Stella Apr 29, 1897
SEE SELBY, Elmer T.
HUDDLESON, Albert B. Little Brindle News Mar 14, 1895
Mr Albert B. Huddleson and Miss Myrtle E. Myers, all of Adams County were married in this city last Wednesday afternoon by Mart Brooks, Esq.
HUDDLESON, Mrs Rosa 5 Years Ago Sep 15, 1892
Mrs Rosa Huddleson married Mr Valentine Sevier.
HUDDLESTON, Jesse Oct 17, 1895
SEE BAKER, Mrs Mary L.
HUDDLESTON, Leon W. Mar 15, 1900
SEE BOLINGER, Miss Clara
HUDSON, Elmer Local Jul 22, 1897
Elmer Hudson and Mabel H. Castle, of Camp Point, have been licensed to wed.
HUDSON, Elmer All Over the County Jul 29, 1897
Elmer Hudson was married to Miss Mabel H. Castle Tuesday, July 20th at the home of G.F. Roberts, Paul H. Castle officiating.
HUDSON, Miss Mollie Dec 22, 1898
SEE ADAMS, Isaac
HUDSON, Orvas Camp Point Apr 12, 1900
Orvas Hudson and Miss Violet Stump were married Tuesday eve of last week by Rev McNabb.

HUFFMAN, Mr Al | Concord | Dec 4, 1890
Mr Al Huffman of Big Neck and Miss Ella Anderson, of Kellerville, were married at Warsaw Thanksgiving Day.

HUFFMAN, Mr Albert | Local | Dec 4, 1890
Mr Albert Huffman and Miss Ella Anderson were married at Warsaw on Thursday.

HUFFMAN, Mr Allie | Local | Feb 21, 1895
It is reported that the marriage of Mr Allie Huffman, of Kellerville and a lady in Missouri will occur this week at the lady's home.

HUFFMAN, Elmer | Neighborhood News | Sep 21, 1893
Married, near Summer Hill, last Wednesday eve, Mr Elmer Huffman to Miss Emma Yeldell, "Pike County Democrat"

HUGHES, Mr | 5 Years Ago | Apr 28, 1892
SEE BAKER, Miss Nora

HUGHES, Miss Ada | Oct 15, 1891
SEE MCFARLAND, Thos.

HUGHES, Miss Amanda L. | 10 Years Ago | Feb 12, 1891
Miss Amanda L. Hughes married Dr Ham Davidson of Kellerville. Both are now gone to thier long home.

HUGHES, Mr Andy | Little Brindle News | Feb 13, 1896
Siloam Herald Mr Andy Hughes and Miss Maggie Lauber were married at Fairview Church Wednesday of last week by Rev Lutener.

HUGHES, Benjamin O. | Local | Nov 23, 1893
Marriage of Benjamin O. Hughes and Miss Jessie Hoffman, both of vicinity of Kellerville occurred Sunday.

HUGHES, Columbus | 10 Years Ago | Feb 15, 1894
Columbus Hughes and Miss Emma Lou Davidson were married at Kellerville.

HUGHES, Cornelius | Feb 1884 | Feb 2, 1899
Married Mr Cornelius Hughes and Miss Emma Davison at Kellerville. They went to Iowa to live, but since returned to this county and live near Kellerville.

HUGHES, David A. | Feb 13, 1896
SEE LAWBER, Miss Maggie A.

HUGHES, Desta | Nov 18, 1897
SEE RENAKER, Chas. A.

HUGHES, Miss Dorothy | Jun 18, 1896
SEE DAVIDSON, Guy L.

HUGHES, Edward | Hazel Dell | Mar 28, 1895
Edward Hughes and Gertrude Hoffman, both of Kellerville, were married in Mt Sterling last Wednesday, the 20th. He is son of William Hughes of Concord. Will live Kellerville.

HUGHES, Miss Emma A. | Jan 5, 1899
SEE BARNES, John A.

HUGHES, Eva | May 10, 1894
SEE HENDRICKS, T.J.

HUGHES, G.W. | 10 Years Ago | Feb 11, 1892
SEE WOMELSDORFF, Mrs Mary

HUGHES, Geo. | 5 Years Ago | Sep 4, 1890
Geo. Hughes and Mrs Kate Bricker were married by Rev Wilken. They reside in McKee.

HUGHES, Geo. | 10 Years Ago | Sep 12, 1895
Geo. Hughes and Mrs Kate Bucker were married at Kellerville.

HUGHES, Geo. W. | Little Brindle | Mar 4, 1897
Mt Sterling Examiner Mr Geo. W. Hughes and Mrs Lilly Belle Baker, nee Smith, both of Kellerville, Adams County were married at his home in this city by Elder Chas. Laycock, Thursday afternoon.

HUGHES, George — City Brevities — Jun 23, 1898
Married in Quincy Tuesday of last week, Mr George Hughes of McKee township and Mrs Mary A. Dumpkin, of Ellington township. Will farm in McKee.

HUGHES, J.W. — Ancient History — Mar 18, 1897
February 1882 Married J.W. Hughes and Cordelia Womelsdorff.

HUGHES, Miss Mary — Local — Nov 9, 1899
Miss Mary Hughes of this place and Mr Bloomberg of Rockford, Illinois were married Wednesday at 7 PM at Rock Island, Illinois. Groom is traveling salesman for some Chicago house. Bride is sister of Mr John Hughes the telegraph man of this city.

HUGHES, Neal — January 1884 — Jan 12, 1899
Married, Mr Neal Hughes and Miss Emma Davison, at Kellerville.

HUGHES, Mr Ol. — Little Brindle — Apr 16, 1896
Mound Beacon Light At his home on Sunday afternoon Rev Lowe married Mr Ol Hughes and Miss Etta Leapley, both of Kellerville.

HUGHES, Mr Preston — Dec 4, 1890
SEE BAKER, Miss Anna

HUGHES, Wm — Elm Grove — Oct 22, 1891
Married last Thursday October 15th at 5 PM, Mr Wm Hughes and Miss Nettie Balfour at home of brides father.

HULETTE, Miss Ida — Oct 2, 1890
SEE ELLIOTT, J.B.

HULL, Cyrus — Dec 1, 1892
SEE STAUFFER, Miss Susie

HULL, Mr and Mrs Granville — Personal — Jun 10, 1897
Mrs Henry Hull went to Carthage to a family reunion to celebrate 44th wedding anniversary of Granville Hull and wife. All the children seven girls and three boys were there--so says the "Gazette".

HULSE, Mrs Martha — Oct 4, 1894
SEE SOLOMON, Dempsey N.

HUMKE, Edward — Nov 24, 1898
SEE MILLER, Fanny

HUMPHREY, Miss Angie — 5 Years Ago — Feb 25, 1892
Miss Angie Humphrey was married to Mr E.D. Anderson.

HUMPHREY, Mr and Mrs W.D. — Golden Wedding — Dec 18, 1890
Mr and Mrs W.D. Humphrey of Jacksonville celebrated their golden wedding the other day, surrounded by their descendants, to the 4th generation. They were married at Springfield by Elder J.P. Henderson of Columbia, Missouri. They settled in Springfield.

HUNSAKER, Columbus C. — Local — Dec 3, 1896
Columbus C. Hunsaker was married January 15th last at Racine, Wisc. to Miss Eunice D. Brents, daughter of Mrs S.D. Brents the proprietress of the Park House at Clayton.

HUNSAKER, Mrs Eunice — Married — Mar 16, 1899
Married in the parlors of the Palace Hotel, Tuesday, March 7th at 2 PM by Rev D.C. Bradford, Chaplain of the House of Representatives, Samuel Nickerson of Bloomington and Mrs Eunice Hunsaker, daughter of Mrs Brents, Clayton, Illinois. Mrs Brents, mother of the bride, of Bloomington attended. This is second marriage of both parties. Groom is in real estate business in Bloomington. Will live Bloomington. "Springfield Register"

HUNSAKER, Eunice Brents and Columbus C. — Jan 5, 1899
City Brevities Among divorces signed by Judge Broody, Saturday was that of Eunice Brents-Hunsaker vs Columbus C. Hunsaker.

HUNT, James — Ill State News — Jan 25, 1894
Married at Jacksonville, James Hunt and Mrs Nellie Walters. Groom is 33 years old and this is his 5th marriage. Two wives died and seperated from two. Bride has also been married before.

HUTCHINSON, Effie May 6, 1897
SEE BOWLING, Albert

HUTCHINSON, Henry Sep 28, 1893
SEE REEDER, Miss Mattie

HYMAN, Capt J.M. and Nora County News May 18, 1899
John M. Hyman yesterday filed suit for divorce from his wife Nora J. Hyman. "Whig"

IMBODEN, Mr and Mrs John Ill State News Dec 28, 1893
Golden wedding of Mr and Mrs John Imboden, residents of Decatur since 1855, each 76 years old was celebrated a few days ago.

IMBRIE, George Feb 13, 1896
SEE SMITH, Miss Nora

INCE, Miss Mellie All Over the County May 13, 1897
Quincy Journal Mrs E.A. Ince and daughter Bessie have returned home from Cincinnati, Ohio, accompanied by Miss Pine of that city, who will attend Miss Mellie Ince at her wedding June 1st to Walter H. Bennett.

INCE, Miss Nellie Carolyn All Over the County Jun 3, 1897
Whig Married at Vermont St. Baptist Church Quincy last eve, Miss Nellie Carolyn Ince, daughter of Rev E. Armstrong Ince D.D. pastor of the church and Mr Walter Henry Bennett, a young member of the Adams County bar.

INGLES, Miss Lureno Personal Oct 30, 1890
Mr and Mrs T.G. Steven's received invitations to wedding of their niece, Miss Lureno Ingles to Mr R.L. Thompson, both of Lexington, Ky November 11th.

INGRAM, Miss Annie Dec 5, 1895
SEE JARVIS, John

INMAN, Miss Frona Local Dec 7, 1893
SEE COGBURN, John

INMAN, Sophronia E. Local Dec 7, 1893
SEE COGBURN, John N.

IRION, Rev Jonathon Ill Brevities Oct 25, 1894
Rev Jonathon Irion and Catherine A. Koch were married at Quincy.

IRWIN, Miss Ora M. Neighbors Jun 30, 1898
Wednesday eve, June 25th, occurred the marriage of Miss Ora M. Irwin and George Griggs, of Bowen. Mr Griggs is in business at Adrian and they will live at that place.

IVENS, Madie Dec 27, 1894
SEE POORMAN, Charlie

JACKMAN, Mr and Mrs John A. Ill State News Nov 30, 1893
Golden wedding of Mr and Mrs John A. Jackman of Bloomington was celebrated a few days since by a family reunion and reception.

JACKSON, Miss Eva Dec 25, 1890
SEE DAVIDSON, Mr I.T. "Gube"

JACKSON, Miss Hattie Feb 18, 1897
SEE HOBBS, Mr Jab

JACKSON, Joseph Neighborhood News Jun 29, 1893
At Quincy July 4th Joseph Jackson a Quincy grocery clerk and Miss Ella Milton of Carthage will be married and make their honeymoon trip in a baloon that will be in charge of Ivy Baldwin.

JACOBS, Mr Edw. Nov 29, 1894
SEE WILLARD, Miss Rose

JAMES, Chas. Jun 15, 1899
SEE SAMMIS, Miss Fay

JAMISON, T.W. Little Brindle News Apr 2, 1896
T.W. Jamison of Clayton and Emma Mikesell of Pea Ridge were licensed to wed today and wedded.

JAMISON, Thomas Pea Ridge Apr 2, 1896
Thomas Jamison, of Clayton and Miss Emma Mikesell of Pea Ridge were married at the court house in Mt Sterling Wednesday of last week. Will live Clayton.
JANSEN, Chris Apr 12, 1894
SEE NEELAND, Miss Fannie
JARVIS, Clay Local Sep 14, 1899
Married, Mr Clay Jarvis and Miss Norine Turner during the week of Settlers meeting at Mt Sterling. They think of going west to make a home.
JARVIS, Henry Personal Aug 24, 1899
Henry Jarvis and bride, nee Loretta Robenau left Sunday for Galesburg after visiting his parents in Concord. They had been to Niagara for their wedding trip.
JARVIS, John Brown County Dec 5, 1895
Married in front of the "Old Flag" by Rev P.L. Turner of Pike County, John Jarvis and Miss Annie Ingram, both of Chambersburg.
JARVIS, Leslie Little Brindle Apr 20, 1899
Married at home of brides parents in Versailles, Illinois, Thursday eve April 6th, Mr Leslie Jarvis and Miss Villa Hibbs by Rev W.N. Rutledge bride is daughter of Mr and Mrs Wm Hibbs of this place.
JEFFERSON, Homer Local Jul 16, 1896
News reached Clayton some days ago of marriage of Mr Homer Jefferson, son of a former Claytonian, Mr Hiram Jefferson to a young lady at Savoy, Texas.
JEFFERSON, Mr T. Elmer May 28, 1891
SEE PEVEHOUSE, Miss Venia
JENNINGS, Miss Della Mar 30, 1893
SEE BOOKMAN, Richard
JEWELL, Miss Gertie All Over the County Apr 29, 1897
Miss Gertie Jewell and lon Boger were married at Camp Point Wednesday.
JEWELL, Gertrude Apr 29, 1897
SEE BOGER, Lawrence
JEWETT, Amanda E. Dec 21, 1899
SEE CHAPMAN, Henderson S.
JIMISON, Thos. W. 5 Years Ago Jan 8, 1891
Thos. W. Jimison and Jennie McCullom were married.
JOHANNES, Charles Oct 13, 1898
SEE MENKE, Miss Frances
JOHNSON, Miss 5 Years Ago Oct 16, 1890
SEE NEWNAN, Elder
JOHNSON, Miss Ada Local Oct 5, 1899
Cards are out by Mr and Mrs S. Johnson of Quincy formerly of the Hotel Hampton of this city announcing marriage of their daughter, Miss Ada, to Mr Ezra Crane who has been mail clerk on the Keokuk branch several months. Wedding will be Monday the 16th inst at Quincy.
JOHNSON, Miss Adah Oct 19, 1899
SEE CRANE, Ezra
JOHNSON, Amanda County News Aug 3, 1899
SEE SMITH, Richard
JOHNSON, Miss Anna Pine Grove Oct 21, 1892
Married, at the home of brides parents, Miss Anna Johnson and Mr Dell Rawson Tuesday eve the 18th. Will live in house vacated by George O. Johnson.
JOHNSON, Charles Little Brindle Feb 9, 1899
Mounds Correspondence of February 2: Married, Charles Johnson and Miss Lena Lucas this eve at 8 PM at home of bride. Groom is farmer of Pea Ridge township, by Rev Vandervoort of Clayton.

JOHNSON, Geo. Ancient History Feb 25, 1897
January 1892: Geo. Johnson and Ella Long were married at Pea Ridge.

JOHNSON, Geo. O. Local Dec 31, 1891
Miss Long, daughter of J.H. Long of Pea Ridge was married to Mr Geo. O. Johnson at high 12 Tuesday.

JOHNSON, Harry T. Neighborhood News Apr 25, 1895
Marriage out of the ordinary was celebrated at Keokuk Wednesday, the contracting parties being, Harry T. Johnson, a negro, to Miss Gertrude B. Smith, white, of Groveland, Illinois. They met while both were employed at the National Hotel in Peoria.

JOHNSON, Hettie Jan 4, 1900
SEE HARRISON, Cyrus

JOHNSON, John S. Jul 5, 1894
SEE BAKER, Emma L.

JOHNSON, Lew Pea Ridge Oct 25, 1894
Mr Lew Johnson and Miss Rosson were married Tuesday of last week. Mr Johnson bought a lot of household goods and will go to housekeeping.

JOHNSON, Mr Pink Pea Ridge Sep 28, 1899
Mr Pink Johnson and Miss Pearl Crawford were married at Mound Wednesday eve September 20th.

JOHNSON, Roy Local May 6, 1897
Siloam will have a wedding today. Mr Roy Johnson, the restaurant man at Siloam and Miss Maude HOuse, daughter of Mr J.B. House.

JOHNSTON, Miss Jennie City Brevities Jun 1, 1899
Marriage of Miss Jennie Johnston of this city to Dr Lewis C. Messner of Potomac, Illinois will occur next Thursday 8th inst at home of Mr and Mrs J.E. Kirkpatrick. Dr Messner is a retired physician and now engaged in banking.

JOHNSTON, Miss Jennie Wedded Jun 17, 1899
Thursday eve at home of Mr and Mrs J.E. Kirkpatrick occurred the wedding of Miss Jennie Johnston, sister of Mrs Kirkpatrick to Dr Lewis C. Messner of Potomac, Illinois by Rev Beadles and Rev Slagle. Will live in Potomac. Present were, Mrs Johnston, Jas Johnston of Breckenridge, Missouri, mother and brother of the bride, Mrs Layton and Mrs Messner of Potomac, Dr Beadles and wife of Quincy, Wm T. Kirkpatrick of Durango, Colorado.

JOHNSTON,Miss Jennie M. Local Jun 28, 1894
Cards received by Mrs Mattie A. Harbison telling of marriage of her niece, Miss Jennie M. Johnston, who visited here three summers ago, to Samuel A. Matthews, June 19th in New York City.

JOHNSTON, Miss Margaret Sep 8, 1892
SEE KIRKPATRICK, Mr J.E. "Everett"

JOHNSTONE, Miss Kate Personal Oct 3, 1895
L.P. and Mrs Hubbs have gone to Warsaw to attend wedding of Miss Kate Johnstone who has frequently visited them here. The groom is Mr Elsie McClure of Carthage.

JONES, Addie Montgomery Jan 26, 1893
SEE LUKER, Joseph H.

JONES, Bruce Oct 31, 1895
SEE MAY, Rosa

JONES, Ella Jun 25, 1891
SEE FERRIS, Elmer

JONES, Mrs Ida B. Jun 28, 1894
SEE GARNER, Dr W.A.

JONES, Miss Mamie May 3, 1900
SEE STOUT, Oliver S.

JONES, Mary E. Mar 12, 1896
SEE FRANKS, Preston M.

JONES, W.H. Apr 24, 1890
SEE MONTGOMERY, Miss Addie
JONES, Wm F. Neighborhood News Apr 13, 1893
Wm F. Jones and Miss Cora Moorley were married at home of brides parents in Camp Point Thursday eve, March 30th by Elder O. Dilley.
JONKIN, Henry Deis Elm Grove Jun 9, 1892
Henry Deis Jonkin married Anna Fruhling last Saturday eve by Rev Darrow of the Trinity Lutheran Church of Golden at his home.
JONSON, Miss Rebecca Feb 6, 1896
SEE DAVIS, Robert
JORDAN, Rev C.L. Little Brindle Dec 28, 1893
Rev C.L. Jordan of Beverly and Miss Thyra Long, daughter of Mr and Mrs Andrew Long, who live near Mound Station were married by Rev E.H. Lugg at noon last Wednesday. Rev Jordan is pastor of ME Church at Beverly.
JOSEPH, Miss Eva May 10, 1900
SEE BAILY, Alex
JOSEPH, Miss Fannie Personal May 27, 1897
Miss Fannie Joseph of Camp Point has married Mr Clay Piper of Mt Sterling. License was issued Wednesday.
JOSEPH, Miss Florence Dec 1, 1898
SEE DEHAVEN, Will
JOSLIN, Joseph Little Brindle Oct 20, 1898
Democrat Message, Mt Sterling: Wednesday afternoon Rev F.P. Douglas was called to home of Dr W.G. Gray to marry Joseph Joslin of Paloma and Mrs Mary Fields, of Fowler, Adams County. Groom is 70 years old and bride is well into 60. Will live Paloma.
JOSLIN, Miss Minnie Our Own Bailiwick Oct 25, 1894
Cards are out for wedding of Miss Minnie Joslin to Robert J. McCray at 6 PM Wednesday October 24th. "Golden New Era"
JUDY, Mark Apr 27, 1893
SEE BURNETT, Miss Carrie
JUETT, Amanda E. Dec 28, 1899
SEE CHAPMAN, Henderson S.
JULIAN, Miss Anna 10 Years Ago Dec 17, 1891
Miss Anna Julian married Charles D. Fullen at Mt Pleasant, Iowa.
JULIAN, Mrs Loretta Local Dec 31. 1891
A telegram from Carthage to St Louis Globe Democrat announces the marriage of Mrs Loretta Julian to Mr S.N. Wagoner on the 23rd inst.
JULIAN, Mrs Loretta Jan 7, 1892
SEE WAGGONER, Mr J.N.
JULIAN, Mrs Rettie Ancient History Feb 25, 1897
SEE WAGGONER, J.N.
JURGEN, John J. Brown County Apr 5, 1900
Marriage license: John J. Jurgens, Damon and Mattie Eckhoff, Damon.
JURKENS, John Damon Apr 12, 1900
At 4 PM Sunday Mr John Jurkens and Miss Mattie Eckhoff were married at the parsonage of the Lutheran Church by Rev Gerken.
KADESKI, Leo.J. May 4, 1899
SEE DOERR, Miss Thea
KALLASH, Miss Anna Dec 8, 1898
SEE COBB, Archibald
KALLASH, Harvey Little Brindle Sep 9, 1897
Brown County Republican: Mr Adolph Kallash of Elkhorn township is having trouble with his younger son, Harvey, age 17 yeasr, who became infatuated with a Miss Nellie Tucker, age over 20 years. Mr and Mrs Kallash objected and took son to the city to put him in reform school, but he told father he had been married in Pittsfield day before. They took the boy home to reconcile.

KAUFMAN, Isaac Mar 30, 1899
SEE MEYER, Miss Bell

KEENER, Chas. C. and Nellie Neighbor May 7, 1896
At Chicago a divorce was granted Mrs Nellie Keener from her husband, Chas. C. Keener. Formerly of Meredosia.

KEITH, Esq. C.W. and wife Little Brindle Apr 22, 1897
Mt Sterling Examiner: Last Thursday, the 8th inst, occurred the golden wedding anniversary of Esq. C.W. Keith and wife.

KELLER, Mrs Carrie Personal Aug 6, 1891
Mrs Carrie Keller, nee Carrie Bostic, with her two children are here visiting her parents. Her sister, Mrs Nellie Price arrived Saturday. Frank Bostic was married to a nice Kansas City girl lately and his brother Fred is there working with Frank for the Medical Springs Company as a driver of a water wagon. Frank has had that job two or three years and receives good wages.

KELLEY, Miss Allie May 31, 1894
SEE AMEN, Philip

KELLY, Miss Allie May 3, 1894
SEE AMEN, Philip

KELLY, Patrick J. Mar 8, 1894
SEE MCLAIN, Miss Mattie C.

KELSO, Artha May 4, 1893
SEE WELTON, C.W.

KELTZ, Josephine Oct 22, 1896
SEE BETZER, Soloa

KEMP, Mr Aldo Personal Apr 6, 1893
Mrs Jos. Cannon returned from Bowen Wednesday where she visited the family of David Kemp and to attend the marriage of their son, Mr Aldo Kemp to Miss Nellie Tarr, both of Bowen.

KEMP, Miss Eva Neighborhood News Nov 1, 1894
The Bowen Chronicle says: Married, Miss Eva, daughter of our friends Mr and Mrs David Kemp of Maple Grove from near Bowen to Fred Barnet also of Bowen.

KEMP, Wm T. Dec 19, 1895
SEE WILLIAMS, Miss Margaret

KENDALL, Otis E. Local Sep 20, 1894
Married at Methodist Church 8 PM Tuesday, Mr Otis E. Kendall and Miss Ada Terrill. Mr C.E. Laughlin was best man. Brode attended by Mrs Anna Flasner, Miss Kendall, sister of groom and Miss Jennie Johnston by Rev J. Glick. Will live Clayton.

KENDRICK, Fred W. and Minnie J. Little Brindle Sep 24, 1896
Divorce was granted to Fred W. Kendrick from Minnie J.

KENDRICK, Jennie M. Local Sep 6, 1894
Clayton friends received cards which read: Married August 30th 1894, Jennie M. Kendricks to James L. Seeley. At home 340 W. 35th St. New York City September 1st to 12th 1894. Mr Seeley is the young gentleman who visited Miss Kendrick here a year or so ago. They became acquainted as members of the Broadball Theatrical Company.

KENNEY, Miss Ella M. Jan 4, 1894
SEE NEWHOUSE, John C.

KERLIE, John 5 Years Ago Feb 18, 1892
SEE WRIGHT, Miss Delia

KERN, Catherine Adams County News Nov 30, 1893
SEE STRICKLER, Wesley

KERN, Jake and wife Local Dec 28, 1899
Uncle Jake Kern and wife celebrated their 49th wedding anniversary Friday.

KERSHAW, Mr and Mrs John — City Brevities — Aug 4, 1898
Friends of Mr and Mrs John Kershaw of Manchester, England, who visited Mr and Mrs John Chapman some years ago, will be interested to hear they celebrated their golden wedding anniversary July 11th last.

KESTNER, Miss Lizzie — Feb 16, 1899
SEE VERING, William A.

KICKEHOFEL, Miss Emma — Mar 15, 1900
SEE CASTLE, Harry

KILBOURNE, Miss Georgia — Jun 18, 1891
SEE SCHOFIELD, Gen. John M.

KIMBALL, Miss — Mar 29, 1894
SEE FORD, Ed

KIMBALL, Mrs Margaret J. — May 24, 1900
SEE PHILLIPS, Green

KIMBOUGH, Mr — Mar 16, 1893
SEE WILLIAMS, Miss Cora

KIMREY, Mrs Sarah — April 1890 — May 17, 1900
SEE MCCAULEY, Chas.

KINCHELOE, Hon C.F. — All Over the County — Feb 11, 1897
Quincy Journal: Hon C.F. Kincheloe is engaged, the marriage will take place in March at Loraine where the bride elect lives. A Quincy dressmaker is now at work on the trousseau.

KINCHELOE, Hon Chas. F. — All Over the County — Apr 22, 1897
Coatsburg Review: The wedding of Hon Chas. F. Kincheloe and Miss Flo Michael was Sunday in the Christian Church at Loraine.

KINDHEART, Miss — Aug 10, 1899
SEE GARNER, Lew

KIPP, Edward — Supplement — Apr 18, 1895
Our Own Bailiwick Edward Kipp and Miss Augusta Taylor were married this afternoon by Rev Shaw at his parsonage. Guy Lewis was best man and Miss M. Holske bridesmaid. Will live 639 Jefferson St. Bride is from Liberty. Groom is a member of the Markley Shoe Company. "Herald, 12th"

KIRBY, Miss Rebecca — Nov 12, 1891
SEE WEST, William B.

KIRBY, Thomas — Feb 27, 1890
SEE GRIFFITH, Miss Hester

KIRBY, Thomas J. — Local — Feb 20, 1890
Thomas J. Kirby and Miss Hattie Griffith, of Pea Ridge were married last week.

KIRKPATRICK, Miss Alice — Locals — Mar 5, 1891
Marriage of Miss Alice Kirkpatrick, daughter of Mr and Mrs M.B. Kirkpatrick to Mr William H. Smith at the home of Mr and Mrs John Cannon at Bowen on Sunday February 22nd 1891 by Rev Hobbs, pastor of Cong'l Church at Bowen. Mr Smith is a compositor on the "Enterprise".

Kirkpatrick,Ella Emma — Local — Oct 10, 1895
Cards are out for marriage of Ella Emma Kirkpatrick, daughter of Mr and Mrs Kirkpatrick to Mr Oscar Gillis Mull Tuesday eve October 17th at Grace ME Church Clayton.

KIRKPATRICK, Ellsworth — Sep 11, 1890
SEE STOUT, Miss Florence

KIRKPATRICK, Frank — Personal — Nov 29, 1894
Frank Kirkpatrick dropped in on us Friday from the far west. He had been to Chicago with a train of cattle from their ranches in Wyoming and stopped by Clayton to see his old home and friends. He went to Wyoming as a boy, 11 years old. He is now a full grown man, has whiskers and a wife since last spring. He is a typical cowboy.

KIRKPATRICK, Mr J.E. "Everett" Married Sep 8, 1892
Reception given by Mrs Mary Kirkpatrick in honor of Mr and Mrs J.E. Kirkpatrick Thursday September 8th the ceremony which united Everett and Miss Margaret Johnston occurred at Brackenridge, Missouri the home of the bride Wednesday.

KIRKPATRICK, Mrs Maude and Webb Little Brindle
Mrs Maude Kirkpatrick was granted a decree of divorce at Fargo, N.D. from her husband, Webb Kirkpatrick. Both were formerly of this city.

KIRKPATRICK, Miss Neva Supplement Oct 26, 1893
7 PM this eve at Methodist Church will be the wedding of Mr Chester Logue and Miss Neva Kirkpatrick by Rev Glick. Reception Thursday at home of W.M. Logue.

KIRKPATRICK, Web Ancient History Feb 25, 1897
January 1886: Web Kirkpatrick married Miss Maude Anderson.

KIRTLEY, Rose Sep 10, 1896
SEE NEICE, James

KLEIN, Will Camp Point Feb 22, 1900
Last Thursday at 6:30 PM occurred the marriage of Will Klein and Miss Lulu Harris by Elder Dilley. Will live on a farm 4½ miles northeast of town.

KLETTKE, William G. Ill Brevities May 31, 1894
William G. Klettke and Miss Wilhelmina J. Halle were married at Quincy.

KLINE, Miss Bertha Feb 15, 1894
SEE BOOTH, Frank

KLOSTERMAN, Miss Amelia Dec 31, 1896
SEE ROWSEY, Lewis

KLOSTERMAN, Miss Lizzie Feb 19, 1891
SEE WANTLAND, Will

KNEELAND, Mr and Mrs C.W. Neighborhood News Jul 23, 1891
Mr and Mrs C.W. Kneeland at Griggsville celebrated their golden wedding July 4th. They have lived at Griggsville almost continuously for 50 years.

KNIGHT, Albert Dec 5, 1895
SEE HOUK, Miss Ida S.

KNIGHT, George J. Little Brindle Mar 18, 1897
Democrat Message: Licensed to wed, George J. Knight, of Pea Ridge age 25 and Ella Garner of Pea Ridge, age 19.

KNIGHT, Miss Hattie 5 Years Ago Sep 4, 1890
SEE BELLOMY, Dr W.T.

KNIGHT, Miss Jettie Apr 25, 1895
SEE GARNER, Mr

KNIGHT, Miss Josie North Pea Ridge Jan 2, 1890
Married, at the bride's home, Miss Josie Knight to John Garner, of Mounds.

KNIGHT, L.H. Little Brindle Jun 30, 1898
Republican: L.H. Knight, of Clayton, and Josie Clarkson, of Pine Grove, Illinois were married in this city by Squire Tom Wallace.

KNOWLES, George and Lilly E. Little Brindle Nov 23, 1893
Mrs Lilly E. wife of George Knowles, Cooperstown tried to commit suicide Sunday. It is reported her husband refuses to live with her is the reason. Married Feb 2, 1892. She is now living with her parents, Martin Clark and wife in this city. "Examiner"

KOCH, Elnora All Over the County Apr 1, 1897
Liberty Bell: Tuesday eve at the home of Mrs Marie Koch, in Columbus township, occurred the marriage of her daughter, Elnora, to Philip J. Deege.

KOHL, Miss Emma Jan 25, 1894
SEE BRENTS, T.H.

KRAMER, Miss Kate — Neighborhood News — Jan 15, 1891
Miss Kate Kramer, a suicide, was buried at Nauvoo the 6th inst. It was to have been her wedding day. On Dec. 30 Fredrick Bangor age 31 of Nauvoo, procured a license to marry Miss Kate Kramer, age 25 years, county clerk Scott, at Carthage received the marriage license by mail with the blank lines used by officiating minister or justice, unfiled. She took poison.

KROSS, John — Pine Grove — Dec 29, 1892
John Kross and Martha Shepard were married Friday at 5 PM by Rev WEst.

KUNTZ, Fred — 10 Years Ago — Nov 10, 1892
Fred Kuntz and Miss Laura Bartlett were married.

LAGUE, Nannie — November 1888 — Nov 3, 1898
SEE CLARK, Benjamin

LAMMA, Miss Laura — Jan 30, 1896
SEE WARE, Charlie

LANDES, Miss Alice — Pike County — Dec 12, 1895
Married at Pittsfield Tuesday afternoon, Miss Alice Landes, daughter of Perry Landes of Pittsfield House to Mr Chas. Shriver of Virden, Illinois.

LANDON, Ed — Camp Point — Jan 26, 1893
Ed Landon came from Chicago last week long enough to get married. Miss Ella Huber being the happy party.

LANE, William — Brown County — Jan 4, 1900
Licensed to wed since last issue of Examiner: William Lane of Damon and Bessie Stoneking of Damon.

LANGAN, Miss Kathryn — May 4, 1899
SEE REDMOND, Thomas

LANTICE, William — Camp Point — Feb 9, 1899
William Lantice and Mrs Matilda Cortney were married Wednesday eve of last week at 6 PM by Elder Dilley.

LANTZ, Joseph B. — Local — Aug 20, 1896
Marriage of Mr Joseph B. Lantz of Chicago and Miss Hattie B. Downing, of this place occurred at Chaddock College in Quincy last Friday by Rev Dr Baker. Joe (groom) lived with the Motters on and off for 3 years and Miss Downing also an attache of the Motter's for several years. Will live Chicago after October 1st.

LARKIN, Miss Addie — Jun 23, 1898
SEE REGAN, John F.

LARKIN, Miss Effie — Jun 15, 1893
SEE CURRY, Charles A.

LASHBROOK, Mr and Mrs — Pea Ridge — Nov 2, 1899
Mr and Mrs Ruby had for their guests Monday Mr and Mrs Lashbrook, of Cass County. They were lately married.

LASHER, Oliver — Little Brindle — May 5, 1898
Examiner of the 30th: County clerk issued a license for marriage to Mr Oliver Lasher and Mrs Barbara Tedrow, of Lee township, Thursday.

LAUBER, Miss Maggie — Feb 13, 1896
SEE HUGHES, Andy

LAUDERBACK, Miss — Elm Grove — Oct 18, 1894
SEE WRIGHT, Tommy

LAUGHLIN, Thos. B. — All Over the County — Jan 28, 1897
Liberty Bell: Mr Thos. B. Laughlin, the P.O. inspector who has relatives here, was married to Miss Myra Lowther at Chicago recently.

LAUGHLIN, William D. and Ida M. — Local — May 3, 1900
Mrs Ida M. Laughlin has filed for divorce against her husband, William D. Laughlin entitled to the June term of court, imcompatibility is assigned as a cause. Seperated a few weeks ago.

LAWBER, Miss Maggie A. | Our Own Bailiwick | Feb 13, 1896
January 29th at Fair View Church, 2½ miles northeast of Chestline, Miss Maggie A. Lawber and David A. Hughes of Chestline were married. Chestline Corr. Baylis Guide

LAWRENCE, Harry G. | Oct 5, 1893
SEE MEISSER, Miss Annie Mae

LEAPLEY, Miss Etta | Apr 16, 1896
SEE HUGHES, Mr Ol.

LEAPLEY, Giles H. | Brown County | Sep 14, 1899
Giles H. Leapley of Kellerville and Mattie A. Stauffer of Fish Hook were granted a license to wed yesterday.

LEASE, Miss Nora | Local | Oct 16, 1890
W.E. Lease is all broke up, his daughter, Miss Nora the joy of his heart, has married Frank W. Evans, formerly a barber in Rube Meats barber shop, without consent. For some time Frank has been working for Mr Lease in the feather renevator business. They went to Quincy on the AM train Monday and were married by Justice McDannold. A note was sent to the mother on the evening train. The note said they were going to Bolling Green, Missouri where they would board. Miss Lease is about 20 years old and was the main stay in the family, Mrs Lease having been an invalid for years. Mr Evans is about 33 years old.

LEE, Geo. F. | 5 Years Ago | Jul 21, 1892
SEE ALLEN, Miss Hattie

LEE, William H. | Brown County | Nov 16, 1899
Five more marriage licenses needed in Brown County to finish record book in use since Dec 1, 1877. First marriage license in book is that of William H. Lee of Mt Sterling 27 years old--occupation, clerk and Jennie Hanna of this 24 years old. They were married Dec 2, by J.C. Sargent at Methodist Minister. Mr and Mrs Lee are still residents of the county living near Mound, engaged in farming.

LEPPER, David N. | Personal | Jan 10, 1895
John Easum and wife went to Springfield last week to attend the China wedding anniversary of David N. Lepper and wife Wednesday eve.

LERHOFF, Antje J. | Dec 16, 1897
SEE FLESSNER, John W.

LESAGE, Miss Joann | 10 Years Ago | May 1, 1890
Miss Joann LeSage was married to Mr E.P. Bryant.

LESLIE, Frank | Feb 9, 1893
SEE WOOD, Miss Hettie

LESTER, J.M. | 5 Years Ago | Mar 5, 1891
SEE RUTLEDGE, Miss Flora

LESTER, Sam H. | Local | Jun 26, 1890
Clayton people were suprised to hear of marriage of Mr Sam H. Lester to Miss Kate Arenz of the Arenz family for whom the town of Arenzeville is named. S.H. has a tonsorial parlor at Beardstown. Jno. W. Lester and brother Dump, of this city and Mrs W.E. Farlow of Chicago went over Tuesday to attend the wedding on the afternoon of that day.

LESTER, S.H. | 10 Years Ago | Jun 27, 1895
S.H. Lester and Miss Kate Arenz were married.

LEWIS, Miss | Nov 7, 1895
SEE MCDOWELL, Moses

LEWIS, Betsey | Local | Sep 21, 1893
Monday, Betsey Lewis, colored, step daughter of Will Ross and about 17 years old and Henry McFaddon, also colored were married in Mt. Sterling.

LEWIS, H.J. | Jun 18, 1891
SEE PIERCE, Miss Jennie

LEWIS, Miss May "Minnie" Little Brindle Jan 25, 1894
Kansas City Star of 3rd inst says: Miss May Lewis of Mt Sterling, Illinois and Henry Sing a Chinese gambler of this city were married yesterday afternoon by Justice J.H. Worthen. Mrs Sing is deaf but by watching the speakers lips can carry on a conversation. The name of bride is given incorrectly in the star, the bride being Minnie, daughter of Wm B. Lewis of Mt Sterling.

LEWIS, Richard Oct 8, 1896
SEE HARBINS, Miss C.T.

LIERLE, Adella 5 Years Ago Feb 4, 1892
SEE LUCAS, John E.

LIERLE, Miss Bessie Personal Jan 20, 1898
Rev E.R. Lierle has gone to Norwalk, Iowa to visit relatives, will perform the marriage ceremony of his grandaughter, Miss Bessie Lierle, daughter of I.A. Lierle to Mr Willet.

LIERLY, Adella Ancient History Mar 18, 1897
SEE LUCAS, James E.

LIGGETT, Mrs Chas. S. Adams County News Jan 4, 1894
Postmaster received letter from Mrs Chas. S. Liggett of Trinidad, Colorado asking about Mr Liggett who says she is his wife and they have one child. Chas. L. is son of David Liggett of Camp Point left home many years ago and was fireman and locomotive engineer all over the west. Was home last winter for first time and while home married Miss Vadie Greenhalgh in March. In summer he went to Kansas leaving his wife at his fathers. He is supposed to be railroading in Kansas. His wife here does not believe story and her brother Ed Greenhalgh is looking for the truth. Postmaster received another letter dated December 28th from Mrs Charles Liggett, Trinidad, Colorado and says she has found her Charley Liggett and he is not the Camp Point Liggett at all. He is from Camden Point, Missouri and they are going to Los Angeles to live. Camp Point Journal

LIKES, Dolly Jan 19, 1899
SEE NIECE, Robert

LIKES, Lou Sep 26, 1895
SEE HENDRICKS, J.R.

LIKES, Robert County News Feb 8, 1900
In circuit clerks office today a petition for Robert Likes, asking the marriage entered into between himself and Flora Winget on Dec 5, 1877 in this county, be annulled. The woman also is known as Flora Curless. Likes is a J.P. near Chestline, this county, says: he lived with his wife until last August when he learned she was the wife of another, Wm Winget, by whom she had two children. Squire Likes gives Oct 14, 1858 as the date of his wife's first marriage which he claims had not been annulled by law or death at the time he married her. Journal "20th"

LIKES, Robert County News May 10, 1900
Judge Broady has signed a decree annulling the marriage of Robert Likes and Mrs Flora Winget this is the case of the couple after having lived together for a number of years, supposing themselves legally married, discovered that the first husband of the woman was still alive. There was no feeling in suit. Both thought this was the only honorable way out of a distressing difficulty.

LIMB, Jas. W. Dec 17, 1891
SEE SLADE, Miss Adella X.

LINDSAY, Miss Belle Jun 19, 1890
SEE HERBIG, Thomas

LINDSEY, Miss Elsie Oct 21, 1897
SEE MIKESELL, Harvey

LINDSEY, Rosa — Feb 7, 1895
SEE NORTON, Lee

LINK, Freda L. — Sep 28, 1893
SEE STOUT, Mr Wm S.

LINN, Miss Anna — Nov 26, 1896
SEE SMITH, Elmer E.

LINN, Charles W. — Dec 9, 1897
SEE GARDNER, Miss Nellie

LINN, Mr Ed — Local — Feb 12, 1891
Mr Ed Linn, son of Mr John Linn of Concord, was married to Miss [illegible] Linn of Oakland, Sangamon County Thursday of last week. We understand they will live on Mr Linn's farm in Morgan County.

LINN, Ed — Local — Feb 19, 1891
The wife of Mr Ed Linn was Miss Belle Lynn. He has rented the old Marrett farm and L.C. and Mrs Marrett will move to town.

LINN, Granville E. — Local — Feb 6, 1896
Marriage license issued Tuesday: Granville E. Linn of Clayton age 21 and Mary E. Yeldell of Clayton age 20.

LINN, John A. — Hazel Dell — Feb 13, 1896
Reception at Glenwood farm, home of John A. Linn Thursday for the groom and his bride. Among guests were Wm Briggs, grandfather of the groom.

LIRELY, Miss Alice — Feb 4, 1897
SEE DAVIDSON, Earl

LITTLE, John T. — Local — Oct 5, 1899
Cards are out announcing coming marriage of Mr John T. Little of Mt Sterling to Miss Julia Gross, daughter of Prof. and Mrs J.D. Gross of this city.

LITZ, Miss Nellie M. — Dec 3, 1896
SEE RIED, Leslie A.

LIVINGSTON, Miss Ida — Dec 20, 1894
SEE EARL, Ben T.

LIVINGSTON, Pearl — Jun 13, 1895
SEE HART, Charlie

LOGSDON, Lillie — Little Brindle — Apr 29, 1897
Lillie Logsdon and Charley F. Friday were married by Parson Madden Wednesday eve with permission from their mamma's.

LOGUE, Chester — Oct 26, 1893
SEE KIRKPATRICK, Miss Neva

LOGUE, Miss Leona — Wedding — Oct 1, 1891
Married at the home of W.M. Logue and wife north of the city Thursday eve of last week, the 24th ult, their daughter, Miss Leona to Mr Gordon Sargent by Rev Abner Clark of Astoria. Mr Sargent is one of our young business men. Will be at home in the property purchased by Mr Sargent opposite the home of T.C. Smith.

LOGUE, Mary — Local — Sep 11, 1890
Card announcing the marriage of Mary, daughter of J.C. and Mrs Logue of Central City, Nebraska to Mr W.M. Traver on the 2nd inst. Miss Mary will be remembered by many of Clayton young folks.

LOGUE, Wm M. — City Brevities — Oct 20, 1898
Mr Wm M. Logue and Miss Ellen Davis were married 37 years ago and celebrated Satruday.

LONG, Miss — Dec 31, 1891
SEE JOHNSON, Geo. O.

LONG, A.C. — Pea Ridge — Nov 23, 1893
Married, A.C. Long of this vicinity and Miss Sarah Hendricks from south of Mt Sterling Tuesday November 14th.

LONG, Albert — Mound Station — Sep 25, 1890
Albert Long and Miss Ella Gooley were married Thursday.

LONG, Miss Anna M. — Oct 30, 1890
SEE CAUGHLAN, Charles W.

LONG, Miss Carrie Anna — Little Brindle — Jun 29, 1899
Cards are out announc ing coming marriage of Miss Carrie Anna Long to Elmore Ellsworth Lowe, Tuesday June 27th at 4 PM at Mr and Mrs Jacob Long's home by William Lowe, of Kansas, a brother of the groom.

LONG, Chas. V. — Neighbors — Feb 17, 1898
At Beardstown, Chas. V. Long married Miss Maud A. Beard.

LONG, Miss Ella — Local — Jan 7, 1892
Married at Mr and Mrs John Long's December 29th, Miss Ella Long of Pea Ridge and Geo. Johnson on same place by Rev Crawford of Mounds at 12 o'clock.

LONG, Florence E. — Nov 16, 1899
SEE MONTGOMERY, George W.

LONG, Fred — Neighborhood News — Nov 30, 1893
At Hamilton, Fred Long was given the choice of marrying Miss Vina Looter or giving her $10. He decided to borrow the dollar for the license and they were married. "Bushnell Record"

LONG, Mr and Mrs J.M. — Mound Station — Nov 19, 1891
Silver wedding of Mr and Mrs J.M. Long at their home north of town last Friday.

LONG, Miss Thyra — Dec 28, 1893
SEE JORDAN, Rev C.L.

LOOMAN, John Henry — Jan 21, 1897
SEE CRAWFORD, Miss Rose L.

LOOTER, Miss Vina — Nov 30, 1893
SEE LONG, Fred

LOUDERBACK, Dan — Pea Ridge — Sep 15, 1892
Dan Louderback was married at high noon Sunday.

LOUDERBACK, Daniel — Little Brindle — Jun 1, 1899
License to marry was issued Tuesday to Daniel Louderback and Mary E. Webster, both of Pea Ridge.

LOUDERBACK, Miss Mary — Jan 9, 1896
SEE TAYLOR, George H.

LOUDERBACK, Nora — Mar 21, 1895
SEE WEBSTER, John

LOWE, Elmore Ellsworth — Jun 29, 1899
SEE LONG, Miss Carrie Anna

LOWE, W.E. — Sep 21, 1899
SEE WILLARD, Miss Carrie

LOWERY, Miss Dora — Nov 11, 1897
SEE CROMWELL, Joseph F.

LOWRY, Miss Dora — Local — Nov 11, 1897
Two young Clayton people went quietly to Mt Sterling last Thursday and were married, Miss Dora Lowry, daughter of J.F. Lowry and wife to Joseph F. Cromwell by Rev McCoy the Methodist clergyman.

LOWRY, Miss Hattie — Sept 1889 — Sep 7, 1899
SEE GRAY, Jas.

LOWRY, Miss Hattie Isabelle — Mar 1, 1894
SEE SCOTT, Calvin Warner

LOWTHER, Miss Myra — Jan 28, 1897
SEE LAUGHLIN, Thos. B.

LOYD, Miss Helen — Jan 15, 1891
SEE COLGATE, Mr John

LOYD, Miss Helen — 10 Years Ago — Jul 4, 1895
Miss Helen Loyd went to Dakota and later married Dick Colgate.

LOYD, John 5 Years Ago Apr 28, 1892
SEE WILTSE, Miss

LUBBEN, Anna Apr 8, 1897
SEE BEHRENS, Ulfert

LUCAS, Allen Married Oct 22, 1891
Married at the home of brides parents, Mr and Mrs J.H. Ratcliff, October 15th 1891 by Rev E.W. Souders, Allen Lucas of Mounds and Miss Mary P. Ratcliff of Clayton.

LUCAS, Chas. Local Jun 11, 1896
At Mounds, an elopement last Sunday, it seems that Chas. Lucas, the dry goods merchant procured a license in Mt Sterling on Saturday to marry Miss Bertha Amrine, daughter of J.H. Amrine without saying anything to parents. On Sunday AM the two met at Sunday school and left for Mt Sterling. Some one told parents who raced after them but the couple were already married at the home of Elmer Stokes before parents arrived.

LUCAS, Mr D.M. Oct 1883 Oct 27, 1898
Married, Mr D.M. Lucas and Miss Hattie Ratcliff.

LUCAS, Mrs Ida M. 5 Years Ago Aug 25, 1892
Mrs Ida M. Lucas married Mr Jas. L. Roy.

LUCAS, James E. Ancient History Mar 18, 1897
February 1887 Married James E. Lucas and Adella Lierly at Mound.

LUCAS, John E. 5 Years Ago Feb 4, 1892
John E. Lucas and Adella Lierle were married.

LUCAS, Miss Lena Feb 9, 1899
SEE JOHNSON, Charles

LUCAS, William Little Brindle Sep 23, 1897
Mound Correspondent to Democrat Message: Mr William Lucas and Miss Lizzie McPhail were married by Rev J.F. Williams Wednesday night at the brides home.

LUKER, Mr and Mrs Locals Dec 14, 1899
SEE SELLS, Mr and Mrs Peter

LUKER, Joseph H. Luker-Jones Jan 26, 1893
Married at the home of J.L. Staker at 7 Pm Tuesday by Rev E.W. Souders, Addie Montgomery Jones of Kansas City, Missouri and Joseph H. Luker of Columbus, Ohio. Left on train for home of Major and Mrs Montgomery in Kansas City today.

LUMMIS, Mr James Mar 23, 1893
SEE ZINN, Miss Ida

LUTHER, Mr J. Apr 26, 1894
SEE RAMEY, Miss Minnie

LYBARGER, Mr and Mrs Solomon G. Ill State News Nov 1, 1894
The 50th wedding anniversary of Mr and Mrs Solomon G. Lybarger was celebrated at their home at Astoria, Fulton County.

LYNN, Belle Local Feb 19, 1891
SEE LINN, Ed

LYON, Miss Emma Sep 7, 1893
SEE HATCH, Dr.

MACGAUGHEY, Rev John Allen May 6, 1897
SEE GIVLER, Miss Jessie

MADDOX, John Sep 12, 1895
SEE BRIGGS, Mrs Catherine and B.F.

MAIN, Miss Lena Jan 5, 1899
SEE STAATS, Eugene A.

MAIRS, Mary O. Mar 26, 1891
SEE CLEMONS, Eugene

MAIS, Miss Rose Oct 4, 1894
SEE SWERINGER, Chet

MALCOMBER, Mary E. 5 Years Ago Jan 26, 1893
Mary E. Malcomber married Samuel Camp in Quincy.

MANARD, Miss Norah E. Mar 23, 1899
SEE DONLEY, Anderson and Jack

MANHOLLAND, Eunice Oakwood Jan 9, 1890
C. Hoke and wife attended the wedding of his niece, Eunice Manholland New Years Day.

MANLEY, Miss Alice B. Jul 16, 1896
SEE SMITH, Vincent V.

MANN, Mr Pea Ridge Feb 27, 1890
Married at 10 AM on Tuesday, Mr Mann and Mrs Nancy Elace.

MANN, Mr and Mrs Geo. D. Personal Oct 3, 1895
Mr and Mrs Wm Shank attended the silver anniversary of Mr and Mrs Geo. D. Mann at Carthage last week.

MANNY, Walter I. Jun 24, 1897
The expected wedding of Walter I. Manny the young state's attorney of Brown County took place at Mt Sterling Wednesday when he was married to Miss Grace L. Webber of the Capitol of Little Brindle, by Rev Dr E. Armstrong Ince of Quincy.

MARLIN, Mrs C.E. Personal Sep 15, 1892
Mrs C.E. Marlin of Orafino, Frontier County Nebraska arrived to visit her parents, Thomas Shockley and wife. Eight years ago a correspondence between Miss Shockley and Mr Marlin resulted in him inviting her to go to Nebraska and become his wife.

MARRETT, Jeptha E. Dec 13, 1894
SEE HOUGH, Miss Marguerite

MARRETT, Louis Cass and Emma F. City Brevities May 4, 1899
Divorce case of Emma F. Marrett versus Louis Cass Marrett was taken up by Judge Broady Saturday AM. Was not concluded that day and was taken up again Monday afternoon. Complaint was drunkenness.

MARRETT, Ralph O. Local Feb 10, 1898
Married, Ralph O. Marrett and Miss Mabel Hedrick at Palmyra, Missouri last week in presence of brides parents Mr and Mrs Wm Hedrick living on a farm one mile southwest of town. Wedding was surprise to grooms parents. A day or two previous to Mrs Marrett went as far as Quincy with Ralph as he started to Eldorado, Kansas, where he had a position in a store.

MARRETT, Mr S.S. Married Oct 16, 1890
At the home of brides parents, this city, Thursday eve October 9th, 1890 at 7:30 by Rev E.W. Souders, Mr S.S. Marrett and Miss Nettie E. Hough. Bride is daughter of Mr and Mrs G.R. Hough. Mr Marrett was raised in this vicinity. Will live with his mother at the old homestead.

MARRITT, Miss Lura Jun 12, 1890
SEE MEREDITH, Benjamin

MARS, John Local Aug 16, 1894
Marriage of Mr John Mars, the popular young Wabash fireman and Miss Birdie Rentschler occurred at the home of brides parents this after noon.

MARS, Johnnie Local Aug 23, 1894
Correction: Last week when marriage of Johnnie Mrsa to Miss Rentschler the ladys name was given wrong. It is Miss Dollie the oldest daughter of Mr Rentschler that married Mr Mars at the home of brides parents Wednesday eve August 15th by Rev Riley Lierly.

MARSH, Charles Local Jan 20, 1898
Last Sunday January 9th at 4 PM the marriage of Mr Charles Marsh and Miss Lena Heubner at the home of brides father, Mr Frank Heubner by J.M. Bell, pastor of C.P. Church, Mt Sterling.

MARSH, Chas. Jan 6, 1898
SEE HUBNER, Miss Lena

MARSHALL, Cora Nov 30, 1899
SEE MCCLINTOCK, David W.

MARSHALL, James — City Brevities — Dec 22, 1898
Marriage of Mr James Marshall, son of Noah K. Marshall and wife of Concord and Miss Clara Six, daughter of Mr and Mrs Marion Six living northeast of Mounds occurred this week.

MARSHALL, Jas. H. — Supplement — Dec 13, 1894
Little Brindle News Married near Mounds, Thursday November 29th Mr Jas. H. Marshall to Miss Ollie V. Hicks, by Rev F.P. Douglas. "Republican"

MARSHALL, Mrs Martha J. Oct 26, 1899
SEE SMITH, Capt J.W.

MARTIN, C.H. — Mounds — Apr 18, 1895
C.H. Martin and Ellen Nolan were married in Mt Sterling on Monday the 15th at 3 by Father Clifford. Will live Mounds.

MARTIN, Charles H. — Local — Apr 18, 1895
Marriage of Mr Charles H. Martin, of Mounds, and Miss Ella Nolan of that vicinity occurred at Mt Sterling Monday afternoon. Mr Martin has been employed as a commercial traveler by the McCormick Reaper Company for years. Bride is a member of one of Brown Counties best families and a sister of the Nolan Brothers. Will probably live Mounds.

MASON, Lewis — Local — Apr 15, 1897
Married, at the home of Mr and Mrs Joseph Mason, in this city at 8 PM Tuesday, Mr Lewis Mason, of McKee township and Miss May Riley of Bowen by Joseph W. Marrett, Esq. Mother of the bride was present. Mr Mason is a young farmer in vicinity of Haselwood, that will be their home.

MASON. Wm — Local — Oct 22, 1891
Wm Mason and Pearl Neece of Adams County were married at the courthouse Tuesday by T.M. Wallace. Brown County "Republican"

MATTHEWS, Peter — February 1889 — Feb 2, 1899
Married, Peter Matthews and Miss Christina Flassner.

MATTHEWS, Pete and wife — City Brevities — Mar 2, 1899
In Quincy last Wednesday night, Pete Matthews and wife celebrated their 10th wedding anniversary.

MATTHEWS, Samuel A. Jun 28, 1894
SEE JOHNSTON, Miss Jessie M.

MAXWELL, Charles W. Jun 16, 1898
SEE BRADNEY, Miss Belle

MAY, Mr Billie — Pea Ridge — Jan 12, 1893
Mr Billie May who lated committed matrimony will live in the house on his father's farm.

MAY, Miss Cora B. — Personal — Mar 21, 1895
The Optic announces marriage of Miss Cora B. May and Mr Edgar S. Potter to take place in a short time.

MAY, Miss Dora Ada Jul 27, 1893
SEE HOOTON, Prof. J.E.

MAY, Miss Ella — Local — Apr 22, 1897
Another wedding at Thomas May's home, on Pea Ridge Sunday eve. The daughter of Mr and Mrs May's, Ella, was married to Mr John Shelley by A.J. Hunsaker, Esq. John has a new house in vicinity of Jud Davis' place ready for the bride where they went Monday.

MAY, Miss Frankie Mar 1, 1894
SEE ROSSON, Frank

MAY, G.T. and Ella T. November 1888 Nov 3, 1898
G.T. May brought suit for divorce from Ella T. May.

MAY, Geo. D. Little Brindle Dec 8, 1898
Examiner: Marriage license issued last Friday to George D. May and Miss Rumple, both of Pea Ridge.

MAY, Miss Ida Nov 14, 1895
SEE WEST, William B.

MAY, Jno. T. 10 Years Ago Apr 6, 1893
SEE WILLIAMS, Miss Laura

MAY, Miss Lizzie 5 Years Ago Feb 6, 1890
Miss Lizzie May was married to Mr Lyman T. Scoggan.

MAY, Rosa Brown County Oct 31, 1895
"Beacon Light" Married at the home of brides parents, J.W. May and wife October 16th their daughter, Rosa, to Bruce Jones by A.J. Hunsaker, Esq.

MAYFIELD, Alta Jun 29, 1899
SEE DEETERLE, Fred

MAYHEW, Charles Mar 10, 1898
SEE CARROLL, Mrs Jsoephine

MEANS, Miss Anna Sep 21, 1893
SEE HERSMAN, Charles G.

MEANS, Miss Florence Apr 15, 1897
SEE FRY, Harvey

MEANS, John H. Little Brindle Apr 22, 1897
Mt Sterling Examiner: Married, Mr John H. Means and Miss Etta E. Greenwood at the home of brides mother, in this city at 7:30 PM Thursday eve the 15th inst by Rev S.A. Glassgow, of Woodson, Illinois.

MEANS, Miss Lena Nov 24, 1898
SEE ATKINSON, William E.

MEATHERINGHAM, Dessie Jan 28, 1897
SEE OMER, Dan

MEATHERINGHAM, James W. Oct 16, 1890
SEE HOKE, Miss Sarah E.

MEATHERINGHAM, John All Over the County Dec 2, 1897
Camp Point Trumpet: John Meatheringham and Minnie Hoke were married Sunday at Pleasant View Church.

MEATHERINGHAM, Mr and Mrs Wm Local Feb 23, 1893
Monday eve Mr and Mrs Wm Meatheringham, west of town celebrated their 25th anniversary.

MEATS, Mr Reuben Sep 18, 1890
SEE FLEMMING, Miss Florence

MEINTS, Grace Oct 1, 1896
SEE BEHRENS, Ulfert Jr.

MEISSER, Annie Mae Local Oct 5, 1893
Miss Annie Mae Meisser was married in Quincy to Mr Harry G. Lawrence, Saturday Review says: Miss Meisser is one of Quincy's leading society young ladies and Mr Lawrence is a rapidly rising young business man and together they will make a happy domestic voyage.

MENKE, Miss Frances Adams County Oct 13, 1898
Cards are out for wedding of Miss Frances Menke, second daughter of H.B. Menke and Mr Charles Johannes at St John's Church October 18th at 8 PM. "Quincy Optic"

MENKE, Miss Ida . County News Oct 12, 1899
Miss Ida Menke, daughter of Mr and Mrs H.B. Menke was married Wednesday at St John's Roman Catholic Church to Emil Weichlein. Bride is eldest daughter of H.B. Menke, President of the Menke Dry Goods Co. "Record"

MENSENDIKE, Miss Lillie Oct 5, 1899
SEE BATES, Will

MEREDITH, Mrs Lura Jan 30, 1896
SEE STRAUSS, Frank X.

MEREDITH, Benjamin Local Jun 12, 1890
A wedding at the county clerks office Thursday afternoon. Benjamin Meredith and Miss Lura Marritt of Clayton by Police Magistrate Brooks. Mt Sterling Democrat Message.

MERRICK, Mrs Minerva Neighborhood News Apr 20, 1893
Mrs Minerva Merrick, of 301 Chestnut, 82 years old adopted a "Prof" Orchardson, a young man 54 years old. We believe that in law its called a marriage. "Quincy Optic"

MESSNER, Dr Lewis C. Jun 1, 1899
SEE JOHNSTON, Miss Jennie

MEYER, Miss Bell Adams County Mar 30, 1899
Wednesday at 1 PM at the home of brides parents, Mr and Mrs Jonas Meyer, 926 6th Ave. North, occurred the marriage of Miss Bell Meyer and Mr Isaac Kaufman, of Pittsburg, Penn. by Rabbi Eppistein. Quincy Record

MEYER, Mr Frank D. Local Nov 10, 1892
Mr Frank D. Meyer and Miss Alberta Gross were married by Father Dechene at 4 PM Thursday at St Joseph Church in Mt Sterling.

MEYERS, Henry Camp Point Mar 24, 1898
Henry Meyers, of Columbus, and Miss Nellie Homer, south of town, were married by Mr O. Dilley last Wednesday at the home of the bride.

MEYERS, Mr and Mrs Mack 5 Years Ago Aug 17, 1893
Mack and Mrs Meyers celebrated their 20th wedding anniversary at Colpitt schoolhouse.

MEYERS, Miss Mary Supplement Jun 29, 1893
5 Years Ago Miss Mary Meyers married John Duke.

MEYERS, Miss Mattie Personal Mar 24, 1898
Miss Sadie Hirons, has gone to Mendon township to attend wedding of her friend, Miss Mattie Meyers.

MICHAEL, Miss Flo Apr 22, 1897
SEE KINCHELOE, Hon Chas. F.

MIKESELL, Miss Addie Local Dec 4, 1890
Marriage of Miss Addie Mikesell, daughter of Henry C. and Mrs Mikesell, to Joseph Cline at the home of brides parents, on Pea Ridge Thanksgiving eve by Rev Wm Lowe. Will live on a farm near Camp Point.

MIKESELL, Miss Carrie Apr 26, 1900
SEE STEVENS, Oscar

MIKESELL, Emma Apr 2, 1896
SEE JAMISON, T.W. and Thomas

MIKESELL, Harvey Little Brindle Oct 21, 1897
Mound Item: Harvey Mikesell and Miss Elsie Lindsey were married Friday eve at Mt Sterling.

MILLER, Ed Local Oct 4, 1894
Marriage of Mr Ed Miller and Miss Hattie Williams occurred at Mt Sterling Saturday eve. Miss Williams has lived in the family of Jas. B. Coe several years.

MILLER, Fanny Adams County Nov 24, 1898
Camp Point Journal: Married at home of Mr and Mrs Benj. Miller of Liberty township on November 10th their daughter, Fanny to Edward Humke, son of Conrad Humke a farmer in McKee.

MILLER, Frank A. Brown County News Sep 14, 1893
Mr Frank A. Miller, of Clayton, and Miss Belle Barlow, of this city were married 7:30 PM Thursday at home of brides parents in this city by Elder Van Dervoort of Clayton. "Examiner"

MILLER, Jessie Local Jul 11, 1895
Mrs L.P. Wyatt subscribed to our paper for her niece, Mrs Jessie Miller. Miss Miller, for she did nor change the last name, married a dentist. They now live at Greenview, Illinois.

MILLER, Mr Jos. S. Local Jan 25, 1900
At the railroad station Wednesday AM were Mr Jos. S. Miller, Miss Rosa Bakerbower, Misses Emma Bakerbower and Tracy Bollinger. Mr Miller and Miss Rosa Bakerbower were to be married at Quincy Wednesday afternoon and the other ladies were going to see the matter properly done.

MILLER, Miss Lillie L. Pea Ridge Mar 6, 1890
Married at the home of brides, Grandmother, Miss Abel Gay in Clayton township, Miss Lillie L. Miller to Mr Edwin K. Owen of this vicinity by Rev Reed of M.E. Church, Clayton.

MILLS, John Neighborhood News Nov 7, 1895
Cards are out for marriage on November 14th of Mr John Mills, formerly of Baylis and Miss Gussie Steeleman, of Curran, Illinois. John is oldest son of Mr and Mrs M.C. Mills of Baylis and is now station agent at Curran.

MILTON, Miss Ella Jun 29, 1893
SEE JACKSON, Joseph

MINER, Miss Augusta Sep 27, 1894
SEE CRANE, F.W.

MITCHELL, Miss Dolly Sep 6, 1894
SEE COX, Miles

MOFFETT, Grant L. Local Jan 3, 1895
Clayton friends of Mr Grant L. Moffett received following card: Mrs George Anna Atkinson announces the marriage of her daughter, Mary Ellen to Grant L. Moffett on Tuesday December 25th 1894 at Denver, Colorado at home, 1618 Fremont St.

MOFFETT, Henry Maynard Local Jan 9, 1896
Cards are out announcing marriage of Mr Henry Maynard Moffett, of this city and Miss Mary Sedgwick January 14th at home of brides parents at Granville, Ohio.

MOFFITT, Henry S. Married Jan 23, 1896
Married Tuesday January 14th at Granville, Indiana, Miss Mary Sedgwick and Mr Henry S. Moffitt of Clayton, Illinois at high noon by Rev Dr. Baldwin. Will live Clayton where groom is a business man.

MONROE, Perry W. Feb 16, 1899
SEE COLLIER, Mrs Jennie

MONTGOMERY, Miss Addie Local Apr 24, 1890
Letter from Major W. Montgomery received this AM tells of the marriage of his daughter, Miss Addie, to Mr W.H. Jones of Kansas City at 7 PM Monday, April 21st by Rev Wilcon of the Presbyterian Church.

MONTGOMERY, Addie Jan 26, 1893
SEE LUKER, Joseph H.

MONTGOMERY, Miss Elva A Decade Ago Jun 15, 1893
Miss Elva Montgomery was married to Fred J. Dykes.

MONTGOMERY, Miss Elva June 1883 Jun 30, 1898
Miss Elva Montgomery, youngest daughter of Major and Mrs Montgomery married Mr Fred S. Dikes, by Rev Hayes.

MONTGOMERY, Frank Married Dec 4, 1890
Married, Wednesday eve at Presbyterian Church, Mr Frank Montgomery and Miss Sadie Evelyn Sweney by Rev E.W. Souders. Mrs B.L. Strother of Abilene, Kansas was on the organ. Bride has lived with sister and brother in law, Mr and Mrs A.F. Jones past six years and last three has taught primary school in Clayton.

MONTGOMERY, George W. Married Nov 16, 1899
Married at home Mr and Mrs Robert D. Long at Mounds at 7 PM Tuesday, Hon George W. Montgomery to Miss Florence E. Long by Rev Slagle. Will live in former home of Mr Montgomery at Clayton.

MONTGOMERY, Mr and Mrs Glen Neighbors Mar 9, 1899
Letters have reached Rushville from Mr and Mrs Glen Montgomery, the juveniles who eloped from that city last week. They went to some point in Michigan, where they were married, and are now at Toledo. It is expected that they will return to Rushville soon.

MONTGOMERY, Miss Jennie 10 Years Ago Jan 2, 1890
Miss Jennie Montgomery and J.L. Staker were married on Xmas Day.

MONTGOMERY, Miss Nellie Mar 19, 1896
SEE FREY, William

MONTGOMERY, Dr Robert Adams County Feb 16, 1899
Dr Robert Montgomery, of Quincy and Mrs Catherine W. Everett, of Elgin were married at Elgin, the 9th inst. Mrs Montgomery's first husband was W.T. Rogers, was at one time Mayor of Quincy, her second husband was Rev William P. Everett, onee of Quincy one of Dr Montgomery's sons married a daughter of his new wife.

MONTGOMERY, Major and Mrs W. 10 Years Ago Sep 11, 1890
Major and Mrs W. Montgomery celebrated their 25th wedding anniversary.

MOORE, Miss 5 Years Ago Oct 23, 1890
SEE FLASSNER, Martin

MOORE, Miss Anna Oct 27, 1898
SEE YELDELL, Ernest

MOORE, Earnest L. All Over the County Apr 29, 1897
Golden New Era Married Thursday at Keokuk, Earnest L. Moore and Miss Edna Selby, youngest daughter of our townsman H.E. Selby. Mr Moore has been here about two years and is in jewelry business. Miss Selby was born and raised here and graduate of Golden High School.

MOORE, Miss Edda Jan 13, 1898
SEE TAYLOR, W.A.

MOORE, Miss Elva Nov 9, 1893
SEE HALL, Calvin

MOORE, J.T. Married Jun 1, 1899
Mr J.T. Moore and Miss Victoria Click, Thursday of last week, the 25th ult. They drove over to Mt Sterling and were married by minister of Christian Church. Tom as a home to take his wife to. Mrs Moore has lived Clayton four years. Mr Moore is member of the dry goods firm Gruber and Moore.

MOORE, Hon.J.W. 5 Years Ago May 30, 1895
May 22, Hon. J.W. Moore and Mrs Lottie Thompson of Mounds were married.

MOORE, James T. Little Brindle Jun 1, 1899
Elder Knoch, at his home in this city Thursday married James T. Moore and Miss Victoria Cleek, both of Clayton.

MOORE, Jno. W. Other Days May 24, 1900
May 1890: Married at Mounds, Hon Jno. W. Moore and Mrs Lottie Thompson.

MOORE, John B. Our Own Bailiwick Mar 8, 1894
SEE WOMELSDORF, Mrs Mary C.

MOORE, Hon John W. May 22, 1890
SEE THOMPSON, Mrs Lottie

MOORE, Miss Lottie Personal Jul 12, 1894
F.W. Burgesser and wife attended the wedding of their cousin, Miss Lottie Moore and Mr Frank Dexter at Mt Sterling, Tuesday night.

MOORE, Miss Mollie Nov 9, 1899
SEE BULMAN, Frank R.

MOORE, Olen Married Feb 4, 1897
Married at the home of Mr and Mrs T.H. Dunlap in this city Wednesday eve January 27th by Rev Paul Heiligman Mr Olen Moore and Miss Mae Dunlap. Mr Moore lived this community several years and is connected with dry goods firm of Gruber and Moore, and restaurant business.

MOORE, Otis Local Oct 12, 1899
Marriage of Mr Otis Moore and Miss Nellie Ripetoe occurred at the home of Mrs Moore, mother of the groom on the eve of the 2nd inst.

MOORE, Polly May 28, 1896
SEE MOORE, William A.

MOORE, Samuel D. Oct 8, 1891
SEE STAUFFER, Miss Lizzie

MOORE, Miss Sarah May 23, 1895
SEE NOKES. Elmer

MOORE, Sollis Local Feb 20, 1896
The Enterprise failed to get the news of the marriage of Mr Sollis Moore and Miss Lucy Ogle of Fish Hook until last week. Bride is sister of Mrs Marshall Love.

MOORE, Miss Tennessee Nov 11, 1897
SEE CAGLE, Wesley

MOORE, Mr Thos. Oct 15, 1891
SEE BOLINGER, Miss Emma

MOORE, William A. Our Own Bailiwick May 28, 1896
William A. Moore of Richfield, age 19 was licensed to marry Polly Moore of Richfield age 16.

MOORLEY, Miss Cora Apr 13, 1893
SEE JONES, Wm F.

MOORMAN, Miss Phoebe Oct 26, 1893
SEE THORNHILL, Henry

MORAN, Clara Jan 4, 1900
SEE STEVENS, Ralph

MORGAN, Harah Ill. Brevities Mar 7, 1895
SEE DIESTERIE, Miss Mary

MORGAN, Miss Sarah Local Feb 28, 1895
SEE HOFFMAN, Albert

MORGAN, Theresa Feb 15, 1900
SEE BRIGGS, Richard M.

MORISON, Miss Ella Local Aug 11, 1892
Married, at the ME parsonage Wednesday eve August 3rd, by Rev W.M. Reed, Miss Ella Morison of Mounds to Mr Clinton Dewitt, of Camden, Ill.

MOSS, Mr Aug 28, 1890
SEE CAMERON, Miss Sallie

MOTTER, Mr Ed S. Jun 12, 1890
SEE PARKER, Miss Lottie L.

MULL, Oscar Gillis Married Oct 24, 1895
Married Thursday at 7 PM at Grace ME Church Mr Oscar Gillis Mull and Miss Ella Emma Kirkpatrick by Rev W.A. Reynolds with a Methodist Episcopal ceremony. Ed Curry was groom's best man. Ushers were Henry S. Moffett and Sam Curry of this place and Gus Skinner and Fred Andrews of Quincy. Bridesmaids were Misses Jessie Givler, Carrie Curry, Laura Pike and Miss Jessie Skinner of Quincy. Little Nelle Potter of Quincy was flower girl. (200 to 300 guests) Mr Mull came to Clayton three years ago and is partner in the well known drug firm. Reception in home of Capt and Mrs James Kirkpatrick. Bride and groom then left for Bowling Green, Missouri on the train, the former home of Mr Mull to visit his parents. Will return this week.

MULLINER, Walter E. Jun 18, 1896
SEE PHILBRICK, Miss Edna E.

MUMFORD, Lottie May 22, 1890
SEE THOMPSON, Mrs Lottie

MUNDT, Prof Carl A. Jan 14, 1897
SEE DISSLER, Miss Rosa or Rose

MURPHY, Miss Ella Dec 1, 1898
SEE REDMOND, Charles

MURPHY, Mr J.D. Dec 26, 1895
SEE HARBISON, Miss Lizzie

MUSICK, George P. Elm Grove Feb 21, 1895
Today (Thursday) at high noon will occur the marriage of George P. Musick to Miss Annie Louise Hopka, daughter of Mr and Mrs Fred Hopka.

MYERS, Flora 5 Years Ago Nov 30, 1893
Flora Myers, of Concord and Thomas Taylor of Mounds were married.

MYERS, Miss Myrtle E. Mar 14, 1895
SEE HUDDLESON, Albert B.

MYERS, Miss Nora June 1888 Jun 30, 1898
SEE DOAK, John

MCARTHUR, A.L. Neighborhood News Aug 4, 1892
Marriage of editor of A.L. McArthur, of the Hamilton Press and Miss Blanche Griffin was last week at the home of her parents, Mr and Mrs Wm Griffin in Hamilton.

MCBRATNEY, Miss Jennie Personal May 14, 1891
Charlie McBratney arrived from St Louis where he has been painting for several weeks. He will attend the wedding of his sister, Miss Jennie, who will give her heart and hand to Mr Ed Crawford, of Hannibal, Missouri at the family home in Griggsville today. Charlie has worked in Kansas City and St Louis since last September.

MCBRATNEY, Miss Mary 5 Years Ago Nov 26, 1891
Miss Mary McBratney was married to Mr R.S. Black. They reside at Mounds.

MCBRATNEY, Samuel Married Apr 3, 1890
Married at the home of brides parents, Clayton, Illinois Wednesday eve March 26, 1890 by Rev E.W. Souders, Samuel McBratney, of the firm of McBratney and Gibson and Miss Josephine Reath, a lady well known to Clayton people.

MCBRATNEY, Miss Sarah Local Dec 19, 1895
Marriage of Miss Sarah McBratney to Mr John Schmitt of Annawan, Ill.

MCCARL, Lyman May 4, 1893
SEE BERRIAN, Miss Hannah

MCCARTY, James E. Personal Nov 2, 1899
Mr James E. McCarty and Miss Bertha Gay, only daughter of Banker Chas. Gay of Camp Point were married at 8:30 PM Sunday at the Gay home. Mr McCarty is ass't cashier in the bank of his father in law.

MCCASKELL, T.L. Little Brindle Mar 26, 1896
T.L. McCaskell and Elizabeth Ritter of Pea Ridge were married at home of Rev C.A. King in Mt Sterling.

MCCASKILL, Wm H. Mar 25, 1897
SEE CLARK, Miss Helen

MCCAULEY, Chas. Other Days May 17, 1900
April 1890 Married, Mr Chas. McCauley and Mrs Sarah Kimrey.

MCCLAIN, Mrs Addie E. Mar 4, 1897
SEE COLPITTS, Joseph A.

MCCLAIN, Chas. City Brevities Jun 22, 1899
Rev E.J. Rice has a wedding at the parsonage Saturday eve, Mr Chas. McClain and Mrs Bertie M. Schreiffler of near Mt Sterling. They will live at Springfield where Charlie has a job as a car inspector.

MCCLAIN, John Local Jan 9, 1896
Sunday at Siloam, the marriage of Mr John McClain and Miss Mary Sullivan, daughter of Mr and Mrs Mike Sullivan of Siloam. Will probably live Clayton, John drives the Siloam and Clayton mail wagon.

MCCLAIN, Robert Local May 18, 1893
Robert McClain of Pea Ridge and Miss Shockey, of the Park House were marries this week. Will live out at Mr Yakley's farm.

MCCLINTOCK, David W. Local Nov 30, 1899
Licensed to wed: David W. McClintock 26, Golden and Cora Marshall 18, Clayton.

MCCLINTOCK, Miss Effie Married Mar 5, 1896
Married at the home of I.T. McClintock in Bowen, Wednesday the 26th ult at 7 PM, their daughter, Miss Effie and Mr Harry McKinzie of Stillwell, Illinois by Rev Westfall. Following day a reception also was held at groom's parents. Present for wedding was Mrs Charlie Kirkpatrick, of Clayton, a cousin of bride.

MCCLINTOCK, Thomas J. Local Mar 25, 1897
Mr Thomas J. McClintock married Mrs Cross at Carthage last Thursday.

MCCLURE, Mr Elsie Oct 3, 1895
SEE JOHNSTONE, Miss Kate

MCCONNELL, Miss Dec 31, 1891
SEE RENAKER, Mr Orson

MCCONNELL, Miss Alice Married Feb 5, 1891
At the parsonage Sunday afternoon by Rev W.M. Reed, Miss Alice McConnell to Mr Wm Purpus. Both from families near Kellerville. Mr Purpus is son of Mr and Mrs Louis Purpus and bride is daughter. of W.H. and Mrs McConnell.

MCCONNELL, Miss Fannie B. Sep 28, 1899
SEE WILLIAMS, Ralph

MCCORKLE, Jesse M. Jun 11, 1891
SEE DYSON, O.E.

MCCORMICK, Miss Anna E. Jun 29, 1893
SEE CHITTENDEN, Samuel F.

MCCORMICK, Miss Eulalia Nov 8, 1894
SEE CAIN, Jos. H.

MCCORMICK, Miss Rosa Nov 3, 1892
SEE HARTMAN, Mr Jos.

MCCOY, Miss Alice Local Jul 21, 1892
Miss Alice McCoy, daughter of Thomas and Mrs McCoy living on LaFayette street was married to Joseph Richardson, Sunday.

MCCOY, Mr and Mrs Chas. H. Local Feb 15, 1894
A peculiar document, entitled a "petition to perpetuate testimony", was filed in circuit court by Mr Chas. McCoy. Its purpose is to create a record of a marriage nearly 30 years ago. Mr and Mrs Chas. H. McCoy were married in 1865 and their four children full grown. Lately it was discovered that through some oversight the officiating minister, Rev R.K. McCoy failed to return the license to county clerk office. Rev McCoy is dead, but several witnesses are living and they went into court to testify to the fact of the marriage so there will be a record.

MCCOY, Miss Ida Local Apr 16, 1891
The home of Mr Thomas McCoy was scene of wedding Sunday afternoon, Miss Ida, their daughter was married to Mr Wm Richardson at 3 PM by Justice Kendrick. Mr Richardson will farm this season.

MCCOY, John and wife Sept 1889 Sep 7, 1899
Friends helped John McCoy and wife celebrate their 25th wedding anniversary.

MCCOY, John W. and Minnie — Local — Nov 28, 1895
John W. McCoy is asking for divorce from his wife, Mrs Minnie McCoy says they were married Apr 16, 1889 and lived together til March 16, 1893 where she deserted him. Asks custody of their one child Sells McCoy now 5 years old. "Democrat Message"

MCCOY, Miss Pearl L. — Mar 20, 1890
SEE WILLIAMS, Mr Hobart M.

MCCOY, Miss Pearl L. — Mar 17, 1900
SEE WILLIAMS, Mr Hobert M.

MCCRAY, R.J. — Dec 17, 1891
SEE WALLACE, Miss Mame

MCCRAY, Robert J. — Married — Dec 24, 1891
Married, Wednesday December 16th Mr Robert J. McCray and Miss Mary E. Wallace at the home of brides parents, Mr and Mrs J.A. Wallace, Sr. near Golden. Groom is in business with his father in Golden, where they will live.

MCCRAY, Robert J. — Oct 25, 1894
SEE JOSLIN, Miss Minnie

MCCULLOCH, Alvin — Neighborhood News — Oct 26, 1893
At Galesburg, Alvin McCulloch married a 17 year old girl to avoid more serious complications. An hour afterwards he deserted her with the avowed intention of not living with her. He was arrested under the new anti wife deserting law and is to appear in court.

MCCULLOM, Miss Angie — Our Own Bailiwick — Apr 16, 1896
Golden New Era Word comes from Kansas that Miss Angie McCullom and Mr Crosby, both former Adams County residents were married at Topeka recently.

MCCULLOM, Jennie — 5 Years Ago — Jan 8, 1891
SEE JIMISON, Thos. W.

MCDANNOLD, Miss Clara — Neighborhood News — Oct 23, 1890
Tuesday afternoon October 14th 1890, Miss Clara McDannold and George C. Dunbar were married at Mt Sterling by Rev Joseph Marshall. Bride is daughter of T.J. McDannold and the sister of the county judge. Was born and raised in Brown County.

MCDELL, Miss Lizzie — Jan 25, 1900
SEE MCMURRAY, Roy

MCDILL, Miss Lizzie — Brown County — Jan 25, 1900
Democrat Message: Wednesday at 4 PM, Miss Lizzie McDill and Roy McMurray, of Clayton, were married at home of William Fuller in this city by Squire J.A. McCabe. Will live on the McMurray farm two miles north of Clayton.

MCDONNALD, Mr Will — 10 Years Ago — Jun 8, 1893
SEE WALLACE, Miss Bettie

MCDONNELL, Miss Lillie M. — Mar 29, 1900
SEE BAGBY, Joseph N.

MCDOWELL, Mr E.E. — Nov 6, 1890
SEE DAVIS, Miss Clara

MCDOWELL, Edgar — Nov 13, 1890
SEE DAVIS, Miss Clara S.

MCDOWELL, Green and Nancy — June 1883 — Jun 30, 1898
Nancy McDowell was divorced from her husband, Green McDowell.

MCDOWELL, Mary E. — May 24, 1894
SEE WATERS, George

MCDOWELL, Moses — Local — Nov 7, 1895
There was a wedding in town Wednesday night, Mr Moses McDowell and Miss Lewis. No cards.

MCDOWELL, Sam K. — 10 Years Ago — Mar 22, 1894
Sam K. McDowell and Miss Addie Caldwell were married at Helena, Mont.

MCDOWELL, Thomas H.W. Jun 21, 1894
SEE WRIGHT, Miss Carrie

MCDOWELL, Tom H.W. Local Jul 5, 1894
Tom H.W. McDowell arrived from Anthony, Kansas with his bride Thursday eve. They were married in the Baptist Church of that city at 5 PM Wednesday and took train an hour later for Clayton. Mrs McDowell was Miss Wright and after leaving college taught school.

MCDOWELL, Wm E. Ancient History Mar 18, 1897
Febraury 1887 Married, Wm E. McDowell and Mattie Wever at Pana.

MCFADDON, Henrietta Dec 29, 1892
SEE POWELL, Gordon

MCFADDON, Henry Sep 21, 1893
SEE LEWIS, Betsey

MCFADDON, Miss Mattie J. Apr 29, 1897
SEE HARBIN, George

MCFADON, Mrs 5 Years Ago Dec 11, 1890
SEE BOSTICK, HENRY

MCFARLAND, Isaac and Annie Our Own Bailiwick Feb 14, 1895
On divorce docket, Isaac McFarland against Annie McFarland, he lives in Golden and was married to Annie Henry in Camp Point on Xmas day 1884. Seperated last February because wife is naturally impotent. Wife is in Omaha.

MCFARLAND, Mr and Mrs John Camp Point Dec 1, 1898
Mr and Mrs John McFarland celebrated their 12th wedding anniversary.

MCFARLAND, Miss Lizzie Feb 9, 1899
SEE BECKETT, Clarence

MCFARLAND, Oliver Our Own Bailiwick Aug 22, 1895
Camp Point items: Oliver McFarland of Camp Point and Sarah E. Griffith of Pea Ridge were licensed at Mt Sterling to marry.

MCFARLAND, Thos. Camp Point Oct 15, 1891
Invitations are out for wedding of Thos. McFarland and Miss Ada Hughes.

MCGAUGHEY, Miss Jessie I. Our Own Bailiwick Dec 26, 1895
Camp Point Journal: Married Wednesday at noon Miss Jessie I. McGaughey, daughter of James F. McGaughey of Quincy to Luther C. Gibbs son of Charles M. Gibbs of Coatsburg.

MCGAUGHEY, Rev John A. Married Aug 19, 1897
Marriage of Rev John A. McGaughey and Miss Jessie Givler, daughter of Mr and Mrs W.F. Givler was at the home of brides brother, Mr Zene Givler at 1959-38th St Chicago at high noon last Thursday, August 12, 1897 by Rev Westerwood, a college classmate of groom. Rev McGaughey is pastor of the Presbyterian Church at Bushnell.

MCGILL, Wm Neighborhood News Jun 16, 1892
Wm McGill and Miss McGraw will be married at Baldwin Park on July 4th.

MCGRAW, Miss Jun 16, 1892
SEE MCGILL, Wm

MCHATTON, Miss Irene Dec 24, 1896
SEE WALLACE, Charles S.

MCHENRY, Miss Feb 27, 1896
SEE DAVIS, F.M.

MCKINZIE, Harry Mar 5, 1896
SEE MCCLINTOCK, Miss Effie

MCLAIN, Miss Mattie C. Local Mar 8, 1894
Miss Mattie C. McLain and Mr Patrick J. Kelly were married in Chicago Monday. Miss McLain was raised in Huntsville township, Schuyler County and Mr Kelly in Quincy. Will live Quincy.

MCMAHAN, Argyil J. Oct 26, 1899
SEE ELDER, Ethel

MCMURRAY, Miss Feb 22, 1894
SEE YEARGAIN, Mr James T.

MCMURRAY, Fred M. All Over the County Jun 24, 1897
Camp Point Trumpet: Married June 6th at the home of Rev W.M. Reed, Mr Fred M. McMurray of Clayton and Miss Ella B. Howe, also of Clayton.

MCMURRAY, Miss Leona Feb 2, 1899
SEE THOMPSON, Gilbert

MCMURRAY, N.F. Local Oct 15, 1896
Mr and Mrs Will Kuntz are up from Fish Hook this week and Mrs Kuntz says they are here "to see our new mother". The marriage of Mr N.F. McMurray and Mrs Ella Hopper was a very quiet affair few people in town knew of the nuptials until several days had elapsed.

MCMURRAY, Miss Nellie Local Apr 29, 1897
Married in Quincy this week, Miss Nellie McMurray, daughter of our former friend, Aaron McMurray, now deceased and Mr F.J. Shusher of Quincy.

MCMURRAY, Roy Brown County Jan 25, 1900
Examiner: Roy McMurray of near Clayton and Miss Lizzie McDell of Keokuk were married by Squire McCabe at the home of Mrs Mary Fuller, Wednesday afternoon.

MCMURRAY, Roy Jan 25, 1900
SEE MCDILL, Miss Lizzie

MCNEAL, Miss May Camp Point Dec 14, 1893
Married the 15th, Elmer Schomp, of Acampo, California and Miss May McNeal of this place. Will live California.

MCNEELY, Marion B. Nov 29, 1894
SEE RICHARDSON, Col. George B.

MCNEIL, Miss Mary E. Feb 2, 1893
SEE PREECE, Elmer E.

MCPHAIL, Laura E. Apr 23, 1896
SEE CHAPMAN, Chas. E.

MCPHAIL, Miss Lizzie Sep 23, 1897
SEE LUCAS, William

MCPHAIL, Miss Sarah J. Feb 20, 1890
SEE WORTHINGTON, Francis M.

MCPHERSON, William and Jennetta County News Dec 14, 1899
Among decrees in divorce signed by Judge Broady Tuesday was that in the case of Jennetta McPherson versus William McPherson.

MCPHERSON, William A. Local Jul 15, 1897
It is now authoritively stated that Mr William A. McPherson and Mrs Nettie Stevens were married at Palmyra, Missouri a week ago Saturday.

MCPHERSON, William A. and Jennettia Aug 24, 1899
County News Jennettia McPherson made application for a divorce from her husband, William A. McPherson, Friday. Says he deserted her less than two months after their marriage which took place June 26, 1897 and she doesn't know his whereabouts. Will be tried in October term.

MCPHERSON, Mr Wm and Mrs Nettie Our Own Bailiwick Sep 17, 1896
Mrs Nettie McPherson of Clayton commenced suit yesterday for divorce from her husband, Wm McPherson and the restoration of her former name of Nettie Stevens. Says they were married at Mt Sterling June 26, 1894 and lived together till July 30 last. Says after about six months of marriage he started to abuse her. Whig "15th"

MCPHERSON, Wm A. Little Brindle News Jul 5, 1894
Married, at the Tinnen house Tuesday eve at 7:30 Mr Wm A. McPherson of this city and Mrs Jennette M. Stevens, of Clayton by Rev Lugg. "Republican"

MCVAY, Miss Ora May 17, 1900
SEE WARD, Mr Elias

MCVEY, Ora Feb 6, 1896
SEE BANKER Edward

NASH, George William Jr. Neighbors Jun 16, 1898
Cards are out announcing the marriage of Mr George William Mash Jr. to Miss Effie May Norris June 22nd at Bowen.

NASH, Mr Lucius Mar 31, 1898
SEE NORRIS, Miss Lulu

NEECE, Pearl Oct 22, 1891
SEE MASON, Wm

NEECE, Dr D.D. Jan 11, 1894
SEE COOK, Miss Inex A.

NEELAND, Miss Fannie Pea Ridge Apr 12, 1894
Wedding at home of Henry Neeland, Tuesday April 3rd, Miss Fannie Neeland of this vicinity to Chris Jansen of Kansas. Mr Jansen owns a large farm in the west where they will depart for in a few days.

NEELAND, Richard Supplement Jun 6, 1895
Little Brindle News Richard Neeland, of Pea Ridge township and Miss Laura Veach of Hastings, Colorado were married last Friday eve at 6 PM at home of Rev C.A. King. Miss Veach lived in this county, but for past two years lived a above state. Will live this county. "Republican"

NEICE, James Our Own Bailiwick Sep 10, 1896
James Neice of Kellerville and Rose Kirtley of Plainville, were licensed to wed.

NEVILLE, Dr L.H. Dec 23, 1897
SEE COX, Miss Daisy

NEVINS, Miss Edith Aug 31, 1899
SEE OMER, Lewis

NEVINS, John A. and Cora A. Locals Jan 1, 1891
Cora A. wife of John A. Nevins, ex County Surveyor and at present Supt. of Public Works at Quincy has brought suit for divorce. Charging extreme and repeated cruelty. They were married at Camp Point a year ago. She was Miss Baughman.

NEVINS, Mr and Mrs John R. Local Jan 8, 1891
Mr and Mrs John R. Nevins have patched up a truce and are living together again as they should do. The divorce suit instituted by Mrs Nevins will be withdrawn. "Herald"

NEWCOMB, Miss Mattie Jun 11, 1896
SEE CRAIN, Fred

NEWHOUSE, Fred Local Jul 3, 1890
Mr Fred Newhouse, a Wabash brakeman, formerly of Griggsville, a nephew of Samuel Newhouse northwest of town and Miss Hattie M. Connor of Camp Point were married last week.

NEWHOUSE, John C. Married Jan 4, 1894
Married, Mr John Newhouse, son of Mr and Mrs Samuel Newhouse, northwest of town to Miss Ella M. Kenney of Creston, Iowa occurred in that city Xmas eve. Came to Clayton Friday eve. Will live in a new house built on Mr Newhouse's farm.
Creston Daily Gazette says: Mr John C. Newhouse of Clayton, Illinois and Miss Ella M. Kenney of this city were married at home of brides parents, Mr and Mrs Leroy Kenney on South Elm Street by Rev L.N. Lafferty, pastor of United Presbyterian Church. Bride has lived here since early childhood. Will live Illinois.

NEWMANN, Miss Cora Mar 11, 1897
SEE BURNES, Mr

NEWNAN, Elder 5 Years Ago Oct 16, 1890
Elder Newnan and Miss Johnson were married at Barry.

NICKERSON, Samuel Mar 16, 1899
SEE HUNSAKER, Mrs Eunice
NIECE, Robert City Brevities Jan 19, 1899
A marriage license was granted last week to Robert Niece of Hazelwood and Dolly Likes, of Chestline.
NOAKES, Miss Birdie M. Local Aug 31, 1893
SEE ROBISON, Fred
NOAKES, Mrs Ellen July 1883 Jul 7, 1898
SEE BIRKETT, Alden S.
NODSON, Mr and Mrs Dec 30, 1897
SEE BLACK, Miss Minnie V.
NOFTZ, Theodore Concord Jan 1, 1891
Mr Theodore Noftz and Miss Hattie Buckner were married December 21st.
NOKES, Albert L. Brown County Jan 4, 1900
Licensed to wed since last issue of Examiner: Albert L. Nokes of Mt Sterling and Florence Tice of Cooperstown.
NOKES, Miss Birdie M. August 1893 Aug 11, 1898
SEE ROBISON, Fred
NOKES, Elmer Little Brindle May 23, 1895
Wednesday night after prayer meeting at Methodist Church, Mr Elmer Nokes and Miss Sarah Moore were married by Rev F.B. Manden. "Examiner"
NOLAN, Miss Ella Apr 18, 1895
SEE MARTIN, Charles H.
NOLAN, Ellen Apr 18, 1895
SEE MARTIN, C.H.
NOLAN, Lewis 15 Years Ago Jul 1, 1897
May 1882: Weddings, Lewis Nolan and Ella Cullinan.
NOLAN, Peter Little Brindle Jul 18, 1895
"Beacon Light" Marriage of Peter Nolan of this place to Miss Boylan of St Louis took place at Mt Sterling.
NORRIS, Miss Allyene Oct 6, 1898
SEE HARDING, Ernest
NORRIS, Allyne E. Oct 20, 1898
SEE HARDING, Ernest E.
NORRIS, Miss Effie May Jun 16, 1898
SEE NASH, George William Jr.
NORRIS, Miss Lulu Camp Point Mar 31, 1898
Miss Maggie Honnold will go to Bowen Wednesday to be bridesmaid at wedding of her cousin, Miss Lulu Morris to Mr Lucius Nash.
NORTHCOTT, Henrietta May 26, 1898
SEE WINSTON, Wm
NORTON, Miss Alice 5 Years Ago Apr 16, 1891
Miss Alice Norton, of Concord married Mr J.A. Bennett.
NORTON, Miss Anna Nov 25, 1897
SEE GROSS, Julius
NORTON, Lee Little Brindle Feb 7, 1895
From Mound Beacon Light Married at home of brides, James Lindsey and wife, Wednesday at 12 by Rev Flemming, Lee Norton, son of B.F. Norton to Rosa Lindsey.
NOYEY, Dr F.C. Dec 26, 1895
SEE BRIERTON, Miss Emma
NYE, Fannie Neighborhood News Feb 4, 1892
SEE SMITH, Miss Fannie
OBRIEN, Mart Camp Point Nov 23, 1893
Mart Obrien and Miss Nellie Howell were married last week.
O'CONNOR, Miss Cornelia 5 Years Ago Oct 13, 1892
Miss Cornelia O'Connor and Mr Jos. Colpitts were married. Mrs Colpitts died a year ago.

O'DONALD, Miss Katherine | | Jan 12, 1893
SEE RINGLING, Dr

OGLE, Miss Lucy | | Feb 20, 1896
SEE MOORE, Sollis

OLIVER, Mr and Mrs Wm L. | Local | Feb 6, 1896
Mr and Mrs Wm L. Oliver celebrated their golden wedding the 13th inst at their home in Kansas.

OMER, Boon | Camp Point | Sep 21, 1899
Boon Omer and Miss Maggie DeHaven were quietly married at the home of Elder Dilley last Wednesday eve.

OMER, Dan | Camp Point News | Jan 28, 1897
Dan Omer and Dessie Meatheringham were married in Quincy Thursday. Dan is agent at the Wabash depot. Miss Meatheringham is daughter of Mr and Mrs Meatheringham, a few miles east of town.

OMER, Daniel B. | County News | Sep 21, 1899
Marriage license issued last week by county clerk to Daniel B. Omer and Maggie L. DeHaven, both of Camp Point.

OMER, Mr and Mrs J. Ed | Our Own Bailiwick | Mar 26, 1896
Camp Point Journal: Mr and Mrs J. Ed Omer went to Keokuk Tuesday and were married a second time. They were married in West Virginia several years ago, when Ed was young and wild and sailing under an assumed name. We afraid it would make trouble in future and decided to be tied up properly.

OMER, Lewis | "Life Sentence" | Aug 31, 1899
Married Thursday of last week, Mr Lewis Omer and Miss Edith Nevins at the home of brides parents, Mr and Mrs Joseph Nevins in the east suburb of Camp Point at 8 PM. Will go to Champaign where he is a student in the State University.

OMER, Pete | Camp Point | Apr 12, 1900
Pete Omer and Miss Hattie DeHaven were married Wednesday eve last week.

OMER, Rob't | All Over the County | Jan 28, 1897
"Herald" Rob't Omer, who was married at the Tremont to Miss Dessie C. Meatheringham is the popular Wabash agent at Camp Point.

OMER, Roy | Local | Jan 14, 1897
Roy Omer, son of Charlie Omer and Miss Maymie Davis were married December 28th at Kirksville. Bride is graduate of Missouri State Normal.

OMER, Will E. | 5 Years Ago | Sep 4, 1890
SEE HASSEN, Miss Jennie

OMER, Wm | Locals | Nov 19, 1891
Wm Omer and Miss Belle Collier, both of Camp Point are licensed to wed.

O'NEIL, Miss Lizzie T. | | Jun 19, 1890
SEE FRANCIS, John T.

ORCHARDSON, "Prof" | Neighborhood News | Apr 20, 1893
MERRICK, Mrs Minerva

ORCHARDSON, Charlie | Local | Jan 9, 1896
Charlie Orchardson's marriage has been declared illegal and he has been deposed as ex. of the will.

ORDING, John C. | Our Own Bailiwick | Oct 31, 1895
Eleborate wedding at 7 AM Thursday morning, John C. Ording and Miss Anna M. Duker, eldest daughter of Mr and Mrs J.H. Duker at St. Boniface Church.

ORR, Matthew City Brevities Apr 21, 1898
Marriage of Mr Matthew Orr of Barry, Illinois and Mrs Jennie D. Ausmus of Quincy occurred in the latter city Wednesday. Mr Orr is brother of Judge Jefferson Orr of Pike County. He has been engaged in business at Barry for some time. Bride has lived Quincy several years. Will live at Barry. As children they were raised together, the farms of the Orr and Davidson families adjoined down in old Pike County. Both were baptized at Northcott Chapel close by. The Davidson family moved and young people seperated.

ORTON, Mr Vandeleur Mar 19, 1896
SEE ROBBINS, Miss Alta C.

OVERSTREET, J.M. 5 Years Ago Mar 12, 1891
SEE CRAIG, Mrs Cina

OWEN, Edwin K. Local Mar 6, 1890
Married at the home of Mrs Gay, north of Clayton, on February 27th by Rev W. Maley Reed, Mr Edwin K. Owen and Miss Lillie L. Miller.

PADGETT, Carrie M. Mar 4, 1897
SEE ARNTZEN, Oscar

PADGETT, Miss Daisy Local Aug 10, 1899
Married at the home of brides parents, Mr and Mrs John Padgett of McKee township at 3 PM Sunday, Miss Daisy Padgett and Mr Emery Peacock, son of Samuel Peacock, Esq. and wife. Mr Padgett is a young farmer of the south part of this county.

PADGETT, John City Brevities Dec 22, 1898
John Padgett of Haselwood, Illinois and May Padgett of Chestline, were Friday granted a license to wed.

PADGETT, May Dec 22, 1898
SEE PADGETT, John

PADGETT, Williams J. Local Sep 15, 1892
Suit for divorce filed October term for Grace Padgett from Williams J. Padgett file shows they were married April 22, 1880 in this county and lived together until September 1888 when she left him because of ill treatment. Formerly lived McKee township.

PALLARDAY, Ed Jul 21, 1892
SEE VANCIL, Miss Viola

PARKER, Miss Alice L. Local Nov 27, 1890
Marriage of Miss Alice L. Parker, daughter of Mrs N.W. Wright, to Mr John Gunn by Rev W.M. Reed at the home of N.W. and Mrs Wright in Concord at 4 PM Thursday.

PARKER, Miss Eliza 5 Years Ago Dec 25, 1890
Miss Eliza Parker was married to Mr John Bartoldos, both of Kellerville.

PARKER, Mrs Emma Jul 23, 1891
SEE WRIGHT, N.W.

PARKER, Miss Lottie L. Married Jun 12, 1890
The marriage of Miss Lottie L. Parker and Mr Ed S. Motter at the home of brides parents, Mr and Mrs E.W. Parker in this city 4 PM Thursday the 5th inst. Present were their parents, their brothers and sisters and perhaps a half dozen friends of the bride. By Rev E.W. Souders. Groom grew to manhood in our midst. He has been connected with R.W. Tansil and Co. Chicago about five years. They went to Chicago the same night.

PARKER, Lucy B. Oct 24, 1895
SEE AUSMUS, Geo. F.

PARKER, Minnie Adelle Local Oct 14, 1897
A card received reads thus: Mr and Mrs Edgar S. Motter request the honor of your presence at the marriage of their sister, Minnie Adelle Parker to Mr Frederick Edward Bryant on Wednesday eve November 10th, 1897 at Grace Episcopal Church Eddy, New Mexico.

PARKER, Mr and Mrs N.H. Neighborhood News Mar 9, 1893
A few weeks ago Mr and Mrs N.H. Parker, of Keithsburg were divorced. Each got lonesome, so they net in joint session entered a motion to reconsider, and drove to the county seat and were married again last week. "Bushnell Record"

PARKS, Miss Lila Local Aug 24, 1899
Last weeks issue of Arlington Kansas paper carries notices of marriage of Miss Lila Parks and Mr Albert Ewing, both of Arlington. Mr Ewing is son of Robert Ewing and wife, formerly of Clayton, who have been in Kansas about 20 years.

PARRICK, Harvey Our Own Bailiwick Jan 30, 1896
Camp Point Journal At Union Church last Wednesday night, Harvey Parrick and Angeline Wild were married by Rev J.T. Parrick.

PARSONS, Mr W.E. Oct 26, 1893
SEE REYLAND, Miss Cad

PARVIN, Miss Sarah Jul 9, 1891
SEE HERMAN, Mr William H.

PAXTON, Hayes Elm Grove Nov 12, 1896
Cards are out for wedding of Hayes Paxton to Miss Lizzie Steed.

PAXTON, J. Hayes Our Own Bailiwick Nov 19, 1896
License has been issued for marriage of J. Hayes Paxton and Miss Elizabeth Steed, two of PineGroves young people. Mr Paxton has rented a farm, now we know why.

PEACOCK, Charles Dec 30, 1897
SEE DEMOSS, Miss Birdie

PEACOCK, Emery Aug 10, 1899
SEE PADGETT, Miss Daisy

PEAIRS, Dr George M. Locals Jan 3, 1895
Newspapers contain the announcements of the marriage of Dr George M. Peairs to Jessie Hayes at Joliet. That is all we know about it.

PEARCE, Miss Saidee Local Feb 22, 1900
Marriage of Miss Saidee Pearce, sister of Jackson R. Pearce, the county treasurer, to Mr William T. Cromwell of LaPrairie, brother of Joe at this place by Rev Beadles Wednesday eve at the home of Mr Pearce. Will live on the Marsh farm 2½ miles northeast of Clayton.

PEARIL, James and Katie Local Aug 11, 1892
James Pearil of Clayton yesterday instituted proceedings for divorce from his wife Katie Pearil. He says he married Katie Walker at Troy, Lincoln County Missouri Sep 11, 1886 and they lived together until November 15, 1889 when she deserted him. They have two children, Dora now 4½ years old and Joe 3. She took Joe with her and left Dora and he asks that he be given custody of her. Mrs Pearil is now at Eolia, Lincoln County Missouri. Sunday Whig.

PEARL, Mr J.E. Mt Sterling Feb 2, 1893
Mr J.E. Pearl and Mrs S.L. Gray, all of Clayton, were married in this city Saturday the 21st by police magistrate Wallace.

PEIPER, Miss Minnie Sep 27, 1894
SEE GROSS, George

PENDLETON, Christ Damon Apr 20, 1899
Marriage of Mr Christ Pendleton and Miss Trintje Hippen at last occurred at home of Mr John Hippen St at 4 PM by German Lutheran minister in English language.

PENDLETON, Christopher T. Little Brindle Apr 20, 1899
Christopher T. Pendleton and Miss Trinkie Hippen were married on Tuesday by Rev Geo. Gerken at home of brides parents in Missouri township, near Damon postoffice.

PENNEY, Mrs Zooetta Oct 28, 1897
SEE HARPER, Frank

PEPPINGER, Kelley Sep 15, 1898
SEE CRAWFORD, Miss Eva

PERKINS, A.J. Feb 23, 1899
SEE FIELDS, Miss Nannie

PERKINS, Joseph and Mrs Amy M. Local Jan 9, 1890
Among the decrees by Judge Marsh, Saturday was that of Mrs Amy M. Perkins, better known to Clayton people as Mrs Amy Smith, from her husband, Joseph Perkins. They had not lived together for about 10 years and he says the cause is she is "too high toned".

PERRY, Miss Minnie Little Brindle Nov 10, 1898
Brown County Republican: Sunday, Miss Minnie Perry and Don S. Harney were married at home of Rev Rigg, the Methodist minister.

PETERS, Edward Local Jan 31, 1895
Marriage of Mr Edward Peters of Clayton and Miss Belle Hipkins of Palmyra, Missouri occurred in Quincy Thursday of last week and next day they arrived in Clayton where they will live. Ed was raised in this community and they will live with his parents.

PETERS, Lucinda 10 Years Ago Nov 30, 1893
SEE WALKER, Rosewell

PETERS, Miss Mae Jul 23, 1891
SEE RYDINGS, Mills

PETRIE, Miss Georgie 5 Years Ago Nov 21, 1890
SEE GROSS, Lieut. Fred

PEVEHOUSE, Miss Emma Local Dec 18, 1890
5 Years Ago Miss Emma Pevehouse was married to Mr H.L. Adair at the home of Esq. Jack Pevehouse.

PEVEHOUSE, Miss Venia Married May 28, 1891
Married at home of brides parents Mr and Mrs J.B. Pevehouse in east part of town Sunday 4 PM by Rev W.M. Reed, their daughter, Miss Venia Pevehouse to Mr T. Elmer Jefferson. Mr Jefferson graduated from Chaddock College last year, is son of a farmer and he to will farm. Miss Pevehouse taught in our school.

PEVEHOUSE, Wm City Brevities Dec 15, 1898
Marriage of Wm Pevehouse and Miss Dora Shields occurred at Mt Sterling last Friday afternoon by Justice McCabe. Groom is oldest son of Joseph B. and Mrs Pevehouse of this city. They are living at present with his parents. Bride is daughter of Mr and Mrs Marion Shields of Mounds.

PHELPS, Lillie M. Mar 30, 1893
SEE HOLMES, Charles

PHILBRICK, Miss Edna E. Our Own Bailiwick Jun 18, 1896
From the city papers we see the marriage notice of Miss Edna E. daughter of Capt J.A. Philbrick the court reporter and head of Quincy Shorthand College and wife. Groom is Mr Walter E. Mulliner, son of Mr and Mrs Ed Mulliner of Quincy. "Whig 16th" Wedding at home of brides parents 1926 Maine St at 8:30 last eve by Rev H.T. Miller of the Presbyterian Church. Bride is daughter of Mr and Mrs James A. Philbrick. Groom works for the Mulliner Box and Paning Co. They will live at 323 S. 16th St. after June 30th.

PHILLIPS, Green Exchanges May 24, 1900
A marriage license was issued last eve to Green Phillips, who gave his age as 52 and to Mrs Margaret J. Kimball age 55 years. Gave their address as Mounds, Brown County. "Rushville Citizen"

PIERCE, Miss Jennie Locals Jun 18, 1891
Miss Jennie Pierce was married to Mr H.J. Lewis at the home of brides - father, Mr Joseph Pierce, one mile east of Camp Point at 1 PM Tuesday by Rev Greer of Camp Point. Groom is son of "Uncle Henry" Lewis one of the first settlers of township. Groom has a 320 acre farm on the Clayton and Camp Point Road.

PILLING, William H. Little Brindle Nov 4, 1897
Golden New Era: Licensed to wed, William H. Pilling and Bertha Bowman, both of Fish Hook.

PIPER, Clay Camp Point Jun 3, 1897
Clay Piper, of Mt Sterling and Miss Fannie Joseph were married at the home of the bride last Tuesday at 4 PM by Rev A.N. Simmonds. Will live Mt Sterling.

PITNEY, Miss Bertha Aug 23, 1894
SEE ROBINSON, Prof J.M.

POLAND, Miss Minerva 10 Years Ago Sep 29, 1892
Miss Minerva Poland married Mr Louis Kesting.

POLAND, Miss Sidney Mar 2, 1899
SEE FRANK, Charlie

POORMAN, Charlie Camp Point Dec 27, 1894
Mr Charlie Poorman of Kansas and Madie Ivins were married Tuesday at the brides home. Will live Kansas.

POPE, Sam Camp Point Jan 5, 1899
Since our last letter the wedding of Sam Pope and Nellie Farlow occurred at home of Squire Bailey.

PORTER, Mr Dec 20, 1894
SEE CHILDS, Misses Nellie and Lura

POTTER, Edgar S. Wedding Mar 28, 1895
Mr Edgar S. Potter and Miss Cora B. May were married Wednesday eve at home of brides mother, 620 Vine St. by Rev J.M. Rudy pastor of Christian Church. She is oldest daughter of Mrs B. May and cashier at Kespohl's. Groom is bookeeper for Wellman and Devire Tobacco Company. They will live at 802 N. 7th st. "Whig 22nd"

POTTOR, J. Will May 1882 Jul 1, 1897
SEE CURRY, Miss Nellie G.

POWELL, Eli and wife Pike County Feb 1, 1900
Eli Powell and wife celebrated their golden wedding anniversary in Pike County at their home near Perry January 31st.

POWELL, Geo. Ill State News Apr 1, 1897
Geo. Powell, wanted at Quincy and elsewhere for alleged forgeries was arrested at Browning, Missouri. He gained notoriety a few months ago by eloping with a young girl and being received with shots from a revolver by her father after the marriage.

POWELL, Gordon Local Dec 29, 1892
A marriage license was issued to Gordon Powell and Henrietta McFadden, both of Clayton.

POWERS, Mr B.F. Married May 10, 1900
Married at the home of the groom in Augusta, Illinois May 1st 1900, Mr B.F. Powers of Augusta, Illinois and Mrs H.M. Rowsey of Clayton by ME pastor Rev Clark at 7 PM.

PRATT, Mrs Julia Jan 2, 1896
SEE ROBBINS, Dr Joseph

PREECE, Elmer E. Mt Sterling Feb 2, 1893
Elmer E. Preece a young farmer of Pea Ridge township and Miss Mary E. McNeil were married at the home of brides parents, Mr and Mrs James Shields in Ripley last Wednesday.

PREECE, Miss Lizzie Ada Mar 17, 1898
SEE CLEAVES, Hobert A.

PRESTON, Mrs Angeline | Ill State News | Jul 27, 1891
SEE WILKERSON, J.J.
PRICE, Miss Helen | | Aug 9, 1894
SEE WARE, Clide N.
PRITCHARD, Ben | Neighborhood News | Mar 30, 1893
Ben Pritchard, who claimed Bushnell as his home in youthful days has been married 9 times, having been married to one woman 3 times.
PROPHATER, Miss Ollie | Local | Jan 23, 1896
Of Miss Prophater who lived in Clayton, the Hamilton Press says: Word received by friends in this city of the marriage of Miss Ollie Prophater, the elder of tow daughters of the Elder Prophater, who lived here a couple of years ago, to a prosperous young farmer, named Smith, near Mt Auburn in Christian County. They was married last fall.
PRORINE, Mr and Mrs | Neighborhood News | Oct 6, 1892
Mr and Mrs Prorine of Vermont, Illinois have been married 54 years. They were born on the same day and the same hour and united with the church on the same Sunday AM.
PUGH, Mr W.D. | 5 Years Ago | Oct 6, 1892
SEE ENNIS, Miss Ella
PURCELL, Ed | | Feb 21, 1895
SEE ADAMS, Miss Hattie
PURPUS, Ida M. | | Jan 23, 1896
SEE HOFFMAN, George
PURPUS, Wm | | Feb 5, 1891
SEE MCCONNELL, Miss Alice
PUTMAN, Mr | | Jan 8, 1891
SEE BELL, Amanda
RAMEY, Miss Minnie | Personal | Apr 26, 1894
Miss Lola Rosson went to Quinvy Tuesday night to attend the wedding of her cousin, Miss Minnie Ramey, to Mr J. Luther, a young gentleman of Quincy. Wedding takes place Wednesday April 25th.
RAND, Miss Eliza | | Jan 5, 1893
SEE DAVIS, Emmor O.
RANIER, Hudson | Married | Oct 16, 1890
Mr Hudson Ranier and Miss Laurissa Hart were married at Camp Point Friday.
RATCLIFF, Mr Chipman | | Nov 12, 1891
SEE HARPER, Carrie
RATCLIFF, Horace G. | Mound Station | Aug 14, 1890
Mr Horace G. Ratcliff and Miss Mattie Henson were married Sunday eve by Rev Van Wey at his home. They have rented the Bruback property and will be at home after first of the month.
RATCLIFF, Idella | | Jun 18, 1896
SEE WRIGHT, Will W.
RATCLIFF, Miss Mary P. | | Oct 22, 1891
SEE LUCAS, Allen
RATCLIFF, Myron | Married | Oct 16, 1890
Mr Myron Ratcliff and Miss Ina K. Davis took the Tuesday train to Quincy and were married that afternoon, returned by evening train. Will live in Concord.
RATLIFF, E.E. | | Apr 29, 1897
SEE BROWN, Miss Fannie
RAWSON, Mr Dell | | Oct 21, 1892
SEE JOHNSON, Miss Anna
RAWSON, Frank | Pea Ridge | Mar 8, 1894
Married, Frank Rawson of Schuyler, to Miss Frankie May of this vicinity Wednesday eve February 28th by Jay Brown Esq.

RAYMOND, Miss Ida 10 Years Ago Aug 8, 1895
SEE STOUT, Oliver

REA, Roberta Y. Married Jun 23, 1892
Married at the home of Mr and Mrs J.M. Rea, Wednesday eve, their youngest daughter, Roberta Y. Rea to Wiley M. Glass son of Mr and Mrs George H. Glass a farmer in vicinity of Clayton by Rev E.W. Souders of Clayton at 6 PM. Mr Glass has taught school in Adams County and Brown County several terms. "Dem. Message"

REATH, Mr Henry Married Oct 26, 1899
Mr Henry Reath, formerly of this city has taken himself a wife in person of Mrs Sarah Hall, of Bedford, Indiana on September 26th. They were school mates in the days of childhood and gew up together. Will live in her home.

REATH, Miss Josephine Apr 3, 1890
SEE MCBRATNEY, Samuel

REDBURN, Miss Florence Jun 8, 1899
SEE WILL, William C.

REDMOND, Charles Little Brindle Dec 1, 1898
Married at St Marys church by Rev D.J. Ryan, Mr Charles Redmond and Miss Ella Murphy both of Pea Ridge last Sunday at 7 PM.

REDMOND, Miss Esther Feb 16, 1899
SEE BRADY, John

REDMOND, Margaret Dec 1, 1898
SEE SCHNEIDER, Charles

REDMOND, Thomas Little Brindle May 4, 1899
Thomas Redmond, of Pea Ridge township and Miss Kathryn Langan of Missouri township were marreid at high noon Sunday last.

REED, Miss Emma May 18, 1899
SEE CANNON, Clarence H.

REED, Henry L. City Brevities Dec 29, 1898
Married at the Hampton House at 3 PM Wednesday Mr Henry L. Reed and Miss Nellie Gibson who has lived in Mr McDowell family several months. by Rev P. Slagle, pastor of Methodist Church of which they are members.

REED, Henry T. October 1889 Oct 5, 1899
Married, Mr Henry T. Reed and Miss Ruth A. Anderson, both of Camp Point.

REEDER, James Local Nov 24, 1892
Mr James Reeder, son of A.L. and Mrs Reeder, formerly of Concord was married Tuesday to Miss Ella Harding of this city by Rev J.H. Terrill, pastor of Baptist Church at the home of the bride and her sister. They met when Mr Reeder lived with parents on the farm in Concord and Miss Harding lived on adjoining farm. Will live Lexington Junction, Missouri.

REEDER, Miss Mattie Local Sep 28, 1893
A letter to Miss Sarah Harding of this city, tells of marriage of Miss Mattie, daughter of A.L. and Mrs Reeder of Lexington Junction, Missouri to Mr Henry Hutchinson, a railroad man. Will live Lexington Junction.

REEN, Wm Married Dec 29, 1892
Married last Sunday, Xmas Day, Wm Reen and Miss Jennie Sharp at the home of Mrs Sharp six miles southwest of Clayton. Miss Hylas Sharp was bridesmaid and Frank Parker groomsman. Married at 4:30 PM by Elder Van Dervoort.

REEVES, Frank Oct 16, 1890
SEE BRYANT, Amelia

REGAN, John F. Little Brindle Jun 23, 1898
Examiner of the 18th: Mr John F. Regan, a attorney of the firm of Regan and Baker and Miss Addie Larkin, daughter of Mary Larkin were married at 4 PM last Thursday at the home of brides mother in this city, by Rev M.S. McCoy.

REID, Joseph Local Mar 15, 1894
Married March 13th 1894 at Presbyterian parsonage, Clayton by Rev E.W. Souders, Joseph Reid of Clayton and Emma A. Clark, of Golden, Illinois.

REID, Ralph Little Brindle Sep 10, 1896
Republican: Ralph Reid and Ida Chenoweth both of Versailles were married at Springfield and went to St Louis for wedding trip.

REIMBOLD, Mr and Mrs Wm Neighborhood News Dec 11, 1890
A nauvoo Rustler claims the oldest married couple in the County live in that city, on the persons of Wm Reimbold and wife, who have been married 50 years.

REIMBOLD, Mr and Mrs Wm Neighborhood News Feb 2, 1893
Mr and Mrs Wm Reimbold, of Nauvoo, have been married 57 years.

REIMHOLD, Mr and Mrs Wm Supplement Dec 25, 1890
Neighborhood News The Nauvoo Rustler claims that Wm Reimhold and wife of that city are the oldest married couple in the County, having been married 55 years.

REINMAN, Mr and Mrs Frederick Neighbors Jan 14, 1897
Nauvoo claims the oldest married couple in the state--Frederick Reinman and wife, both nearly 9 have been married over 64 years.

REMPLE, Amelia Aug 25, 1898
SEE ROYER, Fred

RENAKER, Chas. A. All Over the County Nov 18, 1897
Camp Point Trumpet: Chas. A. Renaker of Clayton, and Desta Hughes of Kellerville, Illinois were married at the Omer Hotel, Camp Point by Elder Chas. Laycock Sunday PM.

RENAKER, Miss Florence Apr 28, 1892
SEE EDMUNDS, James

RENAKER, Mr Orson Local Dec 31, 1891
Father Reed got out of bed last Wednesday long enough to marry, Miss McConnell of Kellerville to Mr Orson Renaker of Concord.

RENAKER, Miss Susan A. Jul 13, 1893
SEE WILSON, Andrew J.

RENAKER, W.G. Brown County May 3, 1900
Marriage license: W.G. Renaker, Clayton over 21 and Jennie Borderick, Clayton age 18.

RENTSCHLER, Miss Birdie Aug 16, 1894
SEE NARS, John

RENTSCHLER, Miss Dollie Aug 23, 1894
SEE MARS, Johnnie

RENTSCHLER, Miss Minnie Sep 13, 1894
SEE FLYNN, John J.

REPLOGLE, Miss Ella Camp Point Jul 7, 1898
Misses Ida and Sarah Derrick left Friday for Iowa to attend wedding of their friend, Miss Ella Replogle.

REYLAND, Miss Cad Neighborhood News Oct 26, 1893
Miss Cad Reyland and Mr W.E. Parsons were married in Jacksonville the 12th inst. Bride is known here, having visited Miss Anna Hazlett, now Mrs Sweetring.

REYNOLDS, Charles A. and Emma Chancery Notice Jan 29, 1891
March term--In chancery divorce: Emma Reynolds, complaintant #4224 vs Charles A. Reynolds, defendent. Charles A. Reynolds lives out of state of Illinois.

REYNOLDS, William C. and Martha J.   Little Brindle   Sep 24, 1896
Divorce was granted William C. Reynolds from Martha J.
RHEA, Miss Effie   Feb 27, 1896
SEE BOGER, Fred J.
RHEA, Miss Effie   Our Own Bailiwick   Feb 27, 1896
Golden New Era: Friends in Golden received invitations this week, Mrs P.J. Thea requests your presence at the marriage of her daughter, Effie, to J. Fred Boger, Wednesday eve February 26, 1896 at her home in Camp Point, Illinois.
RHEA, Miss Grace   Sep 7, 1899
SEE BLOOD, Charles
RHEA, Mary K.   Jul 13, 1899
SEE BOOTHE, Dr John C.
RHEA, Mary Katherine   Jul 6, 1899
SEE BOOTHE, Charles
RHEA, Miss Mollie   Jun 29, 1899
SEE BOOTHE, Dr J.C.
RHEA, Mrs Pamelia J.   Apr 16, 1896
SEE Bailey, Thomas
RICE, Miss   Personal   Dec 27, 1894
SEE SCOGGAN, Alfred
RICE, Miss Maggie   Wedding of Daughter   May 28, 1891
Letter from Rev E.J. Rice   Hamilton, Illinois May 20, 1891 to Enterprise Sunday AM I married Mr Aldridge Busby and Miss Maggie Rice during the service at Wythe Presbyterian Church. She was the little girl who came to Clayton 16 years ago this spring and now is near 18 years old. Mr Busby is a business man of Pueblo, Colo. and will live there. Both members of Presbyterian Church.
RICHARDSON, Col. George B.   Neighborhood News   Nov 29, 1894
At Riverton, Colo. George B. Richardson, 72 years old and on his death bed was married to Marion B. McNeely, 54 years old. Marriage was for the purpose of settling a vast estate upon the woman of his choice who has been his housekeeper for many years. Neither of them had been married.
RICHARDSON, Joseph   Jul 21, 1892
SEE MCCOY, Miss Alice
RICHARDSON, Mr Wm   Apr 16, 1891
SEE MCCOY, Miss Ida
RICHMOND, Miss Maude   Little Brindle   Oct 19, 1893
Last eve at home of Mr and Mrs John T. Hiles, uncle and aunt of bride was marriage of Miss Maude Richmond and Mr Morton L. Schutt of Durango, Colorado by Rev Jonas VanWey. Miss Flora Marion of Rockport, Illinois was maid of honor. Miss Lou Parker of Clayton was at the organ. Will live Durango, Colo.   Mounds Correspondence to Examiner.
RICKEY, Charles F.   Brown County   Jan 11, 1900
Letter received in this city Friday from Colorado Springs, Colorado telling of marriage of Charles F. Rickey, formerly of this place, name of bride is not given and the wedding took place at her home in Nebraska on Xmas. Will live Colorado Springs.
RIED, Leslie A.   Local   Dec 3, 1896
Married at home of Rev Wm R. Lierle November 26th Leslie A. Ried of Liberty to Miss Nellie M. Litz of Clayton.

RIGGS, Miss Alice — Little Brindle News — May 31, 1894
Confusion in Adams and Brown Counties: One Davis, now in jail at Quincy married Miss Alice Riggs, daughter of Risin Riggs at Mt Sterling and moved to Missouri and later seperated, she and two children returned to Mt Sterling. After she left Davis married another woman and lived with her three months when he came to Mt Sterling to live with wife #1. In 1888 he was hurt and taken to home of his father in Missouri and his wife never heard from him until she read of his arrest in Quincy. She went down Thursday with her brother Abe Riggs and had Mr Davis indicted for bigamy.

RILEY, Miss May — Apr 15, 1897
SEE MASON, Lewis

RINGLING, Dr. — Neighborhood News — Jan 12, 1893
Dr Ringling of Riverside sanitarium at Hamilton, Ill. was married on the 20th of last month to Miss Katherine O'Donald of Springfield, MO.

RIPETOE, Miss Nellie — Oct 12, 1899
SEE MOORE, Otis

RITTER, Elizabeth — Mar 26, 1896
SEE MCCASKELL, T.L.

RITTER, Geo. M. — Local — Sep 10, 1891
Carthage Gazette: Geo. M. Ritter and Mary A. Wallace of Clayton were married at the county clerks office yesterday afternoon by Judge Wm R. Hamilton.

ROBBINS, Miss Alta C. — Married — Mar 19, 1896
Married Wednesday eve at brides home in North East township, Mr Vandeleur Orton of Concord and Miss Alta C. Robbins. Will live on Orton homestead in Concord, four miles south of town.

ROBBINS, Dr Joseph — Wedding — Jan 2, 1896
Married, Xmas day, Dr Joseph Robbins and Mrs Julia Pratt at the home of Rev C.F. Bradley, pastor of the Unitarian Church at 3 PM Wednesday. Bride is publisher and ediotr of the "Sunday Optic" in Quincy. Will live in the Permont. "Whig 27th"

ROBBINS, Miss Mary — 5 Years Ago — Oct 19, 1893
SEE CAIN, Harvey

ROBBINS, Mr W.N. — 5 Years Ago — Jan 18, 1894
Mr W.N. Robbins and Miss Ollie Alexander were married.

ROBBINS, Wm and Mary — Elm Grove — Dec 8, 1892
Thursday December 1st, 1892 was the 50th wedding anniversary of Uncle Wm and Aunt Mary Robbins. Brothers, sisters, children, grandchildren, great grandchildren and friends gathered at homestead. Present from a distance were, Mrs N. Balfour and daughter, Mr and Mrs Geo. Eastman of Augusta and Mrs Jennie Hiles Stevenson of Carthage.

ROBENAU, Loretta — Aug 24, 1899
SEE JARVIS, Henry

ROBERTS, Miss May — Local — Apr 23, 1891
Miss May Roberts and W.E. Sprague, of Windsor, N. Dakota were married at the home of Mr and Mrs Alspach by Rev Sadler Friday April 3, 1891 at 9:30 AM. Their romance started in a blizzard Jan 12, 1888. Mr Sprague is said to have gallantly rescued a young teacher from perishing in the storm. Will live Windsor.

ROBERTSON. William — Married — Oct 19, 1893
Married at the home of Capt and Mrs A.J. Griffith last Thursday eve William Robertson of Beverly and Miss Nadine Griffith, the Capt.'s third daughter by Rev J.J. Thomson, the brides pastor. Will live Beverly where Mr Robertson is a prosperous farmer.

ROBINSON, Prof. J.M. — Ill Brevities — Aug 23, 1894
Prof. J.M. Robinson and Miss Bertha Pitney were married at Paxton, Hancock County.

ROBINSON, John 5 Years Ago Mar 12, 1891
SEE GRIFFITH, Miss Tillie

ROBINSON, Miss Myrtle Local Dec 15, 1892
Miss Myrtle Robinson was married to Mr John Ball at the home of brides parents near Versailles last Friday. Miss Robinson lived in this vicinity two or three years. Mr Ball lived Clayton all his life.

ROBISON, Miss Belle Locals Dec 20, 1894
Cards are out announcing marriage of Miss Belle, daughter of James N. and Mrs Robison to Mr James J. Singleton at the family home at Mounds January 2nd. Groom is son of Gen. Jas. W. Singleton, deceased, formerly of Quincy. After wedding they go to Baltimore and then to his plantation in Virginia which will be their home.

ROBISON, Fred Local Aug 31, 1893
Married, at the parsonage of the First Presbyterian Church Thursday eve the 24th inst, by Rev E.W. Souders, Fred Robison and Miss Bridie M. Noakes, both of Mounds, Illinois.

ROBISON, Fred August 1893 Aug 11, 1898
Married, Mr Fred Robison and Miss Birdie M. Nokes, both of Lee township.

ROBISON, Miss Mattie 10 Years Ago Sep 15, 1892
Miss Mattie Robison married Mr Jas. Hoke.

ROBISON, Miss Rae Bell Jan 10, 1895
SEE SINGLETON, James J.

ROCKWELL, Edward Oct 21, 1892
SEE BURGESSER, Miss Clara Blanche

ROCKWELL, Edward W. Sep 29, 1892
SEE BURGESSER, Clara Blanch

ROCKWOOD, Miss Ida Sep 8, 1892
SEE GEISS, Mr Henry

ROGERS, W.T. Adams County Feb 16, 1899
SEE MONTGOMERY, Dr Robert

ROLAND, Miss Elizabeth F. Feb 6, 1896
SEE BOSWELL, Mr L.B.

ROLAND, Miss Nora J. Nov 14, 1895
SEE BOSWELL, Louis B.

ROLLETT, Mr G.S. Local Jun 29, 1893
Mr G.S. Rollett, civil engineer on the Clayton and Pea Ridge Railroad slipped into Libertyville, Iowa and married Miss May Warner, daughter of a wealthy farmer Thursday the 15th inst. Met while he was engineer on railroad running into Iowa. Mr Rollett lives Fort Madison.

ROSS, Miss Lillie Nov 24, 1898
SEE GILBERT, Harry

ROSS, May Aug 29, 1895
SEE EDDINGS, Silas

ROSS, Mr S.M. Jun 16, 1892
SEE BYRNS, Miss Kate

ROSS, Samuel M. Jun 23, 1892
SEE BYRNS, Katie Mae

ROSS, Will Local Sep 21, 1893
SEE LEWIS, Betsey

ROSSON, Miss Oct 25, 1894
SEE JOHNSON, Lew

ROSSON, Mr Allen Oakwood Aug 11, 1892
Mr Allen Rosson, of Creston, Iowa who visited his brother, S.D. last summer was married the 1st of July to a lady of Osceola, Iowa a member of one of the best and wealthiest families in Osceola.

ROSSON. Frank Local Mar 1, 1894
Marriage of Miss Frankie, daughter of Mr and Mrs Wood May of Pea Ridge to Mr Frank Rosson, of Schuyler, occurred at the family home at 6 PM Wednesday.

ROSSON, Geo. A. Married Sep 17, 1896
Married in Quincy, September 10th at the home of grooms aunt, Mrs A.B.-Ramey, Mr Geo. A. Rosson and Miss Katie Carver, both of Clayton by Rev Scott of Grace M.E. at high twelve. Will live Clayton after October 1st, a reception given them Sunday the 13th at S.D. Rosson's.

ROTHGEB, Capt Frank Our Own Bailiwick May 23, 1895
Marriage of Capt Frank Rothgeb and Miss Elizabeth Groom occurred at home of brides mother in Camp Point Wednesday eve. They came to this city on the Wabash same eve and was met by Co. F. in full uniform who fired a salute in honor of their Capt and his bride. After June 1st They will live at 2007 Hampshire St.

ROTTGER, Miss Eugenia A. Oct 26, 1893
SEE CURRY, Frank C.

ROWE, Mr James A. Nov 17, 1892
SEE HARRIS, Miss Anna A.

ROWE, Jas. W. November 1882 Nov 3, 1898
Married Jas. W. Rowe and Sarah E. Curry.

ROWSEY, Mrs H.M. May 10, 1900
SEE POWERS, Mr B.F.

ROWSEY, Lewis Local Dec 31, 1896
Mr Tommie Rowsey was in Quincy Xmas eve to attend the wedding of his brother, Mr Lewis Rowsey and Miss Amelia Klosterman at the home of the bride. Mr Rowsey is a railroad man. Will live Quincy.

ROY, J.A. Jul 14, 1892
SEE AUSMUS, Miss Blanche

ROY, Mr Jas. L. 5 Years Ago Aug 25, 1892
SEE LUCAS, Mrs Ida M.

ROY, Mr and Mrs John Local Nov 30, 1899
Mr and Mrs John Roy formerly of Concord, now of Quincy celebrated their 50th wedding anniversary. Children will gather in the parental home today. Will went down Wednesday.

ROY, Miss Mary 5 Years Ago May 3, 1894
Miss Mary Roy married Thad T. Burke.

ROY, Will Pea Green Feb 2, 1893
Will Roy has taken himself a wife, Miss Ella Varner from near Kellerville some time ago.

ROYER, Fred Little Brindle Aug 25, 1898
Marriage license: Fred Royer, Pea Ridge 18, and Amelia Remple, Pea Ridge 18.

ROYER, Miss Nellie Local Apr 9, 1891
Married in Quincy on Thursday April 20th, Miss Nellie Royer to Mr D.B. Boren, both of this city. Returned on afternoon train and are now living with his father.

RUDDELL, Mr and Mrs John Our Own Bailiwick Apr 23, 1896
Mr and Mrs John Ruddell of Marcaline have celebrated their 64th wedding anniversary.

RUDDLE, Mrs John Local Apr 30, 1896
Mention was made in this paper of the celebration of the 64th wedding anniversary of Mr and Mrs John Ruddle of Marceline, the aged wife has since died. She was an aunt of Mr T.H. Dunlap, of this city.

RUMPLE, Miss Dec 8, 1898
SEE MAY, George D.

RUMPLE, Miss Margaret Feb 7, 1895
SEE BAKER, Bert

RUTLEDGE, Miss Flora 5 Years Ago Mar 5, 1891
Miss Flora Rutledge was married to J.M. Lester. Mrs Lester died about two years ago leaving the husband and sweet little daughter.

RUTLEDGE, J.F. Married Oct 16, 1890
Our young lumber merchant, Mr J.F. Rutledge and Miss Lucie B. Hoxie of San Francisco, California by Rev W.M. Groves of Camp Point at the Occidental Hotel in Quincy 2 PM Tuesday the 7th inst. They arrived here at the home of Mr Rutledge's father that eve and will live with him here in Clayton.

RUTLEDGE, Mary S. Jan 8, 1891
SEE HOUGH, Frank E.

RUTLEDGE, Miss Mollie Local Jan 8, 1891
Miss Mollie Rutledge and Mr Frank Hough were married at the home of the brides parents, Thursday eve. Groom is an engineer on the Wabash.

RYDINGS, Mills Locals Jul 23, 1891
Married Tuesday eve at 9:45 in the ME Church by Rev W.M. Reed. Mr Mills Rydings and Miss Mae Peters.

SALLY, Mr William Little Brindle Oct 6, 1898
Democrat Message: :Last Monday, William Sally of Kellerville and Isabell Smith of Camp Point were married in circuit clerks office by Squire Cronin. Groom was granted a divorce during the present term of court from a previous marriage and decree was not signed yet.

SAMMIS, Miss Fay Adams County Jun 15, 1899
Miss Fay Sammis and attorney Chas. James were married Thursday eve at home of the bride, 529 N. 3rd St.

SAMUELS, Mary L. Ill State News Sep 26, 1896
On September 15, 1846 at Carrollton, Mary L. Samuels was married to William P. Barr they moved to Morgan County in 1861 and stayed. They celebrated their golden wedding in Jacksonville the other day.

SARGENT, Mr Gordon Oct 1, 1891
SEE LOGUE, Miss Leona

SARGENT, Mr and Mrs John Neighborhood News Oct 21, 1892
Mr and Mrs John Sargent of Ruchville celebrated their 50th wedding anniversary.

SARTORIUS, Hannah 10 Years Ago May 21, 1891
Hannah Sartorius and Heye Busbom were married.

SATOREOUS, Miss Minnie Feb 6, 1890
SEE FLEMING, Theodore

SAWIN, Miss Kate Oct 5, 1899
SEE CASTLE, Joe

SAWYER, Miss Hattie E. Supplement Jun 5, 1890
Locals Miss Hattie E. Sawyer, daughter of E.E.B. Sawyer of Camp Point was married to Mr Henson E. Bates, son of Thos. E. Bates, Tuesday eve at 5:30. Bride has been a teacher at Maplewood school. Will live in Galesburg.

SAXER, Fred B. Little Brindle Oct 20, 1898
Examiner, Mt Sterling: At high noon Thursday, at the home of Mr and Mrs J. Saxer, Pea Ridge township, occurred the marriage of their son, Fred B. Saxer to Miss Julia Bouchell. Groom is of Pea Ridge township, bride came to his place only a short time ago from Centralia, Kansas. Groom has exected a dwelling house.

SCHEIFERDECKER, Amelia C. Oct 29, 1896
SEE BALSAR, Lewis A.

SCHLAGENHAUF, Wm Local Nov 3, 1892
Mr Wm Schlagenhauf, a young Quincy lawyer and Miss Lily Eucke were married Wednesday eve by the grooms father. Bride is known to Clayton people and a relative of Mrs F.M. Anderson.

SCHMITT, Mr John Dec 19, 1895
SEE MCBRATNEY, Miss Sarah

SCHNEIDER, Charles	Little Brindle	Dec 1, 1898
Married at St Mary's Church by Rev D.J. Ryan, Mr Charles Schneider of this city and Miss Margaret Redmond of Pea Ridge last Sunday.

SCHOENE, Chistina	Feb 6, 1896
SEE ADEN, Ranke H.

SCHOFIELD, Gen. John M.	Supplement	Jun 18, 1891
Neighborhood News Coming marriage was announced by Gen. John M. Schofield and Miss Georgia Kilbourne of Keokuk. The general is 60 years old and Miss Kilbourne is 26 years old.

SCHOMP, Elmer	Dec 14, 1893
SEE MCNEAL, Miss May

SCHREIFFLER, Mrs Bertie M.	Jun 22, 1899
SEE MCCLAIN, Chas.

SCHROER, Mr Duke	Our Own Bailiwick	Dec 6, 1894
Mr Duke Schroer, the capable Quincy newspaper man, and Miss Mary Brophy, daughter of circuit clerk were married Wednesday after noon of last week and took evening train for Chicago for a week to 10 days.

SCHROLL, M.D.	Jun 14, 1894
SEE CARVER, Miss Katie

SCHUHARDT, Miss Anna	Dec 28, 1893
SEE WHITE, Rev

SCHUHARDT, Charlie	Camp Point	Sep 26, 1895
Wedding reception was given at home of Mr and Mrs Fred Schuhardt, west of town, for their son, Charlie, who was married to Miss Herzog of Missouri.

SCHULTZ, Charlie	Adams County News	Oct 19, 1893
Charlie Schultz and Miss Laura Sparks were married in Columbus township Wednesday afternoon.

SCHUTT, Mr Morton L.	Oct 19, 1893
SEE RICHMOND, Miss Maude

SCHWARTZ, Mr and Mrs	Golden	Mar 15, 1894
Saturday was the 30th wedding anniversary of Mr and Mrs Schwartz.

SCHWARTZBURN, Mrs Eva	Sep 27, 1894
SEE FINKHAUS, William F.

SCHWENK, Mr and Mrs	Neighbbrhood News	Sep 17, 1891
The marriage of Mr and Mrs Schwenk at Macomb brings to light a romance 3 years ago when Mr Schwenk was in college at Philadelphia, Penn. He met Miss Marie Hall who was there visiting friends, they ran away and were married across the Deleware river into New Jersey, that state being the haven for runaway couples. By the laws of that state no license is required or return or record kept of marriages is made. A question of their marriage having arisen and Mr and Mrs Schwenk being unable to find the minister who married them have decided to be remarried in this state, where there is a record kept.

SCOGGAN, Alfred	Personal	Dec 27, 1894
Alfred Scoggan is here from Cowgill, Missouri to visit his brother, Lyman and sister Miss Fannie. He married Miss Rice and they moved away 18 years ago.

SCOGGAN, Miss America	Local	Dec 2, 1897
Married at the home of brides sister, Mrs J.W. Sapp, Miss America Scoggan to Rev H.S. Abbott, of Winchester, Ontario Province, Canada at high noon Thnaksgiving day by Rev Richland, of Canton, Illinois. Will live Canada, leaving on evening train Augusta at 9 PM.

SCOGGAN, Lyman T.	5 Years Ago	Feb 6, 1890
SEE MAY, Miss Lizzie

SCOTT, Calvin Warner | Our Own Bailiwick | Mar 1, 1894
Cards are out announcing the marriage of Calvin Warner Scott to Miss Hattie Isabelle Lowry both of Chicago on February 15th Warren is a Camp Point boy. "Camp Point Journal"

SCOTT, Mr J.V. | Local | Nov 26, 1896
At Mt Sterling Tuesday night occurred the marriage of Mr J.V. Scott and Mrs Anna Moore Flasner. Groom is merchant at Denver, Illinois.

SCOTT, John and Fannie | Our Own Bailiwick | Oct 24, 1895
About 30 days ago John Scott, of near Seehorn, was shot and killed by Edward Tilby, a brother of Scott's wife. Found to be self defense. Thus Tilby came to Quincy and married Effie Brown. Friday Mrs Fannie Scott, widow of the man killed appeared at courthouse and married John Belts of Seehorn. She is 37 and he is 22 years old.

SCOTT, Lola | Neighborhood News | Apr 27, 1893
Lola Scott 17 years old ran away from home in Rushville and married a fellow whom she had met with a theatrical tramp at Wyanet bureau Co.

SCOTT, Mrs Minnie M. | 20 Years Ago | Apr 19, 1894
SEE FORBES, A.R.

SCOTT, Miss Olive Pearl | Dec 1, 1898
SEE BAILEY, William Taylor

SEAMAN, Miss Anna | Mar 15, 1900
SEE SPAULDING, J.W.

SEARS, Miss Iva | Local | Mar 15, 1900
Word received of marriage of Miss Iva Sears, formerly of Clayton, to Mr Souders, who is a nephew of Rev E.W. Souders at Cheny, Kansas which was announced to occur at high noon.

SEARS, Miss Iva | Local | Mar 29, 1900
Married at home of brides parents, 5 miles south of Cheney, Kansas at high noon Mar 13, 1900, Miss Iva Sears to Linneaus Souders. Bride is known in Clayton. Groom is relative of Rev Souders who was formerly pastor of the Presbyterian Church of Clayton.

SEARS, William A. | Married | Nov 4, 1897
Married at home of brides parents in this city, Sunday eve October 31st, Mr William A. Sears and Miss Nevva Glines by Rev Abner Sears, father of the groom. Will soon go to Quincy to live where Will has moved the printing office heretofore used in issuing the Liberty Bell.

SEATON, G.K. | Golden | Feb 8, 1894
Congratulations to our good friend G.K. Seaton on his marriage last Sunday to Mrs Boldin of Elvaston.

SEATON, Tom | Camp Point | Nov 30, 1893
Tom Seaton and Miss Laura Curry were married in Quincy Wednesday eve of last week.

SEDGWICK, Miss Mary | Jan 9, 1896
SEE MOFFETT, Henry Maynard

SEDGWICK, Miss Mary | Jan 23, 1896
SEE MOFFITT, Henry S.

SEELEY, James L. | Local | Sep 6, 1894
SEE KENDRICK, Jennie M.

SELBY, Miss Amata | Dec 3, 1891
SEE STERRITT, C.C.

SELBY, Miss Edna | Apr 29, 1897
SEE MOORE, Earnest L.

SELBY, Miss Electa | Mar 12, 1896
SEE BECKETT, John

SELBY, Miss Ellecta B. Our Own Bailiwick Mar 12, 1896
Golden New Era: Married at Camp Point Wednesday eve, March 4th 1896, Miss Ellecta B. Selby, to John Beckett by Rev Dilley. Bride is daughter of H.E.Selby and wife and groom is son of Joseph Beckett, living a few miles this side of Camp Point.

SELBY, Elmer T. All Over the County Apr 29, 1897
Golden New Era: Elmer T. Selby, of this place and Miss Stella Hucklebury of Brimham, Iowa were married at Keokuk Thursday.

SELBY, Miss Lotta Oct 10, 1895
SEE STEVENS, Charles

SELLERS, Prof J. and wife Neighborhood News May 8, 1898
The Sellers divorce case was continued in Pike County court. This is the cause of Prof J. Sellers, the ex leader of liberty band, against his wife.

SELLS, Mr and Mrs Peter Locals Dec 14, 1899
Mr Peter Sells the millionaire circus man is suing for a divorce from his wife at Columbus, Ohio. Mrs Sells is a daughter of Mr and Mrs Luker, who had the hotel Hampton for many years. Grounds of adultry. Mr and Mrs Joe C. Luker are with Mrs Sells in Columbus.

SEVIER, Mr Valentine 5 Years Ago Sep 15, 1892
SEE HUDDLESON, Mrs Rosa

SEWARD, Mahland Ill Brevities Dec 27, 1894
Mahland Seward age 71 and Mary Edwards age 50 were married at Quincy.

SEWERY, Miss Harriet E. Jun 11, 1896
SEE BERRIAN, John S.

SEXTON, Miss Bernice Jan 2, 1896
SEE ALLARD, Cad

SHAFFER, Mrs Eliza Dec 4, 1890
SEE WILLIAMS, Thomas

SHAFFER, Miss Sophronia Jun 29, 1899
SEE VALLEREUX, Mr F.W.

SHANK, Mr and Mrs Daniel Local Jan 28, 1897
Mr and Mrs Daniel Shank will celebrate their 10th wedding anniversary Saturday eve February 13th.

SHANK, Miss Ella Local Jul 16, 1891
Marriage of Miss Ella, daughter of Daniel Shank, of this place to Mr Louis Ulmer at Jacksonville Thursday eve last week by Rev Howe. Bride has lived at Jacksonville for some time, there she met Mr Ulmer, who is now located at Chicago where they will live.

SHANK, Miss Emma Local Dec 7, 1893
Miss Emma, daughter of Daniel Shank is to be married to Mr Fenstermaker of Jacksonville Wednesday eve. Mr Shank and sons Oscar and George and their wives attended the nuptials. Groom is a farmer. Miss Emma has been living at Jacksonville about 4 years.

SHANK, Miss Emma Local Dec 14, 1893
Jacksonville Journal says: S.F. Fenstermaker, of Davenport, NE. and Miss Emma Shank of this city were married at home of Mr A.E. Gunn, North Vorhees St. Bride is daughter of Daniel Shank, Clayton, Illinois and she has made her home with Mrs Gunn. Groom has many friends in Jacksonville and will stay there till he decides what branch of work he will follow.

SHANK, George Married Sep 15, 1892
George Shank of Clayton and Miss Hattie Byrns, daughter of Dr G.A. Byrns were married at brides home in this city 7 PM Wednesday by Rev J.H. Terrill of Clayton. Will live Clayton. "Mt Sterling Democrat Message"

SHANK, John M. Married Mar 16, 1899
Married at home, John M. Shank of this place to Miss Josephine Cain, of Astoria, Illinois Tuesday eve. Will live in the Reath property spent Wednesday and Thursday in Jacksonville with the two sisters of Mr Shank. Mr Daniel Shank, wife and son Henry attended wedding by Rev George of the Presbyterian Church at Elmwood, Illinois formerly of Lewiston, Illinois and pastor of the brides family.

SHANK, Miss Lydia Married Aug 15, 1895
Marriage of a Clayton lady at high 12 Wednesday August 14th at home of Mr and Mrs Wm Shank, the marriage of Miss Lydia Shank and Mr David M. Crowder of Bethany, Illinois by Rev J.H. Terril the Baptist clergyman. Groom is a retired farmer. Will live Bethany.

SHANK, Rev W.H. 5 Years Ago Jan 2, 1890
Rev W.H. Shank and Miss Mary Burt were married at Pittsfield.

SHANK, William O. Married Oct 15, 1891
Married at the home of brides parents, two miles west of Clayton October 8th 1891 by Rev E.W. Souders, William O. Shank and Miss Ardell Hamilton we understand Mr Shank will associate himself with his brother George in the nursery business in Clayton. He has been in Nebraska for a year or two and we are pleased to welcome him back.

SHANK, Wm Other Days May 17, 1900
April 1890 Married at Carthage Mr Wm Shank and Mrs Mary Goldman. She died a year ago.

SHANK, Wm C. City Brevities Nov 17, 1898
Marriage license has been issued for marriage of Wm C. Shank, Clayton age 26 and Annie L. Smith, Hazelwood age 25. Groom is son of James Shank and bride until recently made her home at F.W. Burgesser's.

SHANKLIN, Rev P.G. Nov 13, 1890
SEE EYMAN, Miss Georgie

SHARP, Amos Camp Point Jan 20, 1898
Amos Sharp and Miss Lizzie Hocamp were married in Quincy last Wednesday. Will live on his farm near Clayton.

SHARP, Miss Eliza Locals Nov 29, 1894
Marriage of Miss Eliza, daughter of Mrs Hylas Sharp of Concord, to Mr Lewis Childs, of Camp Point occurred in Quincy last week.

SHARP, Miss Hylas Mar 18, 1897
SEE BECKMAN, Charles

SHARP, Jack Local Feb 27, 1890
Jack Sharp and Miss Zinck of Concord township were married last week.

SHARP, Miss Jennie Dec 29, 1892
SEE REEN, Wm

SHATZER, Jacob Local Sep 12, 1895
Jacob Shatzer and Mrs Rebecca Bean were married in Mt Sterling Tuesday of last week. They are Concord people.

SHELLEY, John Apr 22, 1897
SEE MAY, Miss Ella

SHELLY, Miss Sophia Jun 24, 1897
SEE BAKER, James V.

SHELLY, Walter Camp Point Sep 23, 1897
Mr Walter Shelly of Bushnell and Miss Lottie Bartells were married at the home of the bride Wednesday eve.

SHEPARD, Martha Dec 29, 1892
SEE KROSS, John

SHEPHERD, Miss Emma Local Jan 1, 1891
Miss Emma Shepherd was married to Mr A.W. Clements Sunday afternoon by Elder Vandervort at the home of Len and Mrs Stevens.

SHEPHERD, Florence Aug 31, 1893
SEE CROQUART, Eugene and Florence

SHEPHERD, Mary F. 5 Years Ago Jan 12, 1893
Mary F. Shepherd married Eugene Croquart.
SHEPPARD, Alice Pea Ridge Mar 16, 1893
Alice Sheppard and Wm Baker were married last week by Elder West.
SHERIDAN, Mr Frank E. Oct 1, 1891
SEE WASH, Miss Nellie
SHERWOOD, Mr Kingdom Aug 27, 1896
SEE BRIDGEMAN, Margaret
SHIELDS, Miss Dora Dec 15, 1898
SEE PEVEHOUSE, Wm
SHIELDS, Miss Fettie Nov 29, 1894
SEE WILLIAMS, Ezra
SHIELDS, John Concord Mar 23, 1893
John Shields and his newly elected bride returned to their home near Augusta Sunday after spending their honeymoon with relatives in this vicinity.
SHIELDS, Miss Nettie Apr 3, 1890
SEE BREWSTER, Mr Haley
SHIELDS, Rev Parker Local May 15, 1890
Rev Parker Shields of Sedill and Miss Emma Austin, of Mendon were married at the brides home on Wednesday eve by Rev S.H. Whitlock. Both were students at Chaddock at one time.
SHIELDS, Miss Zuda Little Brindle Apr 16, 1896
Mound Beacon Light Sunday eve Rev Lowe married Mr Nova Bowen, son of James D. Bowen and Miss Zuda Shields at home of brides parents, Mr and Mrs Marion Shields.
SHILDS, John Local Mar 16, 1893
John Shilds and Retta Simpson, Augusta young people ran away from home and were married at Bowen. The young lady escaped from her room by sliding down a post of the portico.
SHOCKEY, Miss May 18, 1893
SEE MCCLAIN, Robert
SHOCKLEY, Miss Personal Sep 15, 1892
SEE MARLIN, Mrs C.E.
SHOCKLEY, Shepherd Supplement Jun 26, 1890
5 Years Ago Shepherd Shockley and Miss Cora Abbey were married.
SHRIVER, Chas. Dec 12, 1895
SEE LANDES, Miss Alice
SHRIVER, Mr and Mrs Geo. A. Neighborhood News Oct 29, 1891
Mr and Mrs Geo. A. Shriver at Pittsfield celebrated their golden wedding October 21st.
SHRIVER, Mr and Mrs Wm Neighborhood News Oct 27, 1892
October 13th occurred the golden wedding of Mr and Mrs Wm Shriver of Pittsfield.
SHULL, Mr W.S. Local Nov 2, 1899
Mr W.S. Shull went to Keytesville, Missouri and was married to Mrs Thompson on October 24th. Will live Clayton.
SHULL, Mr W.S. Married Nov 9, 1899
Married at home of Mr and Mrs J.W. Thompson, Tuesday at 6 PM, Mr W.S. Shull of Clayton, Illinois and Mrs S.E. Thompson of near Keytesville by Rev G.E. Prewitt. Will live Clayton. Attending wedding were: Mrs Jim Jefferson, Miss Mellie Simper of Keytesville and Mr W.H. Simper, brother of bride of Canton, Missouri.
SHULTZ, Mr and Mrs Local Feb 6, 1896
Monday, January 27, Mr and Mrs Shultz, of East Columbus, celebrated their 10th wedding anniversary. Among guests were Mr and Mrs G.W. Kesting. The ladies are sisters.

SHUSHER, F.J. Apr 29, 1897
SEE MCMURRAY, Miss Nellie
SILLS, Miss Ida Jan 16, 1896
SEE WATERS, Wm
SIMMONDS, Mr and Mrs Sam Camp Point Mar 8, 1900
Mr and Mrs Sam Simmonds celebrated their 10th wedding anniversary last Tuesday.
SIMMONS, Mr Aug 10, 1899
SEE BRIDGEMAN, Miss Jennie
SIMMS, W.D. Neighbors Feb 3, 1898
W.D. Simms of Keokuk who married in Carthage on January 17th to Miss Virginia Thompson, was arrested for bigamy. His first wife has been in Slater, Missouri and she had been granted a divorce from him, but the costs had not been paid nor the decree filed when the marriage took place. He told them divorce had been granted and probably thought it had been.
SIMPSON, Retta Mar 16, 1893
SEE SHILDS, John
SIMS, Adda Sep 12, 1895
SEE YOWELL, Everett
SING, Henry Jan 25, 1894
SEE LEWIS, Miss May "Minnie"
SINGLETON, James J. Local Dec 20, 1894
SEE ROBISON, Miss Belle
SINGLETON, James J. Little Brindle News Jan 10, 1895
James J. Singleton, son of the late Gen J.W. Singleton, Meyerstown, W. Virginia and Miss Rae Bell, daughter of Mrs James N. Robison, of Fargo, this county were married by Rev G.E. Davis at noon Wednesday last week at the home of brides parents. Will leave for their southern home after a few days.
SINTON, George H. and Jane A. Neighborhood News Dec 11, 1890
George H. Sinton of Galesburg wants a divorce from his wife, Jane A. Sinton, whom he alleges is an habitual drunkard, abusing her husband and making his life a burden.
SIX, Miss Clara Dec 22, 1898
SEE MARSHALL, James
SIX, Dr William Oct 14, 1897
SEE HORNEY, Miss Kate
SKINNER, Miss Fannie L. Supplement Apr 18, 1895
Married at the home of Mr and Mrs A.C. Skinner in Quincy Tuesday eve their daughter, Miss Fannie L. Skinner to Mr James W. Clark of Kirksville, Missouri by Rev St Ince. Bride has many friends in Clayton. Mr Clark is one of the business men of Kirksville.
SLADE, Miss Adella X. Neighborhood News Dec 17, 1891
At Pleasant Grove ME Church in Gilmer township December 2nd, Miss Adella X. Slade united in marriage with Jas. W. Limb.
SLAGLE, Miss Nellie Married Mar 16, 1899
Married at home of brides parents in this city, Wednesday March 15th, Mr David H. Harnly of Wilmington, North Carolina, to Miss Nellie Slagle of Chicago by Rev Dr Beadles of the Quincy district and father of the bride of this city. Left on train to visit parents of groom at Auburn, from there to Mattoon to visit grooms former business partner and on to their new home, stopping at Cincinnati and Washington D.C. on the way. Mr Harnly is editor of the North Carolina Fruit and Truck growers Journal at Wilmington. Both received education at Illinois Wesleyan College. Attending from distance was, Mr and Mrs E.R. Slagle of Chicago, Mr and Mrs R.E. Slagle of Chicago, Mr and Mrs H.H. Harnly, of Auburn, Mr J.W. Harnly of Carlinville, Miss Cora Mathias of LaPearl and Frank C. McElvain of Mattoon.

SLOAN, Miss Gracie — Dec 27, 1894
SEE DEMOSS, Leroy

SMITH, Miss — Jul 27, 1899
SEE THOMPSON, Dr.

SMITH, Mr — Local — Jan 23, 1896
SEE PROPHATER, Miss Ollie

SMITH, A.J. — November 1888 — Nov 3, 1898
Married: A.J. Smith, of Huntsville and Sophia A. Peters.

SMITH, Allie — 5 Years Ago — Sep 7, 1893
Allie Smith was married in Pennsylvania.

SMITH, Mr Alva — Kellerville — Aug 17, 1899
Marriage of Mr Alva Smith and Miss Blanche Hoffman occurred last Thursday. Groom is son of Mr and Mrs F.J. Smith and is a young farmer. Bride is daughter of Mr and Mrs M.O. Hoffman. Will live Kellerville.

SMITH, Mrs Amanda — Oct 10, 1895
SEE BREED, Mr

SMITH, Mrs Amy M. — Jan 9, 1890
SEE PERKINS, Mrs Amy M. and Joseph

SMITH, Annie L. — Nov 17, 1898
SEE SHANK, Wm C.

SMITH, Miss Belle — Apr 9, 1891
SEE BAKER, Mr Albert

SMITH, Caroline E. — Sep 28, 1899
SEE HOFFMAN, John

SMITH, Elmer E. — Married — Nov 26, 1896
Married at Palmyra, Missouri Wednesday afternoon last, Mr Elmer E. Smith and Miss Anna Linn in the parlors of the leading hotel there by Rev J.H. Terrill of this city. Returned to Camp Point that night and said nothing. Friends found out Saturday night. Will live at home of brides parents this winter and in spring will build themselves a home.

SMITH, Miss Fannie — Neighborhood News — Feb 4, 1892
Mrs Wm Nye, wife of celebrated humorist, was 20 years ago, then Miss Fannie Smith, a Warsaw school teacher.

SMITH, Frank — Local — Oct 30, 1890
A letter from Frank Smith at Coffeyville, Kansas, who married Miss Alice Haley says that a gasoline stove exploded and burned him badly. It was a narrow escape.

SMITH, George W. — County News — Sep 21, 1899
Marriage license issued last week by County clerk to George W. Smith, of Ellington and Nancy Vance of Siloam Springs.

SMITH, Miss Gertrude B. — Apr 25, 1895
SEE JOHNSON, Harry T.

SMITH, Henry M. — Ill Brevities — Sep 6, 1894
Henry M. Smith and Mrs Cora Brown were married at Jacksonville.

SMITH, Isabell — Oct 6, 1898
SEE SALLY, Mr William

SMITH, J.C. and Mrs — 10 Years Ago — Dec 25, 1890
J.C. Smith and Mrs Smith had been married 15 years.

SMITH, J.H. — 5 Years Ago — Oct 16, 1890
SEE CAMPBELL, Miss Minnie

SMITH, Capt J.W. — Married — Oct 26, 1899
Capt J.W. Smith instead of going to Camp Point Wednesday he went to Quincy to get license and Thursday at high twelve was married to Mrs Martha J. Marshall by Rev E.J. Rice at the home of Capt Smith. Both are old residents of Clayton. Will live in Capt.'s house.

SMITH, John H. — Mound Station — Mar 20, 1890
Married, March 11th by Rev Jacob Crawford, John H. Smith and Miss Mary Graham.

SMITH, Mr John H. 5 Years Ago Feb 12, 1891
SEE FRANKS, Miss Susie
SMITH, Miss Laura May 6, 1897
SEE HOUGH, J.E.
SMITH, Lilly Belle Mar 4, 1897
SEE HUGHES, Geo. W.
SMITH, Lotta Sep 27, 1894
SEE WALKER, John P.
SMITH, Miss M. Adeline Dec 1, 1898
SEE DEVLIN, Stephen
SMITH, Miss Mamie Supplement Jun 26, 1890
5 Years Ago Miss Mamie Smith was married to Mr J.B. Coe at the home of her brother in Pittsford.
SMITH, Miss May 10 Years Ago Feb 9, 1893
SEE BROWN, Alonzo
SMITH, Miss Maymie 10 Years Ago Jun 27, 1895
Married, Miss Maymie Smith to Mr Jas. B. Coe.
SMITH, Miss Nellie Local Oct 18, 1894
Miss Nellie Smith was married to Mr Harper at St Joseph, Missouri the first of month. Bride is daughter of Mr Jas. T. Smith, now deceased and a niece of Mrs Dan Shark of this city.
SMITH, Miss Nora Local Feb 13, 1896
Miss Nora Smith, niece of Mrs Daniel Shank and Mr George Imbrie of St Joseph, Missouri were married last week.
SMITH, Mr and Mrs R.M. Local Oct 31, 1895
Mr and Mrs R.M. Smith celebrated their 18th wedding anniversary Tuesday with about 50 relatives.
SMITH, Mr R.N. Jun 4, 1896
SEE FRANKS, Mrs Mattie
SMITH, Rankin 10 Years Ago Oct 19, 1893
SEE BENNETT, Mrs Addie
SMITH, Richard County News Aug 3, 1899
Prominent colored wedding at Quincy, Richard Smith and Amanda Johnson Wednesday eve. The bride is a widow and had $15,000 worth of real estate. "Quincy Record"
SMITH, Vincent V. Kingdom Jul 16, 1896
Vincent V. Smith about two years ago a student at the University of Tennessee was secretly married in Chattanooga to Miss Alice B. Manley of Harriman after attending a picnic and nothing was said of the marriage. A few months later after he had called on her as usual she left for the north. He went west for a year and the first that was known of the secret marriage is a suit for divorce, he charging her with desertion. He is son of William T. Smith, formerly of here.
SMITH, W. Lee Neighborhood News Nov 27, 1890
Wedding five miles west of Keokuk recently which was novel, W. Lee Smith of Denver, Illinois and Lida Funkhouser of Summitville were married wearing jeans and calico and guests were likewise. Both are from wealthy families.
SMITH, William F. Nov 9, 1893
SEE WATSON, Miss Edith M.
SMITH, William H. Mar 5, 1891
SEE KIRKPATRICK, Miss Alice
SNIDER, Ed Camp Point Mar 14, 1895
Ed Snider and Miss Vada Trout were married at the Francis house Wednesday by Elder Dilley.
SNIVELY, Rev George L. Ill State News Jun 21, 1894
Rev George L. Snively, pastor of Pittsfield Christian Church and Miss Frances Black, daughter of W.L. Black of Virginia, were married recently.

SNIVELY, Elder Geo. Kingdom of Pike Jun 21, 1894
Elder Geo. Snively, pastor of Christian Church at Pittsfield, married Miss Frances, daughter of Mr Lit Black at Virginia. Mrs Mattie Wells attended the wedding.

SOHM, Miss Teresa H. Little Brindle News May 30, 1895
Democrat-Message Cards are out announcing marriage of Miss Teresa H. Sohm, daughter of Mr and Mrs Edward Sohm, to Clarence Eugene Brockman, Thursday, June 6, at St Boniface Church in Quincy.

SOLOMON, Dempsey N. Ill State News Oct 4, 1894
Dempsey N. Solomon age 73 and Mrs Martha Hulse, age 54 both of Palmyra were married at Jacksonville, at the Dunlap house by Rev S.E. Moore of the Christian Church.

SOUDERS, Mr Mar 15, 1900
SEE SEARS, Miss Iva

SOUDERS, Miss Ella Married Dec 29, 1892
Married at the parsonage of the First Presbyterian Church Monday 6:30 PM, Miss Ella, daughter of Rev and Mrs E. Willis Souders to Mr Frank Burnett by brides father. Will live Chicago.

SOUDERS, Miss Ella Local Jan 5, 1893
Miss Ella Souders of Clayton, a pretty girl of Quincy was married Monday eve to Mr Frank T. Burnett of Chicago by Rev Souders, father of the bride. "Quincy Optic"

SOUDERS, Linneaus May 29, 1900
SEE SEARS, Miss Iva

SPARKS, Miss Laura Oct 19, 1893
SEE SCHULTZ, Charlie

SPAULDING, J.W. Brown County Mar 15, 1900
Wednesday eve J.W. Spaulding, formerly of Champaign, but now of Siloam Springs and Miss Anna Seaman of Bloomington were married in the parlors of the Curry House by Rev N.M. Rigg. Groom is scarcely past middle age while bride is about a dozen years younger. Mr Spaulding recently purchased the Siloam Springs property.

SPEARS, Fred Ill Brevities May 31, 1894
Fred Spears and Miss Cora Hatfield were married at Jacksonville.

SPILLARS, Spencer August 1883 Aug 11, 1898
Married, Mr Spencer Spillars and Miss Tillie Wiley.

SPRAGUE, W.E. Apr 23, 1891
SEE ROBERTS, Miss May

STAATS, Eugene A. Neighbors Jan 5, 1899
Wednesday eve at the home of the bride occurred the marriage of Miss Lena Main to Mr Eugene A. Staats, of Griggsville, Illinois. Miss Griggsby of Blandinsville played the wedding march and at 8 PM they entered the parlor andmarried by Rev Huston. Carthage Repbublican.

STAHL, Miss May 8, 1890
Miss Stahl, daughter of Mr Noah Stahl, of Fowler was married to Mr Fred Barrows, son of Arthur Barrows of Brown County Tuesday afternoon.

STAHL, Miss Edith Aug 26, 1897
SEE HENRY, Dr Ed C.

STAKER, J.L. 10 Years Ago Jan 2, 1890
SEE MONTGOMERY, Miss Jennie

STARK, Elder J. Carroll 5 Years Ago Sep 12, 1895
Elder J. Carroll Stark and Miss Phoebe DeFroot were married at LaPrairie.

STARR, Mr and Mrs R.B. Our Own Bailiwick Nov 12, 1896
Invitations are out for silver wedding of Mr and Mrs R.B. Starr next Monday PM.

STATES, Mr and Mrs Eugine Personal Jan 5, 1899
Mr and Mrs Eugine States of Griggsville were here visiting Mrs Wm Shank, the grandmother of the lady. They were married at Carthage the 23rd ult.

STAUFFER, Miss Lizzie Neighbborhood News Oct 8, 1891
Mr Samuel D. Moore and Miss Lizzie Stauffer both of Beverly township were married last week by Elder H.G. Vandervoort of this city.

STAUFFER, Máttie A. Sep 14, 1899
SEE LEAPLEY, Giles H.

STAUFFER, Miss Susie Wedding Dec 1, 1892
On November 23rd 1892 at home of Wm Stauffer, near Chestline, in this county was the marriage of Miss Susie Stauffer and Cyrus Hull of Fish Hook, three bridesmaids and three groomsmen were, Samuel Lawson of Beverly and Miss Mary Stauffer of Griggsville, G.F. Kaylor of Siloam and Miss Ida Hull of Fishhook, S.B. Peacóck of Chestline and Effie Coss of Baylis at 1:30 PM by Rev H.F. Kline of Quincy.

STEED, Miss Elizabeth Nov 19, 1896
SEE PAXTON, J. Hays

STEED, Miss Lizzie Nov 12, 1896
SEE PAXTON, Hayes

STEELEMAN, Miss Gussie Nov 7, 1895
SEE MILLS, John

STEINER, Louisa C. Oct 24, 1895
SEE WALLACE, Shannon

STEPHENSON, Elder J.G. Kingdom of Pike Mar 1, 1894
Elder J.G. Stephenson of the Christian Church of Milton, eloped last Wednesday with Miss Dove Heavener of the same place. He had a wife and three children.

STEPHENSON, Rev J. Gilman Kingdom of Pike Feb 22, 1894
Elopement at Milton, Rev J. Gilman Stephenson pastor of Christian Church and Miss --ove Heavenor, a member of his congregation. Stephenson deserted his wife and three children.

STERN, Miss Blanche Dec 8, 1892
SEE CURRY, Clarence H.

STERNE, Thomas Oct 15, 1896
SEE BURROUGHS, Miss Alice

STERRITT, C.C. Local Dec 3, 1891
At high noon, today, C.C. Sterritt of this place married Miss Amata, eldest daughter of Mr and Mrs H.E. Selby of Golden. Golden Corr.

STEVENS, Charles Local Oct 10, 1895
Last Thursday Mr Charles Stevens, son of Joseph and Mrs Stevens, formerly of Clayton and Miss Lotta Selby were married in St Louis. Bride is daughter of Mr and Mrs H.E. Selby of Golden.

STEVENS, Clarence Married Jan 5, 1893
Married, Miss Anne Gooley, daughter of Mrs Samuel Mitts of Brown County and Mr Clarence Stevens, son of Mr and Mrs James Stevens, also of Brown County. Married at Mt Sterling. Returned home of Mr Mitts for reception. Clarence is connected with butcher business here in Clayton with his uncles, the Stevens Bros. Bride lived Clayton when a child, but has lived on the farm with her mother several years. He has engaged to manage Mr Mitt's farm which will be their future home.

STEVENS, Miss Cora Nov 18, 1897
SEE BROWN, Ray

STEVENS, Miss Edith Mar 7, 1895
SEE BOWEN, William

STEVENS, Mrs Jennette M. Jul 5, 1894
SEE MCPHERSON, Wm A.

STEVENS, Nettie Sep 17, 1896
SEE MCPHERSON, Mrs Nettie and Mr Wm

STEVENS, Mrs Nettie — Dec 17, 1896
SEE CLAIRE, Moses H.
SEE MCPHERSON, William A. — Jul 15, 1897

STEVENS, Oscar — Local — Apr 26, 1900
A license was issued in this county for Mr Oscar Stevens, son of James Stevens of Brown County and Miss Carrie Mikesell, daughter of Henry Mikesell of Mounds. Elder I.G. Williams, of the Christian Church at Camp Point was called here Wednesday to perform the marriage ceremony.

STEVENS, Ralph — Brown County — Jan 4, 1900
Licensed to wed since last issue of Examiner: Ralph Stevens of Mound and Clara Moran of Mound.

STEWART, Mrs Addie — Nov 18, 1897
SEE CRANE, William E.

STIENER, Louisa C. — Local — Oct 31, 1895
Marriage of Louisa C. Stiener to Mr Shannon Wallace was at the home of brides parents on Wolf Ridge then miles southwest of town Wednesday eve of last week by Elder O. Dilley of Camp Point.

STIFFEY, Miss Ella B. — Nov 10, 1898
SEE ANDERSON, Henry S.

STIFFY, Miss Susan — Local — Dec 30, 1897
Married at the home of John Stiffy at 1 PM Saturday Mr George N. Egnor, of St Charles, Missouri and Miss Susan Stiffy of Clayton by Rev Abner Sears. Mr Egnor is a railroad man.

STINSON, C.W. — Golden — Nov 9, 1893
Social event of next week will be wedding of C.W. Stinson and Miss Della Beckett, daughter of our dry goods man on Wednesday by Rev Atkinson.

STINSON, Charles S. — Local — Nov 23, 1893
SEE BECKETT, Della

STONE, Abraham L. — Jul 7, 1892
SEE HIRSHEIMER, Miss Ida B.

STONE, George — Little Brindle — Oct 8, 1896
Versailles Enterprise: Married in Rushville, September 25th 1896 Mr George Stone and Miss Nellie Henderson, both of Versailles.

STONEKING, Bessie — Jan 4, 1900
SEE LANE, William

STOTLAR, Mr — Apr 12, 1894
SEE HESS, Cora

STOUT, Florence — 5 Years Ago — Sep 12, 1895
Florence Stout and Ellsworth Kirkpatrick were married.

STOUT, Miss Florence F. — Local — Sep 11, 1890
Miss Florence F. Stout was quietly married to Ellsworth Kirkpatrick by Rev W.M. Reed at the Me Church parsonage at 7:30 Sunday. They drove to the home of Mr Kirkpatrick and will live in this vicinity.

STOUT, Oliver S. — Married — May 3, 1900
Married Oliver S. Stout and Miss Mamie Jones last week at home of Mr and Mrs S.D. Hyler Wednesday eve at 5:30 by Rev P. Slagle. Will live Moberly. Democrat of that city says: O.S. Stout and Miss Mamie Jones, both of this city were married at Clayton Wednesday at 6 PM at home of his sister, Mrs S.D. Hyler by Rev Slagle. Returned here yesterday AM and will live on Hagood St. Mr Stout is a Wabash engineer. Bride is daughter of Mrs Mary Hogue of West Rollins St.

STOUT, Oliver — 10 Years Ago — Aug 8, 1895
Oliver Stout and Miss Ida Raymond, now of Moberly, Missouri were married.

STOUT, Wm S. Local Sep 28, 1893
Mr Wm S. Stout arrived from St Louis Wed. accompanied by his bride to visit his sisters. She was Miss Freda L. Link, daughter of a highly respected citizen of that city. Will is asst. engineer in the largest wholesale concern in St Louis. Will live at 1214 S. 7th St. when they return from visiting his sisters.

STRAHAN, Miss Lora Oct 6, 1898
SEE HEDRICK, Will C.

STRAHAN, Mary Aug 26, 1897
SEE FLEMMING, Wm

STRATTON, Miss Jan 18, 1894
SEE CHAMPION, Otto

STRAUB, Edward Supplement Sep 24, 1891
Elm Grove Married: Thursday September 17th at 12 oclock, Mr Edward Straub of Galesburg to Miss Emma Alexander at the home of brides parents, Mr and Mrs Wm L. Alexander. Attended by grooms parents Mr and Mrs Albert Straub, and Roy Straub, his brother of Galesburg. Mr Roy Straub was groomsman and Miss Hannah Scully, bridesmaid. Married by J.M. Johnson. Will live Galesburg. Brides father gave them a check for $500.

STRAUSS, Frank X. Local Jan 30, 1896
At Mt Sterling, Mr Frank X. Strauss and Mrs Lura Meredith were married at the home of Elder Laycock, pastor of Christian Church in Mt Sterling, Saturday eve. Mr Strauss is a traveling saleman for a St Louis house and headquarters in Quincy.

STRICKLAND, Mr and Mrs James Neighborhood News Dec 23, 1893
A decade or more ago Mr and Mrs James Strickland of Macomb, were married by a protestant minister. Mrs Strickland was a devout Catholic and of late has been burdened with the idea taught by Catholic Church, that marriage nor sanctioned by the pope are Void so they were married again several days ago by a priest.

STRICKLER, Wesley Adams County News Nov 30, 1893
Wesley Strickler and Catherine Kern were married in Keene township Nov 16, 1843 they both resided in Houston township which at that time was set off in Marguette County in which there was no county offices, the people being opposed to the division of the County, so to make a legal marriage ceremony they went into Adams County to have the marriage solemnized. Last Thursday was the 50th anniversary of the event, and of the witnesses only 5 or 6 are now alive. "Journal"

STUMP, Miss Violet Apr 12, 1900
SEE HUDSON, Orvas

SULLIVAN, Miss Mary Jan 9, 1896
SEE MCCLAIN, John

SUMMEY, Herbert C. Jun 8, 1899
SEE BLOOD, Miss Katherine S.

SWAIN, Miss Gertrude Local Aug 31, 1899
Dr and Mrs Cox received a card announcing marriage of their niece, Miss Gertrude Swain to Mr Ralph Edward Bush, Wednesday eve August 13th at Trinity Cathedral, Omaha, Nebraska the young lady is known here having visited the Dr's family.

SWAN, Mark E. Local Dec 3, 1891
Democrat Message, Mark E. Swan and Miss Jessie Hall of the Ideal Comedy Co., were married in this city on Wednesday AM last by Rev L.A. Powell.

SWEETRING, John Apr 23, 1891
SEE HAZLETT, Miss Anna

SWEETRING, Miss Nellie Local Sep 7, 1893
Miss Nellie Sweetring of Quincy and Mr James Bunda were married on the 28th ult at St Boniface Church and left for Fairfield, Iowa where groom is principal of a business college. Bride is sister of John Sweetring.

SWENEY, Miss Sadie Evelyn Dec 4, 1890
SEE MONTGOMERY, Frank

SWERINGER, Chet Our Own Bailiwick Oct 4, 1894
In St Louis today, Chet Sweringer and Miss Rose Mais will be married at fair grounds while the couple stand in the basket of a baloon and as soon as they are man and wife they will fourney into the skies for their honeymoon. "Whig 30th"

SWISHER, Absalom Little Brindle Dec 8, 1898
Examiner Marriage license issued last Friday, Absalom Swisher of Kellerville and Miss Melissa Burton of Clayton.

SWISHER, Absolem Little Brindle Dec 8, 1898
Mound Correspondence Absolem Swisher of Kellerville and Mrs Malissa Burton of Clayton were in town Thursday and were married by Squire C.H. Martin.

SWISHER, Absolem B. City Brevities Dec 8, 1898
Our good friend Absolem B. Swisher of Concord, has taken himself a wife in the person of Mrs Melissa Burton of this place. She is a sister of Mrs Thornhill. Married by Justice Martin at Mounds Thursday of last week. Will live on Swisher farm.

SWISHER, Miss Belle Oct 21, 1897
SEE BANKS, Ed

SWISHER, Dora Jan 1880 Feb 15, 1900
SEE DUNBAR, Mr

SWISHER, Miss Liola Aug 15, 1895
SEE FALER, Bert

SWOPE, Mr and Mrs Albert Married 50 years Sep 23, 1892
Quincy Herald, Wednesday Mr and Mrs Albert Swope 615 Elm St celebrated their 50th wedding anniversary at the Tremont House. Present were Dr J.M. Swope, wife and daughter, Dr W.A. Swope wife and son, Wheeling, John M. Swope, H.M. Swope wife and children, city.

SYRCLE, John W. Brown County Oct 10, 1895
Mr John W. Syrcle of Adams County near Kellerville, and Miss Martha J. Bean of Buckhorn, this county were married by Mart Brooks, Esq. in this city last Thursday afternoon. The "Examiner"

TAFT, A.H. May 11, 1893
SEE CRAMER, Miss Effie

TANSILL, Robert Weems Jr. Apr 14, 1892
SEE VANBUREN, Minnie

TANSILL, Roy Local Mar 17, 1892
The marriage of Roy Tansill and Miss VanBuren, a Kingston, New York lady is to take place next month. Roy is now at Phildelphia.

TARR, Miss Nellie Apr 6, 1893
SEE KEMP, Mr Aldo

TAYLOR, Miss City Brevities Nov 17, 1898
SEE GRIMES, Dr.

TAYLOR, Miss Augusta Aug 18, 1895
SEE KIPP, Edward

TAYLOR, Mr G.F. Dec 5, 1895
SEE CRUSE, Miss Florence Alice

TAYLOR, George H. Little Brindle News Jan 9, 1896
Beacon Light: George H. Taylor and Miss Mary Louderback both of Pea Ridge were married at the homeof Ben May and wife Sunday by Rev Jacob Crawford.

TAYLOR, Joseph G. Dec 1, 1898
SEE HARPER, Gertrude

TAYLOR, Nettie 10 Years Ago Apr 23, 1891
Nettie Taylor married Dr J.E. Camp at Brooklyn.

TAYLOR, Thomas 5 Years Ago Nov 30, 1893
SEE MYERS, Flora

TAYLOR, Thos Our Own Bailiwick Aug 20, 1896
Camp Point Journal: A marriage license has been issued to Thos Taylor of Camp Point age 60 and Mary C. Wisehart of Camp Point age 54.

TAYLOR, W.A. County Brevities Jan 13, 1898
Camp Point Journal J.E. Meatheringham and wife were in Canton, Missouri last week where he officiated at the marriage of W.A. Taylor of Bowen, Illinois and Miss Edda Moore of Canton. Mr Taylor has taught school and octed a pastor of Christian Church at Bowen.

TAYLOR, Wm Neighborhood News Jul 24, 1890
Wm Taylor, age 18 years son of Dr Taylor of Vermont, and Miss Minnie Wright age 16, step daughter of S.J. Stone, of Astoria eloped last Sunday night.

TEACHENOR, Mr and Mrs October 1889 Oct 5, 1899
Mr and Mrs Teachenor celebrated their 50th wedding anniversary.

TEBO, Mr John W. Nov 5, 1891
SEE CRASKE, Miss Geneva

TEDROW, Mrs Barbara May 5, 1898
SEE LASHER, Oliver

TEDROW, Miss Clara E. Mound Station Sep 23, 1892
After Sunday AM services, Rev F.P. Douglas married Miss Clara Tedrow of this city and Geo. Withrow of Pike County.

TEGMEYER, Frank Local May 13, 1897
Mr Frank Tegmeyer and Miss Lillie Davis were married at Mt Sterling Monday afternoon when they drove to the home of Myron Ratcliff in Concord.

TEGMEYER, Miss Minnie Local Apr 27, 1893
By a letter from Charlie Cox dated Chicago 17th we learn of marriage of Miss Minnie Tegmeyer, daughter of Gus Tegmeyer, to Mr B.C. Epstein a New York silk dealer. Marriage occurred on the 10th inst. Dr Cox and family live at 671 West Erie St.

TERRILL, Miss Ada Sep 20, 1894
SEE KENDALL, Otis E.

TERRILL, Jesse Local Feb 7, 1895
Mr Jesse Terrill, son of our former townsman, James Terrill was married to a Colorado Springs young lady recently. Jesse is manager of R.W. Tansill's New Mexico ranch. He left here as a little boy.

THOMAS, Curt Blacks Station Dec 4, 1890
Curt Thomas, one of the boys of the station and Mis Maggie Farlow of Camp Point were quietly married in that city last week.

THOMAS, Miss Libbie 10 Years Ago Mar 5, 1891
SEE MCCOY, F.A.

THOMPSON, Dr. Local Jul 27, 1899
Marriage of Dr Thompson and Miss Smith occurred at Keokuk last week and the Dr brought his bride to Kellerville where he has a good practice.

THOMPSON, Mrs Nov 2, 1899
SEE SHULL, Mr W.S.

THOMPSON, Mr Edward Sr. Local Nov 23, 1893
The marriage of Mr Edward Thompson Sr. and Mrs Elizabeth Cox, both of this city, will occur at the home of the lady in the east part of town Wednesday eve.

THOMPSON, Ellsworth Supplement Oct 26, 1893
5 Years Ago Mr Ellsworth Thompson and Della M. Alexander were married at Elm Grove where they now live.

THOMPSON, Gilbert Married Feb 2, 1899
Married at Jacksonville, Illinois last Sunday, Mr Gilbert Thompson of Chapin, Illinois and Miss Leona McMurray, of Clayton, Illinois. Will live Chapin where Gilbert is in butcher business. Miss Leona has been in poor health some time and wedding was deferred several months on that account.

THOMPSON, James Golden Feb 20, 1896
James Thompson and Miss Effie Davis near Pine Grove were married February 5th will live on the Ackley homestead. Bride is daughter of James M. Davis and wife.

THOMPSON, Mrs Lottie Local May 22, 1890
Hon John W. Moore and Mrs Lottie Thompson, daughter of Wm Mumford, were married at the home of brides parents in Mound Station at 4 PM last Thursday by Rev L.A. Powell of this city. "Mt Sterling Examiner"

THOMPSON, Miss Minnie Oct 7, 1897
SEE DEJEAN, C.B.

THOMPSON, R.L. Oct 30, 1890
SEE INGLES, Miss Lureno

THOMPSON, Mr R.W. Elm Grove May 5, 1892
Marriage of Mr R.W. Thompson and Miss Mollie Dunn was at the home of C.H. Burke last Sunday 5 PM by Justice C.H. Burke. Mr James Thompson was best man and Miss Louise Hopka bridesmaid.

THOMPSON, Mrs S.E. Nov 9, 1899
SEE SHULL, Mr W.S.

THOMPSON, Miss Virginia Feb 3, 1898
SEE SIMMS, W.D.

THOMSON, Rev John J. Local Jan 25, 1900
Cards have been received by Clayton friends of the Rev John J. Thomson announcing his marriage to Miss Sarah Isabelle Dickson at Tarkio, Missouri Monday January 1st at home 542 S. 25th Ave. Omaha, Nebraska.

THORNBERRY, Miss Ida Nov 28, 1895
SEE YELDELL, Elmer

THORNHILL, Henry Local Oct 26, 1893
Married at the home of Justice Marrett Friday eve, Mr Henry Thornhill to Miss Phoebe Moorman.

THORNHILL, Miss Kate Local Mar 10, 1892
Quiet wedding at home of Mrs Thornhill Thursday eve of last week, Miss Kate, daughter of Mrs Thornhill to Mr William F. Fricke, both of Clayton by Elder H.G. VanDervoort. Miss Kate has spent her life in Clayton. Will live for present with Mrs Thornhill.

THORNTON, Harry Dec 14, 1899
SEE GLINES, Miss Nora

THOROMAN, Miss Florence Feb 25, 1897
SEE DUISSAIR, Mr

THRELKELD, Alfred Local Apr 23, 1896
Mr Alfred Threlkeld of this city and Mrs Ella Harper of Mechanicsburg were married in Jacksonville Wednesday. Will live on Vine St. Quincy Optic.

TICE, Florence Jan 4, 1900
SEE NOKES, Albert L.

TIEKEN, Fred Jr. Local Dec 3, 1896
Marriage of Mr Fred Tieken Jr of Coatsburg and Miss Anna Fuhrken of this township occurred at the home of her father Gerhard Fuhrken in the German Prairie Wednesday. Mr Tieken is a well to do farmer of Coatsburg has 200 acres and a good home.

TILBY, Edward Oct 24, 1895
SEE SCOTT, John and Fannie

TODD, Mr Hugh Jul 5, 1894
SEE TURNER, Miss Minnie

TOLAND, Chas. Neighborhood News Aug 16, 1894
Chas. Toland and Miss Alta Clark, both of Hancock County, eloped and were married at Rushville. Brides father went to Rushville to prevent the marriage, but arrived to late. Groom is 18 years and bride is 15 years old. Both being minors. When last we heard the elopers had not been found.

TOOT, Miss Julia A. Neighbors Aug 27, 1896
At Bloomington the 18th Pres. Baker of Chaddock College married Rev Abner Clark of Quincy and Miss Julia A. Toot of Bloomington.

TOTSCH, Albert Apr 22, 1897
SEE BEHRENS, Miss Ricka

TOTSCH, Charles Local Feb 28, 1895
Marriage of Mr Charles Torsch, son of our friend Jacob and wife and Miss Marie Flesner at the home of brides parents since last week.

TRAVER, Mr W.M. Sep 11, 1890
SEE LOGUE, Mary

TREGO, Prof S.H. Married Jul 28, 1892
Prof S.H. Trego and Miss Eva Burroughs were married yesterday noon at home of brides parents, near State and 30th Sts. by Rev Dr Corbyn. Will live Clayton where Prof Trego has been appointed principal of the high school of that city. Both were teachers in Highland school Riverside township for several years. Whig 21st.

TREGO, Prof S.H. Local Jul 21, 1892
Whig 20th married, Prof S.H. Trego and Miss Eva Burroughs at high noon today at home of brides parents near 30th and State Sts. by Rev Dr Corbyn.

TROUT, Miss Vada Mar 14, 1895
SEE SNIDER, Ed

TUCKER, Miss Nellie Sep 9, 1897
SEE KALLASH, Harvey

TUNIS, Miss Estelle M. Sep 6, 1894
SEE BOND, Sidney J.

TURNER, Harvey Dec 10, 1896
SEE FIELDS, Miss Addie

TURNER, Miss Minnie Little Brindle News Jul 5, 1894
Wedding at Mt Sterling Tuesday eve, Miss Minnie Turner of that city to Mr Hugh Todd of Shelbina, Missouri father of the groom performing the ceremony.

TURNER, Miss Norine Sep 14, 1899
SEE JARVIS, Clay

ULMER, Mr Louis Jul 16, 1891
SEE SHANK, Miss Ella

UMGEBUEHLER, Vanlentine and Lena Our Own Bailiwick Sep 30, 1894
Mrs Lena Umgebuehler started suit for divorce yesterday from her husband, Vanlentine Umgebuehler.

UNDERWOOD, George Adams County Oct 20, 1898
Last Wednesday night George Underwood and Miss Pearl Alexander, who lives in Elm Grove area, eloped taking with them a horse and buggy. George is 18 years old and the girl 14 years old. The girls father is Daniel Alexander is looking for them. Boy is son of Thos. Underwood. Later: Couple returned saying they were married in Michigan. They are now at Thos. Underwood's.

UNGLAUB, Frank Oct 13, 1892
SEE HAZLETT, Miss Lizzie

VALLEREUX, Mr F.W. City Brevities Jun 29, 1899
Marriage of Mr F.W. Vallereux and Miss Sophronia Shaffer, sister of Miss Maud who has lived in family of J.L. Staker, at Mt Sterling at 8 AM Monday. Left for Wyoming on AM train where Mr Vallereux has a good position in the railway service.

VANBUREN, Minnie Local Apr 14, 1892
Nuptial card received reads: Mr and Mrs James VanBuren requests your presence at marriage of their daughter Minnie, to Mr Robert Weems Tansill Jr. on Thursday April 21st at 6 PM at St John's Church, Keyston, New York.

VANCE, Nancy County News Sep 21, 1899
SEE SMITH, George W.

VANCIL, Miss Viola Local Jul 21, 1892
Married Wednesday of last week in Quincy by Rev Wheat, Miss Viola Vancil and Ed Pallarday both of Clayton. Groom is a railroad man on the Wabash.

VANDENBOOM, Miss Catherine May 31, 1894
SEE ABEL, Ewald G.

VANDERVOORT, Miss Ola Nov 26, 1896
SEE CURRY, James S.

VARNER, Miss Ella Feb 2, 1893
SEE ROY, Will

VARNER, Miss May 5 Years Ago Mar 12, 1891
Miss May Varner married Mr Hiram Davis.

VARNER, Miss Rega May 24, 1900
SEE CURRY, Frank L.

VAY, John City Brevities May 11, 1899
SEE BOLINGER, Miss Blanche

VEACH, Miss Laura Jun 6, 1895
SEE NEELAND, Richard

VEACH, Mr Miles Little Brindle News Feb 13, 1896
Siloam Herald Mr Miles Veach, of Fishhook, and Miss Bella Harwood of Barnard, were licensed to wed last week.

VERING, Fred W. Married Jan 22, 1891
Married at home of William Boling and wife Wednesday of last week at high noon by Rev Lierly, Miss Hattie, daughter of Mr and Mrs Boling and Mr Fred W. Vering. Attended by Miss Kate Bradney and Philip Amen of Concord.

VERING, William A. City Brevities Feb 16, 1899
Marriage license issued to William A. Vering of Clayton and Miss Lizzie Kestner, of Haselwood.

VERMILLION, Miss Nellie F. Little Brindle News Feb 13, 1896
Democrat Message: Miss Nellie F. Vermillion, daughter of Mr and Mrs Douglas Vermillion of South Main St. was married Wednesday eve February 5th to Loren M. Briggs of Buckhorn at the home of brides parents at 6:30 PM by Rev L. Royce of Camppoint.

VERRING, Fred W. Jan 15, 1891
SEE BOLING, Miss Hattie

VOLBRACHT, Chris and wife Local Feb 7, 1895
Chris Volbracht and wife had their pictures taken to celebrate their 25th wedding anniversary. Mrs Volbracht has been an invalid for 8 years.

VOLLBRACHT, Miss Emma Dec 29, 1898
SEE HANKE, John

VOLLBRACHT, Geo. and wife Other Days May 17, 1900
April 1890 Geo. Vollbracht and wife had a silver wedding.

VOLLBRACHT, Miss Louisa Locals Mar 28, 1895
Big wedding in Concord Sunday, Miss Louisa, daughter of Mr and Mrs Chris Vollbracht and Mr William Vonholdt, a young farmer and son of Henry Vonholdt lately deceased.

VONHOLDT, Fred Local Mar 11, 1897
Marriage license issued to Fred Vonholdt and Miss Maude Hanke, both of Concord. He has rented C.A. Weaver's farm and they will live there.
VONHOLDT, William Mar 28, 1895
SEE VOLLBRACHT, Miss Louisa
VONHOLT, John W. Brown County Oct 26, 1899
Examiner: John W. Vonholt and Miss Alta Caley, both of Clayton were married by Squire McCabe in this city Sunday.
VORYS, Miss Lauretta Jan 8, 1891
SEE HARBISON, Charles
VOSBURGH, Mr E.A. May 27, 1890
SEE GRAHAM, Miss Nellie Mae
WADE, Edward Supplement May 30, 1895
Neighborhood News A Rockport couple Edward Wade and Mary J. Barley were married in a Louisiana, Missouri, merchants show window.
WAGGONER, Mr J.N. Local Jan 7, 1892
Carthage Gazette Mr J.N. Waggoner and Mrs Loretta Julian were married December 23rd by Rev J.A. Northrup and left to spend the winter in the south.
WAGGONER, J.N. Ancient History Feb 25, 1897
January 1892: J.N. Waggoner and Mrs Rettie Julian were married at Carthage.
WAGONER, S.N. Dec 31, 1891
SEE JULIAN, Mrs Loretta
WALBRIDGE, Boyd L. May 24, 1894
SEE WASH, Miss Addie E.
WALKER, Miss Carrie Sep 8, 1898
SEE ALEXANDER, Wm
WALKER, Charles Brown County Mar 8, 1900
Squire McCabe married Charles Walker and Miss Rosa L. Wing, both of Concord township Adams County in circuit clerk's office Monday AM. Couple attended by C.P. Wing father of the bride. Will live Clayton.
WALKER, Miss Ethel Y. 10 Years Ago Jun 9, 1892
Married, Miss Ethel Y. Walker to G.H. Doolittle.
WALKER, Eugene Oct 7, 1897
SEE COX, Miss Nellie
WALKER, George H. Married Oct 16, 1890
Hon George H. Walker, Mayor of Quincy and Mrs Isabella Byrd, were married at the home of the bride, 1261 Maine St., Quincy Wednesday night by Sean Leman of the Cathedral.
WALKER, J.W. Brown County News Aug 10, 1893
J.W. Walker of Golden and Miss Mary A. Whitechapel of Clayton were licensed to marry by county clerk Reid last week.
WALKER, Mr J.W. Brown County News Sep 14, 1893
J.W. Walker of Golden and Miss Mary A. Whitehead were married August 6th by Squire Wilke Duis at Golden, got their license to wed Brown County on August 2nd. Last Wednesday they got another license and were again married by Esq. J.J. Foraker of Pea Ridge township.
WALKER, Jesse Jr. Elm Grove Aug 10, 1893
Married, Sunday August 6th at Golden, by Rev W.D. Atkinson, Jesse Walker Jr of Elm Grove and Miss Mary Whitehead of Pea Ridge.
WALKER, John P. Ill Brevities Sep 27, 1894
John P. Walker, of Chariton County Missouri and Lotta Smith of Ursa, Illinois were married in Quincy.
WALKER, Katie Local Aug 11, 1892
SEE PEARIL, James and Katie
WALKER, Rosewell 10 Years Ago Nov 30, 1893
Rosewell Walker and Lucinda Peters of North East were married in Quincy.

WALL, John E. County News Oct 12, 1899
In the parlors of the Congregational Church this afternoon at 5, John E. Wall, the ass't states attorney will be married to Miss Belle Conley by Rev Dana.

WALLACE, Anna A. Married Jan 15, 1891
Married in Fort Morgan, Colorado November 27, 1890 O.M. Wilson and Anna A. Wallace. At home after December 6th at LaSalle, Colo. Miss Anna is a Clayton girl, left before Thanksgiving to visit her brother Samuel Wallace at Fort Morgan, Colorado.

WALLACE, Miss Bettie 10 Years Ago Jun 8, 1893
Miss Bettie Wallace and Mr Will McDonnald were wed.

WALLACE, Charles S. Our Own Bailiwick Dec 24, 1896
Golden New Era A high noon today, Rev H.A. Ott, pastor of Luther Memorial Church married Charles S. Wallace and Miss Irene McHatton, both of Golden. Groom is son of Mr and Mrs J.A. Wallace of near Golden. Bride is daughter of Mr and Mrs McHatton, who lives in Golden.

WALLACE, Miss Etta Occ. of Dec 1885 Dec 11, 1890
Miss Etta Wallace married L.W. Bowles, near Camp Point.

WALLACE, Jno. R. 10 Years Ago Aug 23, 1894
Married Jno. R. Wallace and Miss Julia Moffett.

WALLACE, John Jul 14, 1898
SEE FRAZIER, Miss Ada

WALLACE, Miss Mame Local Dec 17, 1891
Rev J.J. Thomson is called to home of J.A. Wallace Sr near Golden this (Wednesday) eve to unite in marriage, Miss Mame Wallace and R.J. McCray of Golden.

WALLACE, Mary A. Sep 10, 1891
SEE RITTER, Geo. M.

WALLACE, Miss Mary E. Dec 24, 1891
SEE MCCRAY, Robert J.

WALLACE, Samuel Local Jun 20, 1895
Married Mr Samuel Wallace and Miss Ella Campbell Thursday upon her arrival in Colorado. She can now be addressed as Mrs Samuel Wallace, Denver, Colorado.

WALLACE, Sarah M. Wedding Aug 15, 1895
Married at home of Mr and Mrs Thos. Wallace in Concord township on Thursday eve the 8th inst, their daughter, Sarah M. to Mr Warren England of Harris, Missouri by Rev G.G. Wilson of Media, Illinois and Rev M.W. Lorimer. Will live Harris, Missouri.

WALLACE, Shannon Local Oct 24, 1895
A marriage license issued to Shannon Wallace, Clayton 23 and Louisa C. Steiner, Camp Point 19.

WALLACE, Shannon Oct 31, 1895
SEE STIENER, Louisa C.

WALLACE, Thomas Local Dec 16, 1897
The 10 acres and little brick house north of town has been sold by James Park to Thomas Wallace who has recently married a Monmouth lady. They will make it their home.

WALTER, Frank Camp Point Dec 21, 1893
Frank Walter and Miss Kate Garrett were married last Thursday.

WALTERS, Mrs Anna Exchanges May 3, 1900
Saturday AM, Mrs Anna Walters was granted a divorce in Pike Circuit court and had her maiden name of Cooper restored, same evening she became Mrs Charles Bradshaw.

WALTERS, Charles Mar 10, 1892
SEE WEAR, Miss Laura

WALTERS, Mrs Nellie Jan 25, 1894
SEE HUNT, James

WALTON, Wesley May 17, 1894
SEE WOODS, Miss Emma

WALTON, Wesley Local Jun 14, 1894
Both Augusta papers tells of marriage of Mr Wesley Walton of Plymouth and Miss Emma Wood, the music teacher who has been visiting in Clayton for a year or two at the Christian Church in Augusta last Wednesday eve.

WANTLAD, G.B. and Mollie Local May 2, 1895
G.B. Wantlad has filed for divorce against his wife, Mollie, he alleges adultery with B.W. Richardson and others. Mollie and Mr Richardson are living in same town in New York state where they went from here. Later: Mrs Wantland came in on train from east Wednesday AM and may have something to say in the mater.

WANTLAND, Geo. B. and Mary June term of Court Jun 20, 1895
An even dozen divorce cases are pending, among them that of Geo. B. Wantland vs Mary Wantland. This is divroce day in court and many a tale of woe will be revealed.

WANTLAND, Will Local Feb 19, 1891
Will Wantland married Miss Lizzie Klosterman Sunday eve at 9. Will live Quincy.

WARD, Miss Della Apr 25, 1895
SEE BYRNS, Mr Sharon

WARD, Mr Elias Local May 17, 1900
Mr Williams the Christian minister at Camppint reported the marriage of Mr Elias Ward of Camp Point and Miss Ora McVay of this township.

WARD, Miss Melissa May 23, 1895
SEE DAVIS, Hope S.

WARD, Rachel Jan 9, 1890
SEE GREENWELL, Geo.

WARD, Tommy (Pipstone) Little Brindle News May 23, 1895
Married in Mt Sterling, Tommy Ward (Pipestone) to Mary Goodwin, this makes the fifth time for Tommy.

WARD, Walter S. Oct 20, 1898
SEE BEALL, Mrs Lina

WARD, Walter Camp Point Oct 20, 1898
Since our last writing the wedding of Walter Ward and Miss Lina Beal took place in Springfield.

WARE, Charlie Local Jan 30, 1896
Dave Ware came in Monday. He has not been well for two years. His son Charlie and Miss Laura Lamma were married a few weeks ago. They now live with Dave and family.

WARE, Clide N. Camp Point Aug 9, 1894
Clide N. Ware and Miss Helen Price were married at home of her parents Wednesday eve.

WARE, Columbus 10 Years Ago Jan 30, 1890
Married, Miss Wiley to Columbus Ware.

WARNER, Miss Etta 10 Years Ago Apr 21, 1892
Miss Etta Warner and Mr W.D. Meisser were married.

WARNER, Miss Lucinda Apr 2, 1896
SEE WILSON, A.L.

WARNER, Miss May Jun 29, 1893
SEE ROLLETT, Mr G.S.

WARNESKE, Anna Mar 10, 1892
SEE HORN, Frank

WASH, Miss Addie E. Little Brindle May 24, 1894
Marriage of Mr Boyd L. Walbridge, of Meeker, Colorado to Miss Addie E. Wash took place Thursday afternoon at the home of brides parents, Mr and Mrs H. Wash by Rev Williams an Episcopolian minister of Chicago.

WASH, Miss Georgia M. | Little Brindle | Feb 16, 1899
Cards are out announcing coming marriage of Miss Georgia M. Wash, youngest daughter of Mr and Mrs Hamilton Wash, of this city and Oscar H. Grover of near Hersman, to take place Wednesday February 22nd at home of brides parents.

WASH, Miss Georgia May | Little Brindle | Mar 2, 1899
Married last Wednesday at 8 PM at home of Mr and Mrs Hamilton Wash of this city, their daughter, Miss Georgia May to Oscar A. Grover, son of Mr and Mrs James Grover of Hersman.

WASH, Miss Nellie | Supplement | Oct 1, 1891
Neighborhood News Mt Sterling had a wedding in high life last week. Miss Nellie, daughter of Col. and Mrs Ham Wash was wed to Mr Frank E. Sheridan of Meeker, Colorado.

WATERS, Miss Agnes | Little Brindl, | Jan 12, 1899
Tuesday AM at St Mary's Church occurred the marriage of Miss Agnes Waters, daughter of Mr and Mrs William Waters of Lee township to Mr Frank Diss of Elkhorn township.

WATERS, George | Little Brindle | May 24, 1894
George Waters of Fish Hook obtained a license on Monday to wed Mary E. McDowell of Buckhorn. "Democrat Message"

WATERS, Wm | Little Brindle News | Jan 16, 1896
Siloam Herald On Decmeber 24th Wm Waters and Miss Ida Sills were married. Groom is son of James Waters and bride is daughter of Harvey Sills, both of this township.

WATKINS, Brock | Little Brindle | Feb 14, 1895
Siloam items in Examiner: Brock Watkins and Miss Louise Grady were married at home of Squire D.F. Cronin last Sunday.

WATKINS, Miss Lottie | Local | Feb 26, 1891
Miss Lottie Watkins, daughter of Mr Watkins, of Hotel Hampton, was married to Mr Bert Hough at Mt Sterling Saturday eve by Rev Little of the First Presbytérian Church. Will live at the Hotel Hampton.

WATKINS, Miss Retta | | Nov 22, 1894
SEE COE, Mr Ed

WATSON, Miss Edith M. | Married | Nov 9, 1893
Married at home of bride near Williamsville, Sangamon County Illinois at 6 PM Wednesday November 1st Miss Edith M. Watson tö Mr William F. Smith by Rev George E. Platt. Mr Smith is a teacher and son of F.H. Smith. Teaches at Kellerville.

WATSON, Elmer A. | Married | May 7, 1896
Married Thursday afternoon, 30th ult., Mr Elmer A. Watson and Miss Bertha M. Curry at Mt Sterling at the home of Mr E. Allen Perry by Elder Chas. Laycock. Groom has job at Canton as pharmacist.

WATSON, M.H. | Local | Apr 19, 1890
The marriage of M.H. Watson to a young lady at Grainville, Ohio occurs this eve (Wednesday). Good wishes Mark.

WATSON, Mr Rob't | 10 Years Ago | Dec 10, 1891
SEE BRIDGES, Miss Alace

WATSON, William C. | Our Own Bailiwick | Jul 12, 1894
Mr William C. Watson and Miss Eva Belmeyer were married in Quincy Monday eve. Bride is daughter of Mr Sol Belmeyer, deputy county clerk.

WEAKLY, P.E. | Neighborhood News | Jan 25, 1894
Sensation at Joetta on account of marriage of P.E. Weakly, the storekeeper and Lillian Beckwith. Weakly is ill nigh unto death and the ceremony is said to have been performed with the groom in bed.

WEAR, Mr | Camp Point | Aug 9, 1894
Mr Wear, of Lincoln, Illinois and Miss Emma Ausmus were married Wednesday eve at brides home.

WEAR, Columbus | 20 Years Ago | Feb 15, 1900
Jan. 1880 Married, Columbus Wear and Miss Wilty both of Concord.

WEAR, Miss Laura | Local | Mar 10, 1892
Married, at Mt Sterling, Thursday of last week, Miss Laura Wear of this place to Mr-Charles Walters by Rev L.A. Powell.

WEBB, Charles and Banche | Local | Feb 22, 1900
A motion for alimony pendete was entered in the divorce suit of Blanche Webb against Charles Webb in Springfield last week. The defendant is the well known Wabash conductor and the family formerly lived in Quincy.

WEBB, Miss Martha | Aug 2, 1898
SEE BENT, George H.

WEBBER, Miss Grace L. | Jun 24, 1897
SEE MANNY, Walter I.

WEBSTER, Miss Annie | Feb 6, 1896
SEE HOGAN, Martin

WEBSTER, John | Little Brindle News | Mar 21, 1895
John Webster and Nora Louderback, all of Pea Ridge were married by Elder Jacob Crawford at home of brides parents last Thursday. "Examiner"

WEBSTER, John W. | Apr 1, 1897
SEE FIELDS, Miss Maggie

WEBSTER, Mary E. | Jun 1, 1899
SEE LOUDERBACK, Daniel

WEICHLEIN, Emil | Oct 12, 1899
SEE MENKE, Miss Ida

WEISTER, Miss Kate | Adams County | Sep 15, 1898
Miss Kate Weister, of Ursa and Mr Wm B. Grimes, also of Ursa were married.

WELCH, Miss Dollie | Apr 8, 1897
SEE FLETCHER, Fred

WELTON, C.W. | Neighborhood News | May 4, 1893
C.W. Welton, son of Frank G. Welton, county clerk of Henry County has been arrested for abducting 14 year old Artha Kelso at Lewistown, whom he married. He is in jail.

WERTS, Ida | Feb 21, 1895
SEE HEINECKE, August

WERTZ, Mr Heye | 5 Years Ago | Feb 12, 1891
SEE BUSS, Miss Hattie

WEST, Miss May | 5 Years Ago | May 3, 1894
SEE CONNOR, C.H.

WEST, William B. | Local | Nov 12, 1891
William B. West quietly went to Scott county week before last and on Friday October 30th was married to Miss Rebecca Kirby, daughter of Thomas Kirby and wife of Clayton by Judge Collins of Winchester. Billie has a home ready on corner adjoining the home of B.F. Jackson ready for his bride.

WEST, William B. | Local | Nov 14, 1895
Married, William B. West and Miss Ida May at home of brides parents, Mr and Mrs Thomas May of Pea Ridge last Wednesday eve by A.J. Hunsaker Esq.

WESTBROOK, O.L. | 5 Years Ago | Jun 12, 1890
SEE HARBISON, Miss Puss

WESTBROOK, Capt U.S. | Neighborhood News | Apr 21, 1892
Capt U.S. Westbrook and Mrs Sarah J. Green of Brown County were married the 13th inst.

WEVER, Mattie | Ancient History | Mar 18, 1897
SEE MCDOWELL, Wm E.

WHEELER, Mrs Maria Nov 11, 1897
SEE CARTER, Lewis
WHITAKER, Dora May Jan 25, 1900
SEE BROWN, Riley
WHITAKER, Nora Dec 22, 1892
SEE GALLAHER, James
WHITAKER, Miss Nora Chestline Dec 29, 1892
Married Wednesday of last week, Miss Nora Whitaker and James Gollier by Esq. Likes.
WHITAKER, Philip Chestline Feb 1, 1894
Mr Philp Whitaker was married last Sunday to Miss Poline Gallaher, Mr Whitaker's second wife. First died about four years ago leaving a lot of small children. His second oldest daughter married into the same family that he was.
WHITAKER, Philip Chestline Feb 8, 1894
In our last we reported the marriage of Philip Whitaker, but he was not married until the 30th ult.
WHITE, Rev Camp Point Dec 28, 1893
Rev White and Miss Anna Schuhardt will be married Wednesday of this week.
WHITE, Miss Addie Occur. of Dec. 1885 Dec 11, 1890
Miss Addie White married Mr Henry Arntzen.
WHITE, James Local Feb 6, 1896
Mt Sterling Message: James White of Quincy and Miss Elizabeth Anderson of Clayton were married at County clerk Purcell's office last Thursday by Squire M. Brooks.
WHITE, James H. Little Brindle News Feb 6, 1896
Republican: James H. White of Quincy was married to Sarah E. Anderson of Clayton in county clerks office Thursday AM by Squire M. Brooks.
WHITECHAPEL, Miss Mary A. Aug 10, 1893
SEE WALKER, J.W.
WHITEHEAD, Mr Alta City Brevities Apr 6, 1899
Married at Mt Sterling, Mr Alta Whitehead and Miss Fannie Hodson of this vicinity. Groom is son of W.H. Whitehead, north of town and bride has lived in family of Wm Logue.
WHITEHEAD, Miss Mary Aug 10, 1893
SEE WALKER, Jesse Jr.
WHITESIDE, Chas. R. Brown County Jan 4, 1900
Licensed to wed since last issue of Examiner: Chas. R. Whiteside of Buckhorn and Sylva Bowen of Lee township.
WIDMAYER, Wm F. Ill Brevities Sep 6, 1894
Wm F. Widmayer and Miss Emily H. Hewitt were married at Jacksonville.
WIGLE, Miss Lizzie V. Aug 25, 1892
SEE ANDERSON, C.N.
WILD, Angeline Jan 30, 1896
SEE PARRICK, Harvey
WILEY, Miss 10 Years Ago Jan 30, 1890
SEE WARE, Columbus
WILEY, Miss Ada August 1883 Aug 11, 1898
Miss Ada Wiley and Mr Edgar Bennett were married.
WILEY, Miss Ida Decade Ago Aug 10, 1893
Miss Ida Wiley married Edgar Bennett.
WILEY, Miss Tillie August 1883 Aug 11, 1898
SEE SPILLARS, Spencer
WILKERSON, J.J. Ill State News Jul 27, 1893
J.J. Wilkerson, age 66 and Mrs angeline Preston age 58 were married at Marshall. 41 years ago Mr Wilkerson made his first matriomonial venture.

WILL, William C. Adams County Jun 8, 1899
Mr William C. Will, foreman of the Saturday Review office announced Saturday afternoon that he would be married to Miss Florence Redburn of Jacksonville. (He is the lame printer who worked on this paper at one time.)

WILLARD, Miss Carrie Brown County Sep 21, 1899
Mound Correspondent Wedding of W.E. Lowe and Miss Carrie Willard occurred Tuesday of this week at the home of the bride in Buena Vista township Schuyler County 7 miles northwest of Rushville by Rev Thompson, pastor of the Presbyterian Church of Brooklyn. Bride a popular school teacher in Schuyler County and only daughter of William Willard and wife. Her father is a prosperous farmer. Groom is a good school teacher, taught six years in this and adjoining counties. His parents live near Springfield, Illinois and are farmers. Wm Willard accompanied the bridal couple to their home in Mound Wednesday. Mr Lowe will begin teaching our school Monday.

WILLARD, Miss Rose Our Own Bailiwick Nov 29, 1894
Miss Rose Willard and Mrs Edw. Jacobs had arranged for a private wedding near Golden, the parents would not have it that way. They invited a great number of their young friends to attend a surprise party at their home. It turned out to be a pleasant surprise as the youngsters had quietly driven to Loraine that afternoon and were married.

WILLET, Mr Jan 20, 1898
SEE LIERLE, Miss Bessie

WILLIAMS, Miss Alice 5 Years Ago May 14, 1891
Miss Alice Williams married Thos. H. Hiles.

WILLIAMS, Miss Cora Local Mar 16, 1893
Miss Cora, daughter of Thomas Williams, was married to Mr Kimbough of Quincy Saturday eve. Will live Quincy where they went Sunday AM.

WILLIAMS, Ezra Little Brindle News Nov 29, 1894
From Beacon Light: Marriage of Mr Ezra Williams to Miss Fettie Shields occurred at the home of brides parents. Groom is son of Ota Williams and bride is daughter of Robert Shields.

WILLIAMS, Geo. W. Local Mar 31, 1892
Mr Geo. W. Williams and Miss Nellie M. Grady all of Clayton were married at 8 AM last Wednesday by Elder D.M. Sharples in the county clerks office. "Mt Sterling Examiner"

WILLIAMS, George Pea Ridge Nov 14, 1895
Mr George Williams and Miss Cora Blansett of Pea Ridge were married at home of brides parents Thursday eve.

WILLIAMS, Miss Hattie Oct 4, 1894
SEE MILLER, Ed

WILLIAMS, Mr Hobart M. Local Mar 20, 1890
Married, at the ME Church Wednesday eve, March 12th 1890, Mr Hobart M. Williams and Miss Pearl L. McCoy by Rev W.M. Reed. Returned to home of brides parents for a banquet.

WILLIAMS, Hobert M. Other Days May 17, 1900
March 1890 Married at ME Church, Hobert M. Williams and Miss Pearl McCoy.

WILLIAMS, Miss Lolah Sep 16, 1897
SEE GRAY, Mr A.E.

WILLIAMS, Miss Margaret Local Dec 19, 1895
Miss Margaret, daughter of Judge Williams was married to Mr Wm T. Kemp at the family home in Quincy Wednesday eve.

WILLIAMS, Ralph Local Sep 28, 1899
Married, Ralph Williams and Miss Fannie B. McConnell both of vicinity of Mounds by Rev J. Shaw at Mounds Wendesday of last week.

WILLIAMS, Thomas | Local | Dec 4, 1890
Thomas Williams, of this place and Mrs Eliza Shaffer of Quincy were married in Quincy last Sunday.

WILLIAMS, W.L. | Little Brindle | Jan 6, 1898
Card written by M.P. Carnahan at York, Nebraska dated Dec 24, ult. asks us to pbulish marriage of W.L. WIlliams of Mt Sterling, Illinois to Miss Millie Carnahan of York, Nebraska on Dec 24, 1897 by the county judge.

WILLIAMS, Wesley R. | Old Pike | Feb 4, 1897
SEE CAIN, Catherine

WILLIAMS, Wilbourne | | Jan 15, 1891
SEE HAMILTON, Miss Fredonia "Dona"

WILLIAMS, Miss Zuda May | | Apr 13, 1899
SEE YOUNG, Mr Ralph

WILSON, A.L. | Neighbors | Apr 2, 1896
Married at Keokuk, Mr A.L. Wilson of the Hamilton Register and Miss Lucinda Warner, of Macomb.

WILSON, Andrew J. | Brown County News | Jul 13, 1893
Mrs Andrew J. Wilson and Miss Susan A. Renaker, all of Concord township, Adams County Illinois were married July 4th at 7 PM at his home in this city by justice of peace Brooks. "Examiner"

WILSON, Charlie | Camp Point | Jan 3, 1895
Charlie Wilson and Jessie French of Chicago were married on eve last week at home of groom in Washington. Bride is niece of Mrs D.G. McFarland.

WILSON, Miss Clara | 5 Years Ago | Apr 28, 1892
Miss Clara Wilson married J.H. Dunkleburk.

WILSON, George H. | Our Own Bailiwick | May 10, 1894
George H. Wilson, a young lawyer of Quincy will be married to Miss Frances Hall of Jacksonville, some time in June.

WILSON, Harve | Little Brindle News | Dec 27, 1894
Married Tuesday eve at 7 by Rev G.A. Little Mr Harve Wilson, the popular tonsorial artist of this city and Miss Maggie, eldest daughter of Mr and Mrs John Harper. "Examiner"

WILSON, Miss Ida | | Jun 13, 1895
SEE GAY, Grant

WILSON, Manford | County News | Jan 25, 1900
Marriage license issued yesterday, Manford Wilson, of Sparland, Marshall county Illinois and Edith Hogan of Clayton.

WILSON, Miss May L. | | Dec 24, 1891
SEE BENTLY, James O.

WILSON, O.M. | | Jan 15, 1891
SEE WALLACE, Anna A.

WILTSE, Miss | 5 Years Ago | Apr 28, 1892
Miss Wiltse became Mrs John Loyd at Clark, Dakota.

WILTSIE, Mrs | May 1887 | Jul 1, 1897
SEE WHIPPLE, Rev W.W.

WILTY, Miss | January 1880 | Feb 15, 1900
SEE WEAR, Columbus

WING, Mr Ezra | | Feb 12, 1891
SEE ANDERSON, Miss Mary

WING, Miss Rosa L. | | Mar 8, 1900
SEE WALKER, Charles

WINGET, Mrs Flora | | May 10, 1900
SEE LIKES, Robert

WINGET, Wm | | Feb 8, 1900
SEE LIKES, Robert

WINSTON, James M. Local Feb 8, 1900
James M. Winston says his wife is a bad woman. He charges her with infidelity and names Ed Shoemaker as the destroyer of his happiness. It all happened on September 1st in Hannibal. Now he wants a divorce. They were married November 10, 1875 and lived together until last September when he learned of her actions. (Whig 7th)

WINSTON, Wm City Brevities May 26, 1898
A license to marry has been issued at Hannibal to Wm Winton and Henrietta Northcott. Young man is son of James M. Winston, formerly of Clayton.

WISEHART, Miss Mary Aug 27, 1896
SEE TAYLOR, Tom

WISEHART, Mr and Mrs Will Camp Point Dec 28, 1893
Mr and Mrs Will Wisehart celebrated their 20th wedding anniversary.

WITHROW, Geo. Sep 23, 1892
SEE TEDROW, Miss Clara E.

WOELKER, Amelia K. Jun 11, 1891
SEE ANDERSON, Robert L.

WOMELSDORF, Mrs Mary C. Our Own Bailiwick Mar 8, 1894
Mrs Mary C. Womelsdorf, a Quincy widow age 36 years went to County clerks office Saturday and all by herself got a license to marry John B. Moore of Camp Point, 44 years old.

WOMELSDORFF, Cordelia Ancient History Mar 18, 1897
SEE HUGHES, J.W.

WOMELSDORFF, Mrs Mary 10 Years Ago Feb 11, 1892
Mrs Mary Womelsdorff and G.W. Hughes married at Kellerville.

WOOD, Miss Emma Jun 14, 1894
SEE WALTON, Wesley

WOOD, Miss Hettie Local Feb 9, 1893
In rhe Benkleman, Nebraska, the marriage of Miss Hettie Wood, daughter of Mr J.D.Wood, former postmaster here, who now lives at Grand Junction, Colorado to Mr Frank Leslie of Benkleman. Past year he has been deputy county clerk. Bride is a prominent member of Benkleman's social and religious circles.

WOOD, John Our Own Bailiwick Apr 12, 1894
SEE BUGBEE, Miss Edith

WOODS, Miss Emma Local May 17, 1894
Marriage of Miss Emma Woods, the lady who has taught music here two years, to Mr Wesley Walton will occur at the Christian Church in Augusta, June 6th.

WOOSTER, Wm Local Oct 12, 1893
Married, Wm Wooster of Spokane, Washington to Miss Phoebe Ferris of Carthage at the home of brides mother in that city Wednesday at 12 M.

WORDEN, Dora E. Carthage Crime Aug 3, 1893
William Dehart of Durham township was charged with rape of Dora E. Worden, a child not yet 14 years old, Thomas Dehart, a brother was examined at same time on charge of abduction but was discharged. About one year ago it is charged that the Worden girl was living with a certain woman in Dunham township had been assaulted by Dehart. Dehart fled soon after Williams' disappearance the Worden girl was spirited away. It is said Thomas Dehart came to schoolhouse and took her away on some plausable pretense and she was not heard of until two weeks ago when Wm was arrested in LaPlatte, Missouri and brought here. Girl was with him. She says she followed Dehart to Texas and was married there to him.

WORSTER, Washington	Local	Feb 3, 1898
Washington Worster of Hamilton, Illinois was married to Miss Ruth Hobbs of Clayton, Illinois in Keokuk yesterday afternoon by Judge Bell in county clerk Rutledge's office. "Quincy Journal 1st"

WORTHINGTON, Francis M.	Local	Feb 20, 1890
Married at the home of brides parents, near Mounds, Brown County Feb 12, 1890 by Rev E.W. Souders, Francis M. Worthington and Miss Sarah J. McPhail.

WRIGHT, Miss	Local	Jul 5, 1894
SEE MCDOWELL, Tom H.W.

WRIGHT, Miss Carrie	Local	Jun 21, 1894
Cards are out announcing marriage to Miss Carrie Wright to Thomas H.W. McDowell at Baptist Church, Anthony, Kansas June 27th. Cards received by Tom's Clayton friends.

WRIGHT, Miss Delia	5 Years Ago	Feb 18, 1892
Miss Delia Wright and Mr John Kerlie were married.

WRIGHT, Della	Ancient History	Mar 18, 1897
SEE KERLEY, John

WRIGHT, Gus	Married	Mar 18, 1897
Mr Gus Wright and Miss Alpha Chase of this city, were married at the ME parsonage at 8 PM March 12th by Rev W.A. Reynolds pastor of Grace ME Church.

WRIGHT, Miss Mamie E.	Feb 27, 1896
SEE GORE, John L.

WRIGHT, Maymie	Wedding	Mar 5, 1896
Married at home of Mr and Mrs N.W. Wright in North East township, Thursday of last week at 4:30 PM their daughter, Maymie and Mr John L. Gore by Rev McDonnold, pastor of LaPrairie Methodist Church. Will live on a farm at Earlton, Kansas.

WRIGHT, Miss Minnie	Jul 24, 1890
SEE TAYLOR, Wm

WRIGHT, Miss Olie	10 Years Ago	Nov 10, 1892
Miss Olie Wright married Allen D. Campbell.

WRIGHT, Tommy	Elm Grove	Oct 18, 1894
Tommy Wright committed matrimony recently with a Miss Lauderback and was so sly about it that he didn't give them a chance to give him the usual reception.

WRIGHT, Will W.	Little Brindle	Jun 18, 1896
Old Flag: Yesterday at his home Rev F.P. Douglass married Will W. Wright of Augusta to Idella Ratcliff of Clayton.

WYATT, L.E.	November 1888	Nov 3, 1898
Married, L.E. Wyatt and Miss Lillie Gay, in Cass County.

WYATT, Mr Lute	5 Years Ago	Nov 30, 1893
Mr Lute Wyatt and Miss Lillie Gay were married.

WYSONG, Joseph	Pine Grove	Oct 13, 1892
Joseph Wysong and Polly Castle were married in Rushville last Thursday.

YAKLE, May	Local	Jun 2, 1892
Married at the home of brides parents, Mr and Mrs Earhart Yakle, on Thursday eve May 19th, May Yakle and John G. Gross, all of Pea Ridge by Rev C.A. King.

YEARGAIN, Mr James T.	Little Brindle	Feb 22, 1894
Wedding at the home of Mr T.C. McMurray, of this place last eve at 7 when the charming daughter of Mr McMurray was married to Mr James T. Yeargain of Quincy by Rev Abner Clark of Quincy.

YELDELL, Elmer E. Married Dec 5, 1895
Married at home of brides parents, Mr and Mrs Joseph Thornberry on Thanksgiving eve, November 28th Mr Elmer E. Yeldell and Miss Ida Thornberry by W.S. Lowe of Mound. Elmer is son of John Yeldell of Concord township.

YELDELL, Miss Emma Sep 21, 1893
SEE HUFFMAN, Elmer

YELDELL, Ernest City Brevities Oct 27, 1898
Marriage of Mr Ernest Yeldell and Miss Anna Moore occurred at the parsonage of Congregational Church in Quincy by Dr Dana at 3 PM Wednesday. Mr Thomas Moore, father of the bride and Miss Tracy Bolinger were present. Will live with Mr and Mrs J.H. Yeldell on the farm.

YELDELL, Miss Mary Married Feb 6, 1896
Married at the country home of Mr and Mrs John H. Yeldell at 4 PM Wednesday, their only daughter, Miss Mary to Mr Granville Linn by Elder W.E. Lowe of Mound. Attended by Mr Elmer Yeldell and Miss Anna Linn, brother and sister of bride and groom. Reception held at home of grooms parents, Mr and Mrs J.A. Linn. Will farm near his parents after March 1st.

YOUNG, George W. and Nancy Ellen Our Own Bailiwick Jan 24, 1895
George W. Young, a farmer of Beverly alleges that in October last his wife Nancy Ellen Young was false to him and to her marriage vows. He wants a divorce and McCarl and Felgenspan will help him get it.

YOUNG, Joe Little Brindle Feb 9, 1899
Joe Young, who has a wife and child here went to Missouri with his grandfather, M.M. Hersman last September and married a Missouri girl in November. Was arrested for bigamy in Jonesbora, Arkansas and taken to Keithsburg, Missouri for hearing.

YOUNG, Mr Ralph City Brevities Apr 13, 1899
Marriage of Mr Ralph Young, grandson of Mrs S. Pevehouse and Miss Zuda May Williams, daughter of Mr and Mrs Stephen Williams, east of town, occurred in Quincy Tuesday afternoon. Groom has a farm in this vicinity and this will probably be their future home.

YOWELL, Everett Pine Grove Sep 12, 1895
Everett Yowell and Adda Sims were married last Sunday.

ZEIGERS, Albert April 1883 Apr 28, 1898
Married, April 12th Albert Zeigers and Louisa R. Runte.

ZIMMERMAN, Miss Personal Oct 20, 1898
Mr J.W. Burnett and little Margaret went to Chicago where she will attend the wedding of her niece, Miss Zimmerman to Mr Brester of Cincinnati, O.

ZINCK, Miss Feb 27, 1890
SEE SHARP, Jack

ZINN, Miss Ida Local Mar 23, 1893
Marriage of Miss Ida Zinn to Mr James Lummis will take place the 28th inst. Miss Zinn lived with her sister, Mrs Rev McKown when they lived here, groom is a merchant at Paloma.

ZINN, Miss Ida Local Apr 6, 1893
At Island Grove parsonage, Berlin, Illinois on March 28th, Miss Ida Zinn of that place and Mr James Lummis of Paloma were married by Rev C.F. McKown, uncle of the bride. Bride made her home with Rev and Mrs McKown during their stay here. Will live Paloma.

ZOLLER, Mr Camp Point Oct 10, 1895
Mr Zoller of McKee and Miss Anna Hornecker were married at the home of the bride, ½ mile north of town at 4 PM last Thursday eve.

ZUMWALT, N.H. and wife Pike County Feb 1, 1900
Mr N.H. Zumwalt and wife, south of Pittsfield celebrated their golden wedding last week.

Heritage Books by
Mrs. Joseph J. Beals, Sr. and Mrs. Sandra Kirchner:

Births and Related Items Abstracted from The Camp Point Journal *of Camp Point, Adams County, Illinois, 1873–1903*

Deaths Abstracted from The Camp Point Journal, *1873–1882, Camp Point, Adams County, Illinois*

Deaths Abstracted from The Camp Point Journal, *1883–1892, Camp Point, Adams County, Illinois*

Deaths Abstracted from The Camp Point Journal, *1893–1903, Camp Point, Adams County, Illinois*

Marriages (1895–1905) and Deaths (1895–1900) and Related Items Abstracted from the Golden New Era *of Golden, Adams County, Illinois*

Marriages and Related Items Abstracted from The Clayton Enterprise *Newspaper of Clayton, Adams County, Illinois, 1879–1900*

Marriages and Related Items Abstracted from the Mendon Dispatch *of Mendon, Adams County, Illinois, 1877–1905*

Obituaries and Death Related Items Abstracted from Clayton Enterprise *Newspaper of Clayton, Adams County Illinois, 1879–1900, Volume 1*

Obituaries and Death Related Items Abstracted from the Hendon Dispatch *of Mendon, Adams County, Illinois, 1877–1905*

CD: Births and Deaths Abstracted from The Camp Point Journal, *Camp Point, Adams County, Illinois, 1873–1903*

CD: Marriages and Related Items Abstracts from the Golden New Era *Newspaper of Golden, Adam County, Illinois, 1895–1905*

CD: Marriages and Related Items Abstracts from the Mendon Dispatch *of Mendon, Adams County, Illinois, 1877–1905*

CD: Obituaries and Death Related Items Abstracts from the Golden New Era *Newspaper of Golden, Adam County, Illinois, 1895–1900*

CD: Obituaries and Death Related Items Abstracts from the Mendon Dispatch *of Mendon, Adams County, Illinois, 1877–1905*

www.ingramcontent.com/pod-product-compliance
Lightning Source LLC
Chambersburg PA
CBHW070912270326
41927CB00011B/2543